Sikhs at Large

Religion, Culture, and Politics in Global Perspective

Verne A. Dusenbery

OXFORD
UNIVERSITY PRESS

OXFORD
UNIVERSITY PRESS

YMCA Library Building, Jai Singh Road, New Delhi 110001

Oxford University Press is a department of the University of Oxford. It furthers the University's objective of excellence in research, scholarship, and education by publishing worldwide in

Oxford New York
Auckland Cape Town Dar es Salaam Hong Kong Karachi
Kuala Lumpur Madrid Melbourne Mexico City Nairobi
New Delhi Shanghai Taipei Toronto

With offices in
Argentina Austria Brazil Chile Czech Republic France Greece
Guatemala Hungary Italy Japan Poland Portugal Singapore
South Korea Switzerland Thailand Turkey Ukraine Vietnam

Published in India
by Oxford University Press, New Delhi

First published 2008

ISBN-13: 978-0-19-568598-5
ISBN-10: 0-19-568598-9

Typeset in Calisto MT 10/12
by Text-o-Graphics, Noida
Printed in India at De-Unique, New Delh
Published by Oxford University P
YMCA Library Building, Jai Singh Road, New

For Liz, my companion along the way

Contents

Acknowledgments

The essays herein have been written and published over nearly three decades based upon research conducted in the United States, Canada, Indonesia, Singapore, Malaysia, Australia, and India. As a consequence, it is virtually impossible to thank all those individuals—relatives, teachers, students, colleagues, friends, informants—and those institutions—schools, libraries, funding agencies, research centres, government and non-government organizations—whose support, encouragement, and/or cooperation have made possible the research and influenced the thinking and writing. I refer the reader to the individual essays for acknowledgment of just some of those to whom I am indebted.

I gratefully acknowledge the following for permission to republish these essays:

Centre for South Asian Studies, University of Toronto for: 'Punjabi Sikhs and Gora Sikhs: Conflicting Assertions of Sikh Identity in North America' in Joseph T. O'Connell, Milton Israel, and Willard G. Oxtoby, (eds), with W.H. McLeod and J.S. Grewal, (visiting eds), *Sikh History and Religion in the Twentieth Century*, Toronto: Centre for South Asian Studies, University of Toronto, 1988, pp. 334–55.

University of California Press and Oxford University Press for: 'On the Moral Sensitivities of Sikhs in North America' in Owen M. Lynch, (ed.), *Divine Passions: The Social Construction of Emotion in India*, Berkeley: University of California Press and New Delhi: Oxford University Press, 1990, pp. 239–61.

The University of Chicago Press for: 'The Word as Guru: Sikh Scripture and the Translation Controversy', *History of Religions*, vol. 31, no. 4 (May 1992), pp. 385–402.

University of Pennsylvania Press for: 'A Sikh "Diaspora"? Contested Identities and Constructed Realities' in Peter van der Veer, (ed.), *Nation and Migration: The Politics of Space in the South Asian Diaspora*, Philadelphia: University of Pennsylvania Press, 1995, pp. 17–42. Reprinted by permission of the University of Pennsylvania Press.

Manohar Publishers for: '"Nation" or "World Religion"? Master Narratives of Sikh Identity' in Pashaura Singh and N. Gerald Barrier, (eds), *Sikh Identity: Continuity and Change*, New Delhi: Manohar Publishers, 1999, pp. 127–44, and 'Socializing Sikhs in Singapore: Soliciting the State's Support', in Pashaura Singh and N. Gerald Barrier, (eds), *The Transmission of Sikh Heritage in the Diaspora*. Columbia: South Asia Publications and New Delhi: Manohar Publishers, 1996, pp. 127–64.

Canadian Ethnic Studies Association for: 'Canadian Ideology and Public Policy: The Impact on Vancouver Sikh Ethnic and Religious Adaptation', *Canadian Ethnic Studies*, vol. XIII, no. 3 (Winter 1981), pp. 101–19.

The University of California Press for: 'The Poetics and Politics of Recognition: Diasporan Sikhs in Pluralist Politics', *American Ethnologist*, vol. 24, no. 4 (Nov. 1997): 738–62. Copyright © 1997, American Anthropological Association.

Institute of Southeast Asian Studies for: 'Diasporic Imagings and the Conditions of Possibility: Sikhs and the State in Southeast Asia', *SOJOURN: Journal of Social Issues in Southeast Asia*, vol. 12, no. 2 (Oct. 1997), pp. 226–60. Reproduced here with kind permission of the publisher, Institute of Southeast Asian Studies, Singapore.

Springer Science and Business Media for: 'Sikh Positionings in Australia and the "Diaspora" Concept', in Melvin Ember, Carol R. Ember, and Ian Skoggard, (eds), *Encyclopedia of Diasporas*, vol. 1, New York: Kluwer Academic Plenn Publishers, 2004, pp. 485–91. Copyright © 2004 by Kluwer Academic/Plenum Publishers, New York. Reprinted with kind permission of Springer Science and Business Media.

Guru Nanak Dev University Press for: 'Who Speaks for Sikhs in the Diaspora? Collective Representation in Multicultural States' in Gurupdesh Singh, (ed.), *Diasporic Studies: Theory and Literature*, Amritsar: Guru Nanak Dev University Press, 2007, pp. 68–83.

Introduction

The essays collected in this volume constitute a selection of articles and book chapters addressing two related topics that have engaged my interest as a socio-cultural anthropologist during more than three decades of research with Sikhs in the United States, Canada, Indonesia, Singapore, Malaysia, Australia, and India. The first is what, following the work of McKim Marriott, I have termed Sikh 'ethnosociology'—that is, Sikh understandings of their social world and their place in it, as reflected in what Sikhs say and what Sikhs do as they live their lives, interacting with other Sikhs and with non-Sikhs. The second is how Sikhs have responded to the fact that in every country of residence they constitute a minority, living under political conditions not of their own making. Of course, the two topics are not unconnected. How Sikhs understand their world affects how they respond to the political settings in which they live their lives—and vice versa. Thus, the book is really about emerging cultural understandings and political stratagems of a paradigmatic transnational religious group—the Sikhs—as I have observed them and engaged with them in multiple global sites over a span of more than three decades.

The past forty years have included many historically important events affecting Sikhs: the Green Revolution in India's Punjab state and its social, economic, and environmental consequences; the accelerated transnational migration of Sikhs taking place in the context of global political concerns over multiculturalism; an unprecedented conversion of non-Punjabis in Western countries to Sikhism; the rise and fall of the Khalistan movement for Sikh sovereignty and of the accompanying state-versus-militant political violence that engulfed Punjab; the liberalization of the Indian economy and an attempted Government of

India rapprochement with the Indian diaspora.[1] Given these developments, one must read these essays aware of their placement within this evolving historical context. To that end, I have made every attempt to indicate the original date of publication of each essay and the time period in which the fieldwork on which it is based was conducted.

***

My own involvement with Sikhs began before either my research subjects or I knew much of anything about Sikhs and Sikhism. To wit, I began my research as a budding anthropologist by spending a summer living in an ashram run by the Healthy, Happy, Holy Organization (3H0), a tax-exempt educational foundation, founded in 1969 by a Punjabi Sikh immigrant to the United States, Harbhajan Singh Puri (aka Yogi Bhajan; aka Siri Singh Sahib Harbhajan Singh Khalsa Yogiji). In 1972, most of the young North Americans who had become 3HO members did not consider themselves Sikhs or even know that Yogi Bhajan was a Sikh. My undergraduate thesis, '"Why would anybody join?" A Study of Recruitment and the Healthy, Happy, Holy Organization' (Dusenbery 1973), notes Sikh influences on the group's ideology only in passing.

By 1974, when I spent a follow-up summer attending 3HO's summer solstice gathering in New Mexico and visiting 3HO ashrams in the western United States and Canada, the 'healthy, happy, holy way of life' was being given a much more explicit Sikh gloss.[2] In fact, 3HO members were being encouraged by Yogi Bhajan to become members of the Sikh Dharma Brotherhood, a registered religious organization, and to participate in 'conversion' and 'baptism' and 'minister ordination' ceremonies to become upholders of 'orthodox' Sikhism in North America. The title of my subsequent master's thesis, 'Straight→Freak →Yogi→Sikh: A "Search for Meaning" in American Culture' (Dusenbery1975) sums up the shared personal journey that 3HO/Sikh Dharma members saw themselves as having undertaken.

During this research in 1974, I became aware of increasing interactions and emerging tensions between the new *gora* ('white') Sikhs of 3HO/Sikh Dharma and the longstanding Punjabi Sikh immigrant communities, especially in California and British Columbia. In fact, I was present in British Columbia when a fight broke out between the two groups in the Khalsa Diwan Society's Ross Street gurdwara in Vancouver. My curiosity as to the source of this tension piqued, I resolved to return to Vancouver to conduct dissertation fieldwork on the interaction of Punjabi Sikhs and Gora Sikhs in North America.

My dissertation research in Vancouver, British Columbia, in 1978–9, introduced me in a more significant manner to Punjabi Sikhs, both new immigrants arriving as a result of the liberalization of Canadian immigration policies and second- and third-generation Sikh Canadians of Punjabi ancestry. My dissertation project was initially conceived as a study of how the Punjabi Sikh 'immigrants' were assimilating into Canadian culture and how the Gora Sikh 'converts' were being incorporated into the Sikh Panth. However, the analytic framework that I subsequently employed in my PhD dissertation, 'Sikh Persons and Practices: A Comparative Ethnosociology' (Dusenbery 1989a), was largely informed by the South Asian ethnosociology project of McKim Marriott and his students and colleagues at the University of Chicago (see, for example, Marriott 1990), an approach seeking to understand alternative notions of persons and their social relationships. Most of the articles in Part 1 of this volume reflect this framework, which seems not only to provide insight into the cultural misunderstandings arising between the Gora Sikhs and Punjabi Sikhs as a consequence of conflicting ethnosociological assumptions, but also to provide a productive way of looking at Sikh discourse and practices more generally.

It was also during my 1978–9 fieldwork that I began to become more familiar with the social and political challenges facing Sikhs as a 'visible minority' in Canada. This led me to explore the effects of changing Canadian ideologies and policies upon Sikh institutions and their political agendas (see Chapter 7). My growing awareness of the different experiences that Sikhs have had in different countries of settlement motivated me to collaborate with Jerry Barrier in inviting other scholars working on overseas Sikh communities to a conference held at the University of Michigan in 1986. This resulted in our co-edited conference volume, *The Sikh Diaspora: Migration and the Experience Beyond Punjab* (Barrier and Dusenbery 1989).

My own brief exposure in 1981 to very different political environments faced by Sikhs in Southeast Asian countries subsequently led me to return to Southeast Asia in 1992–3 to conduct research with Sikh communities in Indonesia (Medan and Jakarta), Singapore, and Malaysia (Kuala Lumpur).[3] This research resulted in case studies and comparative accounts of Sikh experiences under different multiculturalist regimes (see Chapters 8–10). Subsequent fieldwork in Australia (Sydney and Woolgoolga) in 1999 has expanded my comparative base (see Chapter 11). It also led me to collaborate on a social history-cum-ethnography of the Sikh community in Woolgoolga,

New South Wales, undertaken in collaboration with a local Australian Sikh and incorporating the voices of local Sikhs and of other Sikh scholars (Bhatti and Dusenbery 2001).[4]

During all of this fieldwork with Sikhs living outside India, I have been well aware of the ties that link Sikhs globally, both to Punjab and across nodes of the diaspora. Such links are both material and ideational. What makes Sikhs such a good example of a contemporary transnational community is that Sikh persons, goods, capital, ideas, and images readily flow across nation-state borders, reflecting what Arjun Appadurai has called the Sikh construction of a 'new, postnational cartography' (Appadurai 1996b, p. 50). Sikh individuals and ideas come from India to North America and spawn Gora Sikhs. Remittances from Sikh NRIs help fund the Green Revolution. Circulating images of violated Sikh persons spur the Khalistan movement among Sikhs in the diaspora. Bhangra from Punjab gets reworked in the UK and sent back to Punjab and elsewhere in the diaspora as part of world music. Sikh marriage networks literally span the globe.

From the beginning of my research (see Dusenbery 1979), it was clear to me that Sikhs in the diaspora were remitting funds to Punjab for various causes—to build a *pakka* family house, to fund marriages of relatives, to buy agricultural land and inputs, to support various social, political, and religious causes. During the 1980s and early 1990s, the Government of India was, of course, concerned that some of these remittances were funding Khalistani militancy. But I was aware of humanitarian and philanthropic projects, as well, that were being funded by Sikhs living in the diaspora. To further explore this aspect of remittances, Darshan S. Tatla, Director of the Punjab Centre for Migration Studies, and I undertook a collaborative project in 2005–6 on diasporan Sikh philanthropy in Punjab (see Chapter 6).[5] This ultimately led us to organize an international workshop on the topic and to co-edit a volume growing out of the workshop.[6]

In sum, I have pursued an evolving set of projects involving Sikhs over a relatively long period of time. One motivation for the publication of this collection is that the resulting articles, although thematically related, have been published in a wide variety of books and journals. Some have been published in Sikh studies volumes. Some have been published in area studies journals or collections. Some have been published in disciplinary journals. As a result, unless one has been diligent in searching them out, potential readers are unlikely to have encountered them all and thus to have seen the ways in which they are, in fact, related and built upon one another.

***

In entitling this collection, *Sikhs at Large: Religion, Culture, and Politics in Global Perspective*, I pay homage to Arjun Appadurai's influential collection of essays, *Modernity at Large* (Appadurai 1996a), which explored both the ways in which cultural products themselves have become deterritorialized and reterritorialized through the processes of globalization and the ways in which our contemporary theoretical understanding of 'culture' (and related social scientific concepts) must change to better account for a de/territorialized object of study.

In the 1970s, when I began to study Sikhs in North America, disciplinary conventions and area studies perspectives in the fields of anthropology and of South Asian studies were such that it was assumed that 'authentic' Sikh culture was to be found in Punjab and that what one encountered at a distance from the presumed centre was some attenuated, somehow-less-real version of it. Thus, as someone studying Sikhs at large in the diaspora, I found myself somewhat on the periphery, questioned as to why I was not pursuing my fieldwork in Punjab.

But it became increasingly clear to me that, just as Sikhs themselves are not territorially limited to the Punjab but are, in fact, dispersed across the globe, so too Sikh religion, culture, and politics are not simply products of Punjab but also are actively being produced in multiple sites abroad. In fact, Sikhs in the diaspora have been forced to reflect upon and objectify their 'culture' and 'religion' by the very fact of living, working, and interacting with non-Sikhs and non-Punjabi Sikh converts in places where Sikhs have been relatively unknown and lacking in local political standing. And, in the process of reterritorializing themselves, Sikhs have been creating new understandings of their social worlds and new hybrid cultural products. The interaction between Punjabi Sikhs and Gora Sikhs in North America was one clear context in which new understandings were being generated out of initial mutual misunderstandings, but Sikhs in all locales have had to come to terms with what it means to be a Sikh at large in the face of alternate and changing modernities. In fact, many of my more thoughtful and articulate Sikh friends and informants over the years have been well aware of being engaged in a process of making Sikh subjects who can thrive in new and varied social settings without ceasing to be Sikhs.

This volume, therefore, brings together my perspectives on the cultural and political dimensions of Sikh subject making as a consequence of my participant observation in social and religious activities involving Sikhs in several different countries; my reading of various Sikh newspapers, journals, websites, and listservs; and my conversations with Sikhs globally. It is thus an example of what anthropologists would call multisite fieldwork involving polymorphous engagements with Sikhs.[7] In Part I, under the heading 'Sikh Ethnosociology', I have brought together a series of essays that develop my analysis of some of the ways in which Sikhs understand and engage their social world(s).

Chapter 1 ('Punjabi Sikhs and Gora Sikhs: Conflicting Assertions of Sikh Identity in North America') was first published (Dusenbery 1988) in a Sikh studies conference volume from the University of Toronto. It suggests the ways that Punjabi Sikhs and Gora Sikhs initially made sense of one another, in light of the different cultural assumptions and experiences each brought to their interaction.[8] For this volume, I have added a 'Postscript' that provides a brief assessment of how the relationship has developed in the interim.

Chapter 2 ('On the Moral Sensitivities of Sikhs in North America') analyses the continuing importance of *izzat* (honour) as a moral affect in Jat Sikh lives in the diaspora and contrasts that with its absence among Gora Sikhs. The article (Dusenbery 1990b) was originally published in a volume resulting from a conference on the anthropology of the emotions in India.

Chapter 3 ('The Word as Guru: Sikh Scripture and the Translation Controversy') analyses the challenges to translation of the Adi Granth and the reasons why Sikhs might resist using a translation as a focal point in worship. The article (Dusenbery 1992) originally appeared in a special Sikh focus issue of the journal, *History of Religions*.

Chapter 4 ('A Sikh "Diaspora"? Contested Identities and Constructed Realities') questions the unreflective use of the term 'diaspora' in the title of the book that Jerry Barrier and I co-edited (Barrier and Dusenbery 1989) and invites considerations of the multiple sources of shared identity open to Punjabi persons. The article (Dusenbery 1995) was published in a volume that drew together papers first presented in the 1991–2 South Asia seminar on the 'South Asian Diaspora' at the University of Pennsylvania.[9]

Chapter 5 ('"Nation" or "World Religion"? Master Narratives of Sikh Identity') analyses the ways and the contexts in which Sikhs have been commonly represented—by Sikhs themselves or by others—as either a 'nation' or a 'world religion' and suggests possible alternative narratives of Sikh identity. The article (Dusenbery 1999) was published along with other papers first presented at a Sikh studies conference on 'Sikh Identity' held at the University of Michigan.

Chapter 6 ('"Through Wisdom, Dispense Charity": Religious and Cultural Underpinnings of Diasporan Sikh Philanthropy in Punjab') explores the role that Sikh religious teachings and practices, Punjabi cultural understandings and social expectations, and experiences living and working in settings abroad might play in helping motivate diasporan Sikhs to undertake philanthropy in Punjab. This article, written for the international workshop on diasporan Sikh philanthropy in Punjab, is forthcoming in the resulting workshop volume.

In Part II, I have brought together a series of articles that focus on the ways that Sikhs living outside India have experienced and dealt with modern nation-state ideologies, policies, and practices of religious and ethnic management in various countries of residence. This is, in effect, a view of the intersection of multiculturalism and transnationalism from the local Sikh ground up.

Chapter 7 ('Canadian Ideology and Public Policy: The Impact on Vancouver Sikh Ethnic and Religious Adaptation') explores institutional developments from the 1910s through the 1970s among Vancouver Sikhs in light of Canadian differentiation of religion and ethnicity. The paper was first presented at a Canadian Ethnic Studies Association meeting and was subsequently published (Dusenbery 1981) in the association's journal, *Canadian Ethnic Studies*.

Chapter 8 ('Socializing Sikhs in Singapore: Soliciting the State's Support') analyses the 'coinciding interests' of Sikh professional and state bureaucrats that positioned Singaporean Sikhs in the early 1990s as the local 'model minority'. The article, first presented at a Sikh studies conference on 'The Transmission of Sikh Heritage in the Diaspora' at the University of Michigan, was published (Dusenbery1996) in the resulting conference volume.

Chapter 9 ('The Poetics and Politics of Recognition: Diasporan Sikhs in Pluralist Polities') contrasts the very different experiences of Sikhs in negotiating public recognition under Canadian Multiculturalism and under Singaporean Multiracialism from inception through the early 1990s. The article (Dusenbery 1997a) first appeared in the journal, *American Ethnologist*.

Chapter 10 ('Diasporic Imagings and the Conditions of Possibility: Sikhs and the State in Southeast Asia') contrasts the ways that state ideologies, policies, and practices of religious and ethnic management differentially affected Sikhs in postcolonial Indonesia, Singapore, and Malaysia. The paper was originally presented at the Institute of Southeast Asian Studies as part of a seminar on 'Southeast Asian Diasporas' and was subsequently published (Dusenbery 1997b), along with selected papers from the seminar, in the journal, *SOJOURN: Journal of Social Issues in Southeast Asia.*

Chapter 11 ('Sikh Positionings in Australia and the "Diaspora" Concept') argues for an understanding of the differentially positioned Sikhs in Australia and their different ways of belonging to the Australian nation and connecting to others in the Sikh diaspora. The article (Dusenbery 2004), published in the *Encyclopedia of Diasporas*, is a revised version, for a broader audience, of a reflective essay (Dusenbery 2001) included in our book on Sikhs in Woolgoolga.

Chapter 12 ('Who Speaks for Sikhs in the Diaspora? Collective Representation in Multicultural States') draws some conclusions about collective representation through an exploration of the different ways and means by which Sikhs have sought and gained collective representation in four multicultural nation-states where Sikhs now live. An earlier version of this chapter was delivered as the 12th Vidvatva Fulbright Lecture in New Delhi in 2005 and was presented in a seminar on Diasporic Studies at Guru Nanak Dev University in Amritsar. The essay (Dusenbery 2007b) also appears in the resulting seminar volume.[10]

***

Because this is a collection of essays written over a long time span and published in a number of different venues, questions naturally arose about whether or not to update essays, to remove any overlap among essays, and to standardize format across essays. In the end, other than adding a postscript to the first essay and making minor editorial changes, it was decided that it would be most appropriate to republish these essays in their original form. The reader is therefore advised to read each essay as a reflection of the ethnographic particulars, and my interpretation of them, at the time that each essay was originally written. Taken collectively, the essays reflect both the historically and ethnographically varied Sikh experiences in the diaspora and my evolving understanding of these experiences of Sikhs at large.

Sikhs have faced many challenges over their short five-hundred-plus-year history. And the articles here make clear that Sikhs continue to grapple with an array of challenges—over identity, authority, rights, representation, and duty—as they come to terms with modernity in Indian Punjab and in the diaspora. Scholars of the Sikhs have also faced many challenges, especially in rendering Sikh practices fully intelligible to non-Sikh audiences without at the same time finding themselves accused of misrepresentation by would-be Sikh keepers of the tradition (see Dusenbery 1989b and 1994). It is my hope that the approach taken in these articles both conveys my appreciation of the various ways that Sikhs globally are coming to terms with the experiential challenges they face and, at the same time, suggests forms of scholarly analysis that challenge both Sikh and non-Sikh readers without unduly offending the sensibilities of either.

NOTES

1. The 2002 Government of India, Report of the High Level Committee on the Indian Diaspora. New Delhi: Non Resident Indians & Persons of Indian Orgin Division, Ministry of External Affairs. [available at *http://indiandiaspora.nic.in/contents./htm*, accessed 19 August 2007] acknowledges that the Indian diaspora was largely held at arms distance by the GOI until outreach began in the 1990s.
2. This research was funded by a Youthgrant from the National Endowment for the Humanities.
3. This research was funded by a Fulbright Southeast Asia Regional Research Award and by a grant from the Joint Committee on Southeast Asia of the Social Science Research Council and the American Council of Learned Societies with funds provided by the National Endowment for the Humanities and the Ford Foundation.
4. This was a Centenary of Federation project supported with funding from the Commonwealth of Australia.
5. This research was funded, in part, by a CIES Fulbright Senior Research Award.
6. This workshop was co-sponsored by the United States Educational Foundation in India (USEFI) and the Punjab Centre for Migration Studies at Lyallpur Khalsa College in Jalandhar, Punjab, which hosted the event. The forthcoming volume has the working title, 'Sikh Diaspora Philanthropy in Punjab: Global Giving for Local Good'.
7. On multisite fieldwork and polymorphous engagements as anthropological method, see Hannerz 2004, pp. 11–13.
8. A related article, 'The Sikh Person, the Khalsa Panth, and Western Sikh Converts' (Dusenbery 1990a), covering some of the same ground but for a different audience, was published in a festschrift volume for

K. Ishwaran and republished, without the author's knowledge, in the journal *Khera* (Dusenbery 1991). It is not included in this collection.

9. This essay has recently been anthologized in a reader on the sociology of diaspora (Dusenbery 2007a).
10. Note that this collection does not include (a) my introduction (Dusenbery 1989b) or substantive article (Dusenbery 1989c) from *The Sikh Diaspora: Migration and the Experience Beyond Punjab* (Barrier and Dusenbery 1989); (b) my reflective essay (Dusenbery 2001) or co-written chapters from *A Punjabi Sikh Community in Australia: From Indian Sojourners to Australian Citizens* (Bhatti and Dusenbery 2001); and (c) the co-written introduction to our forthcoming Sikh diaspora philanthropy volume. Nor does this volume include any of my published review essays, book reviews, or appreciations listed in the appendix. Interested readers will have to seek these out on their own.

REFERENCES

Appadurai, Arjun, 1996a, *Modernity at Large: Cultural Dimensions of Globalization*, Minneapolis: University of Minnesota Press.

———, 1996b, 'Sovereignty without Territoriality: Notes for a Postnational Geography' in Patricia Yeager, (ed.), *The Geography of Identity*, Ann Arbor: University of Michigan Press, pp. 40–58.

Barrier, N. Gerald and Verne A. Dusenbery, (eds), 1989, *The Sikh Diaspora: Migration and the Experience Beyond Punjab*, Delhi: Chanakya Publications and Columbia, Missouri: South Asian Publications.

Bhatti, Rashmere and Verne A. Dusenbery, (eds), 2001, *A Punjabi Sikh Community in Australia: From Indian Sojourners to Australian Citizens*, Woolgoolga, NSW: Woolgoolga Neighbourhood Centre.

Dusenbery, Verne A., 2006a [1995], 'A Sikh Diaspora? Contested Identities and Constructed Realities' in Ajaya Kumar Sahoo and Brij Maharaj, (eds), *Sociology of Diaspora: A Reader*, New Delhi: Rawat Publishers [reprint of Dusenbery 1995], pp. 772–99.

———, 2007 b, 'Who Speaks for Sikhs in the Diaspora? Collective Representation in Multicultural States' in Gurupdesh Singh, (ed.), *Diasporic Studies: Theory and Literature,* Amritsar: Guru Nanak Dev University Press, pp. 68–83.

———, 2004, 'Sikh Positionings in Australia and the "Diaspora" Concept' in M. Ember, C. R. Ember, and I. Skoggard, (eds), *Encyclopedia of Diasporas,* New York: Springer, pp. 485–91.

———, 2001, 'Punjabi Sikh Positionings in Australia' in Rashmere Bhatti and Verne A. Dusenbery, (eds), *A Punjabi Sikh Community in Australia*, Woolgoolga, NSW: Woolgoolga Neighbourhood Centre, pp. 242–51.

———, 1999, '"Nation" or "World Religion"? Master Narratives of Sikh Identity' in Pashaura Singh and N. Gerald Barrier, (eds), *Sikh Identity: Continuity and Change*, New Delhi: Manohar Publishers, pp. 127–44.

———, 1997a, 'The Poetics and Politics of Recognition: Diasporan Sikhs in Pluralist Polities', *American Ethnologist*, 24 (4) Nov., pp. 738–62.

———, 1997b, 'Diasporic Imagings and the Conditions of Possibility: Sikhs and the State in Southeast Asia', *SOJOURN: Journal of Social Issues in Southeast Asia*, 12 (2) Oct., pp. 226–60.

———, 1996, 'Socializing Sikhs in Singapore: Soliciting the State's Support' in Pashaura Singh and N. Gerald Barrier, (eds), *The Transmission of Sikh Heritage in the Diaspora,* Columbia: South Asia Publications and New Delhi: Manohar Publishers, pp. 127–64.

———, 1995, 'A Sikh Diaspora? Contested Identities and Constructed Realities' in Peter van der Veer, (ed.), *Nation and Migration: The Politics of Space in the South Asian Diaspora*, Philadelphia: University of Pennsylvania Press, pp. 17–42.

———, 1994, 'Review of W.H. McLeod's *The Sikhs: History, Religion, and Society*', *Journal of Asian Studies*, 53 (2) May, pp. 600–2.

———, 1992, 'The Word as Guru: Sikh Scripture and the Translation Controversy', *History of Religions*, 31 (4) May, pp. 385–402.

———, 1991 [1990], 'The Sikh Person, the Khalsa Panth, and Western Sikh Converts', *Khera: Journal of Religious Understanding*, X (1) Jan–March 1991, pp. 20–36 [unauthorized reprint]

———, 1990a, 'The Sikh Person, the Khalsa Panth, and Western Sikh Converts' in Bardwell L. Smith, (ed.), *Religious Movements and Social Identity: Continuity and Change in India*, Delhi: Chanakya Publications, pp. 117–35.

———, 1990b, 'On the Moral Sensitivities of Sikhs in North America' in Owen M. Lynch, (ed.), *Divine Passions: The Social Construction of Emotion in India*, Berkeley: University of California Press and New Delhi: Oxford University Press, pp. 239–61.

———, 1989a, 'Sikh Persons and Practices: A Comparative Ethnosociology', unpublished PhD dissertation, Department of Anthropology, The University of Chicago.

———, 1989b, 'Introduction: A Century of Sikhs Beyond Punjab' in N. Gerald Barrier and Verne A. Dusenbery, (eds), *The Sikh Diaspora: Migration and the Experience Beyond Punjab*, Columbia, Missouri: South Asia Publications and Delhi: Chanakya Publications, pp. 1–28.

———, 1989c, 'Of Singh Sabhas, Siri Singh Sahibs, and Sikh Scholars: Sikh Discourse from North America in the 1970s' in N. Gerald Barrier and

Verne A. Dusenbery, (eds), *The Sikh Diaspora: Migration and the Experience Beyond Punjab*, Columbia, Missouri: South Asia Publications and Delhi: Chanakya Publications, pp. 90–119.

———, 1988, 'Punjabi Sikhs and Gora Sikhs: Conflicting Assertions of Sikh Identity in North America' in Joseph T. O'Connell, Milton Israel, and Willard G. Oxtoby, with W.H. McLeod and J.S. Grewal, (eds), *Sikh History and Religion in the Twentieth Century*, Toronto: Centre for South Asian Studies, University of Toronto, pp. 334–55.

———, 1981, 'Canadian Ideology and Public Policy: The Impact on Vancouver Sikh Ethnic and Religious Adaptation', *Canadian Ethnic Studies*, XIII (3) Winter, pp. 101–19.

———, 1979, 'India's Rural Income Gap' [Letter] in *The Far Eastern Economic Review*, CV (31) 3 August, p. 6.

———, 1975, 'Straight→Freak→Yogi→Sikh: A "Search for Meaning" in American Culture', unpublished MA thesis, Department of Anthropology, The University of Chicago.

———, 1973, 'Why would anybody join…? A Study of Recruitment and the Healthy, Happy, Holy Organization', unpublished BA (Hons) essay, Department of Anthropology, Stanford University.

Hannerz, Ulf, 2004, *Foreign News: Exploring the World of Foreign Correspondents*, Chicago and London: The University of Chicago Press.

Marriott, McKim, 1990, 'Constructing an Indian Ethnosociology' in McKim Marriott, (ed.), *India Through Hindu Categories*, New Delhi and Newbury Park, CA: Sage Publications, pp. 1–39.

PART I
SIKH ETHNOSOCIOLOGY

1

Punjabi Sikhs and Gora Sikhs*

Conflicting Assertions of Sikh Identity in North America

Sikhs claim that theirs is the youngest major 'world religion' and that the teachings of the Sikh Gurus (preceptors) are universal in their truth and applicability. Yet, until recently, Sikhism remained essentially a regional faith, one found among thirteen to sixteen million Punjabis living in India and in scattered Punjabi communities abroad. Over the past five centuries, as the Sikh community in Punjab grew in size and strength, it drew members from the indigenous Punjabi Hindu and, to a lesser extent, Punjabi Muslim communities. But despite more than a century of Sikh migration to other parts of the world, the community has remained an insular one. And norms of endogamy and non-proselytization have ensured that heretofore there has been no significant move on the part of non-Punjabis to embrace the Sikh religion. During the past fifteen years, however, several thousand young North Americans have made unprecedented claims to Sikh identity and have sought to have their 'conversion' to the Sikh *dharma* ('religion', 'moral duty', 'way of life') recognized by both Punjabi Sikhs and the world at large.

In the Punjab, the reaction to these *gora* ('white') Sikhs, as the western converts are commonly called by Punjabi Sikhs, was, at least initially, quite positive. Sikh leaders commented favourably on the apparent

* First published in Joseph T. O'Connell, Milton Israel, and Willard G. Oxtoby, (eds) with W.H. McLeod and J.S. Grewal (visiting eds), *Sikh History and Religion in the Twentieth Century*, Toronto: Centre for South Asian Studies, University of Toronto, 1988, pp. 334–55.

devotion and ritual piety of the converts and held them up as evidence to Punjabi Sikh youth and to non-Sikhs of Sikhism's appeal and relevance to the modern world. In North America, however, the response of Punjabi Sikhs was, from the start, considerably more restrained. Punjabi Sikhs in North America—including the growing number of second and third generation Canadians and Americans of Punjabi Sikh descent—had previously had a virtual free hand in defining for themselves and for the wider public what it meant to be a Sikh. Now this exclusivity was being challenged, and many Punjabi Sikhs thought it prudent to wait and see how the Gora Sikhs would assert their new-found Sikh identity before endorsing their claims and embracing the converts as fellow Sikhs.

This essay explores one aspect of the relationship between the small, but well-organized and highly vocal, group of North American Sikh converts—almost all of whom are members or former members of the Healthy, Happy, Holy Organization (or 3HO) and its religious arm, Sikh Dharma[1]—and the larger, but more diffuse and diverse, population of North Americans of Punjabi Sikh ancestry. The paper suggests that certain of the differences that have arisen between the Gora Sikhs and the Punjabi Sikhs over the assertion of a Sikh identity can be understood as deriving from differing cultural presuppositions about the nature of persons and groups. It argues that contrasting, culturally informed interpretations of Sikh teaching and practices have led the two groups to apply different standards in evaluating each other's assertions of Sikh identity. And it concludes that half a world of difference lies between the 'radical egalitarianism' of North American converts and the 'unity in diversity' perspective of Punjabi Sikhs, approaches that have led the converts to regard most Punjabi Sikhs in North America as no longer Sikhs and most Punjabi Sikhs in North America to regard Gora Sikhs as, at best, Sikhs of a very different kind.

SIKH EGALITARIANISM AND SOCIAL DIVERSITY

Sikh informants and Sikh apologists have commonly emphasized for Western audiences the degree to which Sikh doctrine constitutes a radical departure from Hindu ideology. Thus, they have pointed to the anti-caste pronouncements of the Sikh Gurus and to Guru Gobind Singh's formation in 1699 of the Khalsa Panth ('Brotherhood of the Pure')[2] as evidence of the Sikh obliteration of caste hierarchy. True, some have noted that the institution of inter-caste commensality and consociation in Sikh worship did not lead to inter-caste marriages, even among the

Gurus, and that dropping Hindu caste and clan names in favour of the Sikh name-titles—'Singh' (lion) for males and 'Kaur' (princess) for females—did not push awareness of one's caste affiliation from public consciousness. However, at least in the South Asian context, Sikh teachings and ritual practices have stuck out as radically egalitarian;[3] and the differences in Sikh and Hindu ideology, rather than similarities in social organization, have been emphasized in giving substance to the claim that Sikhism is not only a unique and separate religion but one significantly free of caste distinctions.

Whether in deference to Sikh sensibilities or for lack of familiarity with Sikh social practices, South Asianists have by and large given only passing attention to the question of caste in the Sikh Panth.[4] We are indebted, therefore, to the historian W.H. McLeod for two articles that address directly the persistence of caste observances among Sikhs. It is McLeod's contention that what the Sikh Gurus meant by their teachings and demonstrated through their actions was that 'whereas they were vigorously opposed to the *vertical* distinctions of caste they were content to accept it in terms of its *horizontal* linkages'. Thus, he argues, what they were concerned to deny were (1) the 'soteriological significance of caste' and (2) the 'justice of privilege or deprivation based upon notions of status and hierarchy', while continuing to accept the 'socially beneficial pattern of horizontal connections'.[5] McLeod does not deny hierarchical overtones in the ranking of local Sikh caste groups but argues that the Sikh Panth is and always has been of 'heterogeneous constituency,' being composed of various largely endogamous groups (Punjabi, *zat*; Hindi, *jati*) whose social interaction and status have taken different forms at different times and in different places, yet who continue to assert their own and confirm one another's common membership in the Sikh Panth.

McLeod's formulation, however foreign its solid geometric imagery may be to describing the fluid realities supposed by South Asians, strongly suggests that Punjabi Sikhs do not find it problematic to assert their similarities as Sikhs while simultaneously maintaining other diversities and dissimilarities among themselves as Punjabi persons. Such diversity among those calling themselves Sikhs is not only a matter of the different *zat* groupings to which Punjabi persons continue to belong; it is also a matter of different ritual practices which Punjabi Sikhs follow. For instance, two groups which in the West are considered 'orthodox' and 'heterodox' Sikhs, that is, long-haired *keshdhari* Sikhs and clean-shaven *sahajdhari* Sikhs, are generally regarded by Punjabis as simply different kinds or degrees of Sikhs. In light of prevailing Western conceptions, the persistence of caste observances in the face of Sikh 'egalitarian' teachings and a tolerance of diverse—including what appear to be 'unorthodox'—practices by those calling themselves Sikhs may be considered problematic issues by Western observers.[6] But given the radically different cultural conceptions of persons and social identities they hold, there is no reason to expect these to be problematic issues for Punjabis. Indeed, this essay suggests that the conflicting assertions of Sikh identity and mutual misunderstandings arising in North America between Punjabi Sikhs and Gora Sikhs follow from the radically different cultural assumptions each brings to the interaction.

PUNJABI PERSONS AND SIKH PRACTICES[7]

The Punjabi term *zat* (like its Hindi cognate and synonym, *jati*) is commonly rendered as 'caste', since it refers, among other things, to certain named, loosely ranked, hereditary, primarily endogamous, occupational groupings in Punjabi society that Western-oriented social scientists wish to assimilate to their notion of 'caste'. But as McKim Marriott, and Ronald Inden have convincingly argued,[8] the terms *zat* and *jati* can refer to 'all sorts of categories of things' (for example, male beings as differentiated from female beings, human beings as distinct from animals or divinities) and to a 'whole range of earthly populations' (for example, regional groupings, religious communities, occupational categories, ethnic groups) for which the term 'genus' and its plural, 'genera', seem the most appropriate gloss. Since South Asian genera are ordered paradigmatically, not just taxonomically, each person belongs simultaneously to several kinds of genera. They are intersecting classes.

For Punjabi Sikhs, the most important distinctions of persons within Punjabi society are those based on religion (between Sikhs, Hindus, Muslims, etc.), those based on occupation (between agriculturalist Jats, mercantile Khatris and Aroras, artisan Ramgarhias and Ahluwalias, service Mazhbis and Ramdasis, etc.) and those based on regional origins (between peoples of the regions of the Punjab called Majha, Doaba, and Malwa). These different kinds of persons—by ancestry members of different human genera—are understood to possess different natural substances and moral codes deriving from, respectively and simultaneously, their objects of worship, their means of subsistence, and their territory. Persons' generic substances and codes for conduct of persons are, therefore, not immutable. New substances and new moral codes—altered modes of worship, subsistence, and territory—may transform persons over time.

Being a Sikh, for a Punjabi, implies having one of these kinds of generic features through having incorporated into one's person the natural substance and moral code for conduct of the Sikh Guru (preceptor). Receipt of the Guru's coded substances makes those who bear them partly alike in their personal natures and, without making them alike in other ways, makes of them a recognizably distinct worship genus—the Sikh Panth. But different categories of persons may be recognized within the Sikh Panth based on the kind and degree of Sikh worship substances they have incorporated into their total persons. Minimally, those who incorporate the natural sacred sound (*gurbani kirtan*), the visual emanations (*gurdarshan*), and the edible 'benefits' (*karah parshad*) of the Guru and who mix with other Sikhs in the communality of the *sangat* (congregation) and the commensality of the *pangat* (communal dining hall) may be considered *sahajdhari* (literally, 'one who bears a light-weight [burden]') Sikhs. At the other extreme, those who incorporate the *amrit* (a 'nectar of immortality' including sugar, water, steel, and the Guru's word), shared in the course of the *amrit pahul* (initiation) ceremony, become *amritdhari* (literally, 'nectar-bearing'; the common Christian-style translation is 'baptized') Sikhs and members of the Khalsa Panth.

These *amritdhari* Sikhs, having achieved a higher state of Sikh regeneration through being further united with the Guru's substance and following a stricter moral code appropriate to the Khalsa, are thought capable of uniting others into the Panth by administering the *amrit* to initiates. Standing between the light-burdened *sahajdhari* Sikhs and the more heavily burdened *amritdhari* Sikhs are the *keshdhari* (literally, 'one who bears hair [or a lion's mane]') Sikhs, who maintain the outward Khalsa form (including the uncut hair and other visible markings) without benefit of having incorporated the *amrit* and without the corresponding obligation and prestige of observing the full Khalsa *rahit maryada* (literally, 'prestigious code of discipline'). Finally, *patit* (literally, 'fallen'; the common Christian-style translation is 'apostate') Sikhs are those who once having accepted the *amrit* no longer follow the Khalsa *rahit* (discipline). As their name implies, they are considered to have fallen in purity and rank and thus to be no longer able to induct others into the Panth.

If Punjabi persons are constituted as members of the Sikh Panth (worship genus) through their incorporation and manipulation of Sikh worship substances, they nevertheless continue to belong to their occupational, territorial, and other human genera. Nowhere is this composite nature of the Punjabi Sikh person more clearly illustrated than in the matchings of persons which characterize marriage practices. In keeping with the Guru's injunctions, Sikhs by and large marry other Sikhs; but they marry Sikhs who are relatively more or less like themselves, that is, those with whom they share not only the same worship substances and code of conduct but also the same occupational and territorial coded substances. The fact that endogamy within the Sikh Panth co-exists with an overwhelming preference for 'caste' endogamous marriages and, to a slightly lesser extent, regionally endogamous marriages suggests not that there is some problematic contradiction between Sikh teachings and practices, but rather that ritual transactions, while making Punjabi persons partially alike as Sikhs, do not constitute them as completely identical persons.

Thus, it should not be surprising to find, as McLeod's work makes clear, that persons of different genera may assert their Sikh identity in different ways. For instance, the numerically dominant and influential Jats, though derived from what is sometimes considered a middling Hindu caste, have risen to an elevated rank, especially within rural Punjabi society; and, as McLeod notes, 'the Jat Sikh commonly assumes a considerable freedom with regard to observance of the Khalsa discipline.... In his own eyes and those of other Jats he remains a Sikh even if he cuts his beard or smokes tobacco'.[9] This does not necessarily hold true for other *zat* groups. Though traditionally over-represented in the *sahajdhari* category, once having accepted the visible Sikh markings of a *keshdhari*, the urban Khatris and Aroras have generally maintained the outward form strictly, for 'if a Khatri [or Arora] shaves he is regarded as a Hindu by others and soon comes to regard himself as one'.[10]

The case of what traditionally have been regarded in Punjabi society as lower-caste and outcaste groups is particularly illuminating. As a vehicle of upward mobility, membership in the unpartitioned Khalsa has held considerable appeal. The full, public assertion of Sikh identity entailed in Khalsa membership—or, at the very least, the maintenance of *keshdhari* markings—visibly distinguishes the lower-caste Sikh from his Hindu caste-mates and is essential to the acceptance by others of his claim to being a Sikh. Writing of two such groups, McLeod notes that they have never 'observed to any significant degree the practice of calling themselves Sikhs without observing the outward forms of the Khalsa. For them this would destroy any social advantage implicit in the title of Sikh. Indeed, the title would not have been accepted as valid'.[11] Such a group's transformed nature generally leads its members to take up new occupations and to avoid undertaking marriages with Hindu or Muslim caste-mates. And these actions eventually have led most such groups to be given corporate names distinct from those of their former caste-mates. But despite impressive gains in wealth and reputation made by some of these groups,[12] their partial transformations are rarely acted upon as outweighing other differences included in the group's original nature; and Sikhs of other, more highly reputed, castes generally maintain a policy of non-marriage with them.

It is in light of this understanding of Punjabi persons and Sikh practices that the Punjabi Sikh experience in North America and the conflicting assertions of Sikh identity made in North America by Punjabi Sikhs and Gora Sikhs begin to make sense.

FROM THE DOMINANCE OF JATS TO A DIVERSITY OF *ZATS*

The first substantial Punjabi migration to North America occurred during the first decade of the twentieth century. From that point until the mid-to-late 1960s, the overwhelming majority of Sikhs in North America were Jats from Doaba (the plains area of Punjab between the Beas and Sutlej rivers). The original Sikh immigrants were predominantly labourers and farmers who had served in the Indian army. Most came to North America as sojourners, intent on making their fortune and returning home to the Punjab to retire in comfort on the family farm. The vast majority of these early immigrants eventually settled in British Columbia, where they became concentrated in lumber and lumber-related industries, or in California, where they pursued the traditional Jat occupation as agriculturalists. When, after long and arduous struggle, they were finally permitted to sponsor as immigrants their families left behind in the Punjab, it was their Jat Sikh wives, children, and relatives who came to join them. And it was these original immigrants, plus an intermittent flow of legal and illegal immigrants, and their offspring, who kept alive a Punjabi Sikh presence in North America in the face of significant isolation from the homeland and alternately hostile and indifferent treatment from the host societies.

Individual non-Jats apparently mixed freely with their fellow Punjabi Sikhs and suffered little obvious social impairment on account of caste. In California, the first 'East Indian' elected to the US Congress, Dalip Singh Saund, was a Ramgarhia Sikh. In British Columbia, Mayo Singh, a Mahton Sikh, became a millionaire mill owner and pillar of the Sikh community. Nevertheless, it was Doabi Jat Sikh practices that largely defined the Sikh identity as it developed in North America. One aspect of this Jat dominance was the spreading indifference to the maintenance of the Khalsa *rahit*. In time, a majority of male Sikhs in North America were clean-shaven and turbanless. And eventually most Sikh institutions, including the *gurdwaras* (temples), came to be dominated by clean-shaven Sikhs. New immigrants were urged to shave before or upon arrival in North America so as to facilitate their social and economic adaptation. Administration of the *amrit pahul,* and thus initiation into the Khalsa Panth, virtually ceased. Most Jats in North America designated themselves and their families as Sikh by virtue of their birth and upbringing; and, unless they did something actively to refute the assumption (for example, convert to Christianity or marry a *gora*), that designation was generally not challenged by their fellow Jats.

Whereas British policies in India—especially the requirement that Sikh troops maintain Khalsa *rahit*—had helped to reinforce Khalsa discipline among Jat Sikhs,[13] Canadian and American policies and attitudes worked against the maintenance of the outward Sikh forms. Punjabi Sikhs in North America perceived their beards and turbans to be an impediment in their dealings with non-Sikhs, and most felt obliged to give them up. While this may have made them more acceptable to the non-Sikh public, it did little to change their identities in North America. In their own eyes they remained, for the most part, Doabi Jat Sikhs. And to the wider North American public, clean-shaven or turbaned, Jat or non-Jat, they were (with individual exceptions) regarded as 'Hindoos' or 'East Indians', Canadians and Americans being by and large insensitive to confessional or caste differences within the broader ethnic category.

Naming practices were also affected by North American customs and attitudes. The importance attached to surnames in North American culture and the convention of patronymical inheritance produced a number of onomastic anomalies for Punjabi Sikhs living in North America. Whereas in rural Punjabi society, 'X Singh' could be further identified as 'X Singh of Y village' or 'X Singh, son of Z Singh', and 'A Kaur' could be further identified as 'A Kaur, wife of Y Singh' or 'A Kaur, daughter of Z Singh', North American conventions led not only to a proliferation of 'Mr Singh' but to the creation of 'Mrs Singh' and 'Miss Singh' as well. Pressure from the wider public for a differentiation of 'Singhs' and the Sikhs' own discomfort with the effects of Western naming customs led to modifications in Sikh naming practices. Some Sikhs began to use their family's village name in Punjab as a last name, but by the 1950s it became conventional to use the name of one's *got* ('clan'; exogamous grouping within the *zat*) as a last name, reserving 'Singh' and 'Kaur' for use as middle names. Since *got* names are usually indicative of *zat* as well, Jat identities came to be strongly signalled.

If such accommodation was furthered by the homogeneity which prevailed in North America's Sikh population, that homogeneity did not altogether suppress the development of factional splits for which Punjabis—and Jat Sikhs in particular[14]—are well known. The homogeneity of the community and the chain migration did, however, allow most new immigrants to be incorporated into established social networks (*biradari* or *baradari,* 'brotherhood') of fellow Jat Sikhs who were often kinsmen or village-mates. As a result, the established residents were able to guide the newcomer's adaptation to the new social environment, providing initial housing and job contacts and alerting the newcomer to appropriate local social convention. Of equal importance to the Sikhs, and helping to explain the practice of seeking spouses from India, the newcomer was one who renewed substantive ties to the homeland and provided a conservative counterbalance to any too radical deviation from Punjabi Sikh practices.

The Sikh population in North America began to change rapidly in the late 1960s, and once again the changes were in part the consequence of social policies over which the Sikhs themselves had little control. In the mid-1960s, in response to accusations that their immigration policies were implicitly racist, the Canadian and American governments liberalized their immigration regulations, making it considerably easier for individuals of non-European backgrounds to gain residence. As a result, immigration of Punjabi Sikhs increased dramatically, not only from India but from the United Kingdom, East Africa, East and Southeast Asia, and Fiji as well. During the past two decades, a number of new Punjabi Sikh communities have emerged in North America, especially in the larger metropolitan areas where Sikh professionals have found employment. In the long-established communities of British Columbia and California, old-timers and their descendants have been confronted by newcomers unbeholden to the old-timers for sponsorship, not necessarily having common *zat* membership, and often pushing a visible Khalsa Sikh identity which most old-timers and their offspring had come to regard as an unnecessary encumbrance. Thus, changes in the character of the Sikh population in North America have been profound. Distinctions came to be felt not only between long-time residents and recent immigrants, between 'traditionalists' and 'modernists,' and between India-born and North America-born, but also among those of different national origins or country of last residence, family regional origins in the Punjab, caste, class and—with the emergence of Gora Sikhs—ethnic or 'racial' origins.

To the extent that their fellow Punjabi Sikhs in various countries have constituted their 'significant others', Punjabi Sikhs in North America have remained sensitive to Punjabi differentiations of persons and human genera. The Jat Sikh population had been aware of *zat* relations, and by and large followed Punjabi endo-marital convention, although Jats had traditionally been somewhat 'looser' (that is, more hypergamous) in this regard than other Punjabis.[15] But as most spouses were sought in India and most of one's fellow Sikhs in North America were also Doabi Jats, caste and regional identity had been a relatively infrequent consideration in Sikh social life in North America. The North America-born were raised with far greater concern for the negative consequences for family honour (*izzat*) that would follow from marrying a *gora* (white male) or *gori* (white female) than from marrying the 'wrong' kind of Punjabi Sikh. Indeed, the reputed differences in personal natures of Punjabis of different occupational, territorial, or worship genera paled in comparison to the contrasts that parents drew between Punjabi and Western culture and character.

However, with the increase in non-Jat and non-Doabi immigration during the past two decades has come a greater emphasis on the supposed differences in character and temperament of different kinds of Punjabi Sikhs and increased concern that care also be taken to avoid 'improper' (that is, caste or regionally exogamous) marriages with Sikhs of different kinds. The use of *got* names as last names has conveniently made one's *zat* affiliation public knowledge and those who for whatever reason refuse to use a *got* name are often suspected of trying to obscure low-caste or outcaste origins. To foreclose any suggestion that their personal natures have degenerated as a consequence of transactions undertaken in North America, Punjabi Sikhs of all kinds continue to value actions which serve to 'nourish and sustain'[16] ancestral occupational, territorial, and worship genera. This has led them to minimize certain transactions with alien others (particularly with *gora* society, but also with other 'kinds' of Sikhs) and to maximize transactions with persons of one's own kind. Such concern is manifest not only in formation of factions, in socialization of children, and in arrangement of marriages, but increasingly also in the differentiation of Sikh gurdwaras and secondary institutions by caste, by regional origins, and by ritual practices of members.[17]

It is into an increasingly diverse Punjabi Sikh population in North America that the Gora Sikhs have recently interjected themselves full-force. The reception they have received from Punjabi Sikhs in North America has been shaped in important ways by the Punjabi Sikhs' response to their own internal diversity and by Punjabi Sikh understandings of persons and human genera.

AMERICAN AND CANADIAN SIKHS OF 3HO/SIKH DHARMA[18]

In 1968 Harbhajan Singh Puri, a Khatri Sikh whose family had resettled in New Delhi during the post-partition exodus from Pakistani Punjab, quit his job as a customs official at Delhi International Airport at Palam and left for Canada to take a job as a yoga instructor. Upon reaching Toronto, he found that the promised job had fallen through, but with the aid of a Punjabi Sikh sponsor, he was able to settle in Los Angeles, where he began teaching yoga courses at the East-West Cultural Center. Now calling himself 'Yogi Bhajan', Puri proved to be a compelling teacher. Having found a receptive core of students, he soon established an ashram (spiritual commune) for them. There he taught his 'Kundalini Yoga: The Yoga of Awareness', offered occasional 'Tantric Yoga Intensives', and imposed upon his followers the structure and discipline of what he called 'the healthy, happy, holy way of life'. In 1969, the Healthy, Happy, Holy Organization (or 3HO) was formally incorporated as a tax-exempt educational organization. Puri was now sending his newly-trained 'student teachers' to other cities in North America to teach Kundalini Yoga classes and to establish additional 3HO ashrams. During the early 1970s, the primary orientation of the organization was towards recruiting new members through the yoga classes and establishing new ashrams where, Puri claimed, members were being purified and prepared to accept their calling as Sikhs. At this point, however, Puri 'continued to teach about Sikh Dharma in an indirect way'.[19] 3HO members, most of whom were young, white, middle-class American and Canadian refugees from the counter-culture, tended to regard themselves not as Sikhs but as 'yogis' and 'yoginis' or, in Puri's terminology, 'shaktimen' and 'shaktis'.

Puri had, however, slowly begun to disclose his own Sikh background and introduce Sikh teachings to his closest followers. In 1971, he took eighty-four of them to India, where they visited the Golden Temple and surrounding shrines. At the Akal Takht ('throne of the Timeless One', the highest seat of Sikh religious-cum-temporal authority) the group was cordially received and Puri was honoured for his missionary work.

Returning home with what he represented to be the mandate to spread the message of Sikhism in the West, Puri began to supplement and supplant his primarily yogic explanation of the 'the healthy, happy, holy way of life' with a more explicitly Sikh account. Puri now also began to use the title 'Siri Singh Sahib', a title which he claimed had been given him by the Shiromani Gurdwara Parbandhak Committee (the organization legally empowered to control historic and other Sikh gurdwaras in the Punjab) and which he rendered, liberally, as 'Chief Administrative and Religious Authority for the Sikh Dharma in the Western Hemisphere'. In 1973 he was successful in having the Sikh Dharma Brotherhood (later recast in non-gender-specific language as, simply, 'Sikh Dharma') officially registered as a tax-exempt religious organization legally empowered to ordain Sikh ministers who would have the authority to perform marriages, provide the last rites, and administer the *amrit pahul* ceremony.

Puri's own transformation from 'Yogi Bhajan' to the 'Siri Singh Sahib' corresponded roughly with a change from a primarily yogic to a primarily Sikh identity on the part of 3HO members. The change did not happen overnight; but once convinced by Puri that what he was calling the 'healthy, happy, holy way life' was that of an orthodox Sikh, most 3HO members did not hesitate to make a formal commitment to their new religion. And Puri provided unprecedented opportunities for 3HO members to express their commitment, introducing Sikh initiations and minister ordinations in addition to holding the more traditional *amrit pahul* ceremony. The resultant change from a yogic to Sikh identity on the part of 3HO members also corresponded to a change of emphasis within the organization from the aims of recruiting new members and establishing additional *ashrams* to those of maintaining the established group, raising a second generation, and establishing credibility as upholders of Sikh orthodoxy in North America. With respect to the latter task, the new American and Canadian Sikhs, as they called themselves, exhibited all the fervour and self-assurance one might expect from new converts to any faith.

Whereas most Punjabi Sikhs in North America had been content to keep a low profile, often regarding their visibility as a handicap and sometimes sacrificing their beards and turbans as a necessary adaptation to the demands of life in North America, the new American and Canadian Sikhs of 3HO have asserted their right to a full public expression of their version of Sikh orthopraxy and have sought aggressively to have their 'religious rights' recognized by the North American public. In these efforts, they have made effective use of the media and of administrative and legal channels. 3HO has actively courted publicity and their 'exoticness' (for example, white clothing, beards, turbans, ashrams, mass marriages, and strange 'Indian' names) and their 'good works' (for example, drug rehabilitation programmes, free kitchens) have made them good copy. More significantly, with rare exception,[20] what media exposure they have received has been uncritical in accepting the converts' claim to represent orthodox Sikhism in North America. And such claims have been further reinforced by rulings of human-rights officials and the courts. In a number of cases successfully brought by 3HO members (for example, for seeking exemption from hard-hat and dress-code requirements), North American officials have found the petitioner, as a Khalsa Sikh and a member of Sikh Dharma, to be a Sikh in good standing exercising a legitimate right to the practice of the Sikh religion. All of this activity has made the converts known beyond what their numbers might otherwise warrant. Punjabi Sikhs in North America, in particular, have been made well aware of the existence of the Gora Sikhs, even if they have personally had little or no interaction with them.

GORA SIKHS: PERSONS OF A DEVIANT SECT OR A DIFFERENT GENUS?

It would be inaccurate to suggest that so diverse a population as that of North American Sikhs of Punjabi ancestry has responded uniformly to the assertion of Sikh identity by Gora Sikhs. While few would deny the theoretical right of non-Punjabis to become Sikhs, fewer still accept the idea that Puri and the Gora Sikhs have the authority to speak for all the Sikhs of North America. Beyond that, however, the category 'Gora Sikh' is such a new and in many ways anomalous one that it has taken time to sort out reactions. Early accounts of Gora Sikh–Punjabi Sikh interaction in the Los Angeles area[21] and in northern California[22] reported that initial receptivity to the converts' involvement with the established Sikh gurdwaras gave way to increasing discomfort on the part of Punjabi Sikhs. Agehananda Bharati discusses some of the reasons for the mixed feelings: 'Punjabis candidly admire the strict Sikh ritual discipline of the 3HO, and grudgingly their teetotalitarian ways. [But] they do not approve of the uniformization of the 3HO, especially the 3HO women; and they resent the superior ways the 3HO displays towards them'.[23] In many of their practices, Gora Sikhs seem insensitive to the meanings their actions may have for Punjabi Sikhs. They insist, for instance, that all-white clothing (a mourning colour in Punjab associated with widows), turbans for women (almost unheard of among Punjabis, for whom a turban is a male symbol par excellence), vegetarianism (not a general Sikh—and particularly not Jat Sikh—practice), and yoga (varieties of which were said by the Sikh Gurus to be incompatible with the life of a householder enjoined upon Sikhs) are all orthodox Sikh practices. Yet, at the same time, most 3HO members lack fluency in the Punjabi language beyond the memorization of a few *shabads* (hymns), even though for Punjabi Sikhs the Punjabi language and Gurmukhi script are intimately bound up with Sikh worship. Furthermore, the assertiveness of 3HO women and familiarity between the sexes, although restrained by North American standards, seem excessive to many Punjabis. And, finally, the veneration of Puri by 3HO members verges on what Punjabi Sikhs regard as Hindu-like idolatry. Some of the insensitivity on the part of 3HO members may grow out of naivete and reflect unfamiliarity with Punjabi culture, but some is based on a principled decision that Sikh 'religious' norms—as understood by Gora Sikhs through Puri's presentation of them—must supersede parochial 'ethnic' (that is, Punjabi) custom.

The Goras' assertion of their Sikh identity has tended to provoke one of two responses from Punjabi Sikhs in North America. Some would deny altogether the claims of 3HO members to be Sikh. They maintain that despite the superficial appearance of adhering to Khalsa *rahit*, the Goras have not incorporated Sikh worship substances comparable to those maintained by other persons of the Sikh Panth. Among 3HO practices that are commonly cited as inconsistent and incompatible with the Sikh *dharma* are: inclusion of Kundalini and Tantric yoga practices as a form of Sikh mysticism; distortions of *gurbani* and misquotations and mistranslations from the Adi Granth (the Sikh holy book, which is itself considered to be the reigning Guru); questionable legitimacy and efficacy of *amrit pahul* ceremonies conducted for and by 3HO members; veneration and reverence accorded to Puri over and above that appropriately reserved for the Sikh Gurus, the Adi Granth, and the seats of Sikh spiritual authority; and, finally, formation of organizational structures and an ecclesiastical hierarchy independent of, inconsistent with, and at cross purposes to, the traditional Panthic organization.[24] Together, such considerations lead many Punjabi Sikhs in North America to regard 3HO as a deviant sect or cult with Puri its 'false *guru*'.[25]

A number of parallels have been drawn between 3HO/Sikh Dharma and (a) other North American religious cults and (b) schismatic or breakaway sects in India claiming to be Sikh. Punjabi Sikhs note that young North Americans seem unusually susceptible to religious cults and to brainwashing at the hands of authoritarian cult leaders. Some cynically admire Puri for living the easy life off his gullible North American followers; but most express concern that 3HO members' willingness to take Puri's idiosyncratic teachings as Sikh orthodoxy means that they will accept anything Puri tells them and that their loyalty to Puri will come before their loyalty to the Panth. In the wake of the mass suicide-murder at the People's Temple in Jonestown, Guyana, Punjabi Sikhs asked whether 3HO members might not be capable of the same or a similar act of blind fanaticism. And in the context of the current Punjab crisis they ask: if Puri were to take issue with a ruling (*hukumnama*, *gurmata*) normally considered binding on the entire Panth, would his followers respect Puri's dictates or the collective decision of the Panth?

Recent events in the Punjab also awaken Punjabi Sikh concerns for what can happen if deviant sects which claim to be Sikh are not repudiated at an early stage in their development. Standing out in the minds of many Punjabi Sikhs in North America are the clashes that have taken place in recent years in the Punjab between Sikhs and members of the Sant Nirankari Mandal. This is a group which claims descent from a nineteenth-century Sikh reformist movement and whose leaders maintain an outward Sikh form and use the Adi Granth in public ceremonies. But it is a group that the main body of Sikhs accuses of slandering the Sikh Gurus, misinterpreting and mistreating the Granth, elevating its own leader to the status of Guru and mocking Sikhism in its practices.[26] Several years of clashes between Sikhs and members of the Sant Nirankari Mandal culminated in a fatal encounter in Amritsar on 13 April 1978, and the subsequent assassination of the Sant Nirankari leader in 1980. The provocative actions of the Mandal, and frustrations with the Congress (I) government for allegedly aiding and abetting the provocations, eventually led to a *hukumnama* (decree) issued from the Akal Takht repudiating 'pseudo-Nirankari' claims to being Sikh and ordering Sikhs to cease interaction with members of the Mandal. Some Punjabi Sikhs in North America argue that a similar repudiation should be made of Puri and his gora followers. In fact, resolutions that would declare Gora Sikhs of 3HO to be non-Sikhs and would bar them from participating in Punjabi Sikh institutions have been introduced for consideration by local Sikh societies in North America.

The fact that such resolutions have not been passed should be one indication that this negative view of the Gora Sikhs as a deviant sect is, for the present, a minority one. Indeed, it is more common to hear the Gora Sikhs referred to as 'good Sikhs' than as 'non-Sikhs'. The majority of North American Sikhs of Punjabi ancestry seem willing to look past the Gora Sikhs' idiosyncrasies to note their visible Khalsa form and apparent adherence to Khalsa discipline. This is not to imply that most Punjabi Sikhs in North America are in full accord with the Gora Sikhs' representation of Sikh orthodoxy. Although there are areas of substantive agreement (for example, the significant support given the Gora Sikh efforts to establish a Sikh 'religious right' to maintain the beard, turban, and other Sikh symbols), there is much about the Gora Sikhs' assertion of their identity that Punjabi Sikhs find alien. What I suggest has happened is that, given the Punjabi notion of the person that underlies the 'unity in diversity' of the Sikh Panth, the majority of Punjabi Sikhs acknowledge the converts' claims to being Sikh but nevertheless regard them as persons of a very different—and lower—'kind'.

It is not altogether surprising that Punjabi Sikhs should model their relations with Gora Sikhs along the lines of relations between Punjabi Sikhs of different kinds. When asked to explain to non-Punjabis and to their own North America-born youngsters the persistence of *zat* consciousness and *zat* endogamy in North America, Punjabi Sikhs commonly explain that people of different Punjabi ancestral occupational, territorial, and worship communities are known to have different tastes, temperaments, and ways of doing things which bind them to others of their own 'kind' (*zat*) but which make them difficult to mix with—and unthinkable as recipients of one's daughter in marriage. In short, there are among Punjabi Sikhs many different 'kinds' (*zat*) of people. Such a generic explanation, while doubtless understating Punjabi notions of purity and honour, could easily be applied to make sense of the otherwise anomalous category 'Gora Sikh'.

It is important to realize that most Punjabi Sikhs regard North America not only as alien territory but as a land which all too easily can lead those who inhabit it to undertake indiscriminate and dharmically inappropriate actions that might lower their personal natures. The Western culture of North America is, thus, suspect; and *gora* is a term with pejorative overtones. To be too gora-like (especially, to marry a *gora/gori* or to convert to Christianity) is to risk bringing into question the reputation or honour (*izzat*) of the collectives (for example, family, *got*, *zat*) of which one is a part and to face possible social, if not physical, death. Indeed, before its application to Western converts to Sikhism, the term 'Gora Sikh' was applied censoriously to any Punjabi Sikh whose personal nature was thought to have degenerated as a consequence of improper, 'Western' behaviour. Thus, the new Gora Sikhs of 3HO/Sikh Dharma, even when recognized by Punjabi Sikhs as 'good Khalsa Sikhs', are persons who bear the alienating stigma of being *gora*. And this, in turn, affects the way that Punjabi Sikhs interact with them.

Understanding the Gora Sikhs to be Sikhs of a very different 'kind' allows Punjabi Sikhs to excuse the many idiosyncrasies and insensitivities they detect in Gora Sikh actions. In fact, every idiosyncrasy or apparent insensitivity to Punjabi Sikh cultural conventions is further confirmation of the *goras*' alien nature. Thus even when accepting as appropriate Gora Sikh participation in gurdwara functions and other activities of the Sikh Panth, most Punjabi Sikhs in North America remain circumspect in their interactions with Gora Sikhs. While they might be willing to honour publicly a Gora Sikh for *seva* (service) rendered to the Panth few would go as far as to give their daughters in marriage to persons of what is, in effect, a very different 'ethnic' genus.

In accepting Gora Sikhs as partially transformed *goras* who share a common membership in the Sikh Panth but who in other ways remain alien persons, Punjabi Sikhs are responding much as they have to conversions of low-caste and outcaste Punjabis. From a Punjabi perspective, 'conversion' to Sikhism consists of partial inclusion, intersection, or union into the Sikh Panth and depends on recognized transformations in one's personal nature. Those whose ancestral substance has not been marked previously or marked consistently with Sikh worship substances have generally found initiation into the Khalsa Panth (or, at the very least, attainment of *keshdhari* markings and conduct) crucial to public acceptance of their transformed nature. Thus, like Punjabi converts from low-caste and outcaste groups, Gora Sikhs have found it crucial to their assertion of Sikh identity that they maintain Khalsa *rahit*. And like such Punjabi converts, Gora Sikhs have found that, while entrance into the Panth has resulted in improved markings in the eyes of other Sikhs, it has not removed all differences associated with the converts' original natures. Despite the fact that they, like such Punjabi converts, have avoided undertaking marriage with former 'caste-mates' (that is, non-Sikh *goras*), Gora Sikhs have not yet been accorded by other Sikhs a corporate name which would de-emphasize their *gora* origins. In light of the policy of non-marriage (or, at best, hypergamous marriage) which Sikhs of highly reputed castes maintain with low-caste and outcaste

Punjabi converts, it is not surprising to find that Punjabi Sikhs of all kinds maintain a policy of non-marriage with Gora Sikhs. Gora Sikhs are after all the most recent and most alien of all converts, and their transformed nature is still untested.

PUNJABI SIKHS IN NORTH AMERICA: APOSTATE OR RETROGRADE PERSONS?

If it has served the purpose of a majority of Punjabi Sikhs in North America to treat the Gora Sikhs as Sikhs of a different—and somewhat dangerous and originally inferior—human genus, it has hardly satisfied the Gora Sikhs to be so treated. The source of the converts' discontent goes straight to their interpretation of Sikh teachings, and to the radical egalitarianism they find in Sikhism. It is their understanding of Sikh egalitarianism that leads them to assert a version of Sikh orthodoxy which Punjabi Sikhs in North America find either deviant or different. And it is the same principle that, in turn, leads the Gora Sikh to repudiate many practices of North Americans of Punjabi Sikh ancestry.

The Gora Sikhs make some crucial—and, I would argue, typically North American—assumptions about religion and about persons. They believe that persons are whole and impartible social units, that is, that the 'individual' is a non-divisible entity, and that common personal identity implies full equality. They hold that religious identity is essentially spiritual and personal, achieved through a full and conscious doctrinal choice (for example, through spiritual rebirth, confirmation, conversion) rather than ascribed as a fact of natural birth. And they regard religious norms as universal, absolute, and inviolable, entailing faithful adherence to some moral code of conduct equally enjoined on all believers and protected as a 'religious right'. This contrasts with the assumptions they hold about forms of social identity which they associate with the facts of one's origins and biological descent, for example, race, gender, national origin, ethnicity, and caste. These are regarded as essentially communal and non-volitional forms of social identity, and the associated norms of social action are understood to be arbitrary, ephemeral, and legitimately adaptable in different social settings. In short, the Gora Sikhs are religious absolutists and cultural relativists, arguing that universal religious 'codes for conduct' can be distinguished from and take precedence over particularistic cultural conventions. They thus distinguish that which they identify as a uniquely Sikh duty from that which they regard as mere Punjabi or North American custom. And they hold it incumbent on all would-be Sikhs in all places and at all times consistently to manifest their Sikh identity by maintaining identical Sikh religious practices.[27]

The Gora Sikhs take the creation of the Khalsa in 1699 by Guru Gobind Singh, the last living, human Guru, as a crucial event in the evolution of a distinctive Sikh identity. And they regard undergoing the *amrit* ceremony as crucial in the personal assertion of Sikh identity. They argue that Guru Gobind Singh's intention in setting forth the Khalsa *rahit* was (a) to provide the uniform standards by which to distinguish his Sikhs from other members of society (that is, to give them a unique and distinct identity) and (b) to establish in concrete terms the total (not partial) equality of all those who would assert that identity. Such an interpretation is hardly extraordinary in the context of contemporary Western ideology, where 'the fusion of equality and identity has become established at the level of common sense'.[28] However, set against the understanding given these events by most Punjabi Sikhs, the implications of the Gora Sikh interpretations are radical indeed.

For one thing, because of the central place they give to the Khalsa *rahit* and to the distinctive visible form that Guru Gobind Singh gave his followers, the Gora Sikhs argue that one is not truly a Sikh without wearing the so-called 'five Sikh symbols' or '5 Ks': the *kesh,* unshorn hair (covered by a turban); the *kanga,* a wooden comb; the *kirpan,* a sword; the *kara,* a steel bracelet; and the *kach*, a loin-and-thigh undergarment. In fact, the Gora Sikhs take these observable aspects of the Khalsa *rahit* as a necessary index of Sikh identity. This leads them to reject the notion that there might be different kinds of Sikhs following different codes of conduct and having incorporated varying degrees and kinds of Sikh worship substances. Such a reaction is, of course, culturally informed. As Louis Dumont has cogently noted, '[South Asians] will apply a rank where we in the West would approve or exclude'.[29] Arguing that terms like 'hereditary Sikh' and 'clean-shaven Sikh' are contradictions in terms and that *sahajdhari* Sikhs are 'not yet fully Sikh' and *patits* (as 'apostates') are 'no longer Sikhs', the Gora Sikhs have tried to exclude such people from participation as equals in Sikh affairs and have challenged their right to call themselves Sikhs. To explain why there should be so many of precisely these persons within the Punjabi Sikh communities of North America, the Gora Sikhs suggest that such people have 'sold out' their religious principles to achieve the easy life in North America.[30]

If such a position has effectively alienated the Gora Sikhs from those who for many decades constituted perhaps the majority of all Sikhs in North America, it has not led them in the long run to take any less critical a view of those who have maintained the visible Sikh symbols. While the former are considered 'too North American to be good Sikhs', the latter are often found to be 'too Punjabi to be good Sikhs'. In particular, the Gora Sikhs are sensitive to signs of 'caste consciousness' (a term used broadly to refer to any form of distinction or discrimination of persons among Sikhs), 'subordination of women' (a term used broadly to refer to any form of sex-role differentiation in Sikh practices), and any other evidence of hierarchical or parochial behaviour that the Gora Sikhs regard as inconsistent with Sikh 'egalitarian' teachings.

This conviction leads the Gora Sikhs to take strong stands against a number of established conventions within the Punjabi Sikh communities of North America. As might be expected, they object on principle to caste or regional or ethnic endogamy among Sikhs, arguing that for Sikhs the only legitimate requirement for marriage should be that both partners be good Sikhs. While somewhat sceptical about the present feasibility of marriages between themselves and Punjabi Sikhs (since, they argue, it is so hard to find a North American of Punjabi heritage who is a good Sikh), they have no objection in principle to such marriages. In fact, some were obviously disappointed that Puri gave his own daughter in marriage to another Khatri Sikh rather than to one of his *gora* followers.

In yet another stand against what they regard as retrograde 'caste consciousness', Gora Sikhs raise objections to the use of *got* names by Punjabi Sikhs in North America, arguing that Guru Gobind Singh intended the equality of all Sikhs to be indicated by their common name-titles as well as by their identical external form. As part of their own assertion of their new Sikh identities, Gora Sikhs have been given Sikh names, originally using 'Singh' and 'Kaur' as last names but more recently adopting 'Khalsa' as a non-gender-specifying last name. Ironically, while their intent has been to assert the equality of all Khalsa Sikhs, the fact that they have been virtually alone among Sikhs in adopting this convention means that the last name 'Khalsa' now indexes their membership in the Gora Sikh *biradari* (that is, in Sikh Dharma) in almost precisely the same manner as the use of *got* names indexes the *zat* membership of Punjabi Sikhs.

One final example should suffice to make clear the way in which the Gora Sikhs' version of Sikh orthodoxy has served to separate them from the Punjabi Sikhs of North America. The Gora Sikhs interpret the Gurus' teachings on the equality of men and women not simply as testifying to their equality in the eyes of God and in their ability to accept the coded substances of the Guru but as mandating their equal place in every other aspect of Sikh religious life. Thus, the Gora Sikhs object to what they regard as the 'subordination of women' in Sikh affairs and have pushed for an expanded role for women in the Sikh gurdwaras (for example, as officiants and participants in Sikh services and as members of the management committees of the temple societies). And it is this same insistence on the equality of Sikh males and females that has led the Gora Sikhs to interpret the Khalsa *rahit* as requiring turbans for women as well as men.[31] As with so many of the Gora Sikh efforts to push their brand of radical egalitarianism, the attempts to get Punjabi Sikh women in North America to don turbans and take a more public—and to Punjabi Sikhs a more 'male'—role in gurdwara affairs have been remarkably unsuccessful.[32] The net effect has been only to reinforce the Punjabi Sikh impression of the *goras*' alien natures and to increase the Gora Sikh frustration at the failure of the Punjabis to live up to what the North American converts take to be essentials of the Sikh religion.

CONCLUSION

This essay has argued that the conflicting assertions of Sikh identity on the part of Gora Sikhs and Punjabi Sikhs in North America follow from significantly different assumptions about the nature of persons and social identities. It has suggested that the 'radical egalitarianism' of the Gora Sikhs (that is, the insistence that a common identity as Sikhs mandates a uniform and unitary set of beliefs and practices for all Sikhs) is significantly informed by the understandings of individual persons and totalizing social identities common in Western cultures. And it has suggested that the 'unity in diversity' of the Punjabi Sikhs (that is, the acceptance of multiple *zat* ties among Punjabi persons and varying degrees or levels of incorporation within the Sikh Panth) is significantly informed by understandings of composite persons and partially shared identities common in the South Asian cultures.

As North Americans who could be expected to assert their Sikh identity in a way intelligible to the wider North American public, it is not surprising that the Gora Sikhs have had notable success in convincing the North American media and courts of their orthodoxy. In such situations, they address themselves to an audience which shares with them the same cultural assumptions. On the other hand, to the extent that Punjabi Sikhs in North America look to other Punjabi Sikhs as their significant others, they too can find continuing support for their assertion of Sikh identity. Punjabi Sikhs elsewhere with whom they share the same cultural assumptions do not consider most Punjabi Sikhs in North America to be degenerate and non-Sikh, but continue to match their children in marriage to them as persons of the same kind. Thus, to the extent that they look, respectively, to non-Sikh North Americans and to non-North American Sikhs, each group continues to be reinforced in its assertion of Sikh identity. The conflicts arise most clearly in confronting one another.

But mutual misunderstanding need not be the inevitable and final result of this cross-cultural interaction. As I have suggested elsewhere,[33] there are indications that second- and third-generation North Americans of Punjabi Sikh ancestry may increasingly share current Western cultural assumptions about persons. With the Gora Sikhs having begun to send some of their children to India for schooling, second-generation Gora Sikhs may come to appreciate Punjabi cultural assumptions better than their convert parents have. If, in the face of current misunderstandings and conflicts, a true cross-cultural dialogue can be initiated, then it is possible that ongoing interaction, discussion, negotiation, and debate will generate better mutual translations of the distinctive definitions of Sikh identity maintained by Gora Sikhs and Punjabi Sikhs in North America.

NOTES

1. Admittedly, there have been isolated instances of other Westerners of non-Punjabi ancestry becoming Sikh through intermarriage or individual conversion. Perhaps the most notable of these converts is the Englishwoman, Manjeet Kaur (aka Pamela M. Wylam), the co-editor of the *Sikh Courier* of Gravesend, England. The members of Sikh Dharma are, however, the most numerous, visible, and organized of the *gora* ('white') Sikhs. There are currently some three thousand or more members of Sikh Dharma, including approximately five hundred minor children. They can be distinguished by their distinctive white *bana* (uniform of the Khalsa) and by their turbans for women. All are *keshdhari* ('hair-bearing') Sikhs, and a vast majority of the adults have undergone the *amrit pahul* (initiation into the Khalsa). Most Sikh Dharma members live in or near one of the approximately one hundred 3HO ashrams located throughout North America and in several overseas cities. Membership has held steady over the past decade, which suggests that new converts and children born to members balance those lost to the group by death or departure. Of those who have left the group, an unknown percentage have remained Sikhs; while others, including some of the past leadership, not only have left the organization, Sikh Dharma, but also have totally dissociated themselves from the Panth.

2. Guru Gobind Singh's use of 'Khalsa' seems to have connoted initially that the band of dedicated followers was his 'own' or 'special' community. Secondarily, the connotation of 'pure' has come to be associated with the name Khalsa. Panth, literally 'path', refers to the band or community of Sikhs.—Editors' note [as added on first publication].
3. See, for example, Cole and Sambhi 1978, p. 144; J. Singh 1981.
4. Louis Dumont, for one, is conspicuous in his silence on the issue of caste among the Sikhs. Indeed it is unclear whether he considers the Sikhs to be a renunciatory Hindu sect or a non-Hindu group, although we may infer from what he says of both renunciatory sects and non-Hindu religions in South Asia that he assumes the Sikhs to 'have at the very least *something of caste despite modifications in their ideas and values*' (1980, p. 277, emphasis in the original) since 'a sect cannot survive on Indian soil if it denies caste' (1980, p. 269). Presenting a contrasting model, Veena Das, building on the work of J.P. Singh Uberoi (1967), argues that the essence of the heterodoxy of rebel sects—including the Sikhs—is the 'negation of the conceptual order of Hinduism' (1980, p. 55); but, she argues, the thrust of the negation is not an attack on the caste system itself but on 'the special position of Brahmins as holders of *inherent* ritual merit within the conceptual scheme of Hinduism' (1980, p. 87, emphasis in the original). As if to give substance to this latter interpretation, Satish Saberwal attributes the slackened caste observances in the Punjab to an undermining of the religious supremacy and socio-political influence of the Brahmins (1976, pp. 1–13) but suggests that the egalitarian ideology of Punjabi Sikhs, Muslims, Christians, and Arya Samajists has been used selectively 'to knock the Brahmin down *but to try, if possible, not to concede much opportunity to the lower castes readily*' (1976, p. 30, emphasis in the original). Cf. Marriott and Inden 1974, 1977, for an analysis of caste without recourse to religious/socio-political, orthodox/heterodox, or ideology/practice dualisms. According to Marriott and Inden: 'The Sikhs believe that through initiation they incorporate their teachers, who are believed to be perfect and divine, even though human…[and] that they attain liberation while still belonging to their many original castes' (1974, p. 988).
5. McLeod 1974; 1976, pp. 88–91, emphasis in the original.
6. See, for example, Juergensmeyer and Barrier 1979, pp. 2–3.
7. This section owes much to the 'South Asian ethnosociology' of McKim Marriott, Ronald Inden, Ralph Nicholas, and their students (for example, Inden 1976; Inden and Nicholas 1977; Kurin 1974; Marriott 1980, Marriott and Inden 1974, 1977). For a more elaborated presentation of the analysis herein, see Dusenbery (1990).
8. Marriott and Inden 1977, p. 230.
9. McLeod 1976, p. 98.
10. Ibid.

11. McLeod 1974, p. 83.
12. See, for example, Marenco 1974; McLeod 1974; Saberwal 1976; K. Singh 1977, p. 120.
13. See Barrier 1970, p. xl.
14. See Pettigrew 1975.
15. McLeod 1976, p. 84. See the work of Karen Leonard (1982) on what she calls 'Mexican-Hindu' marriages, that is, some 380 liaisons contracted in California between Punjabi immigrants and Mexican and Mexican-American women in the period from the late 1920s to 1950. As Leonard acknowledges, 'the Mexican-Hindu community in California was a transitory one' (Labrack and Leonard 1984, p. 535), and the offspring of these liaisons were neither socialized into Punjabi culture nor particularly welcomed in California's renascent Sikh communities.
16. Marriott and Inden 1977, p. 231.
17. In 1980, for instance, Vancouver, British Columbia, had three main gurdwaras. One was dominantly Malwai, while the other two were predominantly Doabi. The local Ramgarhia Society, founded in 1972, has talked seriously of Ramgarhias building and maintaining their own Sikh gurdwara, as the numerically and proportionally larger Ramgarhia communities have done in UK and East Africa. Followers of Sant Meehan Singh, a product of the Nanaksar movement, have recently opened their own gurdwara. And even the local Naxalites have their own 'Desh Bhagat Temple'. Diversity of persons is increasingly reflected in diversity of institutions.
18. For greater detail on the development of 3HO, see Dusenbery 1973, 1975.
19. Khalsa and Khalsa 1979, p. 119.
20. See 'Yogi Bhajan's Synthetic Sikhism', *Time*, 5 Sept. 1977.
21. Fleuret 1974.
22. LaBrack 1974, 1979; Bharati 1980.
23. Bharati 1980, p. 249.
24. Sikhism has generally been free of an elaborate hierarchy of religious functionaries. Any good Sikh can serve as a *granthi* (reader of the Adi Granth); and the title *giani* (learned one), a term of respect used in reference and address for Sikh 'priests', does not require formal certification. Since the death of Guru Gobind Singh in 1708, the eternal Sikh Guru has been said to reside jointly in the Panth and the Granth. Decisions in the name of the Guru Panth may in theory be made by any five good Sikhs in consultation with the Guru Granth Sahib. In practice, the *jathedars* (literally, 'commanders'; commonly, 'high priests') of the five historic *takhats* ('thrones') constitute an exalted *panj pyare* ('five beloved'). *Hukumnamas* (decrees) issued on their behalf from the Akal Takht are considered authoritative. The functionary appointed by the Shiromani Gurdwara Parbandhak Committee who serves in the role of

jathedar of one of the *takhats* is respectfully addressed as 'Singh Sahib' ('Lord Singh'). The title attaches to the role, not to the person. Puri's appropriation of the title 'Siri Singh Sahib' (literally, 'Exalted Lord Singh') is seen by many Punjabi Sikhs in North America as suggesting that he considers himself superior even to the *jathedars* of the *takhats*. Most refuse to acknowledge either his use of the title or his right to it. Equally infuriating to many Punjabi Sikhs has been Puri's liberal bestowal of the titles 'Mukhia Singh (Sardarni) Sahib', 'Singh (Sardarni) Sahib' on, respectively, his newly-created 'regional ministers' and 'ministers' of Sikh Dharma.

25. The Punjabi Sikh writer, Trilochan Singh, following a visit to North America to investigate the phenomenon of Western Sikh converts, came to share the views of many Punjabi Sikhs in North America who have been critical of Puri, 3HO, and Sikh Dharma. His work (1977) criticizes the group for deviations from mainstream Sikh practices and characterizes the group as a 'Tantric Yoga Cult'.
26. See, for example, Guru Nanak Dev Mission, n.d.
27. Dusenbery (1981) discusses the radical differentiation of religion and ethnicity in North America (a differentiation of domains not found in Punjabi culture) and explores the implications of this differentiation for Sikh identity and institutional development in Vancouver.
28. Dumont 1980, p. 16.
29. Dumont 1980, p. 191.
30. See, for example, Premka Kaur 1973, 1975.
31. As Paul Hershman notes, in Punjabi Sikh culture 'a woman…wearing a top-knot becomes man' (1974, p. 290). Hershman here mentions specifically the male role adopted by some Sikh widows in village Punjab. The only turban-wearing Punjabi Sikh women in North America whom I encountered in the late 1970s were those from families influenced by Bhai Sahib Randhir Singh's *jatha* (quasi-military 'detachment'). Bhai Randhir Singh was a product of the Basaur Singh Sabha and the reformist ideology of Babu Teja Singh Overseer, whose 'almost fanatical alterations' in Sikh practice included 'that women be given equality in all ceremonies and wear the five k's' (Barrier 1970, pp. xxvi–xxvii. xxiii–xxiv).
32. These positions grow out of radical egalitarian assumptions rather than out of radical feminist ideology. 3HO's own 'Grace of God Movement for the Women of the World' is explicitly opposed to the North American 'women's liberation' movement. 3HO pushes the complementarity of male and female sex roles. Nevertheless, women have from the first taken an active and public role in 3HO and Sikh Dharma; and they seem unwilling to relinquish their public role in dealings with Punjabi Sikhs.
33. Dusenbery 1981, pp. 110–11.

REFERENCES

Barrier, N. Gerald, 1970, *The Sikhs and Their Literature*, New Delhi: Manohar.

Bharati, Agehananda, 1980, 'Indian Expatriates in North America and Neo-Hindu Movements' in J.S. Yadava and V. Gautam, (eds), *The Communication of Ideas*, New Delhi: Concept Publishing, pp. 245–55.

Cole, W. Owen and Piara Singh Sambhi, 1978, *The Sikhs: Their Religious Beliefs and Practices*, London: Routledge & Kegan Paul.

Das, Veena, 1980, *Structure and Cognition: Aspects of Hindu Caste and Ritual*, rev. edn, New Delhi: Oxford University Press.

Durnont, Louis, 1980, *Homo Hierarchicus: The Caste System and Its Implications*, rev. edn, Chicago: University of Chicago Press.

Dusenbery, Verne A., 1973, 'Why Would Anybody Join...?' A Study of Recruitment and the Healthy, Happy, Holy Organization', BA (Hons) essay, Anthropology, Stanford University.

———, 1975, 'Straight→Freak→Yogi→Sikh: A "Search for Meaning" in Contemporary American Culture', MA thesis, Anthropology, University of Chicago.

———, 1981, 'Canadian Ideology and Public Policy: The Impact on Vancouver Sikh Ethnic and Religious Adaptation', *Canadian Ethnic Studies*, 13(3), pp. 101–19.

———, 1990, 'The Sikh Person, the Khalsa Panth, and Western Sikh Converts' in Bardwell L. Smith, (ed.), *Religious Movements and Social Identity: Continuity and Change in India*, Leiden: E.J. Brill and Delhi: Chanakya Publications, pp. 117–35.

Fleuret, Anne K., 1974, 'Incorporation into Networks among Sikhs in Los Angeles', *Urban Anthropology*, 3, pp. 27–33.

Guru Nanak Dev Mission, n.d., *Sikhism and the Nirankari Movement*, Patiala, Punjab: the author.

Hershman, P., 1974, 'Hair, Sex and Dirt.', *Man*, n.s., 9, pp. 274–98.

Inden, Ronald B., 1976, *Marriage and Rank in Bengali Culture*, Berkeley: University of California Press.

Inden, Ronald B. and Ralph W. Nicholas, 1977, *Kinship in Bengali Culture*, Chicago: University of Chicago Press.

Jagjit Singh, 1981, 'Egalitarian Society', *The Sikh Revolution*, New Delhi: Vikas, pp. 115–35.

Juergensmeyer, Mark and N. Gerald Barrier, 1979, 'Introduction: The Sikhs and the Scholars' in Mark Juergensmeyer and N. Gerald Barner, (eds), *Sikh Studies: Comparative Perspectives on a Changing Tradition*, Berkeley: Graduate Theological Union, pp. 1–9.

Khalsa, Shakti Parwha Kaur and Gurubanda Singh Khalsa, 1979, 'The Siri Singh Sahib' in S.P.K. Khalsa and S.K.K. Khalsa, (eds), *The Man Called the Sin Singh Sahib*, Los Angeles: Sikh Dharma, pp. 117–31.

Khushwant Singh, *A History of the Sikhs, vol. 2: 1839–1974*, New Delhi: Oxford University Press.

Kurin, Richard, 1974, 'Sect Formation and Definition in the Indian Context: The Sikh Case', MA thesis, Anthropology, University of Chicago.

LaBrack, Bruce, 1974, 'Neo-Sikhism and East Indian Religious Identification', paper presented at the Midwest Conference on Asian Affairs, Kansas City, Kansas.

———, 1979, 'Sikhs Real and Ideal: A Discussion of Text and Context in the Description of Overseas Sikh Communities' in M. Juergensmeyer and N.G. Barrier, (eds), *Sikh Studies: Comparative Perspectives on a Changing Tradition,* Berkeley: Graduate Theological Union, pp. 127–42.

LaBrack, Bruce and Karen Leonard, 1984, 'Conflict and Compatibility in Punjabi-Mexican Immigrant Families in Rural California, 1915–1965', *Journal of Marriage and the Family*, 43, pp. 527–37.

Leonard, Karen, 1982, 'Marriage and Family Life among Early Asian Indian Immigrants', *Population Review*, 25, pp. 67–75.

Marenco, Ethne K., 1974, *The Transformation of Sikh Society*, Portland, Oregon: The HaPi Press.

Marriott, McKim, 1980, 'The Open Hindu Person and Interpersonal Fluidity', paper presented at the meeting of the Association for Asian Studies, Washington, D.C.

Marriott, McKim and Ronald B. Inden, 1974, 'Caste Systems', *Encyclopedia Britannica,* new 3rd edn, Chicago: Helen Hemingway Benton, 'Macropaedia', 3, pp. 982–91.

———, 1977, 'Toward an Ethnosociology of South Asian Caste System' in K. David, (ed.), *The New Wind: Changing Identities in South Asia*, The Hague: Mouton, pp. 227–38.

McLeod, W.H., 1974, 'Ahluwalias and Ramgarhias: Two Sikh Castes', *South Asia: Journal of South Asian Studies*, vol. 4, pp. 78–90.

———, 1976, 'Caste in the Sikh Panth', in W.H. McLeod, *The Evolution of the Sikh Community: Five Essays*, Oxford: Clarendon Press, pp. 83–104.

Pettigrew, Joyce, 1975, *Robber Noblemen: A Study of the Political System of the Sikh Jats*, London: Routledge & Kegan Paul.

Premka Kaur, Sardarni, 1973, 'Rejoinder'. *The Sikh Review*, 21 (232), pp. 52–56.

———, 1975, 'Listen, O "Patit" and Learn'. *Gurdwara Gazette*, 46 (4), pp. 4–13.

Saberwal, Satish, 1977, *Mobile Men: Limits to Social Change in Urban Punjab*, New Delhi: Vikas.

Singh, Khushwant, 1839–1974, *A History of the Sikhs*, 2, New Delhi: Oxford University Press.

Singh, Trilochan, 1977, *Sikhism and Tantric Yoga*, Ludhiana, Punjab: The author.

Uberoi, J.P. Singh, 1967, 'On Being Unshorn', in *Sikhism and Indian Society* (Transactions of the IIAS, 4), Simla: Indian Institute of Advanced Study, pp. 87–100.

———, 1977, 'Yogi Bhajan's Synthetic Sikhism: The Leader of 3HO Inspires Devotion and Hostility', *Time*, 5 September, pp. 70–1.

POSTSCRIPT

On 6 October 2004, Siri Singh Sahib Bhai Sahib Harbhajan Singh Khalsa Yogiji (aka Yogi Bhajan; aka, Harbhajan Singh Yogi; née Harbhajan Singh Puri) succumbed to heart disease at the age of seventy-five, thus depriving 3HO/Sikh Dharma of its charismatic founder and spiritual leader. Even in death, Harbhajan Singh Yogi remains a polarizing figure among Punjabi Sikhs, especially in North America.[1] In his latter years, legal cases filed against him, his close associates, and the organizations themselves and various exposés by former members provided—and continue to provide—plenty of ammunition to his detractors, both Punjabi and non-Punjabi.[2] At the same time, his personal and political power as a global religious personage of note is well attested to in the letters of condolence and tribute that were received upon his death.[3] A recent ethnography focused on current and former 3HO/Sikh Dharma women captures the ambivalence about this powerful yet flawed man felt even by a sympathetic ethnographer and the women she lived with and interviewed.[4]

But the death of Yogi Bhajan is also an occasion for looking again at the members of 3HO/Sikh Dharma that he left behind and assessing their relations with Sikhs of Punjabi heritage in a post-Yogi Bhajan era.[5] In particular, how has the relationship between the Gora Sikhs and Punjabi Sikhs in North America fared over the past two decades?[6] Are the mutual misunderstandings and conflicting assertions of Sikh identity discussed in my original article still operative? Or, as I suggested at the end of my article, might increased interactions and the coming of age in North America of new generations of both Gora Sikhs and Punjabi Sikhs mean that mutual misunderstandings and conflicting assertions of identity by Gora Sikhs and Punjabi Sikhs have been overcome or negotiated away?

Briefly, my own sense is that Punjabi Sikhs, including a majority of Punjabi Sikhs in North America, continue to be impressed by the ritual discipline and public piety of the Gora Sikhs and appreciative of the battles that 3HO/Sikh Dharma has fought on behalf of Sikh religious rights in North America. Sikhs in Punjab still seem somewhat awed by seeing these westerners wearing full Sikh *bana* (dress), performing *gurbani kirtan* (hymn singing), or doing *seva* (service).

Punjabi Sikhs in North America are less likely than they were during the earlier period to worry that 3HO/Sikh Dharma might be a suicidal cult (like Jonestown) or a heretical sect (like the Sant Nirankaris). The fact that there was no mass falling away or de-conversion of Gora Sikhs after Yogi Bhajan's death has gone a long way towards putting to rest the idea of 3HO/Sikh Dharma as merely a personality cult built entirely on loyalty to one man and not a real transformation of Yogi's followers into Sikhs. At the same time, however, many Punjabi Sikhs still see the Gora Sikhs, even in a post-Yogi Bhajan era, as following a *maryada* (code of conduct) that differs from that of other Sikhs. In that sense, many of them would liken 3HO/Sikh Dharma Sikhs to the members of Akhand Kirtani Jatha or Bhindranwale Jatha or to the followers of a Nanaksar *sant*. That is, they would regard them as a distinctive sect within Sikhism that does not follow mainstream Panthic practices. Of course, the line between being considered a sect within the fold and one considered being heretical is a fine one; and some Punjabi Sikh in North America would still make the argument that 3HO/Sikh Dharma practices have not made them into Sikhs.

Moreover, despite increased interactions over the years, most Punjabi Sikhs in North America still treat Gora Sikhs as Sikhs of a different kind or genus. Some individuals and/or families have come to worship at 3HO/Sikh Dharma-run gurdwaras or have sent their children to 3HO/Sikh Dharma-run schools, including Miri Piri Academy in Amritsar.[7] And 3HO/Sikh Dharma continues to come together with sympathetic Punjabi-run Sikh organizations in North America around shared religious and political interests. But most Punjabi Sikhs in North America have maintained their social distance. Very few have joined 3HO/Sikh Dharma and almost none have entered into marital alliances with Gora Sikhs. In short, most Punjabi Sikhs continue to treat Gora Sikhs as Sikhs of a different *zat*.

For their part, 3HO/Sikh Dharma Sikhs, with greater exposure to Punjabi Sikhs, both in North America and in Punjab, are less morally censorious and publicly dismissive of Punjabi Sikhs in North America than they were in the earlier years. They have come to realize that there are sincere Sikhs of Punjabi ancestry whose understanding and practice of *Sikhi* (the 'way of life') is different from their own. And they have thus had to accept that there are multiple ways of being Sikh today and that they will not be able to bully or shame Punjabi Sikhs into adopting their own version of Sikhi. This has meant that second and third generation Gora Sikhs are more likely to attempt to lead by example rather than by haranguing Punjabi Sikhs or proselytizing among them.[8] This moderation of the rhetoric has taken some of the hostility out of the Punjabi Sikh–Gora Sikh relationship, especially among those who have grown up together in North America.

In sum, differences in how they understand and assert their Sikh identities continue to exist between Gora Sikhs and Punjabi Sikhs in North America, but a good deal of the frustration that once existed on both sides has gone out of the relationship. Today's younger generation of Gora Sikhs and Punjabi Sikhs are likely to find common cause in fighting for Sikh interests in a post-9/11 United States and in shaping a shared understanding of what it means to be a Sikh in North America.[9] And maybe now, with the polarizing figure of Yogi Bhajan having passed from the scene, the further dialogue and mutual translation and shaping of Sikh identities in North America alluded to at the conclusion of my article will move forward apace.

NOTES

1. Since his death, the online Sikh-Diaspora group (*http://groups.yahoo.com/group/Sikh-Diaspora/*March 2006), comprised mainly of Punjabi Sikhs residing in the West, has debated the legacy of Harbhajan Singh Yogi (the name used by most Punjabi Sikhs), with supporters and detractors both well represented.
2. A quick Internet search will uncover a variety of anti-Yogi Bhajan sites, including a site posting relevant court documents (*http://yogibhajan.tripod.com/*March 2006) and an ongoing discussion forum moderated by an ex-3HO/Sikh Dharma member (*http://forums.delphiforums.com/KamallaRose/start* /March 2006). Although both sites are maintained by ex-3HO/Sikh Dharma members, Punjabi Sikh perspectives can also be found there.
3. These condolences, as well as biographical information and testimonials, can by found at the main 3HO website (*http://www.3ho.org/*March 2006) and at a website run by Sikh Dharma members (*http://www.sikhnet.com/* March 2006).
4. See Elsberg 2003, plus my review of her book (Dusenbery 2005).
5. I have not done systematic fieldwork of the type that was the basis for the original article; therefore, my comments here are more impressionistic, based on secondary literature, informal conversations, participation in newsgroups, and perusal of websites.
6. 3HO/Sikh Dharma members prefer today to be called 'American Sikhs' rather than 'Gora Sikhs'. Both are problematic labels. The former because it both marginalizes Sikh Americans of Punjabi ancestry and ignores the fact that many 3HO/Sikh Dharma members are not Americans; the latter because there are 3HO/Sikh Dharma members who are not 'white'. However, I would argue the fact that 3H0/Sikh Dharma members are still generally called '*gora* Sikhs' or 'Yogi's Sikhs' by Punjabi Sikhs supports my argument that they are being defined as of a different genus ('Gora

Sikhs') or a distinct sect ('Yogi's Sikhs'—or what might more appropriately be called '3HO/Sikh Dharma Sikhs').

7. Miri Piri Academy is a residential school, grades 1–12, built on land outside Amritsar given to 3HO/Sikh Dharma on a 99 year lease by the SGPC (see *http://www.miripiriacademy.org*). The school's moto is: 'School of Royalty and Reality. Our first principle is the Love of Discipline.' Currently there are five NRI Sikh children attending Miri Piri Academy, along with over one hundred 3HO/Sikh Dharma children. According to school personnel, most NRI Sikh children that come are not able to take the discipline imposed at the school and soon leave.
8. Yogi Bhajan was infamous for haranguing fellow Punjabi Sikhs in North America in public settings, including gurdwaras. And, as pointed out in my article (n. 32), his chief polemicist, Sardarni Premka Kaur (née Pamela Dyson), wrote widely circulated articles in the 1970s challenging the Sikh identity of Punjabi Sikhs in North America. See also Dusenbery 1989.
9. A recent study of three generations of Punjabi Sikhs in Vancouver, British Columbia, suggests that the younger generation has adopted a 'modern' outlook characterized by 'analytics' (see Nayar 2004 and my review [Dusenbery 2006]). This 'modernity', the product of growing up and being educated in Canada, might suggest the basis for a more productive dialogue between the rising generation of Punjabi Sikhs and Gora Sikhs in North America.

REFERENCES

Dusenbery, Verne A., 1989, 'Of Singh Sabhas, Siri Singh Sahibs, and Sikh Scholars: Sikh Discourse from North America in the 1970s' in N. Gerald Barrier and Verne A. Dusenbery, (eds), *The Sikh Diaspora: Migration and the Experience Beyond Punjab*, Columbia, Missouri: South Asia Publications and Delhi: Chanakya Publications, pp. 90–119.

———, 2005, 'Review of Constance Waeber Elsberg's *Graceful Women: Gender and Identity in an American Sikh Community*', *Contemporary Sociology*, 34 (2) March, pp. 141–2.

———, 2006, 'Review of Kamala E. Nayar's *The Sikh Diaspora in Vancouver: Three Generations amid Tradition, Modernity, and Multiculturalism*', *Journal of Asian Studies*, 65(1) February, pp. 211–12.

Elsberg, Constance Waebner, 2003, *Graceful Women: Gender and Identity in an American Sikh Community*, Knoxville: University of Tennessee Press.

Nayar, Kamala E., 2004, *The Sikh Diaspora in Vancouver: Three Generations amid Tradition, Modernity, and Multiculturalism*, Toronto: University of Toronto Press.

2

On the Moral Sensitivities of Sikhs in North America*

This pride or izzat is one of the Punjabi's deepest feelings, and as such must be treated with great respect. Dearer to him than life, it helps to make him the good soldier that he is. But it binds him to the vendetta.

—Malcolm Lyall Darling, *Wisdom and Waste in the Punjab Village*

The assassination of Indira Gandhi on 31 October 1984, allegedly at the hands of her Sikh bodyguards, provoked mixed reactions from Sikhs in North America. News reports immediately following the assassination included pictures and accounts of Punjabi Sikhs celebrating her death in the streets of New York.[1] Nevertheless, the CBS Morning News, on the day following the assassination, was able to find Sikh representatives who, although upholding the legitimacy of Sikh grievances, were willing to condemn Mrs Gandhi's murder. Thus, viewers of CBS Morning News were presented the comments of Harbhajan Singh Puri (the 'Siri Singh Sahib' or self-styled Chief Religious and Administrative Authority for the Sikh Dharma in the Western Hemisphere) and one of his Gora (literally, 'white'; that is, Western) Sikh followers.

At the time of the CBS broadcast I was outraged that the media should once again have constituted 'Yogi Bhajan' (as Puri is also known) and one of his few thousand Gora Sikh followers as representative of the

* First published in Owen M. Lynch (ed.) *Divine Passions: The Social Construction of Emotions in India*, Berkeley: University of California Press and New Delhi: Oxford University Press, 1990, pp. 239–61.

tens or hundreds of thousands of Sikhs (overwhelmingly of Punjabi ancestry) residing in North America. If CBS considered itself obliged to find a 'moderate' Sikh to condemn the murder, I felt it could have found a more representative Punjabi Sikh than Harbhajan Singh Puri, a former Indian customs official who founded the Healthy, Happy, Holy Organization in 1969 shortly after his arrival in the United States; and CBS certainly need not have included one of his non-Punjabi followers as a spokesperson for the Sikhs of North America.[2]

Subsequently, I have come to rethink my position. In fact, it now seems to me quite appropriate that a Gora Sikh—a North American Sikh 'convert'—should have made the most unequivocal repudiation of the murder by a Sikh that I heard in those confused and emotionally charged moments following the assassination. The different moral sensitivities displayed by the Punjabi Sikh celebrants outside the Indian consulate in New York and by the Gora Sikh spokesman in the CBS studios provide the outlines of what I consider a cross-culturally illuminating morality play.

But before exploring this morality play, let me recount another that came to mind often both in the prelude and aftermath of Mrs Gandhi's assassination. This one concerns an earlier assassination of a public official by a Punjabi Sikh acting, as apparently were Mrs Gandhi's assassins, 'to preserve the honour' of the Sikh community.

The scene is Vancouver, British Columbia, Canada. In 1914, the South Asian community in Vancouver—overwhelmingly Punjabi and Sikh—was a mere ten years old. Nevertheless, it was already a community externally besieged and internally factionalized. Canadian immigration regulations were being manipulated to keep South Asians out of the country and to deport as many immigrants as could be shown deportable. Activities of the Ghadar (Revolution) Party were particularly worrisome to British, Canadian, and Indian authorities. To provide information on the immigrant community in Vancouver, the Canadian Immigration Department had employed W. C. Hopkinson, a Punjabi-speaking Anglo-Indian and former Calcutta policeman.[3] To further his investigations, Hopkinson recruited to his service members of one of the community's factions. One informer subsequently became involved in a shootout in which he killed two and wounded four other Sikhs within the precincts of the local *gurdwara* (temple).[4] Although most Vancouver Sikhs regarded the shooting as an unprovoked and inexcusable sacrilege, Hopkinson was prepared to testify that the man had acted in self-defence. As Hopkinson waited in the courthouse to testify, Mewa Singh, a recent immigrant forest worker and sometime *granthī* (one who reads from and cares for the Guru Granth Sahib [*Gurū Granth Sahib*], the Sikh 'holy book' regarded as the reigning Sikh Guru), shot him dead. Mewa Singh surrendered immediately, pleaded guilty, and was quickly sentenced to death. In a letter to Hopkinson's widow he 'ask[ed] her forgiveness and stat[ed] that he had not acted out of hatred. . . but to wipe off the insults hurled at his countrymen and to preserve their unity' (K. Singh 1964, p. 6). Mewa Singh was hanged on 11 January 1915.

Nearly sixty-five years later, when I came to do fieldwork with the Vancouver Sikh community (a community not merely still extant after decades of isolation but much grown and diversified through recent immigration, natural increase, and even conversion), (martyr) Mewa Singh was still an exemplar to the community. His death was commemorated annually; his name was attached to halls and rooms in the local gurdwaras and invoked in the congregation during the saying of *Ardās* (literally, 'petition'; the communal prayer that includes the remembrance of significant Sikh martyrs); his martyrdom was appropriated by various groups and attached to various causes.[5]

One group that did not invoke Mewa Singh's example to the same degree as others was the group of dozen or so Gora Sikhs at the local Guru Ram Das Ashram. My distinct impression was that these new North American Sikh converts preferred to celebrate the more socially and temporally distant and morally unequivocal heroic martyrdoms of the Sikh Gurus, and other early exemplars, as these are recounted in the Sikh hagiographic tradition. Recent historical figures, whose political and personal motives were perhaps more transparent and, thus, morally more complex to North Americans, seemed to provoke ambivalence. In any case, my Gora Sikh informants repeatedly emphasized that they were a 'religious' group and, therefore, did not involve themselves in Indian 'politics'. As later would be the case in their response to Mrs Gandhi's assassination, their actions indicated that, despite affirming Guru Gobind Singh's teachings that 'when all else fails, it is right to draw the sword', they were not totally comfortable resorting to murder to avenge the 'insult to the Panth' suffered as a consequence of Hopkinson's perjured testimony or Mrs Gandhi's desecration of the Akal Takht.

***

In this essay I want to draw out the implications of these two morality plays—and others involving actions considerably less extreme (from the Western Judeo-Christian point of view) than murder—to suggest that the moral sensitivities of Gora Sikhs and Punjabi Sikhs (and, in this regard, particularly those of the dominant Jat Sikhs) not only differ but also differ in culturally specific ways. In particular, I want to suggest that the notion of *izzat* (honour), apparently so central to Jat Sikh 'moral affect', is not shared by Gora Sikhs.[6] As a consequence, as I will show, Gora Sikhs are largely insensitive to the role of *izzat* in the lives of Jat Sikhs, that is, as it informs both Jat Sikh actions and Jat Sikh reactions to the actions of Gora Sikhs. And this difference in moral affect, I argue, enters into the active estrangement of Gora Sikhs and Jat Sikhs and their (mis)apprehension of one another.

Following Michelle Rosaldo, I use the term 'moral affect' to indicate 'emotions that involve clear conscious, social, and cultural components (and attendant questions of judgment and morality)' (1983, p.136, n. 4). A Western focus upon, and valcrization of, rationalized, readily codified systems of knowledge—as apparent in the anthropologist's search for the norms or rules of an alien culture as in the convert's search for orthodoxy in an adopted religion—has for too long led to inattention to the affective dimensions of other peoples' experience. Yet, ironically, it is precisely in the area of 'emotions', less amenable to direct personal articulation and formal codification than are 'beliefs', that culture shock and cross-cultural tensions are most likely to be experienced and least likely to be reconciled. Yet, because the language of the emotions so often partakes of what Pierre Bourdieu (1976, p.118, n. 1) has called 'the discourse of familiarity', outsiders, whether anthropologists or converts, find it difficult to experience and represent the affective world of others. Moral affects like *izzat*, because they 'involve clear conscious, social and cultural components', are perhaps easier to gain access to with our everyday or conventional social scientific vocabularies than are emotions like fear, anger, or sadness (although these, too, involve moral appraisals of social situations). At the very least, the former are more likely to emerge as overt issues in cross-cultural interaction. This fact leads Rosaldo to argue that anthropologists interested in emotions 'might do well to work from instances like these, where the relevance of culture is clear, *towards* cases where it is more problematic' (1983, p.136, n. 4; emphasis in the original).

But what does this mean operationally? Recent criticism of the classical 'cultures of shame' versus 'cultures of guilt' analyses, such as Ruth Benedict's (1949), has gone beyond contesting the empirical generality of the opposition between the two (Piers and Singer 1953) to emphasizing not only the different kinds of shame and guilt encountered in different cultures (Geertz 1973) but also the different kinds of 'selves' to which these terms can appropriately be applied (Rosaldo 1983, 1984). In the shift from 'culture and personality' to 'concepts of the person' and 'ethnopsychology', 'shame' and 'guilt' have gone from being *explicans* to being *explicandum*. Anthropological attention has correspondingly shifted from using (Western) psychological idioms to characterize cultural differences toward understanding the social and cultural construction of emotions themselves through various culturally constituted social 'selves'. Thus, for example, Rosaldo's (1983) insightful account of 'shame' among Ilongot headhunters, with its exploration of the very different cultural conception of the self that 'shame' presupposes among the Ilongot and among Americans, stands as an exemplary analysis of the social construction of 'self' (as moral agent) and 'emotion' (as moral affect).

***

As might be expected of a moral affect, *izzat* is a multivocalic term defying simple translation.[7] Conventionally it is glossed in English as 'honour,' but it is central to a whole complex of emotionally charged values including honour, respect, reputation, shame, prestige, and status.[8] The term, derived from Arabic and Persian, is tied to very similar concepts among Muslim groups of Southwest and South Asia;[9] but it has also gained wide currency in the languages of the non-Muslims of North India. It infuses Sikh culture to the extent that, since the seventeenth century, the landholding Jats of Punjab, for whom *izzat* is a particular concern, have come to predominate within the Sikh Panth.[10]

It is also a deeply-rooted, affective concept that informants have a hard time defining and discussing, especially with an outsider. In attempting to make the concept intelligible and palatable to this Western researcher, informants often spoke in moral platitudes: '*izzat* means "honour thy father and mother" or *izzat* means "looking out for the good of the family"'. More revealing than direct discussions of it in the abstract, therefore, were after-the-fact discussions of events in which informants asserted that izzat had been involved.

Retention, acquisition, or reacquisition of *izzat* is apparently a common motivating force in Jat Sikh social action. From undertaking migrations, employment, or marriages to seeking retribution (or, in less morally loaded terms, rebalance) for wrongs and injustices (or, in less morally loaded terms, defeats, slights, offences) suffered at the hands of others, informants see *izzat* serving as both impetus and rationale for social action.

Joyce Pettigrew has written in some detail of the role that *izzat* plays in rural Jat Sikh socio-political life in the Punjab. I quote at length from her monograph:

Relationships of extreme friendship and hostility between families were actively involved with the philosophy of life embodied in the conception of *izzat*—the complex of values regarding what was honourable. If a Jat achieved power for his family he automatically enhanced family honour. Power was honour and honour was power. In a situation where a family had no power it was inconceivable that it could have 'honour,' as it would not be able to defend the content of that honour from another family. The rise to power of a family into an 'honourable' position was inevitably accompanied by threats and litigation, and sometimes also by violence and murder.

That aspect of izzat according to which the relationships between families were supposed to be ordered emphasized the principle of equivalence in all things, that is, not only equality in giving but also equality in vengeance. Izzat was in fact the principle of reciprocity of gifts, plus the rule of an eye for an eye and a tooth for a tooth. Giving was an attempt to bring a man of another family into one's debt, and acceptance of the gift involved the recipient in making a return, not necessarily in kind or immediately, but at the moment appropriate to the donor. Not making the return could break the relationships and develop further hostility. Izzat enjoined aid to those who had helped one. It also enjoined that revenge be exacted for personal insults and damage to person or property. If a man was threatened he must at least threaten back, for not to do so would be weakness. The appropriate revenge for murder was likewise murder. Izzat was also associated with sanctioned resistance to another who trespassed into what was regarded as the sphere of influence of one's family. This 'other' might be other Jats belonging to the opposing faction; in the past it also applied to the state and foreign powers. (Pettigrew 1975, pp. 58–9)

Pettigrew's account touches on a number of concerns central to *izzat:* power, reciprocity, protection of one's social domain. The last lines of her account even suggest the way in which outsiders, such as Mrs Gandhi or Hopkinson, may become parties implicated in the pursuit or defence of *izzat.* In a footnote Pettigrew notes other crucial aspects of *izzat,* for example, that for Jat Sikhs *izzat* is attached to landholding and to such occupations as military and administrative service and that it is tied to 'a multitude of rules concerning the behaviour expected of men in relation to women, and vice versa' (1975, p. 240).[11] Although these aspects are perhaps less directly relevant to her concern with political factions, they are crucial to understanding *izzat* in the migrant situation.

As Pettigrew notes, one aspect common to all these concerns is freedom from the constraints and demands of others and a concomitant ability to put others in one's debt or under one's dominion. Pettigrew's own study focuses upon political leadership, and she has, therefore, stressed aspects of the socio-political domination of individuals by other individuals; this is exemplified in the book's title, *Robber Noblemen*. But as a moral affect, *izzat* is pre-eminently a concern for the honour and reputation not of individuals per se but—insofar as personal prestige is subordinate to the collective evaluation of the group—of groups (the family, faction, lineage, village, caste brotherhood, religious community, etc.). Moreover, it is a fluid and relative rather than a fixed and absolute attribute of persons. By this I mean both that it is gained and lost in the give and take of social life and that one may act in the interest of any collective of which one is a part with the honour redounding to all the collectives.[12] Punjabis thus speak of *izzat* as a quality of certain persons that must be zealously guarded and continually expressed in agonistic pursuits.

Migration has long been one way through which Jat Sikh families have sought the means to maintain or raise family *izzat*. By sending away 'excess' or 'wayward' sons (that is, those whose inheritance would otherwise cause fragmentation of family landholdings or whose actions might undermine the family's reputation) and by using migrants' remittances and connections in military or administrative circles, Jat Sikh villagers have sought to further or maintain *izzat* in the ancestral village.[13] Foreign migration, especially to countries in the West, is, however, thought particularly risky. On the one hand, it has been seen as presenting unparalleled opportunities through which a Jat Sikh family might (im)prove its *izzat*. Thus, for example, by frugal living abroad, the migrant will ideally be able to remit large amounts of capital to the family back home for investment in land and farm implements, a *pukka* house, expensive dowries, maintenance of retainers and clients, and conspicuous philanthropy. At the same time, however, foreign migration presents considerable temptations to individuals to pursue actions with negative effects on family or group *izzat*. Thus, it is feared that the migrant may forget his responsibilities to his family by, for example, not saving and sending money home or by engaging in inappropriate sexual or marital relations abroad. A real ambivalence is felt about the risks and benefits of sending family members abroad. Most Jat Sikhs are not, however, averse to taking risks.

Moreover, in most situations of foreign migration, *izzat* is an important concern for Jat Sikhs in both the migrant setting and the home village. That is, accounts of the migrants' actions abroad circulate both within the migrant community and back in the village at home and affect the family's *izzat* in both places. Jat Sikh children living in Western countries thus continue to be socialized in sensitivity to actions that might bring their family or community into disrepute. And, because *izzat* is crucially entailed—and becomes relationally indexed—in political contests and marital matches, much emotional energy in migrant communities continues to be put into intracommunity factional politics and in arranging proper marriages for family members. Consequences of this continuing concern for *izzat* include not only the high degree of Sikh endogamy among Punjabis settled in Western countries but also the apparent willingness to forgo status gains (in Western terms) to ensure the continued good reputation of the family.[14]

Arthur W. Helweg, in his study of migrants from the Punjabi village of Jandiali living in the English town of Gravesend, not only notes the two communities of significant others, villagers at home and fellow-migrants, but also points to a presumed third audience. In his interesting chapter on the role of *izzat* in the lives of his informants (1979, pp.10–19), he writes:

> In Gravesend the Punjabis are deeply concerned about their izzat or *mann* as evaluated by three different audiences: (1) villagers in Punjab, (2) Punjabis in England, and (3) the English host community. The first two categories have the strongest influence on their behaviour but it is interesting to note how the Punjabis have projected their own culture onto the host group. According to their self.assessment of izzat, esteem in the eyes of others is not dependent upon another group sharing a similar concept. Izzat is so entrenched in Sikh Jat culture that an appreciation of it can be projected onto outsiders. Both in England and India, Punjabis are concerned that they and their fellows exemplify bonourable behaviour. In effect, this projection of their own values on the British serves primarily to rally their own sense of superiority over the host population. (Helweg 1979, p. 11)

This Jat Sikh projection of sensitivity to *izzat* onto Western society is also an important factor in understanding Jat Sikh and Gora Sikh misunderstandings and conflicting moral sensitivities. I will return to this point shortly. First, however, I will discuss briefly the Sikh population in North America.

***

Impelled by various push–pull factors (drought, epidemics, rural indebtedness in Punjab; the prospect of ready jobs and cheap passage to North America), Punjabi migrants first settled in Canada and the United States during the first decade of the twentieth century. From that point until the late 1960s, the overwhelming majority of Punjabis in North America were Jat Sikhs from Doaba (the plains area of Punjab between the Beas and Sutlej rivers). The original Sikh immigrants were predominantly male labourers and farmers who had served in the British Indian army. Most came to North America as sojourners, intent on making their fortune and returning home to the Punjab to retire in comfort and honour on the family farm. Although many of these early immigrants returned home within a few years, either through deportation or voluntary repatriation (in fact, a number returned as Ghadarite revolutionaries), the vast majority of those who stayed eventually settled in either British Columbia, where they became concentrated in lumber and lumber-related industries, or in California, where they pursued the traditional Jat occupation of farming.

After long and arduous struggle, the early immigrants were finally permitted to sponsor for immigration their Jat Sikh wives, children, and relatives. Although the relatively few non-Jats among the early migrants apparently mixed freely with their fellow Punjabi Sikhs, the overwhelming preponderance of Jats meant that Doabi Jat Sikh practices largely defined the Sikh identity as it developed in North America.[15] Only since the liberalization of Canadian and American immigration policies in the mid-1960s have significant numbers of non-Jats been a part of an extensive Sikh immigration coming not only from India but from the United Kingdom, East Africa, East and Southeast Asia, and Fiji as well. As I have discussed elsewhere (1981, 1988), this new influx not only has led to establishing new Punjabi Sikh communities, especially in the larger metropolitan areas where Sikh professionals have found employment, but it has also had significant repercussions in the long-established communities of British Columbia and rural California.[16] Nevertheless, within most Punjabi communities in North America, as within the Panth in India, Jat Sikhs continue to (pre)dominate.

If Jat Sikhs in North America are increasingly confronted by other kinds of Punjabi Sikhs (that is, Sikh migrants of other castes), these are at least kinds of Sikhs with whom they are familiar from Punjabi society.

The unprecedented 'conversion' of thousands of Westerners to Sikhism is quite another matter. Making sense of the heretofore anomalous category 'Gora Sikh' has and is taking some effort.[17]

In 1968, Harbhajan Sigh Puri, whose refugee Khatri Sikh family had come to New Delhi from Pakistani Punjab at partition, quit his job as a customs official at Delhi's International Airport and left for Toronto to become a yoga instructor. However, the Canadian who had recruited him for the position had died in the interim. Puri was, thus, without job or sponsor. Fortunately for him, he soon secured sponsorship from a Punjabi Sikh in Los Angeles where he settled and began teaching yoga courses (at the East-West Cultural Center, at a local community college, and out of a storefront). Now calling himself 'Yogi Bhajan', Puri proved a compelling teacher. Having found a receptive core of students (initially middle-age, female, 'spiritual seekers'; subsequently young, white, middle-class refugees from the 'counterculture'), he soon established for them an ashram, a 'spiritual commune', as his students would have it. There he taught his 'Kundalini Yoga:The Yoga of Awareness', offered occasional 'Tantric Yoga Intensives', and imposed upon his followers the structure and discipline of what he called 'the healthy, happy, holy way of life'. In 1970, the Healthy, Happy, Holy Organization (or 3HO) was formally incorporated as a tax-exempt educational organization. By then, Puri was already sending his newly trained 'student teachers' to other cities in North America to teach Kundalini Yoga and to establish additional ashrams. During the early 1970s, the organization primarily sought to recruit new members through yoga classes and establish new ashrams where, Puri now claimed, members were being purified and prepared to accept their calling as Sikhs. At this point, however, Puri 'continued to teach about Sikh Dharma in an indirect way' (Khalsa and Khalsa1979, p.119).

Puri had, however, slowly begun to disclose his own Sikh background and to introduce Sikh teachings to his closest followers. In 1971, he took eighty-four of them to India where they visited the Golden Temple and surrounding shrines. At the Akal Takht, the highest seat of Sikh spiritual and temporal power, the group was cordially received, and Puri was honoured for his missionary work. Returning home with what he represented as a mandate to spread the message of Sikhism in the West, Puri began to supplement and supplant his primarily yogic explanation of 'the healthy, happy, holy way of life' with a more explicitly Sikh account. Puri also began to use the title 'Siri Singh Sahib,' a title which, he claimed, the Shiromani Gurdwara Parbandhak Committee (the organization legally empowered to control the historical Sikh gurdwaras in the Punjab) had given him and which he rendered, liberally, as the 'Chief Religious and Administrative Authority for the Sikh Dharma in the Western Hemisphere'. In 1973, Puri was successful in having the Sikh Dharma Brotherhood (later recast in non-gender-specific language as, simply, Sikh Dharma) officially registered as a tax-exempt religious organization legally empowered to ordain Sikh 'ministers' who would have the authority to perform marriages, to provide the last rites, and to administer the *amrit pāhul*.[18]

Puri's own transformation from 'Yogi Bhajan' to the 'Siri Singh Sahib' corresponded roughly to a change from a yogic to a Sikh identity on the part of 3HO members. The change did not take place overnight; but once convinced by Puri that his 'healthy, happy, holy way of life' was an orthodox Sikh one, most 3HO members did not hesitate to make a formal commitment to their new religion. And Puri provided unprecedented opportunities for 3HO members to express their commitment, not merely holding the traditional *amrit pāhul* ceremonies but introducing Sikh 'initiations' and 'minister ordinations' as well. Members' change from yogic to Sikh identity also corresponded to a change in emphases within the organization from recruiting new members and founding additional ashrams to maintaining the established group, raising a second generation, and gaining credibility as upholders of Sikh orthodoxy in North America.[19]

Today, three to five thousand Gora Sikhs live with their families in or near the approximately one hundred 3HO ashrams in North America (and in scattered cities abroad). Their visibility (for example, their distinctive white uniforms and Indian-sounding names), their aggressive pursuit of 'religious rights' (for example, exemptions from dress codes and safety rules that would require their giving up turbans and other external symbols), and their frequent critical commentary on the practices of Punjabi Sikhs in North America (see Kaur 1973, 1975) have made them known beyond what their numbers might otherwise warrant. Punjabi Sikhs in North America, in particular, are well aware of their existence. And this is particularly so in places, like Vancouver, where Gora Sikhs have attempted to become involved with the local Punjabi Sikh gurdwaras.[20]

***

The contrast between Jat Sikh and Gora Sikh moral sensitivities has emerged at various points in their social interaction in North America. I focus first on two cases from my fieldwork in Vancouver; each suggests different Jat and Gora perspectives on the unfolding interaction. Each case is simultaneously an instance of the Gora Sikh failure to appreciate the considerations of *izzat* that underlie the actions of Jat Sikhs and of the Jat Sikh projection of *izzat* concerns onto the actions of Gora Sikhs.

One Gora Sikh complaint about Punjabi Sikhs in Vancouver is their factionalism—or, as the Gora Sikhs put it, 'East Indian politics'. They express despair and frustration over the factionalism within the Punjabi Sikh community and regard the bitter and often violent struggles for control of the local gurdwaras (and other community institutions both in North America and in India) as incompatible with the practice of the Sikh religion. By the time of my fieldwork in 1978–9, most members of the local 3HO ashram had withdrawn from all but very limited involvement with the management committees of Vancouver's Punjabi-run gurdwaras.

Such had not always been the case. Soon after the founding of a 3HO ashram in Vancouver (*ca.* 1972–3), Gora Sikhs attempted to become actively involved with the two pre-existing Vancouver Sikh gurdwaras, both dominated by Doabi Jats. Their motivation was largely ideological. Convinced by Puri that they were the true upholders of Sikh orthodoxy in North America, Gora Sikhs had become highly critical of certain changes that had crept into local gurdwara protocol in the years since the early migration. Especially egregious to them was the practice of appearing bareheaded in the presence of the Guru Granth Sahib. In pursuing efforts to ensure that this sacrilege not continue and that headcoverings be made mandatory in the main gurdwara, the Gora Sikhs became involved in an escalating conflict between local Sikh factions.[21]

During previous research with 3HO, I had been present in Vancouver during the summer of 1974 when a pitched battle, provoked in part by the Gora Sikhs' attempt to force those entering the gurdwara to cover their heads, erupted at the Khalsa Diwan Society's gurdwara in south Vancouver. In the course of this encounter, both Gora Sikhs and Punjabi Sikhs were assaulted: turbans were pulled off, several people were roughed up, and police were ultimately called in to restore order.[22] The incident included a reported threat in Vancouver on the life of Puri, who was accompanying visiting Punjabi Sikh dignitaries on a North American tour.

The Gora Sikhs' despair and incredulity (and, ultimately, their incomprehension) over the whole situation is well summed up in the title of a letter—'What are the Sikhs doing in Vancouver?'—that the head of the local 3HO ashram wrote to the English-language section of the

Shiromani Gurdwara Parbandhak Committee's journal, *Gurdwara Gazette* (G.R. Singh 1975). Subsequently, the Gora Sikhs grew so frustrated with the factional politics surrounding the gurdwara management committees in Vancouver that they withdrew from the arena.[23] Instead, they chose to continue to spread their version of proper Sikh practices by urging Punjabi Sikh participation in the Sikh Youth Federation of Canada (which they had established with sympathetic Punjabi Sikhs to proselytize among Punjabi Sikh youth and to provide legal support of Sikh 'religious rights'), by attempting to establish an alternative place of worship at the short-lived Siri Guru Sadan (a gurdwara-cum-community centre, also known as 'New Age Community Centre', located in the 'alternative lifestyles' section of town), and by inviting sympathetic Punjabi Sikhs (both local residents and visiting musicians and 'preachers' brought from India) to services held in the gurdwara that they maintained at their own Guru Ram Das Ashram.

Although local Gora Sikhs viewed their withdrawal as principled (that is, eschewing divisive politics in favour of concentrating on practice of the Sikh religion), many Jat Sikhs interpreted the Gora Sikh withdrawal as retreat in the face of a public humiliation suffered in the arena of gurdwara politics. Misunderstanding the Gora Sikhs' motivations to enforce the practice of orthodox ideology, Jat Sikhs misinterpreted their estrangement. For Jat Sikhs, *izzat* rather than ideology provided the explanatory framework.

The Jat Sikh feeling of moral superiority over a potential challenger was reinforced soon thereafter. In attempting to fund their 'Siri Singh Sadan' as an alternative place of worship, the Gora Sikhs twice went before the *sangat* (congregation) at the Akali Singh Society gurdwara to ask for donations. Jat Sikhs were surprised that the Gora Sikhs would so shamelessly solicit and accept charity—in effect, 'lowering themselves' by coming not simply once but twice to ask for assistance and then, in the end, failing in the endeavour anyway. Informants were even more incredulous that, having put themselves in debt to the congregation, Gora Sikhs would dare to continue to voice criticism of Punjabi Sikh practices. Several times informants cited this incident to suggest that the Gora Sikhs knew no shame (that is, were lacking in *izzat*). Their reactions seemed to indicate clearly that Punjabi Sikhs were content to judge the situation morally, using the familiar emotion term of *izzat*, whether or not the converts shared their moral sensitivities.

From the Gora Sikhs' perspective, in attempting to establish the Siri Guru Sadan, they were simply offering to create another public setting for the reading of the Guru Granth Sahib; and by collecting from the congregation, they were offering other Sikhs the chance to contribute toward this religiously meritorious cause.[24] Because they neither consciously related to those at the Akali Singh gurdwara along group lines nor saw this as a matter of collective prestige, they apparently did not feel that success or failure would redound to them as Gora Sikhs. They were disappointed that in the end they did not have the financial wherewithal to keep open this place of worship; but, without a Jat Sikh sensitivity to *izzat*, they never felt humiliated by receipt of Punjabi Sikh largess and subsequent failure of their project. In fact, I think that they never appreciated the negative implications of this incident for their reputation in the local Punjabi Sikh community.

Very briefly, let me add two other examples of public actions that provoked very different reactions from Gora Sikhs and Jat Sikhs. Although the first incident predated my arrival in Vancouver in 1978, it was still actively discussed. In a nearby community a Jat Sikh man had murdered his wayward daughter, who had apparently run off with a *gorā* (white man) and was living openly with him. Rather than continue to suffer this humiliation of his family, her father had killed her in a reportedly brutal manner. Gora Sikhs, like Canadians generally, condemned unconditionally the killing and evinced horror at the very thought of filicide. My Jat Sikh informants, though by no means condoning *to me* the man's actions, nevertheless evinced sympathy with his predicament and recounted other similar stories. In fact, such situations of unapproved, mixed relationships have increasingly arisen in the migrant setting. Other parents have handled the dilemma of wayward children in ways that sought to remove the source of their humiliation by social rather than physical death. Thus, ostracization and outright denial of the wayward family member's existence are common responses to *izzat*-threatening deviance.

The second case, arising subsequent to my departure in 1979, involved the defection of the local 3HO ashram's head and his wife's decision to stay on without him in Vancouver. When the publicly recognized leader of the local Gora Sikhs quit the group, took off his *bāṇā* (the Khalsa uniform), left behind his divorced wife, child, and 'students,' Gora Sikh detractors widely represented this as proof of the superficial nature of Gora Sikh 'conversions'. Even among those generally sympathetic to the Gora Sikhs, the defection dealt a severe blow to the Gora Sikhs' reputation.

Even more illuminating were responses to his wife's decision to stay. No doubt the Gora Sikhs considered the defection of their local leader an unfortunate event, one that their detractors in the Punjabi Sikh community would probably use against them. The leader's wife—whose marriage had been arranged by Puri who had sent them to Vancouver in 1972 to found an ashram—felt torn between her desire to save her marriage and family and her responsibility to the ashram and its projects in the wider Vancouver Sikh community. She represented her ultimate decision to stay as a sign of her commitment to the Sikh *dharma* (moral duty).[25] In effect, she would sacrifice her marriage to remain a Sikh and provide service as well as leadership to her community. Fellow Gora Sikhs applauded her choice which, they hoped, would show the local Punjabi Sikhs that, even though one of their number was an apostate, the rest were steadfast. It is not clear that this was how Punjabi Sikhs responded. Although they told me that her commitment to Sikhism impressed them, even as they expressed shock at her husband's lack of commitment, it is doubtful that many Jat Sikh women would have acted the same. Because the family is a repository of *izzat*, *izzat* suffers when marital discord becomes public. Indeed, Punjabi Sikh families go to great lengths to keep others from learning about the family's intimate life. Women, in particular, have a responsibility to protect the integrity of the family's reputation, even where this might mean maintaining a public fiction. In this instance, informants suggested that a wife's duty would be to follow her husband and, if possible, to work quietly to bring him back into the fold.

I hope by now that my point is clear. The difference between Jat Sikh and Gora Sikh moral sensitivities in North America might well be summed up by suggesting, as did one of my reflective Jat Sikh informants, that the Punjabi Sikh community in Vancouver is, in his terms, 'pre-ideological' but highly sensitive to *izzat* in social relations. In contrast, the Gora Sikhs are highly ideological but operate entirely without recognition of or sensitivity to *izzat* as moral affect.[26]

***

Let me return, at last, to the different responses of North American Sikhs to the news of Mrs Gandhi's assassination. My point is, of course, not that no Jat Sikhs were willing and able to condemn the assassination or that no Gora Sikhs felt that she had, in some sense, brought her death upon herself. Rather, my point is that most Jat Sikhs (including such 'moderates' as Sant Harchand Singh Longowal, the Akali Dal leader who was subsequently assassinated for negotiating an accord with Rajiv Gandhi) felt the destruction of the Akal Takht as a humiliation inflicted upon the Panth, a humiliation demanding some counteraction to restore

Sikh *izzat*. In contrast, the Gora Sikhs regarded the destruction of the Akal Takht as a desecration but the ultimate unfortunate consequence of 'Indian politics'. They responded by urging a cessation of the politics that threatened the religion and demanding a return of Sikhs to their *dharma*.

If the dominant moral sentiments expressed in Gora Sikh pronouncements at the time were righteous indignation and exasperation, those of Jat Sikhs were humiliation and vengefulness. Thus, in the months between Operation Bluestar and the assassination of Mrs Gandhi, Punjabi Sikhs spoke of the needs to remember those Sikhs martyred by government troops, to avenge the death and desecration that occurred in the assault on the Akal Takht, and to restore the honour of the Sikh Panth.[27] At the same time, Gora Sikhs (in such contexts as *Beads of Truth*, the semiannual organ of 3HO), also spoke of the 'martyrdom of Akal Takht' but argued for a 'negotiate-for-solution and do not be revengeful' posture.[28] If most Jat Sikhs felt that the 'martyrdom of the Akal Takht' was occasion for a pledge of vengeance and retribution, the Gora Sikhs felt that it was occasion for a pledge 'to improve any aspect of our individual performance as *gursikhs*' (H. S. Khalsa 1984, p. 44).

***

Reminded by Michelle Rosaldo (1983, 1984), Catherine Lutz (1983, 1986), and Owen M. Lynch (this volume) [1990] that emotions are culturally constructed moral affects constitutive of the self, I am now in a position to pose two questions: What are the different moral affects experienced by Punjabi Sikhs and Gora Sikhs? Moreover, what within the different social selves makes *izzat* such a key moral affect for Punjabis but, in the same social situation, elicits no comparable emotional response from Westerners?[29] To ask the latter question is not to suggest that Punjabis are somehow inherently more emotional and less rational than Westerners. Indeed, the benefit of looking at moral affect is that one need not oppose the emotional and the rational. As long as their socialization experiences continue to differ, Jat Sikhs—raised sensitive to the variable reputations of the collectivities of which they are a part—and Gora Sikhs—raised sensitive to their personal integrity as individuals—will differ in their emotions as appraisals of common situations. But Gora Sikhs can be said to be as emotional as Jat Sikhs; however, the moral affect with which they appraise these contexts is not *izzat* but indignation and exasperation at failure to live up to one's religious duties.[30]

Although the dominant Euro-American ethnopsychology and ethnosociology may continue to regard emotion as antithetical to morality, moral judgments are clearly central to the sorts of appraisals of social situations crucial to a moral affect like *izzat*. This should lead us to rethinking further the classic analytical oppositions between emotion and moral code, sentiment and structure, individual and society, personal experience and cultural construct. As I have suggested, concepts like *izzat* are particularly good candidates for analysis because they so clearly involve both moral and affective dimensions. Yet, the very centrality of *izzat* and related concepts in peoples' emotional lives commonly leads those who experience a particular moral affect to assume its universality (rather than to reflect upon its relativity) and thus to make familiar moral appraisals in new settings and to project a similar moral sensitivity onto others.

But clearly *izzat* is not a universal emotion; rather, it is a socially learned moral appraisal with attendant affective dimensions. The same situation, as I have shown, will elicit very different emotional responses from different persons, depending upon their prior socialization.[31] Moreover, situations as such do not elicit certain kinds of emotions; rather, it is the appraisal of them that is different, and this is identified by an emotional term. We must necessarily be alert, therefore, to the ways in which people of different cultures are socialized into different universes of moral affect. However, because we live in a world of interacting cultures—where, for example, young North Americans are being asked to present the Sikh reaction to major Indian socio-political events—it no longer makes sense to content ourselves with drawing out contrasts between, for example, Ilongot 'shame' and American 'shame' or Jat Sikh 'honour' and American 'honour' as if they were analytic specimens of emotions existing only in separate social universes. Instead, we must also recognize and interpret those instances where cultural differences in moral affect express themselves in mutual (mis)apprehensions of social actors in shared interaction. With Gora Sikhs and Jat Sikhs attempting to incorporate each other in a common moral universe, we can thereby investigate 'moral affect' in the breach. And, because these situations of cross-cultural estrangement will be patterned, knowing the particulars about how, say, *izzat* is entailed and indexed in social life will help make public events—such as the differing Punjabi Sikh and Gora Sikh reactions to Mrs Gandhi's assassination—intelligible. That has been the intent of this analysis.

ACKNOWLEDGMENTS

This essay draws on fieldwork conducted in 1978–9 in Vancouver, British Columbia, with Punjabi Sikhs and Gora Sikhs and on fieldwork conducted in 1972 and 1974 in the western United States and Canada with the Healthy, Happy, Holy Organization. It benefits from continuing archival research and from ongoing conversations with Sikhs throughout North America. I would like to thank Elizabeth Coville, Owen M. Lynch, McKim Marriott, W. H. McLeod, the late Paul Riesman, and the participants in the conference on the Anthropology of Experience, Feeling, and Emotion in India for helpful comments on earlier versions of this essay. I absolve them of any responsibility for the essay's weaknesses.

NOTES

1. See, for example, the *New York Times*, 1 November 1984, p. 13.
2. Puri is from the Khatri (mercantile) rather than Jat (agriculturalist) section of the Sikh Panth (community). Khatris claim elevated status within the Panth by virtue of the fact that Nanak, the first Sikh Guru (preceptor), and his successors were all Khatris. However, although Khatris remain an influential caste in the urban areas of Punjab, Jats have come to predominate within the Panth. This is true among the Sikh diaspora as well as in the Punjab. The concern with *izzat* (honour), the topic of this essay, is especially a Jat Sikh concern. The fact that Puri is a Khatri, not a Jat, may have something to do with his response to the assassination, but it cannot entirely account for the moral sensitivities of his *gorā* followers.
3. The Ghadar Party was a revolutionary organization, centred in North America, which sought the overthrow of British rule in India. Although the leadership of the party came from the Hindu, Muslim, and Sikh immigrant intelligentsia, support of the immigrant Punjabi Sikh masses was crucial to its ability to raise funds and volunteers. Hopkinson had been used elsewhere along the Pacific Coast by Canadian and American agencies interested in gathering information on potentially revolutionary activities among South Asian immigrants. For a detailed analysis of the Ghadar Party, including discussion of Hopkinson's activities, see Puri (1983). Although he does not discuss the concept directly, Puri's analysis suggests that appeals to *izzat* were effective in generating support from the Sikh immigrants of peasant stock, as 'heaped symbols of shame and oppression were used to generate a certain auto-intoxication of disgrace' (Puri 1983, p. 119).
4. *Gurduara* (or *gurūdwārā*) comes from *gurū* (preceptor) + *dvārā* (door) = 'the residence of the Guru'. I employ the more commonly encountered anglicized spelling, gurdwara, throughout this essay.
5. I speak of a 'Sikh community' in Vancouver to the extent that most self-described Sikhs in Vancouver continue to seek to influence one another's lives in the name of common membership in the Sikh Panth. At its 'Desh

Bhagat Temple' the local East Indian Defence Committee—an offshoot of the Indian and Canadian Communist parties (Marxist-Leninist)—celebrates Mewa Singh as one of a line of local Sikhs (including Ghadar revolutionaries, Indian National Army soldiers, and recent Naxalite terrorists) martyred through their involvement in revolutionary anti-imperialist and class struggle. The Khalsa Diwan Society and the Akali Singh Society, at their respective gurdwaras, represent Mewa Singh as a local martyr who, like earlier Sikh martyrs in India, gave his life for the perpetuation of his people and his religion in the face of hostility from the dominant society. The appropriation of Mewa Singh's martyrdom by such different groups suggests that he is a significant collective symbol of a 'Vancouver Sikh community'.

6. I employ the conventional transliteration, *izzat*, which reflects the pronunciation of the term in the Majhi dialect (of the Amritsar–Lahore area) on which literary Punjabi and most Punjabi dictionaries are based. The pronunciation in the dialects of Doaba and Malwa (the areas of the Punjab south of the Sutlej river from which most of my informants originate) is more accurately rendered as *ijjat*.
7. A near-synonym, commonly used in Doabi Jat Sikh conversation, is *mān* (respect, prestige, pride, veneration, arrogance).
8. Malcolm Darling, the British Indian civil servant whose classic books on Punjabi village life (*The Punjab Peasant in Prosperity and Debt*, *Rusticus Loquitur*, and *Wisdom and Waste in the Punjab Village*) constitute a regrettably ethnocentric but nonetheless valuable ethnographic record, recognized both the importance and difficulty of the concept. He notes of *izzat* that it is 'a word for which there is no precise English equivalent, denoting objectively, social position, and subjectively, *amour-propre*' (1934, p. 42, n. 3). See also the discussion of the term in Pettigrew (1975, pp. 58–9).
9. See, far example, Charles Lindholm's (1982) illuminating discussion of personal honour as central to the social organization and emotional life of the Swat Pukhtun of Northern Pakistan.
10. W. H. McLeod (1976, pp. 37–58) discusses in some detail the way in which what people have come to regard as general Sikh characteristics (including the outward Khalsa form and the martial reputation) are largely Jat customs and attributes institutionalized within the Panth. McLeod argues convincingly that the living human Sikh Gurus, all of whom were Khatris, gradually came to adopt Jat practices as Jats came to predominate among their followers. Nevertheless, even today the Panth continues to include those Nanakpanthis who emphasize the more quietistic teachings of the first Guru, as well as those 'orthodox' Sikhs who emphasize the militarism of the Khalsa (whose creation is credited to Guru Gobind Singh, the last human Sikh Guru). If one can speak of emulating the 'dominant caste' within the Sikh Panth, one would have to recognize the remnants of contending Khatri and Jat models. Concern with *izzat* is not normally the intense concern for Khatris that it is for Jats, and this may partially account

for the Jat stereotype that Khatris are, by nature, cowardly and spineless. It appears that Jats and Khatris are socialized with different transactional strategies (see Marriott 1976; especially, pp. 132–3) and, consequently, different moral sensitivities.

11. In his recent, posthumously published book, *Women's Seclusion and Men's Honor* (1988), David Mandelbaum identifies and analyses what he terms a 'purdah-izzat complex' extending—with some regional, caste, class, and religious variation—from Pakistan, throughout most of northern India, to Bangladesh.
12. Mrs Gandhi's assassins will, by having acted to defend the honour of the Panth, also presumably ensure the honour of their families and descendants. In fact, Beant Singh, the Sikh bodyguard and a presumed assasin, slain during the incident, is already being honoured as a martyr in his village; and his shrine will likely continue to be a focal point of veneration by members of his lineage.
13. Sending individuals away from the village is, of course, something quite different from migrating together as a family unit. The preference for the former type of migration, which does not involve relinquishing landholdings in the ancestral village, may distinguish landowning Jat Sikhs from other Punjabi migrants.
14. I do not believe that *izzat* tells the whole story about Sikb endogamy (see Dusenbery 1988, 1990), but it plays a significant role. Vaughn Robinson (1980) notes how concern for *izzat* works against the marriage opportunities of highly educated, British-raised Sikh girls whose sexual purity and ability to submit to the demands of life in her husband's family may be questioned by exposure to Western society. My own research suggests that Jat Sikhs in Vancouver have sought to avoid certain jobs (for example, cleaning, service, sales) that, although they may bear no stigma to non-Punjabi Canadians, are deemed beneath the dignity of a Jat Sikh and detrimental to family reputation.
15. Most of my informants estimated the percentage of Jats among the Sikh old-timers in British Columbia at 90 per cent or more. The lowest estimate known to me is Adrian C. Mayer's, who writes that 'the vast majority of Vancouver Sikhs are from the same caste—the Jat. Perhaps not more than one-fifth represent other castes'(1959, p. 13).
16. For accounts that attempt to assay the effects of the recent immigration on particular North American Sikh communities, see Buchignani, Indra, and Srivast[a]va (1985), Chadney (1985), Dusenbery (1981), La Brack (1983, 1988). For a general overview and specific case studies of Sikh migration and the experience beyond Punjab, see Barrier and Dusenbery (1989).
17. I have discussed this process in greater detail in, especially, Dusenbery (1986, 1988, 1990); see also Dusenbery (1981).
18. The *amrit pāhul* or *amrit saṃskār* ceremony effects the incorporation of one into the Khalsa Panth, the so-called 'Brotherhood of the Pure' (see

Dusenbery 1990). By tradition, any five worthy Khalsa Sikhs can be constituted as the *pañj pyārē* (literally, five beloved) to administer this ceremony. Puri's institutionalization of Sikh 'ministers' is but one of his innovations in building an ecclesiastical hierarchy unprecedented among Sikhs.

19. I analyse the commitment mechanisms used in the early 3HO recruitment process in Dusenbery (1973). I focus on the yogic to Sikh transformation of the organization in Dusenbery (1975).
20. For an account of early Gora Sikh involvement with Punjabi Sikh gurdwaras in Los Angeles, see Fleuret (1974). For accounts of early Gora Sikh involvement with Punjabi Sikh gurdwaras in northern California, see La Brack (1974, 1979) and Bharati (1980).
21. Somewhat conflicting accounts of the factional dispute can be found in accounts commissioned by the British Columbia Police Commission (D. Singh 1975, pp. 39–44), reported in the Sikh press by the head of the local 3HO ashram (G. R. Singh 1975), produced by an outside UNESCO researcher (Scanlon 1977), and presented in a University of British Columbia master's thesis (Campbell 1977, pp. 74–102); see also Dusenbery (1981). The main factional disputants were a 'businessmen' faction, so-called because it drew its strength from the successful, established immigrants who had seen to the building of the present gurdwara in the late 1960s, and a more 'orthodox' faction, representing recent immigrants and numbering among its leaders some non-Jat professionals with whom the Gora Sikhs believed themselves to have some affinity. The source of most of the violence was a 'communist' cadre of Naxalites affiliated with the East Indian Defence Committee and the CCP-ML, a group that each of the two major factions felt was working in league with its opponents.
22. For Punjabi Sikhs, pulling off a man's turban is a serious challenge to his *izzat*. Similarly, roughing up someone in public is as much an assault on his *izzat* as it is on his physical person. For comparative purposes, see the detailed discussion of 'the dialectic of challenge and riposte' in 'the competition of honour' among the Kabyle of North Africa in Bourdieu (1966).
23. Aside from occasionally attending gurdwara functions, the only semiofficial relationship that any Gora Sikh maintained with either of the two main Vancouver gurdwaras was through a 'Sunday school' class taught by the wife of the ashram head at the Akali Singh gurdwara. After I left Vancouver, members of the local ashram ran a Montessori School on Khalsa Diwan Society property, but even that relationship soon dissolved with recriminations on both sides.
24. Contributions toward construction, improvement, or maintenance of a gurdwara are meritorious gifts to the Guru. Because the amount of a donation is public knowledge (amounts of gifts are read to the congregation and subsequently published), conspicuous philanthropy

is both religiously meritorious and secularly good for one's reputation. As a consequence, gurdwaras tend to be quite lavishly endowed institutions in wealthy settings. During my fieldwork, several million dollars worth of property purchases, building projects, or expansions and remodellings were scheduled at some seven present or planned gurdwaras in the greater Vancouver area.

25. I have employed the Sanskritized form, *dharma*, rather than the Punjabi, *dharam*, because that is the form used by the Gora Sikhs. In everyday conversation, Gora Sikhs use 'Sikh *dharma*,' 'Sikh religion,' and 'Sikh way of life' interchangeably.
26. I would argue that, whereas they are insensitive to *izzat* as a moral affect, the Gora Sikhs have a highly legalistic understanding of 'the *dharma*' as a moral imperative underlying their ideology and actions. It seems telling not only that the Gora Sikhs call their religious body, Sikh Dharma, but also that their claims to orthodoxy rest on strict adherence to the 'moral duty' they identify with the Sikh *rahit maryādā* (literally, prestigious code for conduct). A generally accepted version of the *rahit* was formally issued by the Shiromani Gurdwara Parbandhak Commitee in 1950. The fact that most Punjabi Sikhs are ignorant of and indifferent to the exact contents of this document—and, especially in the case of Jat Sikhs, would not feel their identity as Sikhs dependent on strict adherence to its rules of conduct—merely confirms the Gora Sikhs in their conviction that they, rather than the body of Punjabi Sikhs, are the true upholders of 'the *dharma*'. For a further discussion of the 'Gora Sikhs' understanding of religion, see Dusenbery (1981, 1986, 1990). For the text of and commentary on the Sikh *rahit maryādā*, see McLeod (1984, pp. 79–86).
27. 'Blood for Blood' ran the lead headline in Vancouver's Punjabi-language *Indo-Canadian Times* (vol. 7, no. 23) for the week ending 15 June 1984. Elsewhere, the intense emotions Punjabi Sikhs experienced at the time are partially reflected in the following accounts: 'We have suffered and suffered terribly in every respect during the last 2 years. Our prestige has gone down. Our honour has been compromised and the very source of our spiritual sustence [sic] has been cruelly hit' (W. Singh 1985, p. 42). 'Some of us outside Panjab had visualized the possibility of alienation which the entry of troops into gurdwaras would create among the Sikhs. But we had not reckoned with the intensity of the humiliation they have felt. Every Sikh we met was distressed by the Army action. They think that there has been an assault on their identity' (Chowdhury and Anklesaria 1984, p. 143). 'Virtually to a man, the 14 million strong [Sikh] community felt as if it had been slapped in the face. . . . The feeling of hurt and humiliation among Sikhs runs so deep that they seem to feel that they are a persecuted minority' (K. Singh and K. Nayar 1984, pp. 37, 41). 'The Sikhs feel totally alienated and isolated. Their pride and self-respect have been badly hit and the festering wound inflicted

may take decades to heal, though the memory of the tragic happening will remain treasured in the Sikh psyche' (B. Singh 1984: 4a).

28. See, for example, the following articles: Sardarni Premka Kaur Khalsa (1984), Shakti Parwha Kaur Khalsa (1984), Harbhajan Singh Khalsa (1984), Sikh Dharma Secretariat (1984a, 1984b). *Takhat* is an alternative spelling of *Takht*.
29. The articles in Peristiany (1966) on honour and shame in Mediterranean society, although not systematically focused on the contrast of the person in Mediterranean and modern Euro-American societies, nevertheless contain valuable insights into the very different social selves presupposed. Peristiany and other contributors to the volume point out that honour in Mediterranean societies is the concern of equals or near equals interacting in public settings. In Punjabi society, *izzat* as a moral affect is similarly relevant to public relations between would-be elite persons, families, or castes. Within the private sphere of the family and in public interactions with inferiors or superiors, other moral appraisals apply.
30. Punjabi Sikhs and Gora Sikhs construe *dharma* in very different ways. For Gora Sikhs, Sikh *dharma*, as a 'religious' code for conduct, constitutes a privileged source of ultimate morality applicable across all contexts. For Punjabi Sikhs, Sikh *dharma*, however privileged it may be, is but one of a number of moral codes for conduct impinging upon the person. See Dusenbery (1988, 1990) for a more detailed discussion of the different concepts of the person presupposed by Gora Sikhs and Punjabi Sikhs.
31. Even fear of dangerous things in children may be more culturally learned than innate. Catherine Lutz reports that 'academic psychologists have begun to accumulate evidence. . . suggesting that the number of danger response elicitors present from birth is much smaller than was once thought' (1983, p. 257). If this were considered in a cross-cultural context, it might be nil.

REFERENCES

Barrier, N. Gerald and Verne A. Dusenbery, (eds), 1989, *The Sikh Diaspora: Migration and the Experience Beyond Punjab*', Delhi: Chanakya Publications; Columbia: South Asia Publications.

Benedict, Ruth, 1949, *The Chrysanthemum and the Sword*, Boston: Houghton-Mifflin.

Bharati, Agehanand, 1980, 'Indian Expatriates in North America and neo-Hindu Movements' in J. S. Yadava and V. Gautam, (eds), *The Communication of Ideas*, Delhi: Concept, pp. 245–65.

Bourdieu, Pierre, 1966, 'The Sentiment of Honour in Kabyle Society' in J. G. Peristiany, (ed.), *Honour and Shame: The Values of Mediterranean Society*, Chicago: University of Chicago Press, pp. 191–241.

———, 1976, 'Marriage Strategies as Strategies of Social Reproduction' in Robert Foster and Orest Rannum, (eds), Elborg Forster and Patricia M. Rannum, (trans), *Family and Society: Selections from the* Annales Economies, Societies, Civilisations, Baltimore: Johns Hopkins University Press. pp.117–144.

Buchignani, Norman and Doreen M. Indra, with Ram Srivast[a]va, 1985, *Continuous Journey: A Social History of South Asians in Canada,* Toronto: McClelland and Stewart.

Campbell, Michael Graeme, 1977, 'The Sikhs of Vancouver: A Case Study in Minority-Host Relations' Master's thesis, Political Science Department, University of British Columbia.

Chadney, James G., 1984, *The Sikhs of Vancouver*, New York: AMS Press.

Chowdhury, Neerja, and Shahnaz Anklesaria, 1984, 'How the Sikhs Have Taken It', *The Sikh Review*, 32 (368), pp. 143–4.

Darling, Malcolm Lyall, 1934, *Wisdom and Waste in the Punjab Village*, New York: Oxford University Press.

Dusenbery, Verne A. 1973, "'Why would anybody join... ?': A Study of Recruitment and the Healthy, Happy, Holy Organization" Senior honour's essay, Anthropology Department, Stanford University.

———, 1974, 'Straight→Freak→Yoga Sikh: A "Search for Meaning" in Contemporary American Culture', Master's thesis, Anthropology Department, University of Chicago.

———, 1981, 'Canadian Ideology and Public Policy: The Impact on Vancouver Sikh Ethnic and Religious Adaptation', *Canadian Ethnic Studies,* 13(3), pp. 101–19.

———, 1986, 'On Punjabi Sikh-Gora Sikh Relations', in *Aspects of Modern Sikhism: Michigan Papers in Sikh Studies,* (1), Ann Arbor: Center for South and Southeast Asian Studies, University of Michigan, pp. 13–24.

———, 1988, 'Punjabi Sikhs and Coca Sikhs: Conflicting Assertions of Sikh Identity in North America' in Joseph T. O'Connell, Milton Israel, and Willard G. Oxtoby, with W.H. McLeod and J.S. Grewal, (eds), *Sikh History and Religion in the Twentieth Century*, Toronto: Centre for South Asian Studies, University of Toronto, pp. 334–55.

———, 1990, 'The Sikh Person, the Khalsa Panth, and Western Sikh Converts', Bardwell L. Smith, (ed.), *Is Religious Movements and Social Identity: Continuity and Change in India*, Delhi: Chanakya Publications, pp. 117–350.

Fleuret, Anne K., 1974, 'Incorporation into Networks Among Sikhs in Los Angeles', *Urban Anthropology*, 3(1), pp. 27–33.

Geertz, Clifford, 1973, 'Person, Time and Conduct in Bali', *The Interpretation of Cultures*, New York: Basic Books, pp. 364–411.

Helweg, Arthur Wesley, 1979, *Sikhs in England: The Development of a Migrant Community*, New Delhi: Oxford University Press.

Howe, Marvine,1984, 'Among Indians Far From Home, Joyful Celebrations Contrast With Shock and Grief', *The New York Times*, 1, November, p. 13.

Kaur, Sardarni Premka, 1973, 'Rejoinder', *The Sikh Review*, 21(232), pp. 52–6.

———, 1975, Listen, O 'Patit' and Learn, *Gurdwara Gazette*, 46(4), pp. 4–13.

Khalsa, Harbhajan Singh, 1984, 'Message from Siri Singh Sahib Harbajan Singh Khalsa Yogi', *The Sikh Review*, 32(369), p. 44.

Khalsa, Sardarni Premka Kaur, 1984, 'Sikh Dharma Position on Crisis in Punjab', *Beads of Truth*, 2(13), p. 27.

Khalsa, Shakti Parwha Kaur,1984, 'In Memorium', *Beads of Truth*, 2(14), pp. 4–10.

Khalsa, Shakti Parwha Kaur and Gurubanda Singh Khalsa, 1979, 'The Siri Singh Sahib' in S. P. K. Khalsa and S. K. K. Khalsa, (eds), *The Man Called the Siri Singh Sahib*, Los Angeles: Sikh Dharma, pp. 117–31.

La Brack, Bruce Wilfred,1974, 'Neo-Sikhism and East Indian Religious Identification', Paper presented at Midwest Conference on Asian Affairs, Kansas City, Kansas, November.

———, 1979, 'Sikhs Ideal and Real: A Discussion of Text and Context in the Description of Overseas Sikh Communities' in Mack Juergensmeyer and N. Gerald Barrier, (eds), *Sikh Studies: Comparative Perspectives on a Changing Tradition*, Berkeley: Graduate Theological Union, pp. 127–42.

———, 1983, 'The Reconstitution of Sikh Society in Rural California' in George Kurian and Ram P. Srivastava, (eds), *Overseas Indians: A Study in Adaptation,* Delhi: Vikas, pp. 215–40.

———, 1988, *The Sikhs of Northern California, 1904–86.* New York: AMS Press.

Lindholm, Charles, 1982, *Generosity and Jealously: The Swat Pukhtun of Northern Pakistan*, New York: Columbia University Press.

Lutz, Catherine, 1983, 'Parental Goals, Ethnopsychology, and the Development of Emotional Meaning', *Ethos*, 11(4), pp. 246–62.

———, 1986, 'Emotion, Thought, and Estrangement: Emotion as a Cultural Category', *Cultural Anthropology*, 1(3), pp. 287–309.

Lynch, Owen M., 1990, 'The Social Construction of Emotion in India', in Owen M. Lynch, (ed.), *Divine Passions: The Social Construction of Emotion in India,* Berkeley: University of California Press and New Delhi: Oxford University Press, pp. 3–34.

Mandelbaum, David G.,1988, *Women's Seclusion and Men's Honor: Sex Roles in North India, Bangladesh, and Pakistan*, Tucson: University of Arizona Press.

Marriott, McKim, 1976, 'Hindu Transactions: Diversity Without Dualism' in Bruce Kapferer, (ed.), *Transaction and Meaning: Directions in the Anthropology of Exchange and Symbolic Behavior*, Philadelphia: ISHI Publications, pp. 109–42.

Mayer, Adrian C., 1959, 'A Report on the East Indian Community in Vancouver', Working Paper, Institute of Social and Economic Research, University of British Columbia.

McLeod, W. H., 1976, *The Evolution of the Sikh Community*, Oxford: Clarendon.

———, 1984, *Textual Sources for the Study of Sikhism*, W. H. McLeod, (ed.), and (trans.), Totowa, New Jersey: Barnes and Noble Books.

Pcristiany, J. G., (ed.), 1986, *Honour and Shame: The Values of Mediterranean Society*, Chicago: University of Chicago Press.

Pettigrew, Joyce, 1975, *Robber Noblemen: A Study of the Political System of the Sikh Jats*, London: Routledge and Kegan Paul.

Piers, Gerhart, and Milton B. Singer, 1953, *Shame and Guilt*, New York: Charles C. Thomas.

Puri, Harish K., 1983, *Ghadar Movement: Ideology, Organisation and Strategy*. Amritsar, Punjab: Guru Nanak Dev University Press.

Robinson, Vaughan, 1980, 'Patterns of South Asian Ethnic Exogamy and Endogamy in Britain', *Ethnic and Racial Studies*, 3(4), pp. 427–43.

Rosaldo, Michelle Z., 1983, 'The Shame of Headhunters and the Autonomy of Self', *Ethos*, 11(3), pp. 135–51.

——1984, 'Toward an Anthropology of Self and Feeling' in Richard A. Shweder and Robert A. LeVine, (eds), *Culture Theory: Essays on Mind, Self, and Emotion*, Cambridge: Cambridge University Press, pp. 137–57.

Scanlon, Joseph, 1977, 'The Sikhs of Vancouver: A Case Study of the Role the Media in Ethnic Relations', *From Ethnicity and the Media: An Analysis of Media Reporting in the United Kingdom, Canada, and Ireland*, pp. 193–261, Paris: UNESCO.

Sikh Dharma Secretariat, 1984a, *A Factual Report*, Los Angeles: Sikh Dharma.

———, 1984b, *Martyrdom of the Akal Takhat*, Los Angeles; Sikh Dharma.

Singh, Bhag, 1984, 'Sikhs Smarting Under Healing Touch [editorial]', *The Sikh Review*, 32(368), p. 5.

Singh, Dave, 1975, *Some Factors in the Relationship Between the Police and East Indians*, Victoria: British Columbia Police Commission.

Singh, Guru Raj, 1975, 'What are the Sikhs Doing in Vancouver?', *Gurdwara Gazette*, 48(10), pp. 30–4.

Singh, Khushwant, 1964, 'Mewa Singh Shahid: He Died for His Countrymen', *The Sikh Review*, 12(198), pp. 5–6.

Singh, Khushwant and Kuldip Nayar, 1984, 'In the Aftermath of Operation Bluestar', *The Sikh Review*, 32(371), pp. 37–43.

Singh, Waryam, 1984, 'Retrieving the Honour of the Sikhs', *The Sikh Review*, 33(382), pp. 40–3.

3

The Word as Guru*

Sikh Scripture and the Translation Controversy

> The Word enshrined in the Holy Book was always revered by the [Sikh] Gurus as well as by their disciples as of Divine origin. The Guru was the revealer of the Word. One day the Word was to take the place of the Guru. The line of personal Gurus could not have continued forever. The inevitable came to pass when Guru Gobind Singh declared the Guru Granth Sahib to be his successor. It was only through the Word that the Guruship could be made everlasting.[1]

> There seems to be no theological reason why English speaking Sikhs should not use an English copy of the scriptures, not only for study but as the focal point of worship and life.[2]

THE CONTROVERSY

In the absence of a living human *gurū* (preceptor), Sikhs take their sacred scripture, the Ādi Granth or Guru Granth Sāhib, to be their eternal Guru, the source of divine benefits and the central focus of Sikh worship. Yet the language of the text, first compiled in 1603–4 from the devotional songs of medieval north Indian sages and written in what the linguist Chris Shackle has termed 'the sacred language of the Sikhs', is increasingly unintelligible to Sikh worshippers.[3] This is especially so for those born and raised outside Punjab, the ancestral homeland. Some reformist Sikhs and interested outsiders argue that if Sikhism is to be the 'world religion' that its practitioners often claim it to be, then its scriptures should be translated into vernaculars intelligible to all Sikh worshippers and to potential converts. In fact, it has been suggested that resistance to introducing an English or vernacular Punjabi version

* First published in *History of Religions*, vol. 31, no. 4 (May 1992), pp. 385–402.

of the text as a primary focus of worship amounts to 'bibliolatry' and 'idol worship' of a linguistically 'dead' original. Yet even in the contemporary Sikh diaspora there is strong resistance to installing a translated version of the text as a primary focus of worship.

Recent work in the comparative study of scripture and sacred texts has directed attention away from exclusive textualist attention to the meanings inscribed in holy writs and toward greater appreciation of the social uses of oral and written texts in ritual contexts.[4] One result of this growing body of work has been to highlight similarities and differences in texts and their uses between those religions privileging oral transmission, such as Buddhism and Vedic Hinduism, and those privileging the written text, such as Islam and Protestant Christianity.[5] And this has led to considerable discussion of the effects of writing and literacy on religious practice, including both the inscription of formerly unwritten texts and the translation of texts as religious movements across linguistic boundaries.[6] In the context of these discussions, it is surprising that so little attention has yet been paid to the main Sikh scripture, the Adi Granth, and especially to its use in Sikh worship in India and in the diaspora.[7]

Insofar as Sikh scriptures appropriate the inscription of the holy word common to Western monotheistic religions but maintain the sacredness of sound central to the classical Indian traditions, they 'present a Janus head', to use Frits Staal's term, implicitly challenging analytic dichotomies that rigidly oppose oral and written texts or sound and meaning or that foresee an inevitable evolutionary movement between them.[8] Most Sikhs appear to live quite comfortably with a written text retaining crucial oral uses, in which the sound properties of the words have not been subordinated to their meanings. Moreover, given concepts of the person (especially, the personhood of the Guru) and understandings of the properties of language (especially, the powers of the Word) alive among many Sikhs, the advisability—or even the possibility—of translating the Adi Granth and the appropriateness of introducing such a translation as the focal point of worship are considerably more problematic for Sikhs than generally has been recognized.[9]

Nevertheless, W. Owen Cole, the prolific British scholar of Sikhs and Sikhism, has argued forcefully in a number of different contexts that if Sikhism is to be a 'world religion', it must make its 'scriptures' accessible to the world in a variety of vernaculars. Cole, reacting to what he obviously considers half measures adopted by some Sikhs in England and North America—for example, in retaining the original text of the Adi Granth as the reigning Guru and the primary focus of ritual activity but finding a secondary role for the English translation in the service—argues:

There seems to be no theological reason why English-speaking Sikhs should not use an English copy of the scriptures, not only for study but as the focal point of worship and life. There would seem to be something odd, almost amounting to bibliolatry if a book written in a strange language were to be honoured ceremonially while at its side, or a little lower, was the English version from which readings were made and hymns sung during *diwan*.[10]

I would argue that the fundamental issue in the present translation controversy does not lie in Sikh 'theology' (narrowly conceived). Nor is the issue, as Cole would alternatively have it, an impasse caused either by the practical difficulties of 'rendering terse poetry into prose' or by conservative and parochial attachments of Sikhs to Punjabi for Punjabi's sake. Rather, at the heart of the issue is the fact that many Sikhs appear to hold a fundamentally different understanding of the properties of language and the personhood of the Guru than does Cole.

Cole is, of course, correct that the translation controversy is particularly an issue for Sikhs in the English-speaking diaspora. As W. H. McLeod has noted, the issue of the authority and the cohesive role of the scriptures 'is one which must command a particular interest amongst Sikhs living outside India, particularly in those areas where the ability to read Gurmukhi or to understand the actual language of the scriptures is diminishing'.[11] But it is an issue that he fully recognizes must be investigated by actually looking at 'the functional role [of the Ādi Granth] and developments which can be anticipated in the future'.[12] Among the questions he raises regarding contemporary individual and corporate attitudes toward and usage of the Ādi Granth are the following:

How does [the individual] regard the scripture and how is that regard expressed in practice? Does the scripture serve as a source of ideas or rather as a source of inspiration? If the latter, is it a comprehending inspiration or is the scripture treated more as a talisman? Is it an intimate association or is the attitude more distant and infrequent. . . ? What significance (in actual as opposed to purely formal terms) does the scripture command within the gurdwara today...? What benefits are understood to derive from *darsan* of the Guru Granth Sahib? What is the current understanding and actual usage of the *akhand path* [a continuous recitation of the text]?'[13]

Although it would be too much to expect a Sikh consensus on all the issues raised by McLeod, a look at Sikh practices in North America suggests that the translation controversy is rooted in very different understandings of what it means to affirm the Word as Guru.

TWO IDEOLOGIES OF LANGUAGE

It is my contention that to understand the controversy one must recognize two contrasting understandings of the properties of language being brought to the discourse. One, which I term a 'nondualistic' ideology of language, recognizes the material as well as cognitive properties of language (especially articulated speech) and refuses to privilege semantico-referential meaning at the expense of other properties that language is thought to possess. The other, which I term a 'dualistic' ideology of language, privileges reference, semantic meaning, the arbitrariness of signifier and signified, and the context-free cognitive qualities of the text at the expense of the sound properties of the words themselves. While the former lives on among many Punjabis and other South Asians, it is almost entirely submerged in the West, where the latter, dualistic ideology of language has become hegemonic.

It is the adoption of this dualistic ideology of language, long dominant in the West, that makes translation conceivable. Insofar as it separates the material properties of the articulated words from their meanings—and, hence, separates the production and reproduction of the words in recitation from the semantico-referential intentions of the author (or speaker)—one need 'only' decipher common referents and match them with parallel word-vehicles in two languages to effect an 'accurate' translation.[14] Even the distinction of literal versus figurative translation and the recognition of the difficulties inherent in retaining the 'poetic' qualities of the original (considerations that arise, for example, in evaluating the relative quality of various English translations of the Sikh scriptures now available) still do not challenge the prevailing ideology's privileging of reference or meaning at the expense of the sound properties and the substantive effects of the words themselves.

In contrast, what I have termed the nondualistic ideology of language makes translation virtually impossible. The language of the Adi Granth is, after all, *gurmukhī* (literally, 'from the mouth of the Guru'). Insofar as the words of the Adi Granth as originally produced by the Guru and subsequently recited or sung in Sikh worship are simultaneously considered to have efficacious material properties as well as spiritual messages for both reciter and hearer, changing the sound vehicle changes the substantive properties of the text. Each *śabad* ('word') of the Guru's *bāṇī* ('speech') has its own *rāsā* ('flavour'), which at one and the same time is a product of its aesthetic, physiological, and semantic qualities. Moreover, the entire text itself is taken to be the embodiment of the Guru.

Hence, to the extent that this ideology of language persists among Sikhs, one encounters both resistance to translation as a violation of the integrity of the text and recourse by some to the sorts of partial solutions of which Cole is so contemptuous.

Recent works that take as their goal the construction of ethnosocial sciences based upon South Asian first principles make the point that a number of the received dualisms of Western theology, philosophy, and social theory (for example, the oppositions between body/mind, matter/spirit, secular/sacred, natural substance/moral code, actor/action, doxa/praxis, idealism/materialism, and so forth) do not seem to prevail within South Asian cosmologies and conceptual logics.[15] McKim Marriott has thus termed 'monistic' the prevailing South Asian ontology and the ethnosciences it generates, and he and his colleagues have consequently emphasized the fundamental nonduality of South Asian social thought on these matters.[16] Whether one wants to recognize the Sikhs as thoroughgoing monists, it seems clear that one must recognize some strongly nondualistic aspects of sikh social thought and ritual practice, especially in relation to the perceived power of the Word.[17]

In fact, in South Asian ethnosociological terms, being a Sikh means incorporating into one's person the divine 'coded substances' of their Guru. Despite the common English-language translations of *gurū* as 'preceptor' and of *sikh* as 'disciple', the relationship between the Sikh Guru and devotee is not an impersonal and didactic relationship based on formal instruction in religious dogma or doctrine. Rather, Sikh Gurus are thought of as able to transmit to devotees certain divine benefits that are simultaneously both cognitive and physiological. From a Punjabi perspective, rather than merely dispensing religious homilies, *gurūs* serve up a more substantive fare: through channelling divine worship substances to the devotee, they transform the person in body as well as spirit. Receipt of the Guru's substances in the course of Sikh worship, therefore, serves to establish the substantive and moral connectedness of Guru and devotee (despite their differentiation in purity and rank); it serves to make those who receive and exchange the worship substances partly alike in their personal natures (through the 'biomoral' transformation it effects in their persons); and it serves to make of these regenerated persons a recognizably distinct worship genus, the Sikh Panth.[18]

Among the worship substances whose manipulation and incorporation are enjoined by the Sikh *dharma* (moral duty), are the uttered sounds (*Nām, śabad, bāṇī*), the visual or oral emanations (*darśan*), the edible 'benefits' (*kaṛāh praśād*)', and the 'nectar' (*amrit*) of the Guru. Note that, from the Punjabi perspective, not only *praśād* and *amrit* but also uttered sounds (and visual emanations) have substantial properties. Or, as Marriott and Inden put it in talking of a general South Asian ethnosociology, 'Words, like full codes, are thought to be from the beginning embodied... in substances that may have physical attributes, such as sound, shape, matter, force, etc'.[19] Sounds (like the glances, leavings, and other benefits) of divine beings—and of others who can mark one with their coded substances—thus have material/physical/physiological as well as spiritual/mental/cognitive affects upon their recipients.

But is a dichotomy between 'sacred' and 'secular' language central to Sikh thought? Is there a fundamental difference between God and humans such that divine words are categorically different from human words? An affirmative answer to this would seem to be one basis for McLeod's rejection of the term 'monistic' as applied to Sikh thought. Nevertheless, an affirmative answer need not imply that there are consequently different understandings of the properties of sacred and secular language. In fact, it appears that the nondualistic ideology of language can apply equally to all spoken language. Hence, the potentially transformative power of all words, such that certain Punjabi words may be used to curse or do harm, while other words, particularly those from the Adi Granth, have the power to protect or cure.[20] What makes Sikh sacred language—the spoken language of the divinely inspired poets whose words are contained in the Adi Granth—special and unique is its subtlety and power to uplift, not that it alone can affect an audience through its sounds-and-meaning. Whereas having the sight or hearing the words of a benevolent being (such as the Guru) has positive effects upon the recipient, the glance or words of a malevolent being will have negative effects upon the recipient. Thus Punjabi efforts to avoid the 'evil eye' and 'curses' are, in effect, the obverse of seeking to gain *gurdarśan* (the visual emanations of the Guru) and *gurbāṇī* (the speech of the Guru). The entire force of South Asian sociologic suggests that words, like foods and other substances, are media in which interpersonal transactions are made and through which persons are transformed.[21] What makes *gurbāṇī* especially appropriate to Sikh worship is that the words of the Guru are the most refined of all words and have the ability to positively affect the devotee in a way superior to all other words that a Sikh might incorporate in his or her life course.

Thus, when Sikhs, writing for a Western audience, call *gurbāṇī kīrtan* (devotional singing of the Guru's word) 'food for the soul', we should not be too quick to dismiss this imagery as hackneyed metaphor.[22] Such a formulation—joining, as it were, matter and spirit—may well constitute a serious attempt at reflecting a Punjabi appreciation of the positive, substantial qualities of these sacred words, one beyond the normal expressive capacity of everyday English. For those who have internalized a dualistic ideology of language and associated ontological and epistemological dualisms, metaphor is, of course, a primary means by which to overcome conceptual distinctions (as, here, between matter and spirit), bringing together, in images such as these, entities and contexts that are otherwise irrevocably separated in our common sense. But what if we take this metaphor literally, as reflecting those properties of worship substances actually recognized by Sikhs? Then we need to expand our analytic vocabulary to overcome our conceptual dualisms, resorting to such circumlocutions as speaking of the devotee 'imbibing' the 'coded substances' of the Guru, effecting a 'biomoral' transformation of his or her person, and thereby 'nourishing and sustaining' the Sikh Panth. In short, we must find ways to talk about what A.L. Babb has referred to as 'a "physiological engagement" between devotee and the Supreme Being in the person of the guru'.[23]

ENGAGING THE WORD AS GURU

In the case of the Sikhs, this 'physiological engagement' has increasingly come to be effected through the Word of God as transmitted by the Guru and embodied for perpetuity in the Ādi Granth. During the lifetimes of the ten living human Sikh Gurus, physiological engagement with *Akal Purakh* (the divine) came directly through the person of the Guru—for example, by incorporating his *darśan* (visual emanations) or *charan amrit* (foot water), as well as by singing his hymns (*kīrtan*). Since the ascension of the Granth (the Holy Book) and Panth (the corporate assembly) to the status of co-Guru following the death in 1708 of Guru Gobind Singh, exact recitation of the *gurbāṇī,* (the natural sacred sounds of the Adi Granth), and performance of *sevā*, (selfless service to the Panth), appear to be considered especially efficacious in incorporating the Guru's divinely coded substances and to play a central role in recomposing Sikh persons as a divine human genus. In Sikh worship, recitation of the Guru's words takes place primarily through singing the devotional songs from the Ādi Granth, as in *gurbāṇī kīrtan,* or by undertaking a reading of the entire contents of the Ādi Granth, as in an *akhaṇḍ pāṭh*.[24] Note that in reciting *gurbāṇī*, both performer and audience actively take into their persons the natural sacred sounds of the Guru. Recitation from the Adi Granth has also become a crucial feature of all distinctively Sikh life-cycle rituals, in keeping with the logic that, as Guru, the words of the

Adi Granth are the transformative agents.[25] Moreover, the Guru's words are themselves essential components of other worship substances incorporated during Sikh worship. Thus, they are integral to the *karāh praśād* (the blessed 'leavings' of the Guru distributed to worshippers in the gurdwara) and *khaṇḍe-kā-amrit* (the immortal 'nectar' used in the Khalsa *sanskār*), although their co-presence, while absolutely essential, is frequently ignored by Western writers who choose to focus on and enumerate—to their sensibilities—the more tangible ingredients, such as sugar, flour, ghee, water, etc.[26]

Since the divine Word enshrined in the Adi Granth is revered as the reigning Guru, imbibing the sacred sounds has also become central to *darśan* of the Guru Granth Sahib as understood and experienced by most Sikhs. Although *darśan* in the South Asian context normally involves a transaction through seeing, such as to establish a physiological engagement with a superior person or deity, there is no reason within the South Asian sociologic that such a connection cannot also be transacted through hearing. Thus, for most Sikhs of my acquaintance, both sight and sound of the Guru Granth Sahib, making obeisance and receiving a *hukam* ('order') and *karāh praśād* ('leavings'), are essential to a fully satisfying *darśan*. The charges of 'bibliolatry' and 'idol worship' levelled by Western observers at Sikh treatment of the Guru Granth Sahib miss the mark to the extent that they fail to appreciate the *darśan* of the Word and the transformative attributes of sacred sounds according to this nondualistic ideology of language.[27]

Note further the great care that is taken to ensure that these sacred sounds are replicated exactly as they are thought to have been enunciated by the Sikh Gurus and the other poets whose divinely inspired utterances are collected in the Adi Granth. For instance, consider the prestige within the Panth that Damdama Sahib and other centres derive from their long service (in the case of Damdama Sahib, apparently dating to the time of Guru Gobind Singh) as centres for teaching correct enunciation and intonation in reciting the Adi Granth.[28] Additionally, one may note the care with which most Sikhs approach their duty when reciting from the Guru Granth Sahib—for example, making sure to wash their mouths beforehand lest any impurities enter into the sounds they make—and, in the case of an *akhaṇḍ pāṭh* (a continuous reading of the Adi Granth), making sure that the recitation is passed from one reader to the next with no break in the words themselves, that is, with each new reader picking the words up from the line on his or her predecessor's lips. Indeed, given the ritual focus on the accurately recited Word as

Guru, it might be more sensitive for those who have translated the term '*granthī*' as 'custodian of the Book' to recast the English gloss as 'enunciator of the Word'.

I think we can only understand the preceding observations of Sikh practice if we are willing to acknowledge the nondualistic appreciation of the words of the Adi Granth—that is, their significance as worship substance to be actively imbibed and not simply as sacred text to be revered and intellectually contemplated for its moral teachings.[29] This nondualistic logic also explains what appears to so trouble Western observers and some Western-raised Sikhs: to wit, the fact that even those who cannot read and do not understand the meaning of the text are still considered to benefit from their presence in the congregation during Sikh worship. And it is this logic that makes installing the translated version of the Adi Granth as Guru unthinkable in that it would require the wholesale repudiation of the substantial properties of the words and the literal disembodiment of the person of the Guru.

In the face of this inviolability of the person of the Guru, it is not surprising to observe such 'half measures' as the tendency of Sikhs to avoid undertaking a complete translation of the Adi Granth, to avoid having their names attached individually to a complete translation, or—as in the case of the Manmohan Singh translation published by the Shiromani Gurdwara Parbandhak Committee—to avoid publishing the translation itself as a single volume. Given the logic of language and personhood sketched above, only a person recognized by the Panth as a divinely inspired successor in the line of the human Gurus—that is, someone emerging as a new, living, human Sikh Guru—would have the authority to translate the Adi Granth into a modern vernacular and to have such a translation accepted as a successor to or a new recension of the divinely inspired original. Since the mere idea of another human Guru is heretical in the extreme, the sanctity and inviolability of the Adi Granth as Guru Granth Sahib seems assured for the conceivable future.

A dispute between the Akhand Kirtani Jatha and others in the Panth over the Rag Mola underscores the extent to which the currently accepted version of the Adi Granth is considered by virtually all Sikhs to be the inviolable person of the Guru.[30] At issue is whether a short section that concludes the Adi Granth was inappropriately added by the Guru's amanuensis and should, therefore, be eliminated. Followers of Akhand Kirtani Jatha—who trace their lineage back through Bhai Randhir Singh to Babu Teja Singh Overseer and the Bhasaur Singh Sabha—argue that the Rag Mola is inconsistent with the rest of the text and must not have been intended by the Guru, and they 'therefore' refuse to recite it when they hold an *akhaṇḍ pāṭh*. For this, they have been marginalized within the Panth—while even more radical alterations to the Adi Granth by others have provoked even more extreme sanctions.[31]

Clearly, to the extent that the Word as inscribed in the Adi granth is regarded as the reigning Guru, Sikhs understand the integrity and inviolability of the text as crucial to its ability to serve as a source of divine (biomoral) benefits for devotees. Nevertheless, it has proven difficult to maintain the Adi Granth as a text both authentic and intelligible to contemporary Sikhs, and not only because it is challenged by an alternative ideology of language that privileges meaning at the expense of sound.

THE CONTEMPORARY DILEMMA

The inability to hold alive and consistent both the actual *gurmukhī* words inscribed in the text and their literal meaning over the nearly four centuries since the Adi Granth was first compiled presents a dilemma for those who would value both the sounds and their meanings. The dilemma, of course, is that through time and outside the context of a closed linguistic community it has proven nigh on impossible to keep equally accessible to Sikh devotees both the Guru's message and the precise sounds through which the message was first transcribed in 1604. Because languages change over time, and because other languages have entered the picture as a consequence of such factors as migration and inconversion, Sikhs are today confronted with a sacred text increasingly unintelligible to Sikh worshippers. To Western sensibilities, there is an obvious action to be taken: translate.[32] Anything less appears to be a half measure.

For those Sikhs for whom the Adi Granth is simultaneously a source of ideas and other benefits, the dilemma is real, but the options by no means so clear. The nondualistic ideology of language among Sikhs values both sound properties and semantic properties of words. It is not the case that it values the sound properties to the exclusion of meaning (as does the dominant contemporary Western ideology, but in an inverse way). The ideal, therefore, is for all Sikhs to continue to learn the sacred language—both how to reproduce its sounds and understand its meanings—so that all its benefits (spiritual-cum-material, cognitive-cum-physiological) will be immediately available to the worshipper. Thus one frequently finds Punjabi language classes at Sikh gurdwaras in the English-speaking diaspora, where the effort is primarily directed at teaching youngsters to read the Adi Granth. Failing that—and literacy in 'the sacred language of the Sikhs' has always been restricted, even in Punjab—most Sikhs seem hesitant to privilege the ideas at the expense of the other properties of the *gurbāṇī*, as would be the consequence of translation.

It is obviously a trade-off: either you keep the material properties of the sounds and lose the intelligibility or you attempt to retain the intelligibility by translating and, in so doing, sacrifice the sacred sounds of the Guru. The expedient of some Sikhs in England and North America has been to retain the untranslated Adi Granth as the object of worship but to utilize an English translation (or a vernacular Punjabi exegesis) as a means of instruction by providing a gloss on the increasingly unintelligible primary text. Cole's position seems to be that retaining an unintelligible text as a focus of worship, whether or not one employs an English version as a gloss, is bibliolatrous. But the implication that the alternative to a full comprehension of the meaning of the text of the Guru Granth Sahib is that the book itself takes on the character of a 'talisman' (to use McLeod's term) or a 'charm' (to use Cole's term) misrepresents, I believe, the experience of a good many Sikhs in North America.

For many Sikhs who find an intellectual appreciation of the words of the text difficult or impossible, the words of the Guru—*nām*, *gurśabad*, *gurbāṇī*—are still subject to active incorporation in the course of worship. This seems the only way to account for those informants who insisted that it was beneficial for me—and for others not well versed in *gurmukhī*, including their own North American-raised children—to sit in the congregation during the recitation of gurbani despite an inability to comprehend the meaning of the text. Those Sikhs holding this ideology of language may be troubled by other Sikhs whom they do consider guilty of bibliolatry—for instance, those who, to use Cole's own phrasing, hold *akhaṇḍ pāṭhs* 'not in order to listen to the *gurbāṇī* but because of belief that the very practice of reading [does he not actually mean 'having someone else read in their absence'?] the Adi Granth from beginning to end is auspicious'.[33] But their contempt in this case is for the failure of the sponsor to accept the *darśan* of the Word—that is, through failure to recite or to take in the recited words—rather than for a belief in auspiciousness of a continuous recitation of the Adi Granth.[34]

Returning to McLeod's questions posed at the outset—that is, those concerning the contemporary attitudes toward and actual usage of the Adi Granth, it now appears that the question of how individuals treat the Granth may well depend on which Sikhs you are talking about. I certainly do not wish to argue that the actions of all Punjabi Sikhs in North America or England are at this late date informed by the non dualistic ideology of language discussed here. For many, especially of the Western-born and -raised younger generation, paying obeisance to the Guru Granth Sahib upon entering the gurdwara probably can be taken more as a sign of ritual humility before the iconic representation of a transcendent God than as a means of establishing a physiological engagement with God through the transforming powers of the Word of the Guru. For these people, *darśan* no longer exists as a source of tangible biomoral benefits, or, if there are benefits, they are benefits of a different sort than those presupposed according to the long dominant. Punjabi ethnosociology.[35] For them, sitting in the gurdwara listening to words they no longer understand does seem 'odd'. Hence, the increasing instances of *akhaṇḍ pāṭhs* wherein the sponsor neither reads nor hears the words of the Guru Granth Sahib—and calls for translations. Perhaps for these people, whose personal relation to the Adi Granth is distant or detached, Cole's charge of bibliolatry is warranted. But for those who continue to seek the Guru's nourishment, the charge is certainly unwarranted—or, at the very least, misleading—in the connotations it suggests for the Western reader.

Neither would I deny the possible co-presence of dualistic and nondualistic ideologies among previous generations of Sikhs. Indeed, one can find statements from the Gurus themselves that appear to challenge the received monistic understandings of their followers, including points in the text of the Adi Granth itself where the Guru admonishes his followers to understand and not merely recite mechanically the hymns of the Gurus (as was the practice with Vedic mantras).[36] But in that historical context, the Gurus were apparently concerned that the divine Word not be treated as sound without meaning—but without at the same time denigrating the total biomoral affect of the divine sound-and-meaning upon the devotee.[37] Recent Sikh reformers seem to have a more radical goal, that of denying recognition of the sound properties of the *gurbāṇī*. Thus one can read several of the reforms promulgated in this century through the influence of the Singh Sabhas (for example, the antimantra and antiritualistic pronouncements included in the *Sikh Rehat Maryada* issued by the Shiromani Gurdwara Parbandhak Committee) as attempts to undermine practices that would promote an uncontemplative and mechanical incantation of the text.[38] One might note, in a similar vein, the writings of recent Sikh commentators (for example, Taran Singh and S. S. Kohli), whom Cole cites approvingly for having criticized as idolatrous aspects of contemporary Sikh treatment of the Adi Granth.[39]

Given the political, social, and intellectual forces acting on Punjabis over the past century and a half, it is not surprising that there should be a trend toward the hegemony of the dominant Western dualistic ideology of language at the expense of the nondualistic ideology of language. But this recurrent reformist discourse itself suggests a continued appeal to Punjabis of nondualistic understandings of the relationship of devotee and God as transacted in the medium of the Word substance of the Guru. In Vancouver, where I first conducted fieldwork in the late 1970s, Punjabi remains the language of worship and none of the Punjabi-run gurdwaras has, to my knowledge, yet introduced an English (or vernacular Punjabi) version of the Adi Granth into Sikh worship.[40] Only the local group of North American Sikh converts utilize in public worship a translation of the Guru Granth Sahib (in their case, Manmohan Singh's version), but even they use it only as a gloss on the original *gurmukhī* text. Although the pressures of the dominant Western ideology of language are building upon Sikhs in the English-speaking diaspora, when and if the nondualistic ideology of language will ultimately be submerged, subjugated, and silenced among Punjabis remains an open question. For the moment, at least, Sikh understandings are still contestable and contested.

CODA

Finally, to further illustrate just how alien the nondualistic ideology seems to contemporary Westerners—but, nevertheless, to suggest the possibility of its emergence from subjugation even in the West—let me conclude with a lengthy quotation from a recent issue of *Beads of Truth,* the journal of 3HO/Sikh Dharma, an organization of North American Sikh converts.[41] In an article on the nineteenth Pauri of Jap Ji Sahib, a section of the Adi Granth meant to be recited daily, an appropriately named convert, Kirtan Singh Khalsa, begins with the following general insights:

Guru Nanak spoke the *Jap Ji Sahib*. It is the meditation for the soul. It is spoken in the language of a God-enlightened being. It is spoken in perfect *Naad*, that is perfect rhythm, meter and beat to permutate the recesses of the mind. This spoken word transcends our ordinary comprehension. It is spoken at a level that exists beyond time and space in absolute subtlety. The blessing of this *Naad* is that even though one may not understand the language, the words or their meaning, by simply listening to or speaking it, it has the power to affect one's consciousness in an untold positive way. It will change your destiny just to listen to or speak these words.

He continues:

This may sound [*like*] *hokus-pokus to the ordinary* [should he not say, rather, contemporary 'Western'?] *person* but actually there is a very basic law upon which this truth sits and that is the Law of the Word.[42]

After nearly two decades as Sikhs, the converts have finally come to appreciate another, heretofore submerged ideology of language, but it still seems so strange, so 'hokus-pokus', that even writing for fellow converts the author feels the need to acknowledge how alien it all must seem to his Western readers.

The same must be the case for Western scholars. But, to the extent that Western scholars have failed to recognize and affirm this nondualistic ideology of language among Punjabi Sikhs, we must also acknowledge our complicity in its subjugation. Despite the presumed dominance within the Panth of Singh Sabha-inspired understandings—including the apparent repudiation of 'mystical' or supposedly 'non-rational' notions of the power of words, a repudiation consistent with the dominant Western ideology of language—it would be a grave mistake to read directly from the programmatic texts of the reformers to actual Sikh behaviour. One of the mistakes of an earlier orientalism was to assume that South Asian social life corresponded to how it was represented in the classical texts and elite discourses. In the case of Sikh reformist discourse of the past century, Western scholars and Western scholarship have been factors from the outset. Any self-aware Western scholarship must recognize the pragmatics of its own discourse and, thus, its continued involvement along with the discourse of the Sikhs themselves in emergent and contested Sikh understandings.[43]

McLeod is absolutely right. If we are to understand the significance of the Adi Granth for Sikhs, we must look at actual Sikh practice and everyday discourse. And in so doing, what I suggest one finds is that whereas what I have termed the dualistic ideology of language is so firmly entrenched in the West and the primacy of semantico-referential meaning over the sound properties of language so commonsensical for Westerners as to make a nondualistic alternative seem like hocus-pocus, the nondualistic ideology of language lives on among many Punjabi Sikhs—even among those resident in the West. Consequently, in the present state of contested ideologies of language and concepts of the person, the expedient of translation and the suggestion that Sikhs install a translation of the Adi Granth as the focal point of worship are more problematic than Cole and those Sikhs and non-Sikhs who share his opinion seem to realize or might wish to acknowledge.

ACKNOWLEDGMENTS

Earlier versions of this paper were presented at a Sikh Studies Symposium, University of British Columbia, April 1988; the annual Social Science History Association meetings, Minneapolis, October 1990; and the annual South Asia meetings, University of Wisconsin-Madison, November 1990. I thank those audiences and my fellow panelists. Special thanks to Elizabeth Coville, Arthur Helweg, McKim Marriott, W. H. McLeod, Harjot Oberoi, and Frank Reynolds for their encouragement and helpful comments.

NOTES

1. Harbans Singh, 1986, 'Guru Granth Sahib: Guru Eternal for the Sikhs', *Sikh Courier*, 12 (14) Summer, p. 8.
2. W. Owen Cole, 1982, 'The Settlement of Sikhs in the United Kingdom: Some Possible Consequences', *Panjab Past and Present*, 16–17 (32) October, p. 421.
3. Christopher Shackle, 1983, *An Introduction to the Sacred Language of the Sikhs*, London:School of Oriental and African Study.
4. See, for example, Frederick M. Denny and Rodney L. Taylor, (eds), 1985, *The Holy Book in Comparative Perspective* Columbia: University of South Carolina Press; Wendy Doniger O'Flaherty, (ed.), 1979, *The Critical Study of Sacred Texts*, Berkeley: Graduate Theological Union, especially the articles by Joseph Kitagawa, 'Some Remarks on the Study of Sacred Texts', pp. 231–42 and Paul Ricoeur 'Epilogue: The Sacred Text and the Community', pp. 271–6.
5. See, for example, Harold Coward, *Sacred Word and Sacred Text*, 1988, Maryknoll, New York: Orbis Books, William A. Graham, 1987, *Beyond the Written Word*, Cambridge: Cambridge University Press; Miriam Levering, (ed.), 1989, *Rethinking Scripture*, Albany: SUNY Press.
6. See, for example, Jack Goody, 1987, *The Interface between the Written and the Oral*, Cambridge: Cambridge University Press; Lamin Sanneh, 1989, *Translating the Message*, Maryknoll, New York: Orbis Books.
7. An exception is Coward, pp. 130–7; see also David Goa and Harold Coward, 1986, 'Ritual, Word and Meaning in Sikh Religious Life', *Journal of Sikh Studies*, 13 (2) August , pp. 13–31.
8. Frits Staal, 1979, 'Comments: The Concept of Scripture in the Indian Tradition' in Mark Juergensmeyer and N. Gerald Barrier, (eds), *Sikh Studies: Comparative Perspectives on a Changing Tradition*, Berkeley: Graduate Theological Union, pp. 121–4.

9. Coward (n. 5 above) recognizes the difficulty of translating the Sikh scripture, although the terms of his analysis are different from mine: The written words of the Adi Granth function quite differently from the written words of ordinary books or even of other scriptures. In Sikh devotion, the written words fulfil the same function as that of a musical score in relation to the performed music. Just as written music has no value until it is performed, so the written text of the Adi Granth has spiritual power only as it is sung.... This is why the devotional experience of scripture cannot be had from translations—just as it is impossible to translate a Bach fugue into some other form', p. 134. Although I appreciate Coward's music metaphor and believe it helps capture the indigenous notion that in the recitation of *gurbāṇī kīrtan* (hymns of the guru), each *śabad* (word) of the guru's *bāṇī* (speech) is thought to possess its own *rāsā* (flavour), I believe that the analysis needs to address ethnosociology and ethnolinguistics as well as ethnoaesthetics. As further food for thought, I would add a literalized alimentary metaphor to his music metaphor.
10. Cole, 'The Settlement of Sikhs in the United Kingdom', p. 421.
11. W. H. McLeod, 'The Sikh Scriptures: Some Issues', in Juergensmeyer and Barrier, (eds), p. 104.
12. Ibid.
13. Ibid, p. 105.
14. William A. Graham, writing in the Levering volume (n. 5 above), cites Walter Ong, Jack Goody, and others to argue that 'the decisive emphasis upon the written or printed page at the expense of the memorized, recited, and orally transmitted word is tied closely to the circumstances of the modern technological age—an age that first came to maturity in Western Europe between 1600 and 1900' ('Scripture as Spoken Word', pp. 129–69, quote on p. 143). Graham notes that 'with print, words and books lose their dynamism and personal quality and become themselves things—that is to say, mass-produced, impersonal objects' (p. 143). Although Graham does not make the connection, there seems to be a correlation between the resulting Western attitude toward language and translation in the era of the printed book (what Graham calls 'the first truly mass-produced commodity in history') and the emerging capitalist theory of value, insofar as both presume the separation of product from producer and the interchangeability of impersonal products in a market of (potential) equivalences.
15. For a recent summary statement, including citation of earlier work, see McKim Marriott, 1990, 'Constructing an Indian Ethnosociology' in McKim Marriott, (ed.), *India through Hindu Categories*, Newbury Park, California: Sage, pp. 1–39.
16. See, for example, McKim Marriott, 1976, 'Interpreting Indian Society: A Monistic Alternative to Dumont's Dualism', *Journal of Asian Studies*, 36 (1) November , pp. 189–95.

17. In *Guru Nanak and the Sikh Religion*, 1968, Oxford: Clarendon, pp. 164–5, W.H. McLeod argues that he considers 'monism' to be too strong a term for the relation between God and man posited in the works of Nanak, the first Sikh Guru. Yet, as McLeod acknowledges, Nanak 'explicitly declares notions of 'duality' (*dubidha*) to be the essence of man's problem'; he lays stress on 'divine immanence'; and his monotheism 'is not to be construed in the Semitic sense', p. 165. In practice, it makes sense to understand Sikh Panth in *gurū bhakti* terms, wherein receipt of divine substances (especially the Divine Word) channelled through the Guru in Sikh worship establishes a biomoral connection between God and devotee and helps overcome their duality.
18. On the ethnosociology of the Sikh person, see my article, 1990, 'The Sikh Person, the Khalsa Panth, and Western Sikh Converts', *Religious Movements and Social Identity: Continuity and Change in India,* Boeings and Bullock-carts Festschrift Series, 4, Bardwell L. Smith, (ed.), Delhi: Chanakya Publications, pp. 117–35.
19. McKim Marriott and Ronald B. Inden, 1977, 'Toward an Ethnosociology of South Asian Caste Systems', *The New Wind: Changing Identities in South Asia,* Kenneth David, (ed.), The Hague: Mouton, p. 231.
20. Stanley J. Tambiah, 1968, 'The Magical Power of Words', *Man,* 3 (2) June, pp. 175–208, takes a broadly comparative perspective on the pragmatics of ritual speech, emphasizing the importance of authoritativeness over intelligibility as a measure of the effectiveness of words. Tambiah's analysis focuses on the pragmatic force of ritual speech and magical formulas, while mine highlights indigenous understandings of the properties of words; but both of our analyses challenge analytic approaches growing out of the dominant Western ideology of language that focus on semantico-referential meaning as the key to understanding these speech acts and that dismiss nonreferential speech as 'irrational' or pathological.
21. McKim Marriott, 1977, 'Hindu Transactions: Diversity without Dualism' in Bruce Kapferer, (ed.), *Transaction and Meaning: Directions in the Anthropology of Exchange and Symbolic Behavior*, Philadelphia: Institute for the Study of Human Issues, pp. 109–42.
22. See, for example, G.S. Mansukhani, 1976, 'The Value and Importance of Gurbani Kirtan', *Sikh Dharma Brotherhood*, 2 (4) Winter, pp. 9–11.
23. A. L. Babb, 1983, 'The Physiology of Redemption', *History of Religions*, 22 (4) May, p. 307.
24. In addition to the *akhāṇḍ pāṭh*, an unbroken (forty-eight-hour) reading of the Adi Granth, a Sikh can profitably undertake a broken (one-week) *saptahik pāṭh* or a slow-reading (up to several months) *sahaj pāṭh.* In keeping with the belief in the power of the words of the Adi Granth to

bless, protect, and cure, a *pāṭh* is commonly used as a source of strength for those who are ill or by those about to undertake an arduous task. Similarly, words from the Adi Granth are commonly a part of indigenous medicinal recipes.

25. Harjot Singh Oberoi shows this to be an emergent feature of late nineteenth-century Sikh practice, as Sikhs increasingly sought to differentiate themselves from Hindus. Although it took the Singh Sabha/ Tat Khalsa movement to establish the separate identity of a Sikh through establishing a distinct set of ritual practices focused exclusively on the Adi Granth (rather than on Hindu deities, Brahman priests, or on the descendants of the Sikh Gurus), the sociologic and ideology of language by which incorporation of the substance codes of the Adi Granth would differentiate the Sikh person from others predates and made possible this move to neo-orthopraxy. See H.S. Oberoi,1988, 'From Ritual to Counter-Ritual: Rethinking the Hindu-Sikh Question, 1884–1915' in Joseph T. O'Connell et al., (ed.), *Sikh History and Religion in the Twentieth Century*, Toronto: University of Toronto, Centre for South Asian Studies, pp. 136–58.
26. Note how the *amrit* used in Sikh initiation changes from effecting a physiological engagement with the Supreme Being through incorporating the Guru's footwater (during the lifetimes of the living human Gurus) to effecting a physiological engagement through the Guru's Word (when the Granth becomes Guru).
27. Cole, 'The Settlement of Sikhs in the United Kingdom' (n. 2 above), appears to have uncovered the same ethnographic fact among British Sikhs, as he notes that 'Sikhs can be found who speak of receiving *darshan* through the sound of the words', p. 396; but, unfortunately, he fails to incorporate the fact into his analysis.
28. It is said that Guru Gobind Singh compiled the recension of the Adi Granth on which he subsequently conferred Gurudom while staying at the *gurdwara* at Damdama Sahib in 1706. Damdama Sahib is now recognized as one of the five *takhats* (thrones) of the Sikhs. The Damdama Taksihl, from which the Sant Jarnail Singh Bhindranwale first emerged, has taken a leading role in training reciters and explicators of the Word.
29. Note how these different ideologies of language lead to very different pedagogies: the oft-remarked emphasis in indigenous South Asian education on rote learning and recitation versus the so-called critical thinking that Western education has come to value.
30. Consensus among Sikhs accords authenticity to the so-called Kartarpur version, said to be prepared by Bhai Gurdas under the direction of Guru Arjun, to which Guru Gobind Singh later added the compositions of Guru Tegh Bahadur. This is the version that Guru Gobind Singh is said before his death to have anointed as his successor.

31. For all of what N. G. Barrier, 1970, *The Sikhs and Their Literature*, Delhi: Manohar, pp. xxvi–ii, has termed Babu Teja Singh's 'almost fanatical alterations' in Sikh practice, including his insistence on vegetarianism and on turbans for women, it was this attempted alteration of the Guru Granth Sahib that led to a *hukamnāmā* issued from the Akal Takht ordering his excommunication. Similarly, the more recent repudiation, ostracism, and suppression of the Sant Nirankari Mandal was based both on the group's worship of its own *gurū* and its violation of the integrity of the Guru Granth Sahib.
32. At first there would appear to be a direct analogy with the Latin mass in the Roman Catholic Church. It may well be true that a nondualistic ideology of language in the West sustained the Latin mass for centuries, but by the mid-twentieth century it was no longer possible to sustain an argument of untranslatability on the grounds of the superior physiological effects of the Latin sound vehicles. The nondualistic ideology was too submerged in Western Christendom to argue against the vernacular on the basis of the power of the word, in anything other than a metaphorical sense. Hence, the argument against translation was based primarily on aesthetic or conservative grounds. These are not the same grounds of nontranslatability (and the inviolability of the text as the person of the Guru) that sustain the *Gurmukhī* version of the Adi Granth. Thus, the body of the Sikhs do not yet appear ready to accept the arguments for translation (notably: intelligibility and accessibility) that swayed the Catholic powers-that-be.
33. W. Owen Cole, 1982, *The Guru in Sikhism*, London: Darton, Longman & Todd, p. 99.
34. When Cole (ibid.) implicitly criticizes the conduct of *akhāṇḍ pāṭhs* in which the 'emphasis [has] shift[ed] from spiritual nourishment gained by hearing the *gurbāṇī* to the automatic power to remove pollution as a result of reading it', p. 61, he misleads us as to the logic involved by indulging his too radically dualistic Western sentiment: 'spiritual nourishment' and the 'power to remove pollution' are not opposed in a nondualistic ideology of language as they are in Cole's formulation. As long as he does not recognize that fact, he cannot appreciate the practical accommodations that Sikhs have made.
35. Such people may be more intent on seeing and being seen by their peers (and thus experiencing the 'social' benefits of religious participation in the contemporary North American setting) than on establishing a physiological engagement with the Guru (and thus being uplifted through incorporating the beneficent worship substances of the Adi Granth). To the sponsors of an *akhāṇḍ pāṭh*, in particular, accrues social prestige within the local community.
36. On the Gurus' argument that mechanical recitation is not sufficient, see the discussion in McLeod, *Guru Nanak and the Sikh Religion* (n. 17 above),

pp. 215–16. On mantras, see Harvey P. Alper, (ed.), 1989, *Understanding Mantras*, Albany: SUNY Press. On the continuities and discontinuities of Sikh practice with the tradition of sacred revelation developed in the Vedas and found in classical Hinduism, see Staal (n. 8 above).

37. *Nām simaran* (remembering the Name) is a recognized technique for enlightenment in the Sikh tradition. It often involves repetition of a single word or phrase from the Adi Granth. *Nām* is understood to be the immanent or qualitative aspect of God and, thus, a means to physiological engagement with the Supreme Being.
38. See, for example, W.H. McLeod, (trans.) and (ed.), 1984, *Textual Sources for the Study of Sikhism*, Manchester: Manchester University Press, p. 79. Historians who have represented the Singh Sabha movement as having a 'modernist' influence on Sikh discourse and Sikh practice may have in mind just these sorts of attempts to establish 'rational' and 'nonmystical' practices.
39. Cole, *The Guru in Sikhism*, pp. 93–8.
40. Although I am unaware of any use of an English version in public worship, I know Punjabi Sikhs who use an English version as a gloss on the *Gurmukhī* in their private worship—that is, in the room set aside as a *gurdwara* in their home. And, of course, commentary on the text in vernacular Punjabi—or, even, in English—is an accepted part of *kathā* (exposition on the scriptures and on the lives of the Gurus and other exemplars from Sikh history).
41. On relations between the North American Sikh converts and Punjabi Sikh immigrants in North America, see my article, 'Punjabi Sikhs and Gora Sikhs: Conflicting Assertions of Sikh Identity in North America', in O'Connell et al., (eds) (n. 25 above), pp. 334–55.
42. Kirtan Singh Khalsa, 1987, 'The 19th Pauri of Jap Ji Sahib', *Beads of Truth*, 2 (19) Winter, pp. 44–6; emphasis added.
43. For a brief discussion of the continuing power of Western scholarship to help define Sikh realities, see my article, 1989, 'Of Singh Sabhas, Siri Singh Sahibs, and Sikh Scholars' in N. Gerald Barrier and Verne A. Dusenbery (ed.), *The Sikh Diaspora*, Columbia, Mo.: South Asia Publications, pp. 90–119, especially, pp. 105–11.

4

A Sikh 'Diaspora'?*

Contested Identities and Constructed Realities

When does a diaspora come into existence? Does the use of the term necessarily imply a geographically dispersed but unitary 'people' with a common 'culture' and an ancestral 'homeland' (imagined or otherwise) from which they have been 'uprooted', either temporarily or indefinitely (Malkki 1992; Safran 1991)? If, as Peter van der Veer suggests (in the Introduction to this volume [1995]), diaspora and the nation have become inextricably intertwined, is territoriality crucial to the identity of the diasporan person? If so, is there a Sikh diaspora unless and until there is the concept of a 'Sikh homeland'? And does the concept of a Sikh homeland 'naturalize' efforts to realize a separate Sikh nation-state? What, in short, is the conceptual relationship, if any, between the idea of a Sikh diaspora, the assertion that Sikhs are a 'nation', and the call for a territorially separate Sikh nation-state of Khalistan? And how, if at all, has modernist discourse—as reflected, for instance, in colonial administrative directives, Western academic writings, and state policies concerning race, ethnicity, and religion—been implicated in naturalizing connections between people, place, and culture?

My starting point for considering these questions is the conference volume, *The Sikh Diaspora: Migration and the Experience Beyond Punjab*, which I edited with N. Gerald Barrier (1989). In conceptualizing the

* First published in Peter van der Veer (ed.), *Nation and Migration: The Politics of Space in the South Asian Diaspora*, Philadelphia: University of Pennsylvania Press, 1995, pp. 17–42.

topic for the conference and volume, we had taken the existence of a 'Sikh diaspora' to be a relatively unproblematic social fact; but two of the contributing historians, W. H. McLeod (1989a) and Karen Leonard (1989), raised the issue of whether it was in fact appropriate to speak of a Sikh diaspora at the time (late nineteenth and early twentieth century) and among the peoples (Punjabi immigrants in New Zealand and rural California, respectively) with whom they had conducted their research. As McLeod noted (1989a, p. 32), a volume he had preliminarily entitled 'Sikhs in New Zealand' he chose ultimately to publish as *Punjabis in New Zealand* (1986), because 'when we talk about *Sikh* migration we are choosing to use an imprecise adjective' (1989a, p. 32) since 'the Punjabi village of the early twentieth century was no place to go looking for clear-cut normative identities' (ibid., p. 42). Leonard was even more blunt. She argued:

> It has become common to talk of the Sikh diaspora, but there is some question whether or not 'Sikh' is the most appropriate category for analysis of these emigrants from South Asia. While the overwhelming majority of the Punjabi pioneers in early twentieth century California were indeed Sikhs, my research indicates that religion was less salient than other characteristics of these men. It was in fact a Punjabi diaspora, and to go back and emphasize Sikhs and Sikhism does violence to the historical experiences of the immigrants and their descendants. (1989, p. 120)

According to these historians, then, early international migrants from colonial Punjab, whatever their religious practices before or after migration, were not conscious of themselves as forming a 'Sikh diaspora'. For McLeod and Leonard, it was their *Punjabi* identity—their common 'culture', 'place of origin', and 'mother tongue'—that was most meaningful to these early twentieth-century migrants.

The question, then, is when and where and for whom can one legitimately speak of a Sikh diaspora? Both McLeod and Leonard allow that the Sikh aspect of the migrants' identity became increasingly salient as time went by. And it is surely salient in the contemporary context of the political crisis in Punjab and the movement for Khalistan, a separate Sikh state. Was there then a historical moment when the Sikh diaspora came to know itself as a unitary collectivity of people dispersed in geographic space but sharing a common 'culture' and 'homeland', a 'community' structurally distinct from and opposed to equivalent sociological units? If so, what were the terms by which this collective 'identity' was made known and expressed? Was it as a 'nation', defined as a conjunction of people, culture, and place? And has this Sikh diasporan identity become so thoroughly naturalized as to subordinate alternative collective identities?

McLeod and Leonard make an important point in alerting us to analytic anachronisms that may not reflect the subjective experiences of historical subjects but may well reflect an interested retrospective inscription of some putatively collective history. However, in phrasing the issue in the terms of whether this was a Punjabi diaspora or a Sikh diaspora, McLeod and Leonard themselves appear to be overly constrained by high modernist sensibilities that anticipate 'clear-cut normative identities'—including radical distinctions of religious and secular identities (see Dusenbery 1981) and unambiguous mappings of peoples and their cultures on places (see Gupta and Ferguson 1992, p. 8). My argument, by contrast, is: (1) that there are good reasons why the Punjabi village of the early twentieth century was no place to go looking for clear-cut normative identities; (2) that these reasons have had to do with the prevailing understanding of persons and groups that has allowed Punjabis to strategically emphasize different aspects of their partially shared personhood (for example, caste, region, language, religion) in different historical contexts; (3) that the colonial and diasporan experience has confronted South Asians with an alternative modernist discourse of identity that would have them possess—in the possessive individualist sense (see Handler 1988, pp. 50–1)—a fixed, superordinant 'cultural'/'ethnic'/'national' identity, such that Sikhs have increasingly come to represent themselves as an 'ethnoterritorial community' (Oberoi 1987, p. 40); but, finally, (4) that there exist alternative deterritorialized and supraterritorial terms by which Sikhs can, and in fact do, construct their collective identity.

***

McLeod's point about the lack of 'clear-cut normative identities' in Punjabi villages at the turn of the century is an appropriate place from which to begin consideration of a Punjabi ethnosociology. The forty years from 1880 to 1920 were a period of extensive international migration from the hard-pressed villages of central Punjab (see Dusenbery 1989; McLeod 1989a; Fox 1985). It was also a time during which a new cultural elite of neo-orthodox Sikhs, responding to the British colonial and Christian missionary presence in Punjab, successfully sought to 'subsume a variety of Sikh sub-traditions . . . under a monolithic, codified and reified religion' (Oberoi 1988, p. 149). As Harjot Oberoi, writing of the late nineteenth century, notes: 'Far from there being a single 'Sikh' identity, most Sikhs moved in and out of multiple identities' (ibid., p. 137; see also Oberoi 1994). And, as historical work on the British census in Punjab shows (see Barrier 1970), how to categorize and enumerate the population in Punjab was a challenge to the British, who were confused and frustrated by what they perceived to be the lack of clear-cut normative identities among Punjabis.

In Punjab, different kinds of people or different human 'genera' (*zat* in Punjabi, *jati* in Hindi) were locally distinguished by, among other criteria, 'worship', 'territorial', 'occupational', 'linguistic' substances incorporated as a result of their different ritual practices, places of residence, productive modes, and languages used (see Dusenbery 1988, 1990b). Of the indigenous distinctions that Punjabis were making among local people, the British were most cognizant of—and concerned with enumerating and rationalizing for administrative purposes—two identities: occupational genera (which for British purposes becomes reified as 'caste') and worship genera (which for the British becomes 'religion'). By fixing on these identities and then trying to affix said identities to a bounded subpopulation within the province, the British did two things. First, they imposed conceptual boundaries and structural rigidity on a fluid interpersonal and intrapersonal transactive space. This was especially so in the case of caste and religion, where 'cultivating' and 'noncultivating' castes and 'martial' and 'nonmartial' castes were now legally and administratively distinguished, and one was pushed to declare oneself to be unequivocally 'Sikh', 'Hindu', or 'Muslim'. Second, the British made caste and religion increasingly salient political categories around which the local population might organize and be organized, while at the same time making territorial genera (the localized 'regional' identities) less salient and, ultimately, making territory itself a free-floating sign—which, at partition, became aligned with 'communal' distinctions.

One result of modernist discourse among Sikhs (emanating from the Singh Sabha/Tat Khalsa movement) was to help establish this newly emergent canonical Sikh identity, such that it became possible for the Sikh public in the early twentieth century 'to think, imagine and speak in terms of a universal community of believers united by uniform rites, symbols and scripture' (Oberoi 1988, p. 154). If this made sharper and more categorical the distinctions between Sikhs, Hindus, and other 'communities of believers', it still did not make all members of the Sikh worship genus or *panth* (literally, path or way), identical in their personal natures, since they also continued to belong to other, different human genera—territorial, occupational, and even linguistic (given the existence of Sikhs speaking Sindhi and other South Asian languages). A Sikh Jat (agriculturalist) from Doaba (the region of central Punjab between the Beas and Sutlej rivers) and a Sikh Mazhbi (sweeper) from Majha (the region of central Punjab between the Beas and Ravi rivers) might partake of similar worship substances, making them co-equal members of the Sikh Panth, but they would otherwise be distinguished by occupational genus and territorial genus—as is clear from the continued evidence of what becomes reified, in Western sociological terms, as 'caste endogamy' and 'regional endogamy' within the Sikh Panth.

In South Asian ethnosociological terms, the Punjabi person was thus a 'dividual', a confluence of different biomoral substances, partially shared with other persons.[1] Political mobilization and social solidarity in Punjab and among Punjabis abroad have been at different times effected through appeals to these partially shared ties made in the name of caste, religious, linguistic, or territorial 'brotherhood' (the Punjabi terms '*biradari*' and *bhaichara* being potentially applicable to persons thought to share natural substances and codes for conduct). In imposing their own ethnosociology, the British colonial policy of 'divide and rule' made certain fault lines (especially, caste and communal [that is, religious]) that much more rigid and impermeable than might otherwise have been the case. Nevertheless, the historical experience of Punjabis has been of shifting personal and political alliances based on appeals to partially shared personal natures. Many Khatris, for instance, judging their caste similarities (as urban merchants) to outweigh their religious differences, continued to blend and unite Khatri Sikh and Khatri Hindu families long after Jat Sikhs, Jat Hindus, and Jat Muslims had come to marry almost exclusively with coreligionists. The successful Sikh-led, post-independence agitation for Punjabi Suba, a linguistically based state in secular India, could be couched in linguistic terms precisely because Punjabi Hindus, in declaring Hindi rather than Punjabi as their mother tongue, renounced what they could have constituted as their brotherhood with Punjabi Sikhs through a shared language. At the same time, Sikhs themselves have been unable to establish political hegemony in India's reorganized Sikh majority state of Punjab because Mazhbi Sikhs (former 'untouchables') usually have been unwilling to commit their votes to the Jat-dominated Sikh party, the Akali Dal. In the aftermath of the attack on the Golden Temple and the Delhi riots of 1984, however, a sense of shared suffering and dishonour *as Sikhs* was sufficient to override caste differences, sweeping the Akali Dal into power in the Punjab elections of 1985. In Punjab, social, political, and economic interests commonly run along channels laid down in terms of local understandings of persons and their particular natures.

Given these indigenous distinctions of persons, for the early twentieth century at least, one might well talk of a Jat diaspora in North America (since the overwhelming majority of migrants across the Pacific were Jats) or a Ramgarhia diaspora in East Africa (since the vast majority of Punjabi migrants there were of this artisan caste) or even a Bhatra diaspora in England (since the first wave of Punjabi immigrants were from this small peddler caste). Or one could conceivably talk of Malwai, Majhai, or Doabi diasporas, recognizing the indigenous Punjabi territorial distinctions of persons that played a part and continue to play a part in the lives of Sikhs in the diaspora—where marriage networks and even local gurdwaras (Sikh temples) have been organized by Punjabi regions, as well as by caste and sect (see, for example, Ballard 1989).

McLeod and Leonard are right to suggest that Sikh identities were not the only salient identities that early migrants brought with them from Punjab. Not only were the lines between Sikh, Hindu, and Muslim Punjabis not yet drawn as absolutely as they would be by later migrants, but also those who followed different religious practices often shared and were bound together by caste, regional, and linguistic ties. At the same time, however, the notion of a 'Punjabi diaspora' is itself problematic if it implies some clearly delineated, internally undifferentiated cultural-cum-geographic group. Here McLeod and Leonard come close to imposing their modernist sensibilities about the correspondence of culture, language, and place on their informants' subjective understandings of their fluid and relatively unbounded social world. Punjab (literally, [land of] five rivers) might have broad territorial and linguistic referents, but the administrative boundaries that the British drew did not mark off some 'natural' sociocultural or political unit. And turn-of-the-century migrants are likely to have interacted and mobilized on the basis of shared worship, occupational, regional, and/or linguistic ties, but not on the basis of some superordinant 'Punjabi' cultural identity.[2]

Insofar as these indigenous distinctions of persons by worship, occupational, territorial, and linguistic genera have remained salient among Punjabi Sikhs, 'religion' and 'place' would appear to be analytically separate sources of social identity and solidarity. How, then, has a sense of territoriality—of a rootedness to Punjab or Khalistan—

come to be tied to an understanding of the Sikh Panth as a distinct worship genus (*zat*) or brotherhood (*biradari*)? In the ethnosociology sketched earlier, one's territory marked one with the natural substances of the place (that is, the land and its products), making people of the same place into *bhum bhai* (brothers of the earth), whereas one's ritual practices involved incorporating the worship substances—*darshan* (glances), *bani* (speech), *prashad* (leavings), *amrit* (nectar)—of the guru, making those who worship alike into *guru bhai* (brothers of the [same] guru). Members of a Punjabi village might expect to share qualities with their local *bhum bhai* without expecting all fellow villagers to be *guru bhai*. At the same time, Sikhs of different regions within and even outside Punjab might recognize one another as *guru bhai*, without expecting their personal natures to be identical. Worship and territoriality would apparently generate different aspects of a person's nature.

In fact, the collective actions of Sikhs in the diaspora, as reported in the historical and ethnographic literature, suggest that Sikhs have attempted to nourish and sustain the various ancestral genera—worship, territorial, linguistic, occupational—of which the migrants conceive themselves to be a part. Where possible, Sikh migrants have constructed gurdwaras, maintained facility in Punjabi, remitted to and visited the natal village, and avoided inappropriate occupations (see Dusenbery 1990a,1990b). Although it is beyond the scope of this chapter to detail how such actions have been sustained, through stereotyping, gossip, and exclusionary practices (see Helweg 1986, pp. 12–21; Dusenbery 1990a), a Sikh's *izzat* (honour), even in the diaspora, has usually entailed following actions considered appropriate to one's nature as a specific kind of person. And these different aspects of the person continue to be indexed in marriage practices, such that a Punjabi-speaking, Doabi, Jat Sikh living in Vancouver, Yuba City, or Southall will usually seek a spouse of similar personal character. But since this is a dynamic and fluid ethnosociology that can logically incorporate new coded substances, it is also not surprising that for the generation born and raised in the English-speaking diaspora, England, Canada, the United States, Singapore, and Malaysia have over time come to complement Majha, Malwa, and Doaba in imparting their 'territorial' natures—complete with corresponding regional stereotypes and presumed marital compatibilities—to persons.[3]

***

Yet if, as I have been arguing, worship and territorial genera have long been conceptually distinct for Punjabis, how are we to account for the territorial claims in contemporary Sikh political discourse? And how does an inclusive, unbounded Sikh sacred space, defined by the presence of the Guru, articulate with the demand for an exclusive Sikh nation-state defined by territorial boundaries?

The *janam-sakhi* literature, the popular accounts of the life of the first Sikh Guru, recounts Guru Nanak's travels in the late fifteenth and early sixteenth centuries to the extremities of the known world to spread his divinely inspired message. The first Guru is credited with journeys north to Nepal and Tibet, east to Assam and Bengal, south to Ceylon, west to Mecca and Baghdad. The message is of the Guru's expansiveness, of a royal assertion of a Sikh presence throughout the world, of conquest of the world in all four directions along familiar *digvajaya* lines (see McLeod 1989b, p. 20). Like an Indian ruler surveying his domain, the founder of Sikhism in effect circumambulates—and thus metonymically and metaphorically incorporates—the known world. The effect is intentionally outward looking and inclusionary. Far from delimiting a territorial boundary to the Sikh world, the Guru's travels suggest a boundless and boundaryless world of Sikh sacred space which carries itself into the very heart of Hindu, Buddhist, and Muslim lands.

Nor does the distribution of historical Sikh shrines and relics suggest any attempt to define the Sikh realm as coterminous with the boundaries of Punjab. Like their followers in later centuries, the Gurus travelled widely. Shrines and relics said to be associated with the lives of the Gurus can be found throughout India and beyond. The five most important historical shrines associated with the lives of the Gurus, those that have been recognized as the five *takhats* (literally, thrones) of the Sikhs, include two—Patna Sahib in Bihar and Nander in Maharashtra—that are located well outside any of the variable historical boundaries of Punjab.[4] It would appear that the presence of the Guru bestows sanctity on a place, not the reverse.

If Amritsar, the home of Darbar Sahib (the 'Golden Temple') and the Akal Takht (literally, immortal throne; the highest seat of Sikh religio-temporal authority), has over time become a pilgrimage centre of the Sikh world, it is a symbolic centre for a world without boundaries. Unlike caste Hindus, Sikhs suffered no loss of rank or merit from travel overseas. Indeed, Sikhs journeying beyond Punjab, far from Amritsar and the sacred shrines, could take comfort from the pronouncement attributed to the tenth and last human Guru, Gobind Singh, that wherever five Sikhs gather together in the presence of their sacred scripture, the Adi Granth or Guru Granth Sahib, there too is the eternal Guru. Sikhs of the diaspora may be dispersed from ancestral homes in Punjab and far from most of the historical Sikh shrines; but insofar as the Guru is believed to co-reside in the Guru Granth, the divine Word inscribed in the sacred scripture, and the Guru Panth, the corporate community created by the congregation of any five worthy Sikhs, Sikhs are never at a distance from the Guru, whose presence defines the sacred centre. The local gurdwaras (literally, door of the Guru), to be found wherever Sikhs have settled, are sacred spaces in which the Guru's divine substances are made available to any Sikh wherever resident.

Clearly the rhetoric of a territorially delimited Sikh nation-state is not grounded in this vein of Sikh discourse.

***

In one of his many important articles tracing the subjective and symbolic dimensions of Sikh historical experience, Harjot Oberoi has recently explored 'how the expression of Punjab as a homeland was woven into the self-definitions of the Sikh Panth' (1987, p. 27). It is Oberoi's contention that 'the affective attachment with the Punjab is fairly recent, and it does not date back to the early annals of the Sikh community, as some ideologues of 'Khalistan' would like to assert today' (ibid.). Indeed, he presents a convincing argument that it was only with the impending partition of Punjab at the close of the colonial era that Sikhs began to suggest that 'Sikhs belonged to the Punjab; the Punjab belongs to the Sikhs' (ibid., p. 37). Oberoi shows that throughout what he calls the Guru Phase (1600 to 1707), the Heroic Phase (1708 to 1849), and through much of the Colonial Phase (1849 to 1947), including the neo-orthodox Singh Sabha/Tat Khalsa period at the turn of the century, Sikh discourse showed no concern with tying Sikhs and Sikhism to the territory of Punjab. It was the person of the Guru—the human Gurus in their lifetimes and then the scriptural Guru (Guru Granth) and corporate Guru (Guru Panth)—that bound together the Sikhs (literally, disciples).

Only when the British were on the verge of splitting Punjab between Muslims and Hindus—in effect, making territorial groups out of religious communities—did Sikhs demand a 'Sikhistan' based on Sikh 'intimate bonds' to Punjab and, failing to achieve it, bemoan: 'The Hindus got Hindustan, the Muslims got Pakistan, what did the Sikhs get?' Oberoi goes on to show how Sikh commentary over the past four decades has since spread the idea of a special Sikh tie to the 'land of five rivers' (Punjab), with what he calls 'an undeniable nexus between the Punjab and Sikh consciousness' (ibid., p. 39) having been firmly established during the protracted struggle for Punjabi Suba, reinforced by the Green

Revolution miracle in Punjab, and given full voice by proponents of Khalistan. And he concludes by suggesting that the equation of the Sikhs with Punjab—now transformed into Khalistan (the so-called land of the pure)—has become thoroughly 'naturalized'.

Oberoi provides us with the historical time frame in which to place this transformation of Sikhs into an 'ethnoterritorial community'. But how was the symbol of territory added to what Oberoi calls the 'evolving inventory of Sikh ethnicity' (ibid, p. 40)? And what was the impetus for this conceptual or rhetorical shift?

One of the subtle ways in which this reconceptualization has taken place is through increasing substitution in Sikh discourse of the Persian loan word *qaum* (literally, people who stand together) or the English word 'nation' in reference to the Sikh collectivity. The term *panth* seems particularly appropriate to a self-definition that focuses on ritual practice as the source of shared worship substances that unite Sikhs as a brotherhood of *gursikhs* (followers of the Guru). As McLeod has noted, *qaum*, by contrast, 'possesses an ethnic dimension . . . and retains the kind of overtones which have done so much to debase the English words 'community' and 'communal' in their distinctively Indian usage' (1978, p. 294). But precisely for these reasons, *qaum* might serve as an appealing alternative when one is advancing political and territorial claims. All the more would this be the case with 'nation', which even more clearly has come in contemporary political discourse to imply rights to the possession of a sovereign homeland or territory.

This creative tension over how to conceptualize the Sikh collectivity is telling. As McLeod points out, Sir John Malcolm, writing from Punjab early in the nineteenth century, referred to the Sikhs as both a 'sect' and a 'nation'; and 'the two terms have since recurred in the ongoing attempt to find an English word which will accurately describe, in the corporate sense, those . . . who call themselves Sikhs' (ibid., p. 287). It has apparently not been easy for Western observers to categorize Sikhs neatly as either a religious community or an ethnic group. I see this and similar conceptual problems for Western would-be interpreters of the Sikhs (see, for example, Juergensmeyer and Barrier 1979; McLeod 1989b; Dusenbery 1990b) as reflecting deep-seated and recurrent Western ontological and sociological dualisms (for example, spirit and matter, sacred and secular, religion and ethnicity). To the extent that the dominant Punjabi ethnosociology has not been premised on the same dualisms, the issue of Sikh corporate identity presumably has not posed the same problem for Sikhs as it has for Western-trained observers. But, and this is the important point, to the extent that Sikhs do not neatly fall into familiar Western social categories, they may find it useful in given fields of power to manipulate the rhetoric of their personhood so as to represent themselves more or less as a religious community (as may be suggested by the term *panth*) or as an ethnic group or nation (as may be suggested by the term *qaum*). Certainly, as territorially based nationalism became a prevailing discourse of the world in the nineteenth century (see Anderson 1991), it affected discourses of identity and belonging on the Indian subcontinent. Thus, when at partition the British moved to provide Indian Muslims with their own nation-state of Pakistan, it served Sikh purposes as another 'communal' group to emphasize their 'intimate bonds' to the Punjab and the 'rights of the Sikh nation' to 'the creation of a Sikh state', as in the oft-cited Akali Dal resolution of March 1946 which called on the British to create a 'Sikhistan' to be located between India and West Pakistan (quoted in Oberoi 1987, p. 37; see also Madan 1991, p. 620).

***

What Robin Jeffrey (1987) has called modern Sikh 'rhetorical history' is replete with claims that have proven useful to recent proponents of a Sikh nation-state. Foremost among these rhetorical claims is that of past and future Sikh sovereignty. The case for Sikh political as well as religious sovereignty is advanced on many fronts. According to Sikh hagiography, the sixth Guru, Hargobind, was invested with two swords at his installation as Guru, one representing spiritual authority (*piri*; from the Persian, *pir*, a religious teacher) and the other representing temporal authority (*miri*; from *amir*, commander). The Akal Takhat, the pre-eminent 'throne' of the Sikhs (destroyed by the Indian Army in its 1984 raid on the Golden Temple complex), is commonly referred to as 'the seat of Sikh sacred and secular authority' and was intentionally built higher than the palaces or thrones of local potentates. The line, *Raj karega Khalsa* (The Khalsa shall rule), from Ardas, the communal Sikh prayer sung at the conclusion of Sikh worship, is seen by many Sikhs as a prophetic pronouncement of Sikh sovereignty made by the tenth Guru, Gobind Singh.[5] And the reign of Maharaj Ranjit Singh over greater Punjab in the early nineteenth century is taken by some as a 'golden age' in which Guru Gobind Singh's prophecy of Sikh rule was fulfilled. The past century and a half, including both colonial and post-independence Indian history, is then presented as a long series of plots by various parties intent on depriving Sikhs of their rightful sovereignty.[6]

But contemporary Sikh nationalist rhetoric goes beyond reasserting Singh Sabha/Tat Khalsa claims to Sikh distinctiveness—encapsulated in the phrase, *Ham Hindu Nahin* (We are not Hindus)—or reiterating the rhetorical history of Sikh sovereignty—encapsulated in the phrase, *Raj karega Khalsa*. Instead, proponents of a Sikh nation-state attempt to represent Sikh realities as in full conformity with the tenets of modern nationalism, including the correspondence of people, culture, and place. Thus, Mehar Singh Chaddah, in *Are Sikhs a Nation?* starts with a general (modern, Western) definition and proceeds to argue that Sikhs are a separate 'nation' because 'the Sikhs are bound by common race, common language and literature, common land, common history, common religion, common joys and sorrows, and common political aims and aspirations' (1982, p. 79; see also Surjan Singh 1982, pp. 113–18). It is then but a short step from claiming nationhood to demanding statehood, especially in the contemporary world climate of crumbling empires and political devolution. Thus, in a recent joint appeal to the United Nations, the two most powerful mainstream Sikh institutions—the Sikh political party, the Shiromani Akali Dal, and the committee charged with control of Sikh shrines in Punjab, the Shiromani Gurdwara Parbandhak Committee—argue for 'decolonisation of Punjab' on the basis that 'Sikhs are a religious community and a political nation simultaneously. . . . Sikhism and its apotheosis, the Khalsa[,] is a unique political society with a distinct religion, language, culture, ethos, a historic territory and political thought' (Shiromani Akali Dal 1992, p. 6).

In short, the logic of Sikh nationalist rhetoric leads inexorably to the notion that the Sikhs belong to Punjab and Punjab belongs to the Sikhs. Internal homogeneity and historical continuity within fixed spatial boundaries is the dominant imagery, and a unique Punjabi Sikh patrimony is the dominant claim. To make their case, however, Sikh nationalist rhetoricians are perforce required to ignore or explain away such uncomfortable facts as coresidence and intermarriage with Punjabi Hindus, the existence of Sindhi-speaking Sikhs and Euro-American Sikh converts, and long-standing caste, regional, and sectarian differences among Sikhs.[7] The entire thrust of such nationalist rhetoric, with its neatly bounded and differentiated social units, flies in the face of much that we know about the social history of Punjab over the past five centuries. Nevertheless, given that nationalist discourse has become a dominant political discourse of the contemporary world, it is hardly surprising that Sikhs might represent themselves in its terms to advance their claims.

It would be naive to act as though such discourse has had a life entirely unrelated to the changing political economy in which Sikhs have lived their lives. Whatever the sources of these concepts, they find resonance among human agents when conditions are favourable to their propagation. Oberoi's analysis suggests that Sikh claims of constituting a distinct 'ethnoterritorial community' gained general currency on the eve of partition, when Sikhs felt that they, as a 'communal' group, would be net political and economic losers. In the post-independence era, the Government of India acquiesced to the creation of Punjabi Suba only at a time when Punjab was a frontline state and Sikh troops were needed in the 1965 war with Pakistan. Although the demand for a Sikh-majority state within the Indian union had to be cloaked in linguistic rather than religious terms to satisfy the requirements of secular India's constitution, the ultimate acceptance of this demand seemed to confirm in principle the right of the Sikh 'nation' (defined, as earlier in Chaddah's formulation, to include both linguistic and religious referents) to 'self-determination' within a territorial 'homeland' (as the contemporary nationalist slogan would have it). Thus it only temporarily dampened the overt nationalist and separatist rhetoric. After the initial productive success of the Green Revolution, the world and national political economy turned against certain classes in the reorganized state of Punjab, creating a crisis of honour for marginal Sikh farmers and for educated but unemployed Sikh youth. It was in this context that Sant Jarnail Singh Bhindranwale, himself of a small farmer family, and Amrik Singh, head of the All India Sikh Student Federation, found a receptive audience (particularly among youth from less well off Jat Sikh families) for visions of a better, more honourable life that might be realized in a fully sovereign Punjab or an imagined Khalistan.[8] And after the cataclysmic events of 1984 (the assault on the Golden Temple complex and the Delhi riots following Indira Gandhi's assassination), other Sikhs, feeling their own interests and the collective honour of the community to be threatened by the Indian state, found sufficient cause to seriously entertain separatist visions.[9]

***

But why should Sikhs of the diaspora be moved by such imagery, given the presumably very different political and economic situations they are experiencing? The Government of India, particularly under the Congress party rule of Indira Gandhi and Rajiv Gandhi, has made much of the supposed intellectual leadership and material support that the Khalistan movement and 'Sikh terrorists' have received from Sikhs of the diaspora. Clearly, as Arthur Helweg has detailed (1989), specific Sikh individuals and organizations in the United Kingdom, the United States, Canada, and elsewhere have been major proponents of Khalistan, although it is hardly surprising that Sikhs supporting a separatist agenda might find it easier to voice their claims from outside India. As for the charge of widespread material support of and active complicity in 'terrorism' on the part of Sikhs in North America and the United Kingdom, the evidence is less convincing. Indeed, it has even been suggested by credible third parties that Indian agents themselves may have been responsible for some of the violence popularly attributed to diasporan Sikhs (see Kashmeri and McAndrew 1989). Nevertheless, it is true that Sikh nationalists pushing a separatist agenda (which should not to be confused with terrorism) after 1984 established apparent political hegemony, through a combination of moral suasion and intimidation of their critics, among diasporan Sikhs in England, Canada, and the United States, as in Punjab. The question is, given their remove from the immediate political and economic problems troubling the state of Punjab, why has it served some Sikhs of the diaspora to emphasize Sikh nationhood, to proclaim Sikh territorial ties to Punjab, and to promote a new state of Khalistan?

Various explanations have been advanced for diasporan Sikh support for Khalistan. Helweg emphasizes alienation, anomie, and opportunity. That is, he attributes Khalistani sympathies to what he calls a supportive 'psychological and cultural framework' among diasporan Sikhs (1989, p. 331), consisting of a perceived threat of extinction, a migrant's loneliness, and a desire for honour in the eyes of others combined with the organizational capacities of the gurdwaras and the absence of sanctions on nationalist activities. Harry Gouldbourne (1991, pp. 126–69), focusing on the British case, emphasizes the cohesion of the migrant community and its disenchantment with British society, claiming that 'any sense of insecurity in this country tends to encourage articulate Sikhs to support the demand for an independent and secure homeland in the subcontinent' (ibid., p. 152). Mark Juergensmeyer, on the other hand, argues that Sikhs of the diaspora have actively promoted Khalistan mainly because as emigrants they were 'socially marginal to the [home] community [in Punjab]' and 'were looking for a centre to Sikhism and wanted to be associated with it' so as to gain 'a sense of belonging' (1988, pp. 79, 80). Although there is something to be said for these varied explanations, each on its own terms seems unduly general and overly mechanistic. Are diasporan Sikhs, in fact, demonstrably lonelier, more insecure (in their new abode), or more marginal (to their old) than other nonseparatist migrant groups? And, more to the point, are Sikhs of the diaspora who actively support Khalistan lonelier, more insecure, and more marginal than those who do not support Khalistan? My own analysis, therefore, is focused less on the psychological profile of the diasporan Khalistani than on dialectical linkages between (1) Sikh notions of collective identity and personal honour, and (2) the sociology and politics of ethnic representation in those countries with significant Sikh populations. I emphasize this dialectical relationship since, as the discussion here suggests, Sikh identities—including the notion of Sikhs as an 'ethnoterritorial community'—have been constructed in fields of power, where ideologies and policies of the state can significantly affect Sikh self-identity.

Along these lines, Peter van der Veer (in the Introduction to this volume [1995]) has written of the imposition by xenophobia of a negative identity, enhancing among migrants a nationalist sentiment characterized by a 'longing' to be elsewhere. Certainly, the discrimination and hostility that the first generation of South Asian immigrants (overwhelmingly Sikh) experienced in Canada and the United States contributed to the widespread support that they gave the North American-based Ghadar (Revolution) party in the early part of this century. A major ideological motivation for the Ghadar effort to oust the British from India was the perceived failure of the British Indian authorities to protect the interests of South Asian immigrants in North America from hostile, exclusionary actions of Canadian and American authorities. If Indians controlled their own state, it was argued, they would be able to deal effectively on a state-to-state basis with Canadian and American authorities on behalf of the interests of Indian subjects residing in North America. In his definitive account, Harish Puri (1993) shows how an 'autointoxication of disgrace' over their own treatment in North America, as well as that of their 'brothers' in British India, led a significant number of Sikh immigrants to commit their money and lives to this heroic but premature effort to drive the British from India. What is notable about the Ghadar episode is the way in which, as van der Veer suggests, the xenophobia of Canadians and Americans generates a 'nationalist' consciousness among the South Asians. Juergensmeyer labels this the 'Ghadar syndrome', what he defines as 'a militant nationalist movement . . . created abroad by expatriates, for whom the movement is also an outlet for economic and social frustrations, and a vehicle for their ethnic identities' (1979, p. 14; see also Juergensmeyer 1982). But Ghadar was still a pan-Indian nationalist movement, uniting Sikhs, Hindus, and Muslims from various parts of the subcontinent. And accounts focused on Indian nationalism of the Ghadarites have often ignored or underplayed alternative, non-nationalist ideologies present at the same time among North American Sikhs (Dusenbery 1985, Puri 1985). How do we then shift from Indian nationalism to Sikh nationalism among Sikhs in North America?

Ghadar sought primarily to address the political situation in India, with the hope that this would positively affect the situation of South Asians in North America. From the beginning, in Canada, political mobilization to address Canadian authorities on the migrants' concerns as Canadian residents of South Asian origins was consistently channelled through the Sikh gurdwara societies—most notably through the Khalsa Diwan Society in British Columbia. It was not until the 1950s that a nominally pan-'East Indian' organization was founded (again, in British Columbia). And only in the 1970s was a national organization for Canada's 'East Indians' formed. I have advanced situational and cultural factors to explain the failure of South Asians to develop separate religious and ethnic-political organizations in Canada—that is, the demographic predominance of Sikhs among the immigrants and the long-standing tradition among Sikhs of conjoined religious and political authority (see Dusenbery 1981). But the success of the Ghadar party in attracting diasporan Sikh support for an Indian 'nationalist' agenda (as would later be the case with support given the Indian National Army and Indian Congress) suggests that Sikh political action could be mobilized along nonreligious lines.

Let me now implicate the ethnosociology and local politics of the state (what used to be called 'the host country') in this analysis. State ideologies and public policies of race, ethnicity, and multiculturalism pursued in such pluralistic countries as Canada, Malaysia, Singapore and, increasingly, the United States and United Kingdom over the past several decades seem predicated on a common modernist assumption that one's ancestral 'place of origin'—and, in particular, one's 'national origins' or 'country of origin'—in some sense provides the natural building blocks out of which social units—the various ethnic, racial or cultural communities—are constructed in pluralist nation-states. (At the same time, religion is often differentiated from these other identities as private, voluntaristic, and achieved rather than public, essentialistic, and ascribed.)

Given this ethnosociology, it is not surprising that Sikhs in Canada were being encouraged in the 1970s to funnel their public activities through what were at least in theory pan-'East Indian' ethnic-political organizations. While conducting fieldwork in Vancouver, British Columbia, in the late 1970s, I was struck by two contending models and discourses of political mobilization being pursued by local Sikhs. The modernist Sikh elite in Vancouver, including many second-generation and even third-generation Canadians, was active in organizing and providing leadership for a newly established ethnic-political organization, the National Association of Canadians of Origins in India (NACOI). This group accepted the conventional fiction of the Canadian government's new multiculturalism policy (Canada 1971)—to wit, that Canadians of origins in India not only shared a common ancestral place of origin but also a common 'culture' and, it was assumed, similar political interests. The logic of Canadian multiculturalism was of a world of discrete cultures mapped unproblematically onto people who had definitive places of origin. India, as a nation-state, was a recognized place of origin. According to this line of thinking, Sikhs—at least those Sikhs of Punjabi ancestry—like other Canadians whose ancestral roots led back to present-day India, ought to address the government and society-at-large through pan-Indian ethnic-political organization such as NACOI (leaving the gurdwaras and other 'places of worship' to deal with distinctly 'religious' matters). Indeed, the government would actively nurture NACOI to be this umbrella ethnic-political organization.[10]

Struggling to be heard against this logic of Canadian multiculturalism was a popular Sikh alternative, supported especially by the more recent immigrants and enunciated most vociferously at the time by the local Shiromani Akali Dal of Canada—to wit, that Sikhs are 'a separate people' who should be known neither as East Indians nor as Canadians of Origins in India but simply as Canadian Sikhs. Moreover, according to the Shiromani Akali Dal line, political representation of Sikh interests in Canada should come from local gurdwara societies or other representatives 'of the Sikh people', and not channelled through pan-'East Indian' ethnic-political organizations like NACOI—however strong Sikh representation might be in such organizations. When it became clear in the late 1970s and early 1980s that the Canadian government preferred Sikhs to petition the government through ethnic-political organizations, it gave these anti-NACOI Sikhs all the more incentive to promote the message that Sikhs constitute a distinct 'ethnoterritorial community' and, even before the traumatic events of 1984, to join the call for Khalistan.[11]

One of the appeals of Khalistan to diasporan Sikhs may be the creation of a publicly recognized 'country of origin', from which Sikhs may legitimately make claim to their own political voice and to the perquisites of public support for cultural diversity (for example, funding made available under multiculturalism programmes or protection under local human rights codes) in their countries of residence. If the local logic of multiculturalism in these pluralist polities requires a distinctive source 'culture' derived from a recognized homeland or country of origin, then Sikhs who believe their religion, culture, and politics to be indivisible will endeavour to supply the territorial basis for their 'separate identity as Sikhs'.

Since 1984, it has in fact been increasingly difficult to sustain a plausible fiction that Canada's 'East Indians' or Britain's 'Asians' or Singapore's 'Singaporean Indians' share not only a collective identity but also common political interests. And Sikhs seem to realize that in pressing the claims of Sikh nationhood, especially if realized territorially through the achievement of Khalistan, the right of diasporan Sikhs to a separate identity and political voice can be established in local ethnosociological and policy terms. Thus I would argue that much as Ghadar party members sought to end the disgrace following from their treatment in North America by changing the colonial map of India, so too Khalistan supporters in the diaspora can be seen to be attempting to gain a measure of respect and power in countries of the diaspora by changing the contemporary political map of South Asia. In van der Veer's terms, the 'longing' for Khalistan is for some Sikhs a means of and to 'belonging' in their current country of residence.

***

However successfully links between the Sikhs and Punjab or Khalistan may have been naturalized in recent Sikh discourse, there is nothing in fact 'natural' (that is, intrinsic and inevitable and thus beyond human agency) about these links, nor does such discourse exhaust the ways that Sikhs envision their collective identity. And as Richard Handler has forcefully reminded us, anthropologists might do well to distance themselves from a discourse of nationalism and ethnicity that naturalizes such links between people, culture, and place, especially since it is based on a theory of social difference that implicates both 'mainstream anthropology' and 'Western common sense' (1985, p. 171).[12] Thus, it is useful to remind ourselves that understandings of the Sikh collectivity as a 'nation' having a 'homeland' and a 'diaspora' are emergent, contested, and contestable social facts. If in entitling our volume *The Sikh Diaspora* Barrier and I seemed thereby to be committing ourselves to a view of the world or to a political position naturalizing Sikh demands for Khalistan, we were unwitting collaborators. My position is that 'the Sikhs of the diaspora are an integral part of a world-wide Sikh society'

(1989, p. 9). How such social ties—including those with Punjab—are to be conceptualized and represented is an open subject, one of considerable concern to various interested Sikh and non-Sikh parties. Obviously, the stakes are high. As Oberoi notes:

> Having derived sustenance from the stories of territoriality, the Sikhs are now trapped in the depths of a classic dilemma: if they pursue its resolution, they are faced with a situation similar to that of the Basques, the Kurds, and the Palestinians (which are fellow ethnoterritorial communities), but if they abandon this newly constituted emblem they undermine an element of their own identity. One possible way out of the labyrinth would be gradually to invent new myths. (1987, p. 40)

One such possible new myth is not really a new myth at all. By creatively playing within the field of possibilities implicit in the Punjabi notion of a *panth*, Sikhs can plausibly re-emphasize the deterritorialized notion of the Sikh Panth as a 'worship genus' composed of any and all persons who share the Guru's substances, acquired through their 'physiological engagement' with the scriptural Guru and corporate Guru, not with the land of Punjab.[13] Or, if they must represent their collective identity in more familiar Western terms, they can build logically on the supraterritorial notion of Sikhism as a 'world religion' uniting Sikhs of whatever ethnicity or nationality as fellow believers.[14] If such discourse is temporarily submerged by talk of the Sikh nation and of Khalistan, it is by no means dead (see, for example, Sidhu 1989).

Indeed, there are many diasporan Sikhs for whom the 'natural' underpinnings of the Sikh–Punjab nexus are less than compelling. These would include such groups as the recent non-Punjabi North American Sikh converts who, as I have noted elsewhere (Dusenbery 1988), commonly despair of parochial 'Indian politics' contaminating what they take to be a 'universal religion'; many diasporan non-Jat Sikhs, such as Parminder Bhachu's 'twice migrant' Ramgarhias (1985, 1989), who in their move to East Africa and then to Britain have cut their social links to Punjab; members of Sikh sects, like the Namdharis (Tatla 1991), who have reason to fear a fundamentalist Khalistan; and even a good many second-, third-, and now fourth-generation descendants of earlier Jat Sikh migrants, whose own affective ties to Punjab are attenuated. If these Sikhs look to Punjab as a 'spiritual homeland', the birthplace of their Gurus, and the site of historical shrines, and if they remain concerned about the treatment of historic Sikh sites and their fellow Sikhs at the hands of the state, they nevertheless do not necessarily accept the notion that only a

Punjabi can be a Sikh, or that only Sikhs should inhabit Punjab, or that Sikhs should inhabit only Punjab. Not coincidentally, these are among the Sikhs whose very existence is particularly problematic for the nationalist rhetoritcians, who wish to emphasize the Punjabi patrimony (via common language, history, culture, religion, territory, and blood) of the Sikhs. It is hardly surprising, therefore, that these Sikhs have been among the least ardent Khalistan supporters or that, in pursuing Sikh collective interests in their countries of residence, they have (at least in North America) commonly used the rhetoric of 'religious rights' rather than those of 'race', 'ethnicity', or 'national origins' in pressing claims of Sikh social distinctiveness.[15]

In their recent postmodernist celebration of deterritorialization and reterritorialization, Akhil Gupta and James Ferguson note that 'remembered places have often served as symbolic anchors of community for dispersed peoples' (1992, p. 11), but that the 'naturalizations' of people, place, and culture underlying such images are often analytically problematic, even if politically potent (ibid., p. 12). As we have seen, for Sikhs in Punjab and dispersed beyond, the notion of Sikhs as an 'ethnoterritorial community' bound by natural ties to Punjab/Khalistan has recently served as one powerful way to conceptualize their place in the world. And representations, in academic or popular discourse, of Sikhs outside Punjab as constituting a 'diaspora' may well serve to further strenthen the Sikh–Punjab nexus. Yet this territorialization has never been 'the *only* grid on which cultural difference could be mapped' (ibid., p. 20). Sikh collective identity has been and can be envisioned and bespoken in other, nonterritorialized terms—as, for example, in Sikhs understanding themselves to be a particular 'worship genus' or an inclusive 'world religion'. The terms by which Sikhs know and represent themselves ultimately must be determined by Sikhs as human agents operating within multiple fields of power. At the moment, Sikh identity remains contested; and it would, therefore, be premature to represent the issue and the terms of debate as closed.

NOTES

1. On South Asian ethnosociology, see Marriott 1990. On the ethnosociology of the Sikh person, see Dusenbery 1988, 1990b.
2. In any case, 'Punjabi' was rarely a term by which the early migrants were known in the diaspora. North Indians in Southeast Asia were known as 'Bangalees'; South Asians in North America were known indiscriminantly as 'Hindoos' or 'East Indians'.

3. I do not mean to be seen as making an essentialist argument. Not only is this Punjabi ethnosociology flexible enough to incorporate new languages, territories, and occupations, but also it is and long has been challenged by alternative ethnosociologies through which Sikhs can understand their social world. What seems notable to me has been the persistence among many diasporan Sikhs, even after long residence abroad, of what I take to be the dominant Punjabi socio-logic.
4. The other three *takhats* are the Akal Takhat in Amritsar, Keshgarh at Anandapur Sahib, and Damdama Sahib near Batinda. Nominally, the *jathedars* (lit., commanders) of the five *takhats* constitute an exhalted *panj pyare* (lit., five beloved) who can, in consultation with the Guru Granth (the scriptural Guru) make pronouncements in the name of the Guru Panth (the corporate Guru). In practice, since they are appointed by different administrative bodies, they rarely function as a cohesive consultative board.
5. See Dhanoa (1990) and Singh and Dhillon (1992) for conflicting views on whether the phrase *Raj karega Khalsa* necessarily implies the establishment of a territorial state under Sikh rule.
6. Dilgeer and Sekhon (1992) present the most sustained argument on how Sikh sovereignty has been thwarted by various parties over the past two centuries.
7. In advancing his claim that Sikhs are a distinct 'race', Chaddah (1982: 75) goes to heroic lengths to minimize the significance of non-Punjabi Sikh converts, whose emergence on an unprecedented scale in the early 1970s had been heralded by Sikh leaders in Punjab as a sign that Sikhism is a modern world religion of mass appeal and not simply a parochial faith (see Dusenbery 1988). Furthermore, as Andrew J. Major has pointed out, it is not easy to sustain the nationalist's claim for 'commonality of blood' when 'everyone is aware of the commonplaceness of marriages between Sikhs and non-Sikhs, especially Punjabi Hindus' (1985: 178).
8. For analyses of some of Bhindranwale's imagery, see Pettigrew (1987), Juergensmeyer (1988), and Madan (1991).
9. It might only be fair to note that the territorial association of Sikhs with Punjab has probably been most compelling for Jat Sikhs, the traditional landholding class/caste of central Punjab, whose honour as Jats has been significantly tied to their independence gained from maintaining the family homestead. Those Sikhs from castes less tied to the land, may in general be less moved by naturalizing the links to Punjab. This seems to be one lesson to be derived from the work of Parminder Bhachu (1985, 1989) on the 'twice migrant' Sikh Ramgarhias who, having resettled in England after their expulsion from East Africa, have cut their marital and property ties to Punjab. But since Jats predominate within the Panth, their moral and political visions tend to dominate Sikh discourse.

10. The Canadian folk category 'East Indian' has been used to refer to all people of South Asian ancestry. But under the logic of Canadian multiculturalism, each nation-state in South Asia could serve as a separate 'country of origin' for purposes of self-identification and political organization. This meant, for example, that the numerically smaller Pakistani Canadian community was able to get official recognition and support for their separate ethnic-political organization, while Canadian Sikhs were being urged to use NACOI to advance their political agenda.
11. On the rise and eclipse of NACOI, see Dusenbery (1981) and Paranjpe (1986), (especially pp. 76–7). It should be noted that despite its lack of popular support among Sikhs, NACOI continues to represent all 'Canadians of Origins in India' on the Canadian Ethnocultural Council (CEC), a representative body that advises the government on multicultural issues. A recent attempt by the World Sikh Organization (Canada) to gain a seat on the CEC was turned down largely on the basis of NACOI's argument that it already represents Canadian Sikh interests (personal communication, Anna Chiappa, Executive Director, Canadian Ethnocultural Council).
12. Handler's argument is that essentialistic anthropological and popular Western concepts of culture, which commonly align an ahistoric 'culture' with a 'people' and a 'place', have proven useful to nationalist ideologues. Handler argues for a 'destructive analysis of our shared presuppositions' as 'the anthropologist's contribution to a dialogue that respects natives by challenging rather than romanticizing them' (1985, p. 181).
13. The term 'physiological engagement' is taken from Babb (1983). I explicate its logic as it applies in the Sikh case in Dusenbery (1992).
14. On the significance of world religions as 'the longest lasting of civilization's primary institutions' and as a source of 'self-identification', see Hefner (1993). Part of the unfinished project of religious rationalization begun by Singh Sabha/Tat Khalsa reformers at the end of the 19th and beginning of the 20th century was to make Sikhism into a world religion on par with Hinduism, Islam, and Christianity (see Oberoi 1994).
15. As I have noted elsewhere, in the Canadian human rights codes and in Canadian multiculturalism funding, a radical distinction is made between discrimination, whether negative or positive, on the basis of 'religion' or on the basis of 'race, ethnicity, and national origins' (see Dusenbery 1981). A similar distinction is operative in the United States. In North America, Sikhs have commonly sought protections and exemptions (for example, from dress codes that would require giving up turbans) as a matter of fundamental 'religious rights'. In the United Kingdom, by contrast, Sikhs have apparently used laws against 'racial' discrimination (see Wallman 1982) to pursue similar ends. As McLeod suggests (1989b, p. 106), the effect of British law and public policy might be to further strengthen among British

Sikhs the Punjab–Sikh nexus and thus 'ethnoterritorial community' over 'world religion' rhetoric and social identities.

REFERENCES

Anderson, Benedict, 1991, *Imagined Communities: Reflections on the Origin and Spread of Nationalism*, revised edition; original 1983, New York and London: Verso.

Babb, Lawrence A., 1983, 'The Physiology of Redemption', *History of Religions*, 22 (4) May, pp. 293–312.

Ballard, Roger, 1989, 'Differentiation and Disjunction amongst the Sikhs in Britain' in Barrier and Dusenbery, *The Sikh Diaspora*, pp. 200–34.

Barrier, N. Gerald, 1970, *The Sikhs and Their Literature*, Delhi: Manohar.

Barrier, N. Gerald and Verne A. Dusenbery, (eds), 1989, *The Sikh Diaspora: Migration and the Experience beyond Punjab*, Columbia, Mo.: South Asia Publications, Delhi: Chanakya Publications.

Bhachu, Parminder, 1985, *Twice Migrants: East African Sikh Settlers in Britain*, London: Tavistock.

———, 1989, 'The East African Sikh Diaspora: The British Case' in Barrier and Dusenbery, *The Sikh Diaspora*, pp. 235–60.

Canada, 1971, 'Canadian Culture: Announcement of Implementation of Policy of Multiculturalism within a Bilingual Framework', *House of Commons Debates*, 8 October.

Chaddah, Mehar Singh, 1982, *Are Sikhs a Nation?* Delhi: Delhi Sikh Gurdwara Management Committee.

Dhanoa, S. S., 1990, 'The Meaning of Raj Karega Khalsa', *The Sikh Review*, 38 (12), December, pp. 24–6.

Dilgeer, H.S. and A.S. Sekhon, 1992, *The Sikhs Struggle for Sovereignty: An Historical Perspective* in A.T. Kerr, (ed.), Oslo: Guru Nanak Institute of Sikh Studies.

Dusenbery, Verne A., 1981, 'Canadian Ideology and Public Policy: The Impact on Vancouver Sikh Ethnic and Religious Adaptation', *Canadian Ethnic Studies*, 13 (3) Winter, pp. 101–19.

———, 1985, 'Review of Harish K. Puri's *Ghadar Movement*', *South Asia in Review*, 9 (3) March, pp. 5.

———, 1988, 'Punjabi Sikhs and Gora Sikhs: Conflicting Assertions of Sikh Identity in North America', in Joseph T. O'Connell et al., (eds), *Sikh History and Religion in the Twentieth Century*, Toronto: Centre for South Asian Studies, University of Toronto, pp. 334–55.

———, 1989, 'Introduction: A Century of Sikhs beyond Punjab' in Barrier and Dusenbery, *The Sikh Diaspora*, pp. 1–28.

———, 1990a, 'On the Moral Sensitivities of Sikhs in North America', in Owen M. Lynch, (ed.), *Divine Passions: The Social Construction of Emotion in India*, Berkeley: University of California Press, New Delhi: Oxford University Press, pp. 239–61.

———, 1990b, 'The Sikh Person, the Khalsa Panth, and Western Sikh Converts' in Bardwell L. Smith, (ed.), *Religious Movements and Social Identity*, vol. 4 of 'Boeings and Bullock-Carts', festschrift for K. Ishwaran, Delhi: Chanakya Publications, pp. 117–35.

———, 1992, 'The Word as Guru: Sikh Scripture and the Translation Controversy', *History of Religions*, 31 (4) May, pp. 379–96.

Fox, Richard G., 1985, *Lions of the Punjab: Culture in the Making*, Berkeley: University of California Press.

Goulbourne, Harry, 1991, *Ethnicity and Nationalism in Post-Imperial Britain*, Cambridge: Cambridge University Press.

Gupta, Akhil, and James Ferguson, 1992, 'Beyond 'Culture': Space, Identity, and the Politics of Difference', *Cultural Anthropology*, 7 (1) February, pp. 6–23.

Handler, Richard, 1985, 'On Dialogue and Destructive Analysis: Problems in Narrating Nationalism and Ethnicity', *Journal of Anthropological Research*, 41 (2) Summer, pp. 171–82.

———, 1988, *Nationalism and the Politics of Culture in Quebec*, Madison: University of Wisconsin Press.

Hefner, Robert W., 1993, 'Introduction: World Building and the Rationality of Conversion' in Robert W. Hefner, (ed.), *Conversion to Christianity: Historical and Anthropological Perspectives on a Great Transformation*, Berkeley: University of California Press, pp. 3–44.

Helweg, Arthur W., 1986, *Sikhs in England*, second edition, New Delhi: Oxford University Press.

———, 1989, 'Sikh Politics in India: The Emigrant Factor' in Barrier and Dusenbery, *The Sikh Diaspora*, pp. 305–36.

Jeffrey, Robin, 1987, 'Grappling with History: Sikh Politicians and the Past', *Pacific Affairs*, 60 (1) Spring, pp. 59–72.

Juergensmeyer, Mark, 1979, 'The Ghadar Syndrome: Nationalism in an Immigrant Community', *Punjab Journal of Politics*, 1 (1) October, pp. 1–22.

———, 1982, 'The Ghadar Syndrome: Ethnic Anger and Nationalist Pride', *Population Review*, 25 (1 & 2), pp. 48–58.

———, 1988, 'The Logic of Religious Violence: The Case of the Punjab', *Contributions to Indian Sociology*, n.s. 22 (1), pp. 65–88.

Juergensmeyer, Mark and N. Gerald Barrier, 1979, 'Introduction: The Sikhs and the Scholars' in Mark Juergensmeyer and N. Gerald Barrier, (eds), *Sikh Studies: Comparative Perspectives on a Changing Tradition*, Berkeley, Calif.: Graduate Theological Union, pp. 1–9.

Kashmeri, Zuhair, and Brian McAndrew, 1989, *Soft Target: How the Indian Intelligence Service Penetrated Canada*, Toronto: James Lorimer.

Leonard, Karen, 1989, 'Pioneer Voices from California: Reflections on Race, Religion and Ethnicity' in Barrier and Dusenbery, *The Sikh Diaspora*, pp. 120–40.

Madan, T. N., 1991, 'The Double-Edged Sword: Fundamentalism and the Sikh Religious Tradition' in Martin E. Marty and R. Scott Appleby, (eds), *Fundamentalisms Observed*, Chicago: University of Chicago Press, pp. 594–627.

Major, Andrew J., 1985, 'Sikh Ethno-Nationalism, 1967–1984: Implications for the Congress', *South Asia: Journal of South Asian Studies*, n.s. 8 (1 & 2), June and December, pp. 168–81.

Malkki, Liisa, 1992, 'National Geographic: The Rooting of Peoples and the Territorialization of National Identity among Scholars and Refugees', *Cultural Anthropology*, 7 (1) February, pp. 24–44.

Marriott, McKim, 1990, 'Constructing an Indian Ethnosociology' in McKim Marriott, (ed.), *India Through Hindu Categories*, Newbury Park, Calif.: Sage Publications, pp. 1–39.

McLeod, W. H., 1978, 'On the Word *Panth*: A Problem of Terminology and Definition', *Contributions to Indian Sociology*, n.s. 12 (2), pp. 287–95.

———, 1986, *Punjabis in New Zealand*, Amritsar: Guru Nanak Dev University Press.

———, 1989a, 'The First Forty Years of Sikh Migration: Problems and Possible Solutions' in Barrier and Dusenbery, *The Sikh Diaspora*, pp. 29–48.

———, 1989b, *Who Is a Sikh? The Problem of Sikh Identity*, Oxford: Clarendon Press.

Oberoi, Harjot S., 1987, 'From Punjab to 'Khalistan': Territoriality and Metacommentary', *Pacific Affairs*, 60 (1) Spring, pp. 26–41.

———, 1988, 'From Ritual to Counter-Ritual: Rethinking the Hindu-Sikh Question, 1884–1915' in Joseph T. O'Connell et al., (eds), *Sikh History and Religion in the Twentieth Century*, Toronto: Centre for South Asian Studies, University of Toronto, pp. 136–58.

———, 1994, *The Construction of Religious Boundaries: Culture, Identity and Diversity in the Sikh Tradition*, New Delhi: Oxford University Press.

Paranjpe, A. C., 1986, 'Identity Issues among Immigrants: Reflections on the Experience of Indo-Canadians in British Columbia' in Richard Harvey Brown and George V. Coelho, (eds), *Tradition and Transformation: Asian Indians in America*, Williamsburg, Va.: College of William and Mary Studies in Third World Societies, (38), pp. 71–94.

Pettigrew, Joyce, 1987, 'In Search of a New Kingdom of Lahore', *Pacific Affairs*, 60 (1) Spring, pp. 1–25.

Puri, Harish K., 1985, 'Singh Sabhas and Ghadar Movement: Contending Political Orientations', *Punjab Journal of Politics*, 7(2) July-December, pp. 12–26.

———, 1993, *Ghadar Movement: Ideology, Organisation and Strategy*, second edition, Amritsar: Guru Nanak Dev University Press.

Safran, William, 1991, 'Diasporas in Modern Societies: Myths of Homeland and Return', *Diaspora*, 1 (1) Spring, pp. 83–99.

Shiromani Akali Dal, 1992, 'Appeal by Shiromani Akali Dal and Shiromani Gurdwara Parbandhak Committee to the United Nations', *World Sikh News*, June 26, pp. 6–7.

Sidhu, M.S., 1989, 'The Punjabi-Sikh Nexus', *Sikh Courier*, 29 (67) Spring-Summer, pp. 22–24.

Singh, Kharak and Gurdarshan Singh Dhillon, 1992, 'Raj Karega Khalsa' in Kharak Singh, Gobind Singh Mansukhani, and Jasbir Singh Mann, (eds), *Fundamental Issues in Sikh Studies*, Chandigarh: Institute of Sikh Studies, pp. 187–95.

Singh, Surjan, 1982, *Case for Republic of Khalistan*, Vancouver: Babbar Khalsa.

Tatla, Darshan Singh, 1991, 'A Note on Namdhari Sikhs in Britain', *Khera*, 10 (1) January-March, pp. 50–7.

Veer, Peter van der, 1995, 'Introduction' in Peter van der Veer, (ed.), *Nation and Migration: The Politics of Space in the South Asian Diaspora*, Philadelphia: University of Pennsylvania Press, 1995, pp. 1–16.

Wallman, Sandra, 1982, 'Turbans, Identities and Racial Categories', *RAIN* (*Royal Anthropological Institute News*), 52 (4).

5

'Nation' or 'World Religion'?*

Master Narratives of Sikh Identity

This paper considers alternative constructions of a 'Sikh' collective identity in India and outside, especially two of the dominant master narratives—Sikhs as a 'nation' and Sikhism as a 'world religion'—through which Sikhs have commonly represented themselves to others (and, thereby, to themselves and to one another). My argument is that these master narratives are (a) historical products of modernist discourse and a related Western ethnosociology, which (b) conceptually map out different social spaces, that (c) find greater or lesser resonance or impetus in different socio-historical contexts, and (d) hold varying appeal to differently-situated constituencies among those calling themselves Sikhs, since they tend to (e) entail Sikhs in different sorts of claims vis-a-vis the state and civil society. A few years ago, it was fashionable for postmodern theorists to pronounce the end of 'master narratives', the collective stories people tell about themselves as subjects and agents of history and society. Thus Jean-François Lyotard proclaimed that 'the grand narrative has lost its credibility, regardless of what mode of unification it uses, regardless of whether it is a speculative narrative or a narrative of emancipation' (1984, p.37). And while it may be true that postmodernist sensibilities have led to a recognition of the historical constructed-ness of such narratives, thus inviting a deconstruction of their claims to be natural or neutral reflections of some external social reality, it is not clear that even academic scholars have ultimately escaped the master

* First published in Pashaura Singh and N. Gerald Barrier (eds), *Sikh Identity: Continuity and Change,* New Delhi: Manohar Publishers, 1999, pp. 127–44.

narratives that modernist realism has bequeathed us for making intelligible our social world.[1] What is clear is that (*pace* Lyotard), for most people in the world, familiar high modernist master narratives continue to animate collective identities, aspirations, and self-representations.

This is hardly surprising since, as has been increasingly noted, globalization, transnationalization, the End of Empire have neither erased social difference in the world nor precluded the human need for narratives that would account for differences and commonalties among peoples. Indeed, in our contemporary 'Age of Revolution' (Comaroff 1995), transnational forces that impel the movement of people, capital, goods, and ideas around the globe provide an impetus for translating particularistic (local, micro) identities into the now global 'identity vocabulary' of modernist social realism (which conceives the world as made up of so many discrete 'nations', 'cultures', 'religions', 'races', 'ethnic groups', etc.). Hence, in the contemporary global 'politics of identity', claims for collective recognition from the state or from other powers commonly entail appropriating proven narrative strategies through which difference is made intelligible and collective aspirations advanced (even if this means adopting classificatory terms and concepts introduced from orientalist, colonial, and/or neocolonial discourse).[2]

The case of the Sikhs is illustrative for many reasons. As a transnational community, historically influenced by involvement with the British Empire and now well-represented in English-speaking countries, Sikhs have a long history of self-representation to audiences of non-Sikhs. In both India and the diaspora, Sikhs have been in a position of soliciting states, international bodies, and the institutions of civil society for recognition as a distinct social group. In recent years, many Sikhs, especially those promoting territorial sovereignty for the imagined nation-state of Khalistan, have made a strong argument that 'Sikhs are a nation', emphasizing ways in which the Sikh collectivity meets one or another standard definition of what constitutes 'nationhood'. But just a few years earlier, in the wake of mass migration from Punjab and a wave of conversions by young, non-Punjabi North Americans and Europeans, it was at least as common to hear it said that 'Sikhism is a world religion', with the emphasis placed on the ways in which Sikhism transcended its Punjabi roots. These two narratives are each powerful, but they position Sikhs in different social space, entailing different inclusions and exclusions and invoking quite different poetics and politics of recognition.

Although analysing, as I intend to do here, the social construction and historical use of these master narratives may have the effect of denaturalizing them, it is *not* my purpose to undermine Sikh claims (about social identities and political rights) animated by them. Unlike other scholars, I am not interested in whether or not Sikhs meet some authoritative definition of what constitutes 'a nation' or 'a world religion'. Rather, I am interested in what ways and under what conditions Sikhs might want to advance claims to belonging to a nation or world religion. In pursing this line of inquiry, my hope is that Sikhs and scholars alike can consider the implications (especially the various inclusions and exclusions) involved in adopting these master narratives and contemplate alternative socio-logics and discursive claims entailed in Punjabi notions of personhood and collective identity without the acrimony that has greeted much recent scholarship on Sikhs and Sikhism.[3]

Western scholars (and British colonial administrators before them) have long grappled with 'the problem of Sikh identity', to use the subtitle of Hew McLeod's recent book (McLeod 1989; see also Juergensmeyer and Barrier 1979, Dusenbery 1990). And one of their main concerns has been a problem of how to classify the Sikhs using conventional Western ontological and sociological categories. Sir John Malcolm, one of the first of the British to write extensively on the Sikhs, felt compelled in his writings of the early nineteenth century to refer to the Sikhs as both a 'sect' and a 'nation' (1810:198 cited in McLeod 1978). As Juergensmeyer and Barrier put it in 1979, the 'problematic issue'—at least for Western observers—has been that Sikhs appear to constitute 'both a social group with a long history and a present-day community of faith' such that 'one is born into the Sikh community; but one may also voluntarily leave [or join] it' (Juergensmeyer and Barrier 1979, p. 2).

Implicit in the way that 'the problem' is laid out by western observers is a radical distinction between conceiving Sikh identity to be based on being born into 'a social group with a long history' (for which the terms 'ethnic group' or 'nation' might be appropriate glosses) and conceiving Sikh identity to be based on voluntarily leaving or joining 'a present-day community of faith' (for which 'sect' or, more expansively today, 'world religion' might be an appropriate gloss). From this perspective, Sikhs appear to blur a set of modern, western distinctions: between 'secular' and 'sacred' domains; between birth-groups and associational groups; between relationships through shared natural substance and through shared moral code for conduct; between 'ascribed' and 'achieved' identities, etc. In short, as the neologism 'ethno-religious group' suggests,

Sikhs do not fit neatly into a dualism employed in the modern West which would radically distinguish racial, national, ethnic identities from religious identities.

This definitional 'problem' has also provided an opportunity for Sikhs, depending upon the context in which Sikhs have found themselves, to adopt either the master narrative of 'Sikhs are a nation' or of 'Sikhism is a world religion' as a narrative of emancipation. Although each narrative has had its own pragmatic motivations and political effects, the two together, since they map out different social space, have raised an existential 'problem' of reconciling who stands within the boundary of the Sikh collective.

SIKHS AS A NATION

As noted, early British chroniclers (for example, Malcolm 1810, Thornton 1846, Cunningham 1849), encountering the kingdom of Maharaja Ranjit Singh, referred in their writings to Sikhs as a 'nation'. And present-day Sikh nationalists make frequent reference to these writings to support their claims that Sikhs constitute a nation. But even during the nineteenth century there was an awareness that the use of the term in the Punjabi context did not entirely match the term as it was coming to be understood in a European context. Thus, for instance, the British civil servant-cum-social historian Vincent Smith wrote that '(t)he Sikhs are not, and never have been, a nation in any intelligible sense' (1958, p. 432), apparently because they were not seen as having fully carved out a space apart from Hindu society. As a consequence, as McLeod reminds us in his consideration of the appropriateness of the term in historical reference to the Sikh collectivity:

> After the collapse of Ranjit Singh's kingdom, the British themselves used the word very loosely. . . . Only as the Muslim League claim to nationhood crystallized and produced the threat of partition did the concept of a Sikh 'nation' begin to attract serious attention. . . . In times of communal crises it waxes strongly and in recent years its radical exponents have dramatized the claim as a demand for Khalistan. (1989, p.107).

Clearly, the prevailing social history in the West sees Sikh claims to being 'a nation' as episodic and the product both of particular historical conditions and of changing meanings of the term.

Yet the discursive history provided by exponents of Sikh nationalism runs in quite different directions. The genealogy in this narrative usually begins with Guru Gobind Singh's creation of the Khalsa (citing especially the *Raj Karega Khalsa* couplet from Ardas) or with Guru Arjun's martyrdom and his son, Guru Hargobind's adoption of the *miri-piri* policy and *sant/sepahi* ideal or even with Guru Nanak's institutional innovations. Having located the origins of the Sikh Nation in the Guru period, exponents of Sikh nationalism commonly point to Maharaja Ranjit Singh's kingdom as the flowering of Sikh nationhood. Both the British Raj and the Delhi Raj (post-independence India) are represented as periods of thwarted sovereignty of the Sikh Nation. Details of the negotiations at partition are used to buttress the claim that Sikhs all along saw themselves as a separate nation but that the British and the Congress party betrayed them in dividing India on the basis of a two-nation (Muslim and Hindu) basis. Subsequently, the Indian government is seen as not following through on assurance provided to Sikh leaders that Sikhs in India would be treated as a distinct people. For Sikh nationalists, the movement for Khalistan is thus represented as the logical culmination of a long struggle to gain political and territorial sovereignty for a Sikh nation which has in fact existed for several hundred years.[4]

But contemporary Sikh nationalist rhetoric goes beyond simply reiterating the rhetorical history of Sikh sovereignty. Proponents of a Sikh nation-state also attempt to represent Sikh social realities as in full conformity with the tenets of modern nationalism, including the correspondence of people, culture, and place. Thus, Mehar Singh Chaddah, in *Are Sikhs a Nation?*, starts with a general (modern, Western) definition and proceeds to argue that Sikhs are indeed a separate 'nation' because 'the Sikhs are bound by common race, common language and literature, common land, common history, common religion, common joys and sorrows, and common political aims and aspirations' (1982, p. 79).

It is clearly but a short distance from claiming nationhood to demanding statehood, especially in the contemporary world climate of crumbling empires and political devolution. Thus, it is not surprising that in various public appeals—to British colonial authorities (as in the Akali Dal resolution of March 1946), to the Government of India (as in the Anandapur Sahib Resolution of 1978), to the United Nations (as in the joint Akali Dal–SGPC appeal of 1992), or to the American public (as in an advertisement entitled 'The Sikh Nation' on the Op-Ed page of the *New York Times* in 1995), Sikhs would emphasize their 'nationhood' (in terms of territory, language, history, culture, blood, etc.) as a prolegomena to claims for greater political sovereignty in Punjab and/or territorial independence for Sikhistan/Khalistan.[5] The strategic advantage of projections of a 'captive nation' are clear. So long as the modernist norm of 'for every people their own state' holds, the emancipatory narrative of 'Sikhs are a [captive] nation' provides Sikhs a certain amount of moral leverage and public sympathy to represent the collectivity as a full-fledged 'nation' that has been denied sovereignty or self-determination in its own homeland.

To make such a case as convincing as possible, however, requires that Sikh nationalist rhetoric emphasize internal homogeneity and historical continuity within delimited spatial boundaries as its dominant imagery and a unique Punjabi Sikh patrimony (blood, language, history, culture) as its dominant claim. Sikh nationalist discourse must explain away such uncomfortable sociological facts as co-residence and intermarriage with Punjabi Hindus, the existence of Sindhi-speaking Sikhs and Euro-American Sikh converts, and long-standing caste, regional, and sectarian differences among Sikhs as well as ignore an alternative discourse of an inclusive, deterritorialized Sikh sacred space (see Dusenbery 1995, pp. 23–5). The effect is to marginalize many self-identified Sikhs who do not identify fully with the Punjabi patrimony. And, not surprisingly, these Sikhs tend to be among those least invested in the narratives of Sikhs as a nation, since the parochialism of this master narrative calls into question their Sikh identity. But, as I have argued elsewhere (1995), while much of this narrative of the Sikh nation flies in the face of the social history and contemporary sociology of the Sikhs, it is hardly surprising that *some* Sikhs would have an interest in representing their collective identity in nationalist terms, given its dominance and utility in contemporary global political discourse.

SIKHISM AS A WORLD RELIGION

As noted above, early British accounts not only referred to the Sikh 'nation' but also referred to the Sikhs as a religious 'sect', recognizing that Sikh allegiance to the teachings of the Sikh Gurus and the institutions of the Panth differentiated Sikhs in Punjab from other Punjabis. If the lines of demarcation between these groups were thought to be fuzzy, there were still apparently sufficient resemblances to recognize the Sikhs as at least a partially separate people. And this separate identity was, in part, based on a separate religious orientation derived from respect for the teachings of the Sikh Gurus and from the set of social institutions and ritual practices that had grown up around the community. In using the term 'sect', most of these early European observers apparently saw Sikhs as deviating from orthodox Hinduism (McLeod 1988, p. 39), which was taken to be the ur-religion. But during the period of British rule in Punjab, we now recognize one of the main thrusts of the Singh Sabha movement (especially under the leadership of the Tat Khalsa) as differentiating 'Sikhism' as a unique and systematic religion from what was coming to be understood as 'Hinduism'. Having accepted the modernist notion of exclusive religious identities and recognizing 'sect' to be a slighting label, the Tat Khalsa made differentiating Sikhism from two other local variants of recognized 'world religions' (Islam and Hinduism) and a new imported 'world religion' (Christianity) a major project in the late nineteenth and early twentieth centuries.

Kahn Singh Nabha's *Ham Hindu Nahin*, 'We are not Hindus', published in 1898 became a key text of the period asserting Sikh identity distinct from Hinduism (see Nabha 1984[1898]). And, as Harjot Oberoi (1994) has shown us, the Singh Sabhas' successful introduction of a set of distinctive life-cycle rituals further justified that claim. With the success of the Gurdwara Reform Movement, Sikhism gained an institutional mechanism (through the creation of the SGPC) that would further separate Sikh religious authority from Hindu influence. Thus, the 1925 Sikh Gurdwaras Act implicitly reflects the Tat Khalsa understanding of the Sikh religion as distinct from and structurally equal to other religions when it defines a Sikh as one who has 'no other religion'.

As a consequence of the success of the Tat Khalsa reformers, Sikhs in the early twentieth century came 'to think, imagine and speak in terms of a universal community of believers united by uniform, rites, symbols and scripture' (Oberoi 1988, p.154). Ideologically, if not always in practice, the Sikh religion was now distinguishable from Hinduism and religious identities were taken to be exclusive. Thus, Sikh representatives reacted with anger when the 1950 Constitution of India declared the Sikh religion to be a sect of Hinduism and failed to establish a separate personal law for Sikhs. And Sikhs have continued to be sensitive to portrayal of Sikhism as a Hindu sect in English-language texts, even to the point of denying historical connections between Sikhism and Hinduism.[6]

If Sikhism had come to be represented, at least by Sikhs, as a separate and distinct religion, it was still thought of by most people—Sikh as well as non-Sikh—as primarily a regional faith of some Punjabis rather than as a major world religion. Despite the efforts of Singh Sabha writers and sympathizers (such as Macauliffe) to represent the Sikh religion to the English-speaking public, world religion textbooks and comparative religionists largely ignored Sikhism (see Juergensmeyer 1979). And, as a non-proselytizing religion, Sikhism tended to be firmly encapsulated within Punjabi communities. I would argue that it was not until the late 1960s and early 1970s that a number of convergent events allowed Sikhs to effectively make the claim that Sikhism is a major 'world religion' rather than a parochial faith.

First, celebrations of the 300th birthday of Guru Gobind Singh (1966–7), the 500th birthday of Guru Nanak (1969), and the 100th anniversary of the Singh Sabha movement (1973–4) provided multiple occasions for Sikhs to represent themselves and their religion to a wider audience, as these celebrations generated an outpouring of activities and published material intended for public consumption in India and abroad. Second, renewed scholarly attention from western academics—especially the work of W.H. McLeod (beginning with *Guru Nanak and the Sikh Religion* in 1968), but also the contributions of N. Gerald Barrier, Mark Juergensmeyer, W. Owen Cole and others—made Sikhism a legitimate topic of intellectual contemplation and discussion in the West. As Mark Juergensmeyer notes in a recent review of Sikhism in religious studies (1993a), having a chronicler of McLeod's stature (however critically his work may have been received in some Sikh quarters) has ultimately helped legitimate Sikhism as a religious tradition worthy of academic study in western universities. Third, the global dispersion of Sikhs from Punjab and, perhaps more importantly, the unprecedented mass conversions of non-Punjabi westerners to Sikhism introduced Sikhs and Sikhism to new audiences, made Sikhism part of the menu of religious options available to religious seekers in the West, and ultimately made it plausible to assert that Sikhism was global both in its spread and in its appeal. All of the above were, of course, aided by the increased collective wealth of the Sikhs which helped underwrite the publications, celebrations, Sikh Studies chairs, travelling *ragi jathas*, missionaries, etc. which dispersed both Sikhs themselves and Sikh images globally.

If the master narrative of Sikhs as a nation is focused on the Punjabi patrimony of the Sikhs, the master narrative of Sikhism as a world religion has focused on the transcendent appeal and relevance of the Guru's teachings. Since at least the Singh Sabha period, a frequent refrain in representations of Sikhism to non-Sikhs has been the ecumenical character of the religion. Thus much is made of the fact that the Sikh scriptures contain the compositions of Hindus and Muslims as well as those of the Sikh Gurus, that Sikh gurdwaras are open to persons of all backgrounds, and that the Gurus themselves were respectful of other religious traditions. Another frequent claim about Sikhism has been of its modernity. As 'the youngest major world religion', it is represented as being particularly relevant to the challenges of the contemporary era.[7]

In the late 1960s and early 1970s, claims about the expansiveness and modernity of Sikh religious teachings were made in leading English language Sikh publications, in some ways defensively in light of concern at the time over Sikh youth in India and the diaspora falling away from the faith and failing to maintain the *rahit*.[8] For Sikhs, beginning to feel insecure about whether they could hold on to a generation coming of age outside Punjab or in the modernizing Punjab itself, the evident appeal of Sikhism to non-Punjabis in the West was thus something of a godsend. The Gora Sikh followers of Yogi Bhajan were a visible demonstration — both to the outside world and to doubtful Sikhs—that Sikhism was indeed a world religion, relevant to all kinds of people living in the contemporary world and that the Truths enunciated by their Gurus were accessible to all. In short, the existence of the Gora Sikhs made it increasingly plausible to claim that Sikhism was a world religion rather than simply a parochial faith of some Punjabis. And Sikh authorities in Punjab were quick to make such claims, while the Gora Sikhs themselves were happy to claim that they were a fulfilment of a prophecy attributed to Guru Gobind Singh which was said to foresee the rise of the Khalsa in the West.[9]

As the anthropologist Robert Hefner has noted (1993), world religions are 'the longest standing of civilization's primary institutions' and have long been a primary source of 'self-identification'. The master narrative of Sikhism as a world religion thus provides Sikhs with a strong claim to collective identity, and a narrative of Sikhism as a world religion has had strong appeal in recent years. But if Sikhism is to be regarded as a 'world religion', this opens it up to the sort of expectations that others have come to take for granted of religions in the modern world. For one thing, it invites the kinds of academic analysis to which other world religions have been subjected. This means, it has to come to terms with new forms of historical and textual analysis. And this sort of attention, as we know from the unhappy fate of Sikh Studies chairs in North American universities, has not been received well in some Sikh quarters. For another thing, it makes Sikhism subject to the sorts of political controls that many states exert over recognized religions and forces Sikhs to accommodate themselves to the prevailing local ideologies and policies governing the extension of rights and the entailment of responsibilities of recognized religions. If constitutional guarantees of freedom of religion have been a source of certain protections to Sikhism, state policies that mandate a strict separation of religion and politics can be seen as a challenge.[10]

QAUM AND *PANTH*

Whether talking about Sikhs as a 'nation' or Sikhism as a 'world religion' we are, of course, using English terms from the vocabulary of high modernism. Moreover, because of the long-standing separation of church and state, religion and politics, sacred and secular identities in the West, Sikh self-representation as simultaneously a 'nation' and a 'world religion' is, as already suggested, 'problematic' to many western observers. One problem, as I have attempted to illustrate above, is that the ways in which national and religious identities have come to be narrated in late twentieth century identity politics have meant that identity claims about the 'Sikh nation' and about the 'Sikh religion' are not coterminous, but rather entail different inclusions and exclusions and, at times, a forced choice between the two.[11]

The case of the so-called Gora Sikhs—the Western converts to Sikhism—illustrates nicely the difference. Those who claims membership in the Sikh nation by virtue of patrimonial inheritance and those who claims membership in the Sikh religion by virtue of conversion may in fact contest (implicitly, if not explicitly) one another's identities. North American Sikh converts in the 1970s challenged the Sikh identity of many Punjabi Sikh immigrants since, they argued, 'you can be a Punjabi no matter what you do and no matter where you go but you cannot call yourself a Sikh unless you are living as a [practicing, religious] Sikh' (Premka Kaur 1973, p. 53). This notion of an exclusive and uniform religious identity has fed an ongoing dispute over orthopraxy and the boundaries of the religion community.[12] In turn, many Sikh nationalists in the 1980s felt compelled to ignore, deny, or repudiate the converts and the possibility of conversion so that they could plausibly advance the claim that 'the Sikhs are bound by common race, common language and literature, common land, common history, common religion, common joys and sorrows, and common political aims and aspirations' (Chaddah 1982, p. 79). The existence of non-Punjabi Sikh converts in the West helps substantiate the master narrative of 'Sikhism as a world religion'; and, consequently, Sikh authorities in India were in the 1970s proud to show off their new Western converts. But the existence of these same non-Punjabi Sikhs proved awkward to those who in the 1980s were intent on proclaiming that 'Sikhs are a nation' based on a common Punjabi patrimony.

Undoubtedly, both local and international political structures provide the conditions favourable to advancing certain narrative claims. When the British rulers in Punjab privileged religion as a basis for enumeration of the local population and for reservation of legislative seats, it provided an impetus to those who would distinguish exclusive Sikh and Hindu religious identities. On the contemporary international stage, so long as international law continues to be based upon a world of territorial nation-states, Sikhs with grievances about their status in India find it useful to emphasize the narratives of nationalism to justify claims for greater political sovereignty and self-determination in the imagined homeland. A similar dynamic has been at work in the diaspora, where Sikhs have had to be responsive to the discursive conditions under which they represent themselves. Thus, for example, the promise of the extension of religious rights to recognized religions in North American has been an impetus to Sikhs in the United States to claim that Sikhism is a world religion whose followers should consequently enjoy the rights and benefits that the state accords to recognized religions (for example, in the Sikh case, a religious exemption from hard-hat requirements or helmet laws or weapons restrictions).[13] At the same time, where distinct 'national origins' is a primary basis for the extension of recognition and public support in multicultural regimes (such as that in Canada), it makes sense that Sikhs might want also to emphasize their separate identity by employing the narratives of Sikh nationhood (see Dusenbery 1995).[14] In short, both master narratives — 'Sikhs are a nation' and 'Sikhism is a world religion' — have proven useful to Sikh interests in certain socio-historical situations. And, in many ways, they have been naturalized in Sikh discourse. But what if we were to re-cognize some of premodern terms of identity used by Sikhs as being appropriate to our postmodern age? Why should Sikhs have to work so hard to make their collective identity fit the identity vocabulary of high modernism and risk either being challenged for failing to live up to normative expectations of what constitutes a 'nation' or 'world religion' or being forced to choose between the two when there are Punjabi concepts that might have resonance for the existential situations that Sikhs encounter at the end of the twentieth century? Why adopt what Partha Chatterjee (1986), speaking of nationalism in India and other former colonies — but his comments could equally well apply to narratives of world religion — has characterized as a 'derivative discourse'?

As McLeod has noted, 'for many Sikhs "nation" has served as a translation for the word *qaum*.' But, as McLeod goes on to note, 'In its original Arabic form *qaum* designates "a people who stand together" and this meaning has survived its adoption into Punjabi usage' (1989, p. 107). As McLeod goes on to suggest (1989, pp. 107–8), the Punjabi notion of *qaum* is thus not strictly the same as the English notion of 'nation'. While *quam* entails a notion of collective identity and common interests, it does not appear to entail the same patrimonial, territorial, and sovereignty claims that the term 'nation' has come to acquire in this century. At a time when the future of the nation-state as the primary institution of social and political life is increasingly in question (see, for example, Guéhenno 1995) and when Sikhs have come to constitute almost a paradigmatic example of a transnational community, might there not be some advantage to furthering a de-essentialized and de-territorialized discourse of identity that would incorporate rather than marginalize diasporan Sikhs and Sikh converts? Sikhs have shown that they can maintain a collective identity and unite behind common interests even without a fully sovereign homeland and even while dispersed around the globe. They thus constitute a broadly inclusive, situationally-defined *qaum*. A narrative that focuses identity more on collective agency (as the concept *qaum* does) and less on an essentialistic subject (as the term 'nation' does) would seem to be of potential appeal to a transnational community like the Sikhs. In fact, rather than relying on the narrative of territorial nationhood, Sikhs might wish to take the lead in thinking us beyond the vocabulary of high modernism. Indeed, Arjun Appadurai has recently suggested that Sikhs are constructing 'a new, postnational cartography in which ethnos and demos are unevenly spread across the world' such that 'this topos of Sikh "national" identity is in fact a topos of "community" (*qom*), which contests many national maps . . . and contains one model of post-Westphalian cartography' (1996, p. 50).

Similarly, McLeod has argued (1979, 1988, pp. 39–40) that the term *panth* (literally, 'path' or 'way') does not readily translate as 'sect' or 'church' or 'nation'—some of the terms by which it has been glossed. I have suggested (1988, 1990) that one gloss for Panth might be 'worship genus', which suggests a collectivity identified through shared religious practices that mark them with the same biomoral worship substances (that is, the Guru's *bani, prasad, amrit*, etc). This seems to me one sense in which the term '*Panth*' has been and still largely is applied within the Sikh community. Thus one can talk of the Khalsa Panth or the Sikh Panth or Nanakapanthis without assuming the terms cover the same people and without labelling Sikhs who are not Khalsa as non-Sikhs. Rather, they are members of the Sikh Panth by virtue of their biomoral engagement with the Gurus but are not members of the Khalsa Panth, since they have not incorporated the amrit or taken on the discipline of the Khalsa *rahit*. This notion of the Panth as a particular kind of 'worship genus' seems to have certain advantages over the notion of Sikhism as a world religion, if the latter implies a doctrinal religion whose membership is determined by an all-or-nothing adherence to a uniform code-for-conduct. Of course, this premodern concept has been challenged and transformed by the evolving narrative of Sikhism as a world religion, which, in order to make Sikhism the ontological equivalent of other 'world religions', has tried to codify its doctrinal rules and police its boundaries. What I am suggesting here is that this acceptance as a 'world religion' has had its costs.

In conclusion, although master narratives of 'Sikhs are a nation' and 'Sikhism is a world religion' provide emancipatory discourses through which Sikhs can resist impositions of hostile states or indifferent publics, investing wholeheartedly in modernist narratives tends to obscure premodern Punjabi narratives that may, in fact, be well adapted to our postmodern condition.

NOTES

1. Anthropologists, for example, are still trying to figure out how to think themselves beyond the notion of a world of discretely-bounded, internally-homogenous, historically-continuous cultures. And, as Richard Handler (1985) has pointed out, such essentialist anthropological and modern Western concepts of culture—aligning an ahistoric 'culture' with a 'people' and a 'place'—have proven discursively useful to nationalist ideologues.
2. Thus, for example, Terry Turner notes in late-capitalism 'the elevation of "culture" as a new category of collective human rights, [which] defines it, as such, as a legitimate goal of political struggle for equal representation in the public domain' (1993, p. 425). While Turner emphasizes the empowering potential of these emancipatory narratives, Eric Wolf (1994) notes their darker, exclusionary implications.
3. Thus, unlike W.H. McLeod (1979, 1988, pp. 39–41, 1989, pp. 106–8), W. Owen Cole (1983), and Mark Juergensmeyer (1982), I am not so much concerned with whether Sikhs live up to some academic definition of a 'nation' or 'world religion' but rather in how and why and to what ends Sikhs have represented their collective identity in these terms.
4. See, for example, Pritam Singh Gill's *History of the Sikh Nation* (1978), Mehar Singh Chaddah's *Are Sikhs a Nation?* (1982), and H.S. Dilgeer and A.S. Sekhon's *The Sikhs' Struggle for Sovereignty* (1992).
5. Thus the Akali Dal resolution of March 1946 emphasizes Sikh 'intimate bonds' to the Punjab and the 'rights of the Sikh nation' to 'the creation of a Sikh state' (see Oberoi 1987, p. 37). The Anandapur Sahib Resolution

of 1978 begins: 'Whereas, the Sikhs of India are a historically recognized political nation ever since the inauguration of the Khalsa in AD 1699, and Whereas, this status of the Sikh nation had been internationally recognized by the major powers of Europe and Asia . . . (Maharaja Amarinder Singh 1992, p. 134). In their 'Appeal' to the United Nations, the Shiromani Akali Dal and Shiromani Gurdwara Parbandhak Committee argue for 'decolonisation of Punjab' on the basis that 'Sikhs are a religious community and a political nation simultaneously . . . . Sikhism and its apotheosis, the Khalsa[,] is a unique political society with a distinct religion, language, culture, ethos, a historic territory and political thought' (Shiromani Akali Dal 1992, pp. 6–7). 'The Sikh Nation' piece placed in *The New York Times* by the Khalistan Affairs Center asserts: 'We Sikhs are a proud people united by our religion, history and culture . . . . We Sikhs are one nation, one people . . . 'captured' in the map of India' (Khalistan Affairs Centre 1995, p. A11).

6. For a critique of the representation of Sikhism in English-language encyclopedias, for example, Kharak Singh (1992).
7. The collection of essays by Kapur Singh, published posthumously as *Sikhism: An Oecumenical Religion* (1993), contains notable examples of this vein of discourse. Particularly noteworthy is his differentiation of Sikhism (as 'transcending all particularism') from Judaism (one of the 'religions that are ethnic'), pp. 176–81 and his assertion that 'Guru Amar Dass mapped out the blueprint organization of Sikhism as a World Religion by appointing twenty-two Sikh bishops over as many bishoprics coterminus [sic] with the temporal Mughal Indian empire' (p. 47). This focus on Sikhism as an ecumenical 'world religion' is perhaps surprising, since Kapur Singh is commonly thought of as one of the foremost recent proponents of Sikh nationalism. But this fusion of discourses may make sense in the context of what Mark Juergensmeyer (1993b) has termed the rise of global 'religious nationalism'.
8. See, for example, articles of this period by B.S. Josi (1970), T. Singh (1971), and K. Singh (1973) in *The Sikh Review*. See also Kapur Singh's claim that 'Sikhism, as a World religion, and as spiritual impulse will have failed to establish its claim as such unless it can successfully meet the challenge that is implicit in their [*sic*] present situation and predicament as successfully as it did in the past . . . '(1993, p. 92).
9. For Indian accounts that represent Western converts as evidence of Sikhism's global appeal, see, for example, Hukam Singh (1974), *Gurdwara Gazette* of October 1974, Bhatia (1979). On the North American converts as fulfilment of Guru Gobind Singh's prophecy, see Premka Kaur (1975, p. 7).
10. See Dusenbery (1981 and 1996) for case studies that touch on the relationship between Sikhism and the state in Canada and Singapore, respectively. Dusenbery (forthcoming) is a comparative case study.

11. This seems to be what J.S. Neki is getting at when he asks: 'What is the root cause of the strife between two different types of parochial loyalties [among Sikhs]—the national and the Panthic? Is there a possibility of rapprochement between the two?' (1994, p. 82).
12. See my arguments concerning this dispute in Dusenbery (1988) and Dusenbery (1989).
13. Indeed, America's religious freedom and the benefits accorded to recognized religious organizations have been a boon to Sikh organizations in the United States. According to his biographers, Yogi Bhajan (née Harbhajan Singh Puri; aka Siri Singh Sahib Bhai Sahib Harbhajan Singh Khalsa) 'foresaw that the greatest protection available to Sikhs in America would be the constitutional guarantees of freedom of religion' (Khalsa and Khalsa 1979, p. 120).
14. In the United Kingdom, the Race Relations Act of 1976, which defined a 'racial group' as 'a group of persons defined by reference to colour, race, nationality, or ethnic or national origins', led Sikhs to employ the narrative of 'Sikhs are a race' to qualify for protection of turbans in the *Mandla v. Lee* case. See Walman (1982) and McLeod (1989, p. 106) for discussion of this (mis)use of the term 'race' in reference to the Sikh collectivity. My point would be that the state provided Sikhs the conditions for the possibility of advancing this particular narrative of identity.

REFERENCES

Appadurai, Arjun 1996, 'Sovereignty without Territoriality: Notes for a Postnational Geography' in Patricia Yaeger, (ed.), *The Geography of Identity,* Ann Arbor: University of Michigan Press, pp. 40–58.

Barrier, N. Gerald, 1970, *The Sikhs and Their Literature*, Delhi: Manohar.

Bhatia, S. Rajinder Singh, 1979, 'A New Chapter in Sikh History' in Premka Kaur Khalsa and Sat Kirpal Kaur Khalsa, (eds), *The Man Called the Siri Singh Sahib,* Los Angeles: Sikh Dharma, pp. 410–11.

Cole, W. Owen, 1983, 'Sikhism: A World Religion', *Studies in Sikhism and Comparative Religion,* 1 & 2, pp. 1–10.

———, 1988, 'The Sikh Diaspora: Its Possible Effects on Sikhism' in Joseph T. O' Connell et al., (eds), *Sikh History and Religion in the Twentieth Century*, Toronto: Centre for South Asian Studies, University of Toronto, pp. 388–402.

Comaroff, John L., 1995, 'Ethnicity, Nationalism and the Politics of Difference in an Age of Revolution' in J.L. Comaroff and P.C. Stern, (eds), *Perspectives on Nationalism and War*, Luxemburg: Gordon and Breach Publishers, pp. 243–76.

Chaddah, Mehar Singh, 1982, *Are Sikhs a Nation?* Delhi: Delhi Gurdwara Management Committee.

Chatterjee, Partha, 1986, *Nationalist Thought and the Colonial World: A Derivative Discourse*, London: Zed Books.

Cunningham, J.D., 1849, *A History of the Sikhs from the Origin of the Nation to the Battles of the Sutlej*, London: John Murray, Reprint, New Delhi: S. Chand & Co., 1985.

Dilgeer, H.S. and A.S. Sekhon, 1992, *The Sikhs' Struggle for Sovereignty: An Historical Perspective* in A.T. Kerr, (ed.), Oslo: Guru Nanak Institute of Sikh Studies.

Dusenbery, Verne A., 1981, 'Canadian Ideology and Public Policy: The Impact on Vancouver Sikh Ethnic and Religious Adaptation', *Canadian Ethnic Studies,* 13, (3) Winter, pp. 101–19.

———, 1988, 'Punjabi Sikhs and Gora Sikhs: Conflicting Assertions of Sikh Identity in North America' in Joseph T. O'Connell et al., (eds), *Sikh History and Religion in the Twentieth Century*, Toronto: Centre for South Asian Studies, University of Toronto, pp. 334–55.

———, 1989, 'Of Singh Sabhas, Siri Singh Sahibs, and Sikh Scholars: Sikh Discourse from North America in the 1970s' in N. Gerald Barrier and Verne A. Dusenbery, (eds), *The Sikh Diaspora: Migration and the Experience Beyond Punjab*, Delhi: Chanakya; Columbia, Missouri: South Asia Books, pp. 90–119.

———, 1990, 'The Sikh Person, the Khalsa Panth, and Western Sikh Converts' in Bardwell L. Smith, (ed.), *Religious Movements and Social Identity*, 4, 'Boeings and Bullock-Carts,' festschrift for K. Iswaran, Delhi: Chanakaya Publications, pp. 117–35.

———, 1995, 'A Sikh Diaspora? Contested Identities and Constructed Realities' in Peter van der Veer, (ed.), *Nation and Migration: The Politics of Space in the South Asian Diaspora*, Philadelphia: University of Pennsylvania Press, pp. 17–42.

———, 1996, 'Socializing Sikhs in Singapore: Soliciting the State's Support' in Pashaura Singh and N. Gerald Barrier, (eds), *The Transmission of Sikh Heritage in the Diaspora*, New Delhi: Manohar, pp. 113–47.

——, 2007, 'The Poetics and Politics of Recognition: Diasporan Sikhs in Pluralist Polities', *American Ethnologist*, 24 (4), pp. 738–62.

Guéhenno, Jean-Marie, 1995, *The End of the Nation State*, Victoria Elliott, (trans.), Minneapolis: University of Minnesota Press.

Gill, Pritam Singh, 1978, *History of Sikh Nation*, Jullundur: New Academic Publishing Co.

Handler, Richard, 1985, 'On Dialogue and Destructive Analysis: Problems in Narrating Nationalism and Ethnicity', *Journal of Anthropological Research*, 41 (2) Summer, pp. 171–82.

Hefner, Robert W., 1993, 'Introduction: World Building and the Rationality of Conversion' in Robert W. Hefner, (ed.), *Conversion to Christianity:*

Historical and Anthropological Perspectives on a Great Transformation, Berkeley: University of California Press, pp. 3–44.

Hukam Singh, 1974, 'Sikhs in UK and Americas, Part III', *Gurdwara Gazette* [English-language section] 45, (12) December, pp. 6–19.

Josi, B.S., 1970, 'Sikhism's Universality', *The Sikh Review,* 19 (207) February, pp. 16–18.

Juergensmeyer, Mark, 1979, 'The Forgotten Tradition: Sikhism in the Study of World Religions' in Mark Juergensmeyer and N. Gerald Barrier, (eds), *Sikh Studies: Comparative Perspectives on a Changing Tradition*, Berkeley: Graduate Theological Union, pp. 13–23.

———, 1982, 'The Future of Sikhism as a World Religion', *The Sikh Times*, July, pp. 7–11.

———, 1993a, 'Sikhism and Religious Studies' in John Stratton Hawley and Gurinder Singh Mann, (eds), *Studying the Sikhs: Issues for North America*, Albany: SUNY, pp. 9–23.

———, 1993b, *The New Cold War? Religious Nationalism Confronts the Secular State*, Berkeley: University of California Press.

——— and N. Gerald Barrier, 1979, 'Introduction: The Sikhs and the Scholars' in Mark Juergensmeyer and N. Gerald Barrier, (eds), *Sikh Studies: Comparative Perspectives on a Changing Tradition*, Berkeley: Graduate Theological Union, pp. 1–9.

K. Singh, 1973, 'Sikhism as a Universal Religion', *The Sikh Review*, 21 (235), June, pp. 30–8.

Khalistan Affairs Centre, 1995, 'The Sikh Nation' [paid op-ed infomercial], *The New York Times*, Monday, 18 December, p. A11.

Khalsa, Shakt Parwha Kaur and Gurubanda Singh Khalsa, 1979, 'The Siri Singh Sahib' in Premka Kaur Khalsa and Sat Kirpal Kaur Khalsa, (eds), *The Man Called the Siri Singh Sahib,* Los Angeles: Sikh Dharma, pp. 117–31.

Kharak Singh, 1992, 'Encyclopedias and Sikhism', *Abstracts of Sikh Studies*, July, p. 98–111.

Lyotard, Jean-Francois, 1984[1979], *The Postmodern Condition: A Report on Knowledge*, Minneapolis: University of Minnesota Press.

Maharaja Amarinder Singh, 1992, 'Anandapur Sahib Resolution' in Harbans Singh, (ed.), *Encyclopedia of Sikhism*, vol. 1, Patiala: Punjabi University, pp. 133-41.

Malcolm, John, 1812, *Sketch of the Sikhs*, London: John Murray.

McLeod, W.H., 1978, 'On the word *panth*: A problem of terminology and definition', *Contributions to Indian Sociology*, n. s., 12 (2), pp. 287–95.

———, 1988, 'A Sikh Theology for Modern Times' in Joseph T. O'Connell et al., (eds), *Sikh History and Religion in the Twentieth Century,* Toronto: Centre for South Asian Studies, University of Toronto, pp. 32–43.

——, 1989, *Who is a Sikh? The Problem of Sikh Identity*, Oxford: Clarendon Press.

Nabha, Kahan Singh, 1984 [1898], *Sikhs ... We are Not Hindus*, Jarnail Singh, (trans.), Willowdale, Ontario: The Sikh Social & Educational Society.

Neki, J.S., 1994, 'The Sikh Sociology', *The Sikh Review*, 42, (8) August, pp. 79–82.

Oberoi, Harjot S., 1987, 'From Punjab to 'Khalistan': Territoriality and Metacommentary', *Pacific Affairs,* 60 (1) Spring, pp. 26–41.

——, 1988, 'From Ritual to Counter-Ritual: Rethinking the Hindu-Sikh Question, 1884–1915' in Joseph T. O'Connell et al., (eds), *Sikh History and Religion in the Twentieth Century*, Toronto: Centre for South Asian Studies, University of Toronto, pp. 136–58.

——, 1994, *The Construction of Religious Boundaries: Culture, Identity and Diversity in the Sikh Tradition*, New Delhi: Oxford University Press, Chicago: University of Chicago Press.

Premka Kaur, 1975, 'Sikh Dharma: Past, Present, and Future', *Sikh Dharma Brotherhood,* Winter, pp. 2–7.

Smith, Vincent, 1958, *The Oxford History of India*, Oxford: Oxford University Press.

Taran Singh, 1971, 'Guru Nanak's Religion and its Relevance for Modern Times', *The Sikh Review*, 19 (216) November, pp. 17–24.

Thornton, Thomas Henry, 1846, *History of the Punjab and the Rise, Progress & Present Condition of the Sect and Nation of the Sikhs*, 2 vols., London: W.H. Allen Reprint, Patiala: LDP, 1970.

Turner, Terence, 1993, 'Anthropology and Multiculturalism: What is Anthropology That Multiculturalists Should Be Mindful of It?', *Cultural Anthropology*, 8 (4), pp. 411–29.

Wallman, Sandra, 1982, 'Turbans, Identities and Racial Categories', *RAIN* (*Royal Anthropological Institute News*), vol. 52, p. 4.

Wolf, Eric, 1994, 'Perilous Ideas: Race, Culture, People', *Current Anthropology*, 35 (1), pp. 1–12

6

'Through Wisdom, Dispense Charity'

Religious and Cultural Underpinnings of Diasporan Sikh Philanthropy in Punjab

sachai saramai bāhare agai lahih na dādi
akali eh na ākhīai akali gavāīai bādi
akali sāhibu savīai akali pāīai mānu
akalī parhi kai bujhīai akalī kīchai dānu

(They who are bereft of truth and hard service, receive not appreciation hereafter.
The wisdom which is wasted in wranglings; this by no means can be called wisdom.
Through wisdom, one serves the Lord and through wisdom one obtains honour.
Through wisdom, man is instructed by reading and through wisdom, he rightly gives in charity.)

—Guru Nanak, Ādi Granth, p. 1245[1]

Travel to any village in Doaba or surrounding areas of central Punjab, key sites of international emigration, and you are likely to see a newly built or refurbished gurdwara and an impressive village gate. You may also find a newly constructed village sports stadium or public gathering place. If it happens to be larger village, a new school or college or hospital may also have been constructed in recent years. And, if you are visiting at the right time of the year, a *kabaḍḍī* tournament or a medical camp may be taking place. Now, if you look closely at the donor plaques or sponsor lists, you are likely to find, prominently listed, the name or names of diasporan Sikhs from the village.

While no official figures are available on the extent of remittances from abroad being used to fund philanthropic projects in Punjab, the amounts have been estimated to be considerable. A sample survey in nine development blocks in Doaba, conducted in 2002 by the NRI Sabha Punjab, found that Non-Resident Indians (NRIs) had donated almost two billion rupees in 477 villages to six different types of village projects : health, education, sports/stadia, street/streetlights/sewage, community centres, and gurdwaras /religious places.[2] And, in recent years, NRIs have begun to undertake extensive infrastructural improvement projects in selected Punjabi villages, as detailed, for instance, in the cover story of *Simply Punjabi* for March 2006.[3]

The Government of India and the Government of Punjab have both awakened to the idea that NRI contributions might play an important role in the development of the state. After years of fear that Sikh remittances from abroad were funding political unrest in the state, the central and state governments now see remittances as a potential source of needed capital to fund infrastructure improvements and social services. Accordingly, the central government has committed itself to removing impediments to the international transfer of funds and the state government has offered to partner with NRIs to make matching grants for development projects in Punjab through its CD 2.35 'Mera Pind Initiative'.[4]

This essay explores the role that Sikh religious teachings and practices, Punjabi cultural understandings and social expectations, and experiences of living and working in settings abroad might play in helping motivate diasporan Sikhs to undertake philanthropy in Punjab.[5] The paper argues for appreciation of the multiple, complex, and sometimes conflicting motivations underpinning diasporan Sikh philanthropy in Punjab, including both the initial decision to undertake philanthropy and subsequent decisions about which projects to support.

SIKH RELIGIOUS TEACHINGS AND PRACTICES

In undertaking research on the philanthropic projects in Punjab supported by NRIs whom we have identified as being part of the 'Sikh diaspora', my colleague, Darshan S. Tatla, and I have already identified 'Sikh' as an important component of the philanthropist's identity.[6] In fact, the government itself has not used a religious designation for the NRIs whose social investments they seek, and NRI Punjabis of various religious and non-religious backgrounds are involved in philanthropic projects in the state. However, since the vast majority of those going abroad and remitting money to villages of Punjab are from Sikh backgrounds or, at the very least, grew up in an environment permeated with discourses derived from the Sikh tradition, it makes sense to explore some of the discourses on giving and service that are found in Sikh religious teachings and practices. In short, it suggests that we investigate possible imaginative sources for a philanthropic ethic within the Sikh tradition.[7]

Selfless Giving, Selfless Service : Textual Sources

Giving charity (*dān*) and performing selfless service (*sevā*) to others are two of the most important and praiseworthy acts discussed by the Sikh Gurus and incorporated not only into the Adi Granth and Dasam Granth but also into Sikh popular literature and folk sayings.[8]

On the importance of charity, the following *shalok* of Guru Nanak's from the Adi Granth is among the most often cited :

> *ghāli khāi kichhu hathahu dehi.*
> *nānak rāhu pachhāṇahi seai.*
> (One who eats what he earns through his earnest labour and from his hand gives something in charity,
> O Nanak, he alone knows the True way of life.)
>
> —Guru Nanak, AG, p. 1245

And this message is reiterated elsewhere in the Adi Granth. The following verse, from Guru Nanak's *Sidh Gosht* 36, is one basis of the popular formula for spiritual liberation, *nām, dān, ishnān* (the divine Name, charity, and bathing [spiritual purification]), further elaborated upon in the *janam-sakhi* literature[9]:

> *guramukhi nāmu dānu isanānu*
> *guramukhi lāgai sahaji dhiānu*
> *guramukhi pāvai daragah mānu*
> *guramukhi bhau bhanjanu paradhānu*
> *guramukhi karaṇi kār karāe*
> *nanak guramukhi meli milāe*
> (The pious person is blessed with the Name, charity, and purity.
> The pious person's attention remains fixed on the Lord.
> The pious person obtains honour in the Lord's court.
> The pious person attains the Supreme Lord, the Destroyer of Dread.
> The pious person practices virtuous deeds and actions.
> Nanak, the pious person unites in the Lord's union.)
>
> —Guru Nanak, AG, p. 942

One of the most popular expressions of Sikh religious duty is the following proverb, with its explicit invocation of giving. Indeed, the concept of '*vaṇḍ chhako*' (sharing with others) is probably the most (re)cited phrase when informants provide a Sikh explanation of their philanthropic motives:

> *Nām japo, kirat karo, vaṇḍ chhako.*
> (Repeat the divine Name, work honestly, and give a share [of your wealth to others less fortunate])
>
> —proverb summarizing duties of a Sikh, commonly attributed to Guru Nanak

According to the Gurus, such giving should be heartfelt and based on compassion (*dayā*), neither performed through compulsion nor done mechanically:

> *sachu tā paru jāṇīai jā sikh sachī lei*
> *daiā jāṇai jīa kī kichhu punnu dānu karei*
> (Then alone is the mortal deemed to be true, when he receives true instruction.
> He shows mercy to living beings and gives something in charity.)
>
> —Guru Nanak, AG, p. 468

> *badhā chaṭī jo bhare nā gunu nā upakāru*
> *setī khusī savārīai nānak kāraju sāru*
> (In the fine the prisoner pays there is neither merit nor any goodness. Nanak, the act which the mortal performs with his sweet will is the best.)
>
> —Guru Angad, AG, p. 787

Moreover, according to Sikh teachings, the ideal recipient of charity is a needy person, not a mendicant or a Brahmin (traditional recipients of *dān* among Hindus):

> *nīchā andari nīch jāti nīchī hu ati nīchu*
> *nānak tin kai sāngi sathi vaḍiā siu kiā rīs*
> *jithai nīch samālīani tithai nadari terī bakhasīs*
> (Those who are of low caste among the lowly, rather the lowest of the low;
> Nanak seeks the company of those. Why should he rival the lofty?
> Where the poor are looked after, there does reign the look of Thy grace, O' Lord.)
>
> —Guru Nanak, AG, p. 15

kabīr ko suāmī garīb nivāj
(Kabir's Lord is the cherisher of the poor.)
—Bhagat Kabir, AG, p. 331

gurū ke sikh garīb dī rasanā gurū kī golak jānaṇī.
(The Gursikh should regard a pauper's mouth as the Guru's alms-box.)
—Chaupa Singh's Rahit-nama[10]

During the period of the Gurus, *dasvandh*, the practice of giving one. . . .tenth of one's earnings in the name of the Guru for the common good, was instituted.[11] In a *Tanakhāh-nāmā* popularly attributed to Nand Lal, a contemporary of Guru Gobind Singh, the following is put forth as the Guru's perspective on those who do not give *dasvandh*:

dasvandh gurū nahi devai jhūth bol jo khāi
kahe gobind singh lāl jī tis kā kachhū nā bisāhi
(He who does not give a tithe [*dasvandh*] to the Guru, and he who utters lies.
The word of Gobind Singh, [Nand] Lal, is that you should never put trust in him)
—Bhai Nand Lal's *Tanakhah-nama*, verse 24[12]

And those taking *amrit* receive the following injunction as part of their initiation into the Khalsa:

āpaṇi kamāi vichon guru kā dasavandh deṇā.
(From your own earnings, you should give one-tenth for the common good)
—from the Amrit ceremony

For Sikhs, *sevā* (service) is of equal, if not greater, importance than *dān* (charity) as a moral and ethical imperative and as a means to spiritual enlightenment.[13] The Adi Granth is full of verses extrolling *sevā*,[14] including the following:

vichi duniā sev kamāīai
tā daragah baisaṇu pāīai
(In this world perform the Lord's service.
Then [shalt thou] get a seat in the Master's Court.)
—Guru Nanak, AG, p.26

sevā karāt hoi nihakāmī
tisu ko hot parāpati suāmī
(He who performs Guru's service without desire for reward,
Attains to the Lord.)

—Guru Nanak, AG, pp.286–7

dāsani dās dās hoi rahīai jo jan ram bhagat nij bhaīā
(The person, who has become the Lord's own servant;
Be thou the slave of the slave of his slave.)

—Guru Ram Das, AG, p.834

viṇu sevā dhrig hath pair hor nihaphal karaṇī
(Without seva, cursed are the hands and feet,
Useless are all the virtues.)

—Bhai Gurdas's *Vārān*, 27.10

And service, like charity, is most appropriately directed to the poor and needy. Here is Guru Gobind Singh's linking of the two in his *Savayya*:

sev karī in hī kī bhavat aur kī sev suhāt na jīko
dān dayo in hī ko bhalo aru ānako dān na lāgat nīko
āgai phalai in hī ko dayo jag mai jasu aur dayo sabh phīko
mo grah mai tan te man te sir lao dhan hai sabh hī inhīko
(To serve them [the poor] alone is a pleasant and acceptable. To serve others is not to my liking.
To give charity to these people is good thing. To give charity to others is fruitless.
And that charity grows that is given to these people. Otherwise it is a waste.
In my body and in my mind, poor as I am, all my wealth that I have is theirs.)

—Guru Gobind Singh, *Dasam Granth*, p.717

Moreover, both giving *dān* and performing *sevā* should be done with humility and without ego (*haumai*) or pride (*māṇ*)—hence, 'selfless giving' and 'selfless service' (*nishkām sevā*) are emphasized. The following verses address this point:

anik bhānti kari sevā karīai
jīu prān dhan āgai dharīai
(In various ways render thou service unto the Lord.
Place thou before him thy life, soul and wealth.)

—Guru Arjan, AG, p.391

braham giānī kai garībī samāhā
braham giānī paraupakār umāhā
(Lord's realizer is steeped in humility.
Lord's realizer takes delight in doing good to others.)
—Guru Arjan, AG, p.273

tīrath barat aru dān kari man mai dharai gumānu
nānak nihaphal jāt tihi jiu kunchar isanānu
(Whosoever going on pilgrimages, fasting and giving alms takes pride in his mind,
Nanak, these deeds of his go in vain like an elephant bathing.)
—Guru Tegh Bahadur, AG, p.1428

Finally, the communal Sikh prayer *Ardās*, the collective recitation of which concludes almost all Sikh worship, captures both the notions of humility in giving and of concern for others, describing the congregation's gifts to the Guru as *til phul* ('this little offering') and concluding with a humanitarian appeal for *sarbat dā bhalā* ('welfare of all').

Historical Exemplars: Personifying the Sikh Ethic of Giving and Serving

In addition to these textual sources, Sikh discourse on the lives of the Gurus and other exemplary historical figures emphasizes their acts of charity and service. Thus, in the *janam-sākhīs*, the popular accounts of the lives of the Gurus, there is a story of Guru Nanak providing service by giving water to thirsty people in Delhi. A gurdwara, Nanak *Pio*, commemorates the spot where this service is said to have been undertaken. Similarly, Amar Das's service as a water-carrier to Guru Angad is said to have been a sign to the Guru that Amar Das should succeed him. And, of course, the establishment of *gurū kā langar* (the communal kitchen and dining hall), dating from at least the time of Guru Amar Das, is seen as institutionalizing charity and service within the Sikh tradition.

One of the most inspirational of Sikh historical figures is Bhai Ghahnaiya (also spelled Ghaniya or Kanhaiya) who was recognized by Guru Gobind Singh for the radical humanitarian act of serving water to the injured enemy, as well as to his own compatriots, during the battle of Anandpur. He was the inspiration for the *sevā-panthī* sect and, more recently, for various Bhai Ghahnaiya societies dedicated to social welfare. In modern times, Bhagat Puran Singh, founder of the All India

Pingalwara Charitable Society, is recognized as a *sevādār* of first class for his service to the sick and destitute in Lahore and Amritsar, before and after partition.

Giving to the Guru: Socializing the Gift

As suggested above, the Sikh ethical imperative for giving *dān* and performing *sevā* is that the charity and service be done 'selflessly' (*nishkām*). And giving money, goods, or service to the Guru via the gurdwara (literally, 'door to the Guru') so that the Panth might collectively undertake charitable and humanitarian projects has long been the way that Sikhs have socialized their giving (that is, made it socially meritorious) in Punjab. Indeed, in one of the few works devoted specifically to philanthropy among Sikhs, J.P. Singh goes so far as to claim that 'all philanthropy among Sikh [*sic*] is carried out in the name of the Gurus' (2001, p. 60) and 'the key institution for providing philanthropic help is the Gurudwara' (2001, p. 62). And Taran Singh, in his entry on '*Dān*' for *The Encyclopaedia of Sikhism*, claims that 'in the Sikh tradition, all *dān* or offering is in the name of the Guru and, usually, through *golak* (treasure, or receptacle kept in the gurdwara for the devotees, offerings) of the Guru or the Panth representing the Guru' (1992, p. 503). Thus ideally, the Guru Panth collectively, rather than named individuals, provides for and serves others (for example, through the institution of *gurū kā laṅgar* or by the establishment of schools, dispensaries, or other facilities attached to gurdwaras).

J.S. Neki, in his entry on '*Sevā*' for the *Encyclopaedia of Sikhism*, explains the Sikh rationale as follows :

> *Sevā* through material means (*dhan*) or philanthropy (*dān*) was particularly sought to be made non-personal. The offerings (*kār bheṭā*) made to the Gurus and the *dasvandh* (tithe) contributed by the Sikhs went straight into the common coffers of the community. Personal philanthropy can be debasing for the receiver and ego-entrenching for the giver, but self-effacing community service is ennobling (1998, p. 85).

This Sikh tradition of socializing one's charity by giving to the Guru (via *golak* at the gurdwara) and of the role of the 'gurdwara as pivot' in providing social services (Singh 2001, p. 16) continues to be important. Recent surveys of charity in Punjab villages suggest that over half of the total funds contributed by NRIs have gone to religious places; and, beyond the family, the gurdwara is usually the first institution of the village to benefit from remittances from Sikh villagers living abroad.[15] Even among Sikhs of the diaspora, therefore, there has been a historical tendency to socialize one's charity by giving to the Guru via the gurdwara in the expectation that the Panth will see to its wise use.

However, for some diasporan Sikhs, the humanitarian injunction to give to the needy and the ethical imperative to provide service to others have been generalized beyond the gurdwara so as to allow for the possibility of private philanthropy. Thus, in recent years, one sees an increasing number of projects initiated 'funded' and run by individuals or groups of individuals directly rather than through the village gurdwara, a sant's *ḍerā* (religious commune), or an organization such as the SGPC. However, such undertakings run the risk of being seen as self-interested or ego-inflating by others. Hence, even private philanthropy is often undertaken in the name of one of the Gurus, with religious elements incorporated in the philanthropic act.[16] We will return to this tension over the appropriateness of private philanthropy and the presumed intentions of philanthropists below.

PUNJABI CULTURAL UNDERSTANDINGS AND SOCIAL EXPECTATIONS

Sikh religious teachings and practices regarding *dān* and *sevā* are a part of the moral and ethical discourses that diasporan Sikh philanthropists are likely to have encountered through family socialization and their participation in the *saṅgat* (congregation at the gurdwara), both in Punjab and abroad. But, to the extent that they are Punjabis, one can suggest other, sometimes countervailing, cultural discourses that might motivate their social action.

Sikhi vs Sardari

Insofar as Jats are the dominant caste among Sikhs, especially in the villages of rural Punjab, village life in rural Punjab and among Punjabi villagers abroad is influenced not only by Sikh religious teachings about egoless giving and selfless service (aspects of *Sikhī*) but also by Jat notions of *izzat* (honour) and *sardārī* (supremacy of self).[17]

Sardārī is ultimately tied to the ongoing contest of domination–subordination through which honour and prestige are gained or lost in Jat Sikh society. Historically, one of the main goals of Jat Sikh social life has been to gain recognition as a *sardār* (literally, 'chieftan'), a person of honour, one who stands out in the crowd. This ideal of the public recognition of one's independence from and dominion over others is captured in various Punjabi folk sayings commonly attributed to Jats: 'Men may come and men may go, but I go on forever', 'Where I am, no one else is'; or, as we saw written on the back of an oversized sports utility vehicle careening aggressively past us on the GT Road, 'All eyes on me'.

Giving and receiving are two means by which status or reputation is judged. In Punjabi culture, the giver stands in a position of dominance with respect to the receiver. For example, within the traditional village context, the *sardār* (the Jat patron) gained prestige and enhanced his reputation as a 'nobleman', to use Joyce Pettigrew's (1975) term, through his largesse to his (largely non-Jat) clients and his success in competitive display with other Jats. For a Jat, having to ask for charity or to accept a gift from another continues to be an act that lowers one.[18] And Jats have commonly gone out of their way to keep face by avoiding situations in which they become dependent upon another Jat. To do so would be a threat to one's sense of *sardārī* and a risk to one's *izzat*. But, in the competition for honour among Jats, to put another into a position of subordination serves to raise one's prestige.[19]

The *sardār* thus seeks independence by avoiding being put in the debt of others, but he gains honour and enhances prestige by dispensing patronage to others. As Pettigrew puts it: 'To give, to have the ability to offer, is an indication of superiority; the giver is the powerful man and those who accept are inferior and not his equals. A man will secretly nurse a grudge that he has had to accept anything from another ....' (Chaudhri [Pettigrew] 1971, p. 42). Competitive gifting is, therefore, one way in which the contest of honour among Jats is played out.[20]

To be in a position to dispense patronage is, thus, to be able to demonstrate *sardārī* and to enhance *izzat*. Maharaja Ranjit Singh, whose reign in Punjab from 1799–1839 is regarded as something of a 'golden age' by Sikhs, exemplified the notion of the political leadership and reputation built upon dominion over others sustained in large measure through generous acts of personal and public patronage.[21] As Pettigrew notes in general of political leadership among Jat Sikhs : 'A leader's power depends on those who have given it to him. His power has legitimacy so long as he receives their continued support. This he does receive so long as he uses his own resources and those of the political system to bestow benefits' (Pettigrew 1975, pp. 45–6). Patronage is thus a crucial element of leadership and a source of status in Punjab.

If patronage has traditionally been a crucial means through which a Jat Sikh gains power and status, then it is not surprising that philanthropy might be interpreted as a form of patronage, a display of power, and a source of prestige. As Pettigrew notes of the value system: 'Power consists in bestowing benefits and can only be sustained by so doing. Thereby prominence is gained and prominence is a value to which honour is attached. The honourable man shares his power and his resources and this results in the egalitarianism upheld by the Jats as a value" (Chaudhri [Pettigrew] 1971, p. 61). The philanthropist, as one who shares his power and his resources, is thus well-positioned to enhance honour and prestige; and, so as not be to eclipsed, other families with whom he is competing for honour are likely to attempt either to undermine his projects or to outdo him with their own, since 'it is particularly a matter of prestige and pride for a family not to let other families to rise above it economically and to outdo its achievements in any sphere' (Chaudhri [Pettigrew] 1971, p. 66).[22]

In short, philanthropy, as a form of giving, is potentially implicated in contests of honour characteristic of Jat Sikh social life. Through one's ability to engage in personal philanthropy, one demonstrates *sardārī* and gains or enhances *izzat*. It is in this cultural context that we need to understand the observation made by J.S. Neki that '(p)ersonal philanthropy can be debasing for the receiver and ego-entrenching for the giver' (1998, p. 85).

But do those who have lived and worked abroad continue to be influenced by such considerations ? Research in the diaspora (see, for example, Chaudhri [Pettigrew] 1971, Helweg 1986, Dusenbery 1990, Nayar 2004) suggests that *izzat* remains an important consideration for many Punjabis, even into the second and subsequent generations. To the extent that Punjabi social networks are now transnational, both Punjab and the diaspora become settings where reputations can be made or broken. But to ensure one's reputation back in Punjab, the diasporic subject must demonstrate and display one's status there as well.

From 'Conspicuous Consumption' to 'Conspicuous Philanthropy' ?

Pnina Werbner quotes a Punjabi diasporic proverb, 'If peacocks dance in the jungle, who can see them?' She notes that,

> For diasporans, achievements of wealth and status are hollow unless they can display them before an audience living elsewhere, at home, in the cultured

heartland of their imagined collectivity... This means, in effect, that diasporans must constantly confront their invisibility through active acts of mobilization and hospitality, and through public demonstrations of generosity which reach out beyond their locally constituted territorial communities (2002, p. 10).

And generous philanthropic work in Punjab becomes one means of erasing invisibility and displaying one's status. Bruce La Brack, in an important early work on remittances from diasporan Sikhs, makes the following observation: 'Since a remittance is usually viewed as primarily an economic activity, the practical use of remittances tend to overshadow other latent or not-so-latent social functions. My own fieldwork contains examples of remittances being employed to enhance status, *gain philanthropic prestige*, maintain *izzat* or honor ...' (1989, p. 263; emphasis added). And, later in the same article, enumerating the different types of remittances that his Sikh informants in northern California sent back to Punjab, he notes: 'The third type [of remittance] might be called "local philanthropy". Generally, such remittances were funds given in the name of the donor for local Sikh projects or causes that would not benefit the lineage or any individual directly in any financial sense. Rather such transfers would enhance family *izzat* or honor' (1989, p. 270). Finally, La Brack notes that the wealthy Sikhs of the diaspora have become what he calls 'the new patrons', able to gain status and prestige through 'conspicuous consumption, philanthropy, sponsorship of religious ceremonies, and a wide spectrum of activities formerly only available to the more affluent in India' (1989, p. 277).

While leading Jat Sikh families have been the traditional contestants in the 'battle for honour' in Punjab state and village politics, one of the effects of international migration has been a change in the economic resources available to other castes. Thus non-Jats are now in a position to improve their status through some of the same cultural means long available to the landowning Jats, even, putting themselves in direct status competition with the latter.[23] Initially this was via 'conspicuous consumption' (fancy houses, expensive marriages, new consumer goods); increasingly, it has also come to include 'conspicuous philanthropy' as well.[24]

La Brack's 'new patrons', have gained further prominence in the years since he originally wrote his article. We were told during our research, 'NRIs are the new VVIPs'.[25] As villagers explained, when an NRI from the village shows up to announce a project, they have reason to believe that the project might actually come to fruition; whereas, when a government official shows up to announce a grant or a project, there is great scepticism about whether the village will ever see the goods. As the state (whether in the guise of the Government of Punjab or the Government of India) has proven an unreliable patron (especially in the provision of education, health care, infrastructure, and basic social services), NRIs have stepped in to fill the breach. Since patronage has been a traditional means of gaining prestige in Punjabi society, the new patrons from among the NRIs gain a reputation but also make themselves a mark for other parties whose prestige they might eclipse. Thus, even if their intentions are purely humanitarian, it is easy to understand that others might try to undercut them by accusing them of being ego-driven (*shoharāt*) or possessing excessive pride (*ahankār*).

Indeed, the claim that NRI philanthropy in Punjab is a matter of ego-satisfaction gains prima facie credence from the way in which donations are regularly made public knowledge in Punjab, as a means of recognizing and honouring donors. Those who give, advertise it unabashedly, with the donor's name and the amount given prominently featured in plaques on buildings or in news reports in local newspapers. Private philanthropy may be philanthropy undertaken by private individuals but it is commonly done in a very public way.[26] Culturally, the public display of one's generosity not only honours the donor but also serves as a potential spur to the donor's family, friends, and allies to contribute generously to the cause. At the same time it is also a potential spur to one's status competitors, who may feel compelled to defend their honour by undertaking an even grander scheme.

Long ago, Thorstein Veblen, in his famous study of the new 'leisure class' who had gained wealth in the transition from pre-industrial to industrial society in nineteenth century America, made some comments that appear germane to the move from 'conspicuous consumption' to 'conspicuous philanthropy' on the part of diasporan Sikhs in Punjab. The leisure class's 'exemption from pecuniary stress', having initially fuelled 'conspicuous consumption' and 'invidious comparison', eventually led some to move beyond 'pecuniary standing' and to engage in 'non-predatory pursuits'. According to Veblen:

> The tendency to some other than an invidious purpose in life has worked out in a multitude of organizations, the purpose of which is some work of charity or social amelioration. These organizations are often of a quasi-religious or pseudo-religious purpose, and are participated in by both men and women (2005[1899], p. 255).

However, Veblen goes on to note:

It is of course not intended to say that these efforts proceed entirely from other motives than those of a self-regarding kind.... It is a matter of sufficient notoriety to have become a commonplace jest that extraneous motives are commonly present among the incentives to this class of work—motives of a self-regarding kind, and especially the motive of an invidious distinction. To such extent is this true, that many ostensible works of disinterested public spirit are no doubt initiated and carried on with a view primarily to enhance repute, or even to the pecuniary gain, of their promoters (2005[1899], p. 256).

It would be naïve on our part—and would do injustice to the assessments of many Punjabi villagers to deny that, in the context of status competition among Punjabis, concerns for individual and collective reputation may contribute to diasporan Sikh's philanthropic activities in Punjab.

EXPERIENCES OF WESTERN MODERNITIES

Of course, diasporan Sikhs are influenced not only by Punjabi cultural understandings and social practices but also by the cultural understandings and social practices of the respective countries to which they emigrated. Given their international migration patterns, the majority of Sikh emigrants have experienced some form of western modernity. Indeed, the vast majority of diasporan Sikhs currently live in the UK, Canada, or the United States. And Sikhs from western countries are the major source of funding for various philanthropic projects in Punjab.[27]

Part of the experience of western modernity was the carving out of the space of civil society, apart from the state and the market. During the industrial revolution, it was the religious associations and private voluntary organizations of civil society that took upon themselves, through acts of philanthropy, the collective projects that neither the market nor the state were seen as addressing. Alexis de Toqueville, the French observer of the new American nation, noted early on the propensity for civic participation and voluntary organizations in the new democracy.[28] And, in the United States, the so-called 'robber barons' of the late nineteenth and early twentieth centuries used the wealth they had accumulated in the market to create charitable trusts and philanthropic foundations through which to address perceived social needs of the population not otherwise being addressed by the government or the market.[29] Religious charities, whether Catholic, Protestant, or Jewish, also took it upon themselves to address perceived needs of the destitute and needy. In Canada and the UK, where the twentieth century state assumed greater responsibility for the social welfare of the population, the space and perceived need for private philanthropy was perhaps less. Nevertheless, traditions of private and religious-based charity work have developed in those countries as well.

Living in the West, Sikhs have encountered vibrant civil societies that include a strong tradition of both religiously-based and secular philanthropy. They know that their non-Sikh neighbours are likely to donate to various charities and to see giving as part of active civic participation. And they know that the state encourages its citizens to donate through tax concessions extended for charitable donations. Indeed, an implicit part of the social contract in these nation-states is that one should give back in some manner to society for the good fortune that one has achieved as a result of the economic and political system in place.

Of course, another aspect of modernity, has been its sense of progress and of bringing 'development' to those less developed. The sorts of charities founded in the late nineteenth and early twentieth centuries often took upon themselves the task not only of meeting the needs of the destitute but also of reforming the underclass. Thus the temperance movement and other 'missions of improvement' and 'moral uplift' were undertaken in the name of philanthropic work. To the extent that the philanthropists themselves were products of the successful upper and middle classes, the norms and values that they extolled were those of their own class—thus the focus on temperance, literacy, hygiene, etc. And this same attitude manifested itself in attitudes towards other 'traditional' cultures (such as the tribal and peasant societies of Africa, Asia, and Latin America), which were seen as also needing 'modernity' and 'development'. Thus domestic charity led to international charity work, often with an evangelical or reformist zeal.

When diasporan Sikhs experience the Western culture of giving, they are confronted with the question of how to accommodate Punjabi and local norms of giving and of socializing one's wealth. Giving generously to the local gurdwara is one option, consistent with both Punjabi and Western practices. After all, most charitable giving in the United States is to religious organizations, and Sikhs have traditionally socialized their giving by going through the gurdwara. One could give to local charities run by other religious groups or private voluntary organizations—the Red Cross, the Lions Club, etc.—to demonstrate that one is part of the local community. One could give to one of the new transnational Sikh religious charities—Khalsa Aid, United Sikh, etc.—that seek to put a Sikh face to humanitarian relief operations. One could fund and open one's own local charity to undertake philanthropic work on projects of concern in one's country of residence. Or one could fund philanthropic work back in Punjab, either individually or in collaboration with others.

Most diasporan Sikhs now involved in philanthropic projects in Punjab have actually undertaken some or all of the various forms of philanthropy suggested above. That is, they may have given to the local gurdwara in their country of residence, donated to Sikh and non-Sikh charities, and done some private philanthropic work abroad. In fact, many understand that it is important for Sikhs to be seen as contributing in their current countries of residence.[30] But they commonly come to believe that giving back to their natal village or to Punjab-based projects is the best use of their charitable funds and/or time because of perceived level of need, return on investment, accountability, and personal satisfaction. Thus the following explanations are advanced for the decision to focus one's philanthropic giving on Punjab: (a) the local gurdwara in the UK, Canada, or the US may not have the need and may not have evolved social mechanisms for spending the donations or using the service on wider humanitarian concerns; (b) non-Sikh charities in those countries have lots of potential donors and the local needs are not so pressing; (c) transnational Sikh charities are new and unproven and the donor has little contact with the beneficiaries; (d) the needs addressed by charities in the West are dwarfed by the current needs in Punjab, where one's funds go much further.

Of course, as suggested above, when one gives to a project in Punjab one is making a statement about how one envisions or imagines a 'modern' Punjab. In choosing to fund a sewage treatment facility, a hospital, a school, a library, or a sports tournament, the donor is making an assessment of what Punjab in general or the village in particular 'needs' to be the kind of place that the donor wants it to be or imagines that it should be. Although donors talked of consultation with villagers about local needs and priorities, it was clear that majority of the projects visited had a strong donor-input in their conceptualization and planning. Most donors had a sense that they were addressing what they saw as a facility or programme lacking in the local environment vis-à-vis what they had experienced living in the West. Thus, what these donors were bringing back from the diaspora to the village, along with the capital, goods, and persons responsible for the specific projects, were the accompanying ideas and images for a new, improved, rebuilt, 'modern' Punjab.[31]

DECIPHERING PHILANTHROPIC MOTIVES

How, then, are we to make sense of the various factors underpinning diasporan Sikh philanthropy in Punjab? Clearly the conditions for diasporan Sikh philanthropy in Punjab were created by a combination of opportunity and need. That is, on the opportunity side, the increasing wealth of the Sikh communities in the diaspora and the fact that many diasporan Sikhs had already taken care of their own extended families; the liberalization of the Indian economy and the outreach to NRIs for their capital and expertise; the possibility of tax deductions for charitable contributions in their countries of residence. On the needs side, the financial and political crises of the state in meeting basic human needs (health, education, infrastructure, social services) and the perceived failure of either the capitalist market or Sikh religious institutions in Punjab to step into the breach to effectively meet these needs.[32]

But if this set of factors has provided the opportunity and conditions for NRI philanthropy, what has motivated those individuals who have risen to the occasion? Here, one must acknowledge that individual motives may well be complex and mixed, including a combination of Sikh religiousity (*dān* and *sevā*) and of Punjabi competitive individualism (*izzat* and *sardari*); a combination of humanitarianism (helping 'the needy') and of nationalism (helping 'my people'); a combination of altruism ('meeting their needs') and of self-interest ('making the village liveable so my kids will visit'); a combination of the impersonal ('welfare of humankind') and the personal ('seeing to my village'). Rarely has it been possible to identify a single motivating or sustaining factor at work.

Religious teachings and practices were, for some philanthropists we interviewed, a quite explicit motivating factor. Even those highly critical of Sikh religious authorities in Punjab and of the projects undertaken by the SGPC or by various Sikh *sants* and *bābās* commonly brought up aspects of their own religious philosophy to explain their involvement in philanthropy and/or they included religious symbols prominently in their projects. On the other hand, presumably out of concern that they should not be seen as ego-driven, most philanthropists were less willing to acknowledge that they had undertaken a project for reasons of enhancing *izzat*. Yet it was hard not to see many of these same people as involved in competition with others and doing little to downplay their own philanthropic accomplishments. In fact, the grounds of philanthropic competition in Punjab seem to be ever evolving—from gurdwaras and village gates to *kabaḍḍī* tournaments and eye clinics to rural hospitals and colleges to entire village infrastructure projects. Some acknowledged the influence of experiences in the West both on their development of a philanthropic ethic and on their choice of particular philanthropic undertakings. Others claimed that their experiences in the West had little influence, yet their own choices of projects to initiate or to fund often suggested that their experiences abroad had affected their social *imaginaries*.

We must conclude, therefore, both that mixed motives and mixed agendas characterize contemporary diasporan Sikh philanthropy in Punjab and that, at times, the motivations and intentions of philanthropists have themselves been points of contention and contestation.

CONSEQUENCES, INTENDED AND UNINTENDED

Finally, we must ask a series of questions about the consequences of all this recent NRI philanthropy in Punjab.

If, as suggested above, there is an element of competition for prestige underpinning the conspicuous philanthropy visible today in Punjab, what has been the net effect? Several years ago, Roger Ballard had some useful insight into a similar dynamic as it has played out among Sikhs in Britain. His comments seem relevant to the current situation in Punjab:

> On the face of it, the establishment of rival gurdwaras within a few hundred yards of one another, the installation of taller and taller *nishan sahibs* (flagpoles), the construction of larger and larger *langar* halls, marriage halls, sports halls, car parks and so forth would seem to be a waste of scarce resources: pooled facilities would undoubtedly have resulted in superior outcomes because of economies of scale. But that is to miss the point. It is precisely because of their vigorous pursuit of internal rivalries that Sikhs everywhere have managed to build communal facilities which are the envy of other, less quarrelsome groups (1989, p. 232).

How many gurdwaras, *kabaḍḍī* tournaments, rural hospitals are needed in Punjab today? As philanthropists compete to fund them, these 'goods' proliferate with little apparent coordination or rationalization. As Ballard suggests, there appears to be a waste of resources and a lack of economies of scale. In fact, too many rural hospitals within the same area would seem to be a recipe for financial disaster. Is there a place for rationalization of giving, either coordinated by the state or by philanthropists themselves, that might maximize the effectiveness of giving without at the same time undermining the very vitality that competitive giving has produced?

Moreover, given the uneven patterns of international migration from Punjab, what is the effect of leaving so much social investment in the hands of NRI philanthropists? If diasporan Sikhs are giving primarily to their own villages, do the rich (that is, those areas and those social groups with more NRIs) get richer? The early evidence from the Mera Pind Initiative is that NRIs from Doaba have jumped at the opportunity to take advance of matching funds for village improvement projects. Will Majha and Malwa villages also benefit to the same extent? How will the government ensure equity across regions and social groups? And what responsibility does the government have, anyway, to meet basic needs for health, education, infrastructure, and social welfare rather than to expect private philanthropy and the market to accomplish the job?

If, as suggested above, much of the impetus for philanthropic projects in Punjab has been donor-initiated, what does that suggest about stakeholder buy-in and sustainability? Do the priorities of givers reflect villagers' perceived needs? What plans have been made by NRIs, villagers, or the state to sustain projects once initiated? To what extent does the ongoing operation depend on the continued vision, funding, and direction of paternalistic founder donors? How and when do local people take ownership and responsibility for the projects initiated in their name and for their presumed benefit?

And, finally, what kind of modernity is being constructed by way of diasporan Sikh philanthropy in Punjab? What do their own projects suggest about how the philanthropists envision Punjab? And how do those projects themselves transform Punjab in the image held by the philanthropists?

Clearly, diasporan Sikh philanthropists active in Punjab are working toward a transformation of aspects of the physical, socio-cultural, economic, and political environment of the state—something that they would most likely identify as 'progress' or 'development'. Those involved in village infrastructure projects see clean water, sewers, sewage treatment plants, street lights, crematoriums, parks, and public spaces as a means of ensuring health, hygiene, and safety. The continued interest in giving for clinics/hospitals and for schools/colleges, suggests that effective public health and universal education are two goals sought by many. Support for stadiums, sports tournaments, and sports academies are indicative of the hopes that many put on organized sports as character-building for young people. The continued support that philanthropists have given for female education and training suggests a desire to further empower Punjab's females in what is still a male-dominated society. In short, one can see in many of the projects that diasporan Sikh philanthropists have chosen to fund the kind of place that they would have a modern Punjab be—cleaner, healthier, better educated, more egalitarian, etc.

But, beyond this, one of the greatest effects that this dynamic NRI philanthropy is having is in itself creating a more vibrant civil society in Punjab—that is, creating space outside the government, market, or gurdwara for the operation of various non-governmental organizations (NGOs), private voluntary organizations (PVOs), non-profit organizations (NPOs), and philanthropic foundations (PFs) of the sort that they themselves have been creating.[33] And, insofar as these civil society organizations themselves come to model transparency, integrity, and collaborative decision-making in their operations—if, in short, through wisdom, they dispense charity, they can potentially have a demonstration effect spurring greater openness and accountability on the part of government, business, and religious institutions in the state.[34] If this were one outcome of their endeavours, I believe that most diasporan Sikh philanthropists we talked to would be ecstatic about the revolution they had wrought in Punjab.

NOTES

1. For consistency's sake and despite its limitations, all translations from the Ādi Granth (hereafter, AG) are taken from the Manmohan Singh (1969) translation, authorized by the Shiromani Gurdwara Parbandhak Committee (SGPC).
2. I am indebted to Satnam Chana, Media and Field Director, NRI Sabha Punjab, for sharing these survey results. The official distinction made between a Non-Resident Indian (NRI), a person living abroad who maintains Indian citizenship, and a Person of Indian Origin (PIO), a citizen of another country who traces ancestral roots to India, is elided in common usage such as that followed here, where 'NRI' covers both categories. The distinction is important, however, for reporting donations to Indian charities, since PIO donations are treated as 'foreign contributions'.
3. Ramesh Vinayak, 'Good fellas: Public-spirited expats are striving to improve the rural landscape of the state' in *Simply Punjabi*, 2(3), March 2006, pp. 4–8. The article highlights village development projects inspired by the Village Life Improvement Project (VLIP) initiated by Raghbir S. Bassi and by Gurdev S. Gill in Kharoudi village, Hoshiarpur district.
4. See *Report of the High Level Committee on the Indian Diaspora* (Government of India 2002). The CD 2.35 'Mera Pind Initiative' of the Government of Punjab seeks to identify 'integrated village development projects',

especially 'water management services and village infrastructure projects', that will be funded on a 50 : 50 match between the government and NRIs. As of January 2006, forty-three such projects (total cost: Rs 7,44,08,590) had been approved, the majority of the projects being located in villages in Nawanshahr and Hoshiarpur districts.

5. The focus here on religious and cultural factors is not meant to suggest that political and economic factors (for example, availability of tax concession for charitable gifts, ease of transfer of goods and capital, visa requirements, licensing and permit processes) do not also affect giving.
6. Darshan S.Tatla, Director of the Centre for Migration Studies at Lyallpur Khalsa College in Jalandhar, and I, as a Fulbright Senior Research Scholar affiliated to the Centre, jointly conducted the research in Punjab on which this paper is based. The paper draws upon our interviews with philanthropists and villagers and on our site visits to philanthropic projects in Punjab between August 2005 and May 2006, as well as on the previous research work that each of us has conducted with Sikhs living in the diaspora. I am indebted to Dr Tatla for his generosity and assistance with the paper and to a CIES Fulbright Fellowship for research support, and to W.H. MacLeod, LizCoville, and paticipants at the international workshop on 'Diasporan Sikh Philantrophy in Punjab' for helpful comments on earlier drafts of this essay.
7. There is no exact Punjabi equivalent of the English word 'philanthropy' (literally 'love of humanity'; commonly understood to entail 'private giving for public good'). We see elements of a philanthropic ethic in the distinctively Sikh understandings of *dān* and *sevā.*
8. In his *Historical Dictionary of Sikhism,* W.H. McLeod defines *dān* and *sevā* as follows: '*DAN*: Charity. A gift given to the poor. *Dān* is frequently enjoined in the Adi Granth' (2002, p. 66). *SEVA*: Service. This may be rendered to the Guru, either in money or kind or duties performed, or it may be directed to ordinary people ... (2002, p. 191).
9. In the *rahit-nama* popularly attributed to Bhai Nand Lal, his *Tanakhāh-nāmā,* the following exchange with the Guru is reported: 'Tell me', Nand Lal asked the Guru, 'what should a Sikh do and what should he avoid?' The Guru answered him: 'These are the deeds required of a Sikh, Nand Lal. Let him perform only those which reflect the threefold rule of the divine Name, charity and purity (*nām dān iśnān*)' (McLeod 1984, p 77).
10. Transliteration and translation are from W.H. McLeod's *The Chaupa Singh Rahit-nama* (1987, pp. 60, 151).
11. W.H. McLeod in his *Historical Dictionary of Sikhism,* defines *dasvandh* as follows:

    '*DASVANDH*: A tithe, the portion of one's income that is given for community service. Gifts to the gurdwara are an example, frequently donated before the Guru Granth Sahib upon entry and thence into the

Guru's *golak* (treasure chest). Its distinction from *dān* (charity) is not clear, some say that *dān* is included in *dasvandh* and some saying it is separate' (2002, p. 69). Authors of separate entries in the *Encyclopedia* of *Sikhism* disagree. On the one hand, Taran Singh, writing the entry on *dān* says: 'The second institutionalized channel for *dān* [beyond *gurū kā langar*] is *dasvandh* .... Contributions may be made at any recognized centre—the local *gurdwārā*, any historical shrine, an orphanage, school, charitable hospital, and the like' (1995, p. 503). On the other hand, Wazir Singh, writing the entry on *dasvandh* says: 'This is their religious obligation—a form of *sevā* or humble service ... to be distinguished from *dān* or charity' (1995, pp. 533–34). In practice *dasvandh* has not been fully institutionalized within the contemporary Panth.

12. The translation is from W.H. McLeod's *Sikhs of the Khalsa* (2003, p. 282). McLeod asserts that the *Tanakhāh-nāmā* certainly was not written by Nand Lal himself (2003, p. 15).
13. The *Sikh Rehit* [*sic*] *Maryada* ('The Sikh Code of Conduct'), published by the SGPC, says the following of *sevā*: '*Sevā* is a fundamental feature of Sikhism' (1950, p. 32). It proceeds to provide examples of *sevā* (sweeping the gurdwara, serving *langar*, cleaning shoes of worshippers). Note that McLeod's definition above (n. 8) includes service beyond the context of the gurdwara.
14. Verse indexes to the Adi Granth suggest that there are four times as many verses on *sevā* as on *dān*. See, for example, the search engine at *http://www.srigranth.org/*
15. See papers by Chana (2006), Kullar & Toor (2006), and Mann & Mann (2006) which suggest that over half of all funds donated by NRIs in villages they studied had gone towards religious places through the time of their respective studies; but, since their accounts lack a full temporal dimension, it is unclear that *current* giving follows the same proportions as does historic giving. Moreover, it is not always clear whether gifts to 'religious places' include gifts only for buildings themselves or gifts both for buildings and for the philanthropic activities run by gurdwara societies.
16. Indeed, if one takes an expansive view of *dān* and *sevā*, then one is doing one's religious duty whenever one gives to or serves others—or, as J.S. Neki puts it, 'service rendered to humanity (that is, God in man) is indeed considered a form of worship' (1998, p. 84). But channelling such charity and service through the Guru Panth seems to have heretofore been the socially sanctioned means of delivery.
17. Birinder Pal Singh sees a conflict between the social egalitarianism of Sikh teachings and practices and the attempt to establish *sardārī* (supremacy) of oneself within with the contest of domination–subordination characteristic of Jat society. He argues that 'this conflict of values is manifest in all movements and institutions dominated by the Jutt Sikhs' (2002, p. 208). Joyce Pettigrew, however, sees the 'principle

of equality' and 'the value of honour' as self-reinforcing such that '(t)he opposition and competition between families that ensues [as each struggles to defend its honour] thus brings about in reality the equality that people ascribe to' (1975, p. 46).

18. This disapprobation of accepting gifts from others, plus the religious injunction to live by one's own honest labour, is said to account for why one sees so few Sikhs begging or living on charity.
19. *Izzat* accrues to collectivities (for example, family, lineage, *birādarī, bhāī chārā, got, zāt,* faction, village, *ilāqā*), not just to individuals. An individual who becomes a person of honour brings prestige to the collectivities of which he is a part. Conversely, one can bring disrespect to the collective by engaging in dishonourable activities. Thus, philanthropy must be looked at not only in individualistic terms, since decisions about undertaking and supporting projects may be collectively motivated in the interest of the repuration of the collectivity.
20. As Pettigrew notes: 'Giving was an attempt to bring a man of another family into one's debt, and acceptance of the gift involved the recipient in making a return, not necessarily in kind or immediately, but at a moment appropriate to the donor' (1975, p. 58).
21. It was Maharaja Ranjit Singh, for instance, who was responsible for donating and for seeing to the installation of the original gold gilding of Harimander Sahib, or the 'Golden Temple'.
22. The gendered nature of the discussion here is telling. A *sardār* is a male. (The female is *sardārnī*.) And it has been males that have traditionally been the public competitors in the battle for honour. This may explain why most of the philanthropists we encountered were male, even when females were contributors to the project. But cf. Purewal (2006) on the emergence of female philanthropists in the diaspora.
23. See, for example, Archana B. Verma's *The Making of Little Punjab in Canada* (2002) for the ways in which Mahtons from Paldi village, Hoshiarpur district, used remittances from successful *birādarī* members in Canada in the early 20th century to enhance their local status vis-à-vis Jats. In the early 21st century, Ravidasis, the major Dalit group in Doaba, have launched an impressive array of high-profile philanthropic projects, including the construction of what purports to be the largest *Diwan* (public meeting hall) in Punjab at Ballan village, Jalandhar district.
24. When one looks at the use of remittances in Punjab villages, there seems to be a definite evolution from contributing toward the family's reputation through conspicuous consumption to conspicuous philanthropy. Having built the fancy house back in the natal village and settled one's children, the returning NRI can afford to think in terms of broader concerns and contexts.
25. In India, there is a hierarchy of officialdom, with appropriate symbols of rank, running from 'very, very important person' (VVIP) through 'very important person' (VIP) to 'important person' (IP).

26. It is interesting and instructive to note that making public the amount of individual donations extends even to gurdwaras, where plaques honouring donors are prominently featured and where, at the conclusion of *Ardās*, the names and amounts contributed to guru kalaṇgar or to other gurdwara-sponsored activities are commonly read out. Cf. J.S. Neki quote above.
27. Tatla (2006) and Barrier (1989) analyse the significant early giving by Sikhs from the Far East and East Africa, two sites of early Punjabi settlement. But many African Sikhs have subsequently resettled elsewhere; and many Southeast Asian Sikhs have either moved on or have become less connected to their villages. Sikhs in the UK, Canada, USA, and Australia, in particular, seem to have both sufficient resources to make donations and ongoing or revitalized ties to Punjab such that they would want to stay connected though their philanthropy.
28. See Alexis de Toqueville, *Democracy in America* (1840), especially Vol. II, Sect. II–VI.
29. The Carnegie, Mellon, Rockefeller, and Ford Foundations all are products of the socialization of the wealth of this early generation of American capitalists. Different foundations have focused on different kinds of philanthropic projects (for example, Carnegie is associated with the building of libraries across America). Today's successful American capitalists (for example, Bill Gates, John D. MacArthur, William Hewlett) continue the tradition of using their wealth to endow philanthropic organizations that focus on addressing different kinds of social issues. At the same time, smaller charitable organizations exist at the grassroots. These tend to survive on direct appeals to individual donors or through joint appeals coordinated through the annual United Way fund drive.
30. Especially after 11 September 2001, Sikhs in the West have come to believe that greater visibility in civil society through undertaking and publicizing local Sikh philanthropy might shield them from the kind of anti-Muslim backlash provoked by terrorist attacks on Western targets—that is, that local philanthropic undertakings in the West might garner positive recognition of Sikhs as a distinctive, non-Muslim, part of the local multicultural civil society.
31. A major implication of Arjun Appadurai's pathbreaking work on the cultural dimensions of globalization is that we see transnational flows of capital, goods/technologies, people, ideas, and images as both having material effects and opening up new 'social *imaginaires*' (that is, conceptual resources for imagining alternative ways of being in the world). The title of Appadurai's collection of essays, *Modernity at Large* (1996), suggests that ideas of modernity itself may be deterritorialized and reterritorialized as a consequence of these global flows.
32. See the gloomy report on Punjab finances and human development by the World Bank (2004).

33. It is worth noting that, as per information available from Charities Aid Foundation-India (*http://www.cafonline.org/cafindia/i_search.cfm,* March 2006), and from the Government of India's Ministry of Home Affairs, Foreigners Division (*http://mha.nic.in/fcra.htm*, March 2006,), Punjab currently has relatively few registered NGOs and charitable organizations compared to other states of India. See also the statistics provided in Kapur, Mehta, and Dutt (2004, pp. 185, 187) and in Thandi (2006).
34. See Walton-Roberts (2006) for an analysis of the ways in which ongoing influences from the diaspora have affected the operational practices of one high-profile philanthropic project in Punjab—the Guru Nanak Medical Mission and Educational Trust—at Dhahan-Kaleran, Nawanshahr district.

REFERENCES

Appadurai, Arjun, 1996, *Modernity at Large: The Cultural Dimensions of Globalization*, Minneapolis: University of Minnesota Press.

Ballard, Roger, 1989, 'Differentiation and Disjunction Amongst the Sikhs in Britain' in N. Gerald Barrier and Verne A. Dusenbery, (eds), *The Sikh Diaspora: Migration and the Experience Beyond Punjab*, Delhi: Chanakya Publications and Columbia, Missouri: South Asia Publications, pp. 200–34.

Barrier, N. Gerald, 1989, 'Sikh Emigrants and their Homeland: The Transmission of Information, Resources and Values in the Early Twentieth Century' in N. Gerald Barrier and Verne A. Dusenbery, (eds), *The Sikh Diaspora: Migration and the Experience Beyond Punjab*, Delhi Chanakya Publications and Columbia, Missouri: South Asia Publications, pp. 44–89.

Chana, Satnam, 2006, 'NRI Investment in Social Development Projects in Punjab', Paper for international workshop on Diasporan Sikh Philanthropy in Punjab, Lyallpur Khalsa College, Jalandhar.

Chaudhri [Pettigrew], Joyce J. M., 1971, *The Emigration of Sikh Jats from the Punjab to England*, unpublished final report, SSRC [UK] Project HR 331/1.

Dusenbery, Verne A., 1990b, 'On the Moral Sensitivities of Sikhs in North America' in Owen M. Lynch, (ed.), *Divine Passions: The Social Construction of Emotion in India*, Berkeley: University of California Press and New Delhi: Oxford University Press, pp. 239–61.

Government of India, 2002, *Report of the High Level Committee on the Indian Diaspora*, New Delhi: Non Resident Indians & Persons of Indian Origin Division, Ministry of External Affairs. [*http://indiandiaspora.nic.in/diasporapdf/chapter34.pdf*]

Helweg, Arthur W., 1986, *Sikhs in England: The Development of a Migrant Community,* rev. edn, New Delhi: Oxford University Press.

Kapur, Devesh, Ajay S. Mehta, and R. Moon Dutt, 2004, 'Indian Diaspora Philanthropy' in P. Geithner, P.D. Johnson, and L.C. Chin, (eds), *Diaspora Philanthropy and Equitable Development in China and India*, Cambridge: Harvard University Press, pp. 177–213.

Kullar, Inderpreet Kaur and M.S. Toor, 2006, 'The Socio-Economic Impact of Foreign Remittances on Central Punjab Farmers', Paper for international workshop on Diasporan Sikh Philanthropy in Punjab, Lyallpur Khalsa College, Jalandhar.

LaBrack, Bruce, 1989, 'The New Patrons: Sikhs Overseas' in N. Gerald Barrier and Verne A. Dusenbery, (eds), *The Sikh Diaspora: Migration and the Experience Beyond Punjab*, Delhi: Chanakya Publications and Columbia, Missouri: South Asia Publications, pp. 261–304

Maan, Charanjit Kaur and Gurmej Singh Maan, 2006, 'Empowering Shankar: A Case Study of Diaspora Sikh Sponsored Projects in a Doaba Village', Paper for international workshop on Diasporan Sikh Philanthropy in Punjab, Lyallpur Khalsa College, Jalandhar.

McLeod, W.H., 2003, *Sikhs of the Khalsa: A History of the Khalsa Rahit*, New Delhi: Oxford University Press.

———, 2002, *Historical Dictionary of Sikhism*, New Delhi: Oxford University Press.

———trans., 1987, (and ed.), *The Chaupa Singh Rahit-nama*, Dunedin: University of Otago Press.

———, 1984, *Textual Sources for the Study of Sikhism*, Manchester: Manchester University Press.

Nayar, Kamala E., 2004, *The Sikh Diaspora in Vancouver: Three Generations amid Tradition, Modernity, and Multiculturalism*, Toronto: University of Toronto Press.

Neki, Jaswant Singh, 1998, 'SEVĀ' in Harbans Singh, editor-in-chief, *Encyclopaedia of Sikhism*, vol. IV, Patiala: Punjabi University Press, pp. 84–5.

Pettigrew, Joyce J.M., 1975, *Robber Noblemen: A Study of the Political System of the Sikh Jats,* London and Boston: Routledge & Kegan Paul.

Purewal, Navtej K., 2006, 'Gender, Seva and Social Institutions: A Case Study of Bebe Nanaki Gurdwara and Charitable Trust, Birmingham, UK.' Paper for international workshop on Diasporan Sikh Philanthropy in Punjab, Lyallpur Khalsa College, Jalandhar.

Shiromani Gurdwara Parbandhak Committee, 1950, *Sikh Rehat Maryada: The Sikh Code of Conduct*, English (trans.), Amritsar: SGPC.

Singh, Birinder Pal, 2002, *Violence as Political Discourse: Sikh Militancy Confronts the Indian State*, Simla: Indian Institute of Advanced Study.

Singh, J.P., 2001, *Sikh Philanthropy in Ahmedabad*, Ahmedabad: Indian Institute of Management.

Singh, Manmohan, (trans.), 1969, *Srī Gurū Granth Sāhib*, 8 vols, Amritsar: SGPC.

Singh, Taran, 1995, '*DĀN*' in Harbans Singh, editor-in-chief, *Encyclopaedia of Sikhism*, Patiala: Punjabi University Press, pp. 502–4.

Singh, Wazir, 1995, 'Dasvandh' in Harbans Singh, editor-in-chief, *Encyclopaedia of Sikhism*, Patiala: Punjabi University Press, pp. 533–34.

Tatla, Darshan S., 2006, 'Diaspora Sikh Philanthropy in Punjab: Origins, Growth and Contemporary Trends', Paper for international workshop on Diasporan Sikh Philanthropy in Punjab, Lyallpur Khalsa College, Jalandhar.

Thandi, Shinder S., 2006, 'Diasporas and Development: Can Diasporan Philanthropy Deliver Human Development in Punjab?' Paper for international workshop on Diasporan Sikh Philanthropy in Punjab, Lyallpur Khalsa College, Jalandhar.

Toqueville, Alexis de, 1840, *Democracy in America,* II, Henry Reeves, (trans.), *http://www.gutenberg.org/etext/816.*

Veblen, Thorstein, 2005[1899], *The Theory of the Leisure Class: An Economic Study of Institutions*, Delhi: Aakar Books.

Verma, Archana B., 2002, *The Making of Little Punjab in Canada: Patterns of Immigration*, New Delhi: Sage Publications.

Vinayak, Ramesh, 2006, 'Good fellas: Public-spirited Expats are Striving to Improve the Rural Landscape of the State', *Simply Punjabi*, 2(3), March, pp. 4–8.

Walton-Roberts, Margaret, 2006, 'The Role of 'Vision', Transformation and Sustainability in NRI Healthcare Philanthropy', Paper for international workshop on Diasporan Sikh Philanthropy in Punjab, Lyallpur Khalsa College, Jalandhar.

Werbner, Pnina, 2002, *Imagined Diasporas Among Manchester Muslims: The Public Performance of Pakistani Transnational Identity Politics*, Oxford: James Currey and Santa Fe: School of American Research.

World Bank, 2004, *Resuming Punjab's Prosperity: The Opportunities and Challenges Ahead*, Washington and New Delhi: The World Bank.

PART II

SIKHS AND THE STATE

7

Canadian Ideology and Public Policy*

The Impact on Vancouver Sikh Ethnic and Religious Adaptation

Vancouver's Sikh community is the oldest, most heterogeneous, and perhaps still the largest and most influential Sikh community in Canada.[1] For seventy-five years [1904–79], despite periods of relative isolation from the Indian subcontinent and alternately hostile and indifferent treatment from the wider Canadian society, the community has persisted. During the 1970s, the community has experienced considerable growth and internal diversification brought on, in part, by a tremendous upsurge in Sikh and non-Sikh 'East Indian' immigration from South Asia, Britain, East Africa, East, and Southeast Asia, Fiji, and the Caribbean;[2] the coming of age of a sizeable Canadian-born and raised generation of Punjabi Sikh immigrant offspring; and the emergence of an organized and vocal group of *gora* (white) Canadian and American Sikh converts.

Prior anthropological accounts (Smith 1944; Mayar 1959; Ames and Inglis 1973; Srivastava 1974; Chadney 1976, 1977a, b) seem to support James Chadney's assessment—at least through the time of Chadney's fieldwork in the early 1970s—that the Vancouver Sikh community was undergoing a process of 'ethnic adaptation', that is, 'accommodating the larger Canadian society by foregoing some aspects of traditional Punjabi culture' (Chadney 1977a: 5912–A). Nevertheless, these accounts suggest that this adaptation did not involve widespread behavioural, structural, or marital assimilation into white Canadian society. Rather, taking into account the often conflicting social and cultural pressures emanating

* First published in *Canadian Ethnic Studies*, vol. XIII, no. 3 (Winter 1981), pp. 101–19.

from the host and sending societies, these analyses stressed changes internal to a community which continued to differentiate itself from the wider Canadian society.

One area of adaptation little noticed in previous accounts has been that of institutional adaptation.[3] For most of the community's seventy-five years, the original gurdwara (temple) society fulfilled the traditional role of institutional centre for the various activities of the Sikh community. Increasingly, however, new institutions have arisen to take on significant responsibility for these activities. Thus, today, one finds active Sikh participation in a number of ethnic organizations with explicitly political, cultural, social, and social service objectives.[4] Gurdwaras, in the meantime, flourish, but with more narrowly religious concerns.

Demographic and social changes, in and of themselves, are not sufficient to account for the new institutional make-up of the community. Nor can factional and interpersonal disputes within the community be entirely responsible for the proliferation and diversification of institutions. Instead, I will argue, institutional developments within the community—and, especially, a differentiation of ethnic and religious identities, institutions, activities, and leaders—can best he understood as reflecting the increasing impact of Canadian ideology and public policy.[5]

'RELIGION' AND 'ETHNICITY' IN CANADIAN IDEOLOGY AND PUBLIC POLICY

As befits its New World ethos, religion in Canadian ideology is conceived in terms of notions of pluralism (that is, many religions and religious denominations co-exist harmoniously), voluntarism (that is, the individual is free to belong to and participate in the activities of the religious group of his or her choice), and freedom (that is, the state neither endorses one particular religion nor allows limitations to be placed on the individual's legitimate religious expression; and, at the same time, the state bestows certain special statuses on all recognized religious organizations). This Canadian ideology with respect to religion is reflected in Canadian governmental policies in the form of the legal protection of individuals' rights of religious affiliation and expression (for example, as set forth in the Canadian Bill of Rights (1960), the Canadian Human Rights Act (1978a), and the various provincial and municipal human rights statutes) and in such advantages as the tax-exempt status accorded the property of religious organizations when such property is used for religious purposes (for example, see the B[ritish] C[olumbia] Religious Institutions Act (1960) and the Vancouver Charter (Chpt. 55, Sec. 396(c)iv)).

The Canadian ideology with respect to ethnicity is reflected in the commonly-accepted image of Canadian society as a 'mosaic'—a pluralistic society in which, unlike the American 'melting pot', the constituent elements are discrete 'ethnocultural' groups which retain their unique ethnic identity and cultural integrity despite social interaction. The most explicit statement of this ideology in the area of public policy is, of course, in the federal policy of 'multiculturalism within a bilingual framework', first enunciated by the Liberal government in 1971 (Canada 1971). Here, the government does not simply guarantee certain human rights to individuals of all races, colours, ancestries, national origins, etc. (for these, see the Bill of Rights, the Human Rights Act, and the provincial and municipal human rights statutes), but takes positive steps to ensure the recognition and vitality of ethnocultural organizations and their activities.[6]

There is much to notice about the representation of religion and ethnicity in Canadian ideology beyond their common pluralism. While social scientific definitions of 'ethnicity' commonly list 'religion' as one of the bases of ethnic identity and solidarity (see, for example, Isajiw's (1974) review article), it appears that in Canadian ideology, religion and ethnicity are viewed as generally separable and potentially cross-cutting sources of social identity and social solidarity and relatively distinct generators of social norms. Furthermore, not only can religious and ethnic identities, groups, and norms be distinguished according to Canadian ideology, they can also be seen to contrast. Thus, whereas religious identity is viewed as essentially voluntary and individualistic (membership being achievable through the symbolic action of re-birth, confirmation, and conversion), ethnic identity—like the even more extreme racial identity—is viewed as essentially communal and non-volitional (membership being ascribed on the basis of common ties of origin and descent).[7] Furthermore, as a corollary of the preceding, whereas religious norms are seen as absolute and inviolable (generally involving faithful adherence to some 'code for conduct' enjoined on all believers and protected as 'religious rights'), ethnic norms are seen as relatively loose and non-specific (generally involving the retention of only a few 'cultural markers' sufficient to index one's membership in a particular ethnic category).[8] Finally, implicit in the ideology and crucial to its public-policy implementation is a separation of sacred and secular domains such that religious institutions (for example, churches, temples, mosques, and other 'houses of worship') which benefit from certain taxation and incorporation policies can be distinguished from the ethnic institutions (for example, ethnic-political, ethnic-cultural, ethnic-social, and ethnic-social service organizations) which are the intended beneficiaries of multiculturalism programmes and other forms of public funding.[9]

TRADITIONAL SIKH IDEOLOGY AND INSTITUTIONAL STRUCTURES

It would be a serious mistake to assume that traditional Sikh ideology corresponds to Canadian ideology with respect to the differentiation of religion and ethnicity.[10] Since Sikhism has heretofore been essentially a regional faith, the Sikh and Punjabi identities of its adherents have been largely conjoined. And even when Sikhs have settled abroad, their insularity—reflected in norms of endogamy and non-proselytization—has meant that they have gone virtually unchallenged in defining as they please the meaning of the term 'Sikh'. It is not surprising to find, therefore, that it is commonly asserted of and by Punjabi Sikhs that the Sikhs constitute a distinct religious-cum-social-cum-political-cum-cultural community and that it is either impossible, unwarranted, or ill-advised to attempt to delineate components of this unique Sikh identity. Chadney pinpoints this traditional Sikh ideology when he asserts:

> It is this constant blending of sacred and secular identities, goals, structures, and functions, which, at the emic level, helps explain the important continuance of Sikhism in Vancouver .... For it is not simply a religious identity, it is an identity of *Sikh* which is an identity incapable of being categorically isolated into disparate and separate sacred and secular identities (Chadney, 1976, p.195; emphasis in original).

Rich symbolic support for this ideological unity of the sacred and secular domains is to be found in Punjabi Sikh culture in the *miri/piri* and *degh/tegh/fateh* concepts. According to traditional Sikh hagiography, the sixth Sikh Guru (teacher), Hargobind, was invested with two swords at his installation as Guru, one representing spiritual power (*piri:* from the Persian word, *pir*, used to denote a religious teacher) and the other representing temporal power (*miri:* from another Islamically-introduced word, *amir*, meaning commander of the faithful). Besides encapsulating the long-standing Sikh notion of worldly involvement co-existing with spiritual enlightenment, the pairing of *miri* and *piri* reflects the ideal of

Sikh religious and socio-political unity and sovereignty. A more recent symbolic development, first popularized at the time of the ninth and tenth Gurus (that is, in the late seventeenth century), was the pairing of the terms *degh* (cooking pot) and *tegh* (sword) to emphasize that 'the use of arms is an extension of the giving of alms' (Cole and Sambhi 1978: 30) and their conjunction with *fateh* (victory) in reference to the temporal and spiritual victory of God and God's Khalsa Panth (the orthodox Sikh community).

Historically, one could enumerate numerous examples of the continued blending of what from the perspective of contemporary Western ideology would be distinguished as 'religious' and 'non-religious'. Institutionally, one can observe this in the jointly political and religious aspirations of the Sikh communal party, the Akali Dal, which has periodically agitated for a separate Sikh homeland and against incorporation into a secular Indian state; in the political as well as religious activities of the Shiromani Gurdwara Parbandhak Committee (the organization legally empowered to run the affairs of the historical gurdwaras in the Punjab); and in the often parallel leadership of these most dominant of Punjabi Sikh organizations.

However, the institutional framework wherein the difference in ideologies is best observed is in the scope and function of the Sikh gurdwara, the central Sikh institution at the local level. It is conventional in English to translate gurdwara (literally, 'the Guru's door') as 'temple'. This is unfortunate, since, as virtually every Sikh scholar has pointed out, Sikh gurdwaras traditionally have been—and in most cases continue to be—more than simply 'houses of worship', as religious buildings in the West are commonly considered. If we wish to apply our conventional Western understandings to an explanation of the traditional role of gurdwaras in Sikh social life, it would be more appropriate to speak of them as religious, social, political, cultural, and social service centres for the local community.[11]

INSTITUTIONAL DEVELOPMENTS WITHIN THE VANCOUVER SIKH COMMUNITY: 1907–47

Given this place of the gurdwara in Punjabi Sikh society, it is not surprising that a gurdwara was formed in Vancouver in 1908 following the arrival of some five thousand Sikh immigrants and that from the very beginning it served a multiplicity of apparently religious and non-religious purposes. In its early years, the Khalsa Diwan Society's gurdwara on West Second Avenue was truly a religious, social, political, cultural, and social service centre for the entire South Asian immigrant population of the lower mainland. In this building, regular readings from the Guru Granth Sahib (the collected Sikh Scriptures regarded as the reigning Sikh Guru) were conducted; the traditional *langar* (free kitchen) operated; and shelter was provided for the homeless. In addition, the gurdwara was a place where the overwhelmingly working-class, male population came together to socialize, discuss issues, air conflicts, and reach decisions affecting the community.[12] Gurdwaras subsequently built in other areas of Sikh settlement in British Columbia became legally affiliated branches of the Vancouver Khalsa Diwan Society. Thus, during this period, the Vancouver Khalsa Diwan Society could legitimately claim to speak on behalf of all the Sikhs—and thus the overwhelming majority of all South Asian immigrants—in British Columbia.

It was not inconsistent with Sikh ideology for a 'temple' organization such as the Khalsa Diwan Society (hereafter, KDS) to engage in political activities, and the KDS quickly took the lead in fighting against the exclusionary Canadian immigration policies and for the extension of full civil rights to all South Asian immigrants in British Columbia. Having played a central role in the community's rejection of a governmental proposal which would have seen South Asians relocated to British Honduras, the KDS found itself deeply involved in seeking redress of the community's many grievances against the British, Canadian, and British Columbian authorities. Causes championed by the KDS in the period from 1909 to 1947 included sending delegations to Ottawa and London to argue for the lifting of the 'Orders-in-Council' which effectively barred further immigration from the Indian subcontinent, supporting court challenges to the legality of Canadian immigration policies, offering material and legal support to the passengers and would-be immigrants of the ill-fated *Komagata Maru,* and assisting individual immigrants facing deportation orders. In addition, the KDS worked to bring about favourable decisions from Canadian officials which eventually allowed South Asian immigrants to sponsor for immigration their wives and dependent children and extended domiciliary rights to illegal immigrants who had been successfully established in the country for a certain period of time.[13] Finally, the KDS was the institutional voice for the community in its ultimately successful efforts to achieve the federal, provincial, and municipal franchise, an important victory which allowed South Asian Canadians in British Columbia not only the right to vote but also the right to enter certain professions (notably, law and medicine) otherwise closed to them.[14]

During the community's first decades in Canada, sporadic attempts had been made to found what could be regarded as separate ethnic-political organizations (see Lal 1976; Buchigniani 1979). For the most part, these organizations failed to attract sufficient support from the community to sustain their activities.[15] Political successes which could be claimed, most notably on the part of the United India League, had to be shared with the KDS. As Norman Buchigniani points out, the Sikhs did not lack in political organization during their first decades in Canada even if they did lack in explicitly ethnic-political organizations.[16] It was simply the case that so long as the South Asian immigrant population remained small, overwhelmingly Sikh, and relatively united (if only in respect to the perceived intransigence of government authorities), the KDS and its gurdwara were regarded by community members as the logical institutional centre for meeting the community's varied needs. And so long as the various levels of government regarded the KDS as speaking on behalf of South Asian Canadians, the KDS was able to sustain an active political role.

INSTITUTIONAL DEVELOPMENTS WITHIN THE VANCOUVER SIKH COMMUNITY: 1948–69

By 1947, the South Asian immigrant population in the lower mainland—still almost exclusively Sikh—had shrunk to little over one thousand persons. However, following changes in Canadian immigration and citizenship policies, the community slowly began to expand after decades of contraction and retrenchment. Ironically, the KDS, which had worked to bring about these changes, was itself significantly affected by them. An influx of newcomers helped stir up incipient factional conflict between what other anthropologists have termed the 'modernist' and 'traditionalist' segments of the Sikh community. In 1952, a dispute arose over requirements for election to the KDS executive committee, with the 'traditionalists' arguing unsuccessfully for the exclusion of clean-shaven and turbanless Sikhs from KDS leadership positions. Following their defeat, a group of 'traditionalists' broke with the KDS to found a second Vancouver gurdwara and a second society, the Akali Singh Sikh Society. Shortly thereafter, a parallel split occurred in Victoria, where a 'traditionalist' minority there broke away from the KDS gurdwara to form yet another independent gurdwara society. With the unity of the province's Sikh gurdwaras under the umbrella of the KDS now broken, the affiliated KDS gurdwaras themselves began to seek independence from the Vancouver KDS. And these developments, together with an increase in non-Sikh South Asian immigration, effectively undermined the credibility of the Vancouver KDS as the sole organization speaking to the wider Canadian society on behalf of the entire South Asian immigrant community.[17]

Out of this newly unsettled situation emerged what could be regarded as an ethnic-political organization—the East Indian Canadian Citizens' Welfare Association. Though dominated by the sizeable Sikh population and sharing some leadership with the KDS, this was an overtly non-religious organization, formally independent of any gurdwara. By setting its objectives as working for the benefit of the entire 'East Indian' population throughout the country, it implicitly accepted the Canadian view of social reality—which is, that there exists a distinct 'East Indian' ethno-cultural group sharing certain unique interests and activities. Thus it was at this juncture that the Welfare Association—as it came to be called by community members—began to take on some of the more political functions (for example, pressing the government for increased immigration quotas for India) previously undertaken by the KDS.[18]

During the 1950s and early 1960s, the community gradually grew in number on the strength of sponsored relatives, small quotas of independent immigrants, and Canadian-born offspring. For the most part, evidence from this period points to continuing accommodation to certain Canadian norms. While the influx of newcomers—and especially the practice of seeking spouses in India—served to counteract assimilative tendencies, the new immigrants generally deferred to the established immigrants—often their relatives and fellow villagers—for direction in adapting to Canadian customs. Thus, to give but one example, most male Sikhs took the job-hunting advice of earlier immigrants and were clean-shaven and turbanless upon or shortly after their arrival in Canada.

As the 1960s drew to a close and the KDS prepared to move into its impressive new gurdwara overlooking the Fraser river, leadership of the KDS and the Welfare Association was in the hands of those 'modernists' who largely counselled accommodation and who had themselves succeeded in Western terms.[19] With the community prospering, suffering little overt hostility, and anticipating more open immigration, the Welfare Association had become less politically active. Meanwhile, the gurdwaras, as the social centres for the Sikh community, were now more than ever functioning like Western-style 'houses of worship', opening their doors primarily for weddings, funerals, and Sunday services. However, certain events had been set in motion or were about to be set in motion, which in the course of the past decade have significantly changed the community makeup and altered both the organizational structures and leadership patterns.

INSTITUTIONAL DEVELOPMENTS WITHIN THE VANCOUVER SIKH COMMUNITY: 1970–80

First of all, changes in Canadian immigration policies in 1962 and especially in 1967 (and lasting until modified in 1973 and 1974) significantly liberalized regulations affecting the immigration of South Asians. Increased immigration and increases resulting from a significant excess of births over deaths within the Sikh community help explain the perhaps fourfold increase in the Sikh population of the lower mainland to current estimates of upwards of forty thousand persons. At the same time, the make-up of the 'East Indian' population as a whole (now including Ismailis, Pakistanis, Fijians, and others of South-Asian ancestry) has gone from overwhelmingly Sikh to a point where Sikhs represent only one-half to two-thirds of all 'East Indians' in the lower mainland. Furthermore, rapid growth and increasing diversity within the Sikh community itself (resulting from Sikh immigration not only from India but from Britain, East Africa, Fiji, and other Commonwealth countries) has meant some attenuation of the influence of the old family and village ties which had served to integrate new immigrants into the community, and which had served as power bases for certain community leaders. While such ties continue to be important generators of solidarity within the community, no one person's ties are by themselves sufficient to ensure power and position within the Sikh community. At the same time that diversification and internal growth in the Sikh community has worked against the continued dominance of the old Sikh leaders, similar factors conspire to challenge any assumption of continued Sikh dominance— either locally or nationally—within the collective 'East Indian' ethnic category.[20]

The 1970s has also seen the introduction of the federal multiculturalism programmes and the passage of human rights legislation at the federal and provincial levels. One effect of these policies has been to make clear that in the Canadian context 'East Indians' are seen as constituting a distinct ethnocultural group and that the Canadian government would prefer to deal with pan-'East Indian' ethnic organizations. At the same time, while Canadians generally remain insensitive to confessional and conventional differences among South Asians and persist in lumping all those of South Asian ancestry in a single category, the term 'Hindu' which was once applied indiscriminately—and largely inaccurately—to those of South Asian ancestry in Canada has for the most part been replaced by 'East Indian' as the common ethnic label.

While other Canadians may assume that 'East Indians' share common ethnocultural traits and common socio-political interests, Canadians of South-Asian ancestry are themselves aware of the increasing diversity of backgrounds and interests among those considered 'East Indians'. Thus it is not surprising that, as John Wood (1978) makes clear, 'East Indian' participation in the process leading to the new Immigration Act of 1976 was marked by disparate and often conflicting presentations. By the mid-1970s, there was no organization, either local or national, which could accurately be said to represent the interests of a united 'East Indian' community. In Vancouver, the Welfare Association was only sporadically active and had been stricken from the Provincial Register of Societies, the KDS was increasingly immobilized by internal struggles for control of the executive, and the Akali Singh Sikh Society continued its generally quietistic ways. The only organization presuming to represent the entire community was the soon discredited East Indian Defence Committee, a Maoist group (now affiliated with the Albanian-leaning Communist Party of Canada Marxist-Leninist (CPC-ML)) which had organized vigilante actions to defend 'East Indians' in Vancouver from physical and verbal harassment by whites.[21]

To fill this void in ethnic-political organizational solidarity exposed by the immigration policy review, an all-Canada 'East-Indian' umbrella organization was formed in 1975–6. Drawing its leadership and support largely from the Indo-Canadian elite (that is, the Western-educated, English-speaking professionals, bureaucrats, and business people) and, at the local level, from those with prior experience in dealing with Canadian governmental bureaucracy (for example, through private or government employment and/or leadership of the KDS or Welfare Association during their activist phases), the organization called itself the National Association of Canadians of Origins in India (NACOI) and set as its aims and objectives:

1. To encourage Canadians of origins in India to fully participate in Canadian Society;
2. To provide a national voice to Canadians of origins in India;
3. To provide a forum for exchange of ideas, issues and common concerns;

4. To facilitate communication within and with other organizations;
5. To assist in the orientation and adaptation of Canadians of origins in India to the Canadian milieu and bring about a better understanding of Canada and other Canadians;
7. To formulate guidelines for improving the collective image of Canadians of origins in India;
8. To assure due recognition of the contributions of Canadians of origins in India to Canada (NACOI 1977).

While at the local level, NACOI's British Columbia Chapter has been dominated by the Vancouver Sikh elite (and suffers, says its detractors, from elitism), it would be unwarranted to assume that the Sikh community in Vancouver has been united in accepting the wisdom or necessity of participation in a pan-'East Indian' ethnic-political organization. Given the traditional Sikh ideology of religious-cum ethnic distinctiveness, it is not surprising that there should be residual support for the position, most vocally enunciated by the local Shiromani Akali Dal of Canada, that Sikhs are a 'separate people' who should be known not as 'East Indians' or 'Canadian of origins in India' but as 'Canadian Sikhs' and whose political interests should be looked after by the gurdwara societies or other representatives of the Sikh Panth (community). In general, however, local Sikh participation in the 'establishment' ethnic-political organizations (for example, NACOI. the revived and revitalized East Indian Canadian Citizens' Welfare Association, and the fledgling Fraser Valley East Indian Canadian Welfare Association) as well as the 'leftist' alternatives (for example, the aforementioned East Indian Defence Committee, the rival Indian Peoples' Association of North America and the recently-founded East Indian Workers' Association) suggests a significant acceptance of the position that to compete for funds and recognition in the wider Canadian society it may be necessary to organize into what are at least in theory pan-'East Indian' ethnic-political organizations.[22]

As suggested earlier, the rise in ethnic-political organizations has gone hand-in-hand with a proliferation of ethnic institutions of various sorts. Thus, with the establishment of groups such as the Punjabi Cultural Association, the Punjabi Literary Association, and of independent Punjabi schools, one finds that ethnic-cultural activities are no longer the exclusive province of the gurdwaras. Likewise, groups like the India Club of Vancouver, the International Punjabi Society, the India Mahilla (Women's) Association, and various sporting clubs function as ethno-social organizations independent of the gurdwaras. Finally, ethnic-social services, once almost exclusively the institutional province of the gurdwaras, have now largely been taken over by governmental agencies or semi-governmental organizations like the Immigrant Services Centre or the local Neighborhood Houses which increasingly employ 'East Indians' to deliver services to largely 'East Indian' clients.[23]

One might suspect that this proliferation of ethnic organizations taking over what were once the multiple responsibilities of the gurdwaras might leave the gurdwaras themselves deserted and lifeless. This has not been the case. Gurdwaras continue to enjoy high attendance and tremendous material support from the Sikh community. Several new gurdwaras have been built, are being built, or are being planned in the lower mainland. Indeed, the past ten years have seen something of a religious revival within the Vancouver Sikh community. Calls for greater religious orthopraxy have resulted in increasing ritual elaboration in the established services as well as the reintroduction of Sikh ceremonies and gurdwara protocol which had nearly died out in Vancouver. The election for the 1979 term and subsequent re-election of an 'orthodox'-dominated executive committee of the KDS has been seen by many as a consolidation of 'orthodox' control over gurdwara affairs and a repudiation of lapses in religious orthopraxy perpetrated over the years in the interests of social accommodation.[24]

The present leadership of both the KDS and the Akali Singh Sikh Society appear to view their mandates primarily in terms of promoting a return to religious orthopraxy and not as necessitating political activism. Thus, they have concentrated their energies on maintaining the gurdwaras as a context for the practice of what they regard as appropriate Sikh religious activities and have involved the Societies only indirectly in ethnic-political activities.[25] For the old-guard KDS leadership, the loss of power in a gurdwara which was built under their leadership and which practices a brand of Sikhism with which they felt comfortable has been a blow.[26] On the other hand, as they have withdrawn from gurdwara society affairs, many of these people have become increasingly involved in the ethnic organizations, finding them to be a more rewarding forum for their interests and expertise. In light of these changes in orientation and leadership of the community's institutions, it is not surprising to find that many of the qualities which Chadney (1976, pp. 154–68) had earlier identified as crucial to KDS leadership (for example, professional or business occupation, lengthy residence in Canada, 'modernity', and bilingualism) are now important for leadership of the ethnic-political organizations but of lesser importance today as criteria for election to the executive committees of the gurdwara societies.

SIKH SUPPORT FOR THE DIFFERENTIATION OF 'RELIGION' AND 'ETHNICITY'

The proliferation and diversification of religious and ethnic institutions, activities, and leaders within the Vancouver Sikh community is a fact of life. To what extent it represents a fundamental, irreversible, conscious acceptance of Canadian ideology with respect to religion and ethnicity remains to be seen. It should be noted, however, that support for the differentiation of 'religion' and 'ethnicity' can be found among those two categories of persons within the Sikh collectivity who, having been born and reared in Canadian society, would be most likely to interpret social action and social identity in terms of the prevailing Canadian ideology. These two groups are the now sizeable and maturing second and third generation of Canadians of Punjabi Sikh ancestry, and the small but vocal and visible group of non-'East Indian' Canadian and American Sikh converts. While the two groups tend to define themselves in vastly different ways with respect to the Vancouver Sikh community as a whole, their very existence speaks to the separability of religion and ethnicity in the Canadian context.

What is striking about the second- and third-generation Canadians of Punjabi Sikh ancestry is their strong ethnic identity. Second- and third-generation Canadians of Punjabi Sikh ancestry have largely avoided transgressing the implicit norms (for example, by marrying out or converting out) which govern inclusion in 'our community'. Pressures both from within and without have reinforced the norm of Sikh endogamy, so that intermarriage with Canadians of other ethnic backgrounds—and thus any question of conflicting ethnic allegiances—is still uncommon. Moreover, during the 1970s, the ethnic consciousness of many of these people has been significantly politicized. The increase in overt anti-'East-Indian' hostility on the part of other Canadians, although largely directed at the new immigrants, has been sufficiently generalized so as to affect the second and third generations as well. And these people, sensitive to an injustice being done to all 'East Indians', have regarded the ethnic-political organizations as the appropriate institutions for mounting a response.[27]

On the other hand, many of these same people express estrangement from the recent Sikh religious revivalism, regarding it as an unfortunate return to aspects of life in 'village India' with little relevance to, or positive implications for, the community's situation in Canada. To such people, the issue of religious orthopraxy should rightfully be an individual one, distinct from and subordinate to the community's efforts to better their position as 'East Indians' in Canadian society. Thus, for many of these people, the orientation of the ethnic-political institutions and the challenge they provide in bridging the gap between the ethnic community and the wider Canadian society is more compelling than the activities of religious organizations from which they feel largely estranged. It is from these people that one gets the clearest statement that it may be possible to be 'ethnically' Sikh (or Punjabi or 'East Indian') without being 'religiously' Sikh.[28]

One receives just the converse message from the *gora* (white) Sikh converts.[29] For them, solidarity with Vancouver's 'East Indian' Sikhs is based not on a shared Punjabi heritage but on common adherence to a universal Sikh *dharma* (variously translated as 'religion', 'way of life', 'duty'). The converts make a clear ideological distinction between religious accommodation (for example, the giving up of beards, turbans, and other Sikh 'religious symbols') which they consider neither necessary nor excusable, and ethnic adaptation (for example, an end to residual Punjabi 'caste consciousness' and the 'subjugation of women') which they accept and would encourage.[30] The converts' major contention vis-à-vis the 'East Indian' Sikh community in Vancouver is that in the process of accommodation to Canadian norms those Canadians of Punjabi Sikh ancestry who have violated what the converts take to be inviolable religious norms are *patit* (literally, 'fallen'; the converts' translation is 'apostate') and thus 'East-Indians' (or 'Punjabis') but no longer 'real Sikhs'.[31]

Since they define themselves in religious terms, the converts have viewed the gurdwaras—their own as well as those which are predominantly Punjabi Sikh—as the appropriate institutions for their religious involvement with 'East Indian' Sikhs. In the gurdwaras, they have generally aligned themselves with 'orthodox' elements, helped sponsor visits by Sikh 'missionaries' from India, performed *gurbani kirtan* ('hymns of the Gurus') at services, and (at the Akali Singh gurdwara) introduced 'Sunday school' classes for the children. Furthermore, since they hold such an unequivocal notion of their own identity as 'religiously' but not 'ethnically' Sikh, the converts are able to draw a sharp distinction between 'religious' discrimination and discrimination based on 'race', 'ethnicity', or 'national origins'. Thus the converts, as individual litigants or as co-counsel through the Sikh Youth Federation of Canada, have been particularly aggressive in seeking to secure and expand Sikh 'religious rights' in Canada. Basing their arguments on the principle that religious codes for conduct are privileged and inviolable, they have enjoyed noteable success in appealing instances of perceived religious discrimination to the courts, Human Rights Boards, and other public bodies. They have ensured, for example, that 'orthodox' Sikhs can retain their beards, turbans, swords, and other religious symbols without fear of discrimination and with full understanding that such religious symbols are being retained on religious principle and are not merely a perpetuation of bizarre 'East Indian' ethnic customs.[32]

CONCLUSION

It is somewhat ironic that while the ethnic-political organizations serving the Sikh community are often castigated for their impotence in defining and defending ethnic interests, it is once again an explicitly-religious organization and individuals acting in the name of religion who have brought about some small—but, to many Sikhs, significant—changes in Canadian policies affecting them. This should serve as a reminder not to overlook channels of power which may be open to ethnic groups aside from the expressly political. However, this should not obscure the main point of this analysis, which has been to account for the proliferation and diversification of institutions within Vancouver's Sikh community. In this regard, it seems appropriate to conclude that the de facto differentiation of religious and ethnic-political institutions, activities, and leaders within the Vancouver Sikh community represents a significant departure from traditional Punjabi Sikh ideology and social structure. This departure can also be seen as constituting adaptation to Canadian ideology and public policy.

If so, what more general implications are there in these developments within the Sikh community? Are these developments peculiar to the Sikh situation in Canada, deriving from the unique interaction of Punjabi Sikh and Canadian ideologies and institutional forms? Or are the developments noted here for the Vancouver Sikhs common to other 'ethno-religious' groups in Canadian society—for example, to Canadian Doukhobors, Mennonites, Hutterites, Orthodox, Old Believers, Jews? I would suggest that in responding to Canadian ideology and public policy each 'ethno-religious' group is likely to have a somewhat different experience reflecting (1) the unique intersection of Canadian and the group's traditional ideology and institutional structures, and (2) the nature and extent of interaction between the group and the wider society. But if, as has been suggested, a distinction between 'religion' and 'ethnicity' is a commonplace of Canadian ideology, then it should not be surprising to find an increasing differentiation of religious and ethnic identities, organizations, activities and leaders taking place within these 'ethno-religious' communities over time. And if political power is a secular rather than religious prerogative in Canadian ideology, one might also expect to observe over time the emergence of ethnic–political organizations serving these communities and a corresponding de-politization of their religious institutions. If this is so, we need to know more about the institutional developments within these 'ethno-religious' communities, for the outlines of a general theory await further substantiation by others.

ACKNOWLEDGEMENTS

A version of this paper was first presented at the Biennial Canadian Ethnic Studies Association Meetings in Vancouver, 12 October 1979. The paper is based on archival research and on fieldwork conducted in 1978–9 with the Vancouver Sikh community. The research builds on previous research conducted in 1972 and 1974 with the Healthy, Happy, Holy Organization (3HO), whose members are now known more widely as Canadian and American Sikh converts. Funding for the latter research was provided by the US National Endowment for the Humanities (Youthgrant #AY-20553-74-398). I would like to thank Brenda Beck, Norm Buchignani, Elizabeth Coville, Gary Downey, Rich Handler, and John Wood for their helpful comments on earlier drafts of this paper.

NOTES

1. I use the term 'Sikh community' in a broad sense to include all those living in greater Vancouver who consider themselves to be Sikhs. Unfortunately, accurate statistical information on the Sikh population in Canada is hard to obtain, not least because 'Sikh' is not a category of enumeration (either religious or ethnic) in Canadian census data. While Toronto's and Vancouver's Sikh populations are by far the largest in Canada, it remains an open question as to whether Toronto's has yet to surpass Vancouver's as the largest.
2. I put quotation marks around 'East Indian' because while it is the conventional categorical label for all those of South Asian ancestry in Canada, many persons so labelled find it misleading and derogatory and would prefer another general label (for example, 'Indo-Canadian'

or 'Canadian of origins in India') or a more specific one (for example, 'Sikh Canadian' or 'Fijian Canadian') or none at all.

3. 'Institutional adaptation' should not be confused with 'structural assimilation'. While the latter refers to the 'large-scale entrance of immigrant group members into the cliques. clubs, and institutions of the host society on a primary group level' (Gordon, 1964, p. 71), the former refers to changes of institutional structures *within* the immigrant community with respect to institutional forms sanctioned by the host and sending societies.
4. By 'ethnic-political' organizations, I mean those institutions whose primary activities involve lobbying for the interests of a particular ethnic community and mediating between the ethnic community and the social institutions—and particularly the political institutions—of the wider society. By 'ethnic-cultural', I refer to organizations primarily concerned with promoting the folk arts, history, and language of the ethnic group's 'traditional culture'. 'Ethnic-social' organizations arc those providing social and recreational opportunities for members of the ethnic community. 'Ethnic-social service' organizations are those delivering social services to the ethnic community. These are, in a sense, ideal-type institutions. Organizations can be and often are involved in more than one type of activity. Nevertheless, I feel justified in my characterization of various organizations within Vancouver's Sikh community on the basis of their dominant orientation.
5. Like 'adaptation', the term 'ideology' is a theoretically loaded one which deserves careful definition. Following one common anthropological usage (see Nicholas, 1973, pp. 75–80; Geertz 1973, pp. 193–233; Schneider 1976, p. 220), I regard ideology as the natives' social theory. Understood in this way, ideology is a non-evaluative theoretical concept—that is, one expressing actors' ideas about/ideals for their society. While ideologies build upon and draw their authoritativeness from pervasive and persuasive cultural symbols, the natives' social analysis (1) is 'prey to the same problems of coherence and authority as are other cultural systems' (Nicholas 1973, p. 76), and (2) 'is not the same as the analyst's theoretically constructed view of the native culture' (Schneider 1976, p. 220). Given this definition of ideology, it becomes apparent that one can hold 'ethnocultural pluralism' to be the prevailing Canadian ideology without thereby endorsing it as one's own social scientific analysis of Canadian society and culture. Understanding this, it is possible to agree with John Porter's conclusion that '(i)f not its one distinctive value, that of the mosaic is Canada's most cherished' (1965, p. 558) without disputing those who present evidence of ethnic hierarchy or fluid ethnic boundaries or a widespread adoption of common cultural premises across ethnic boundaries.

6. The Canadian ideology with respect to ethnicity and the government's policy of multiculturalism have been variously criticized by social scientists for inaccurately portraying the structural realities of Canadian society (Porter 1975), for confusing the analytic notions of 'ethnicity' and 'culture' (Burnet 1976), and for co-opting the legitimate human rights concerns of immigrant groups by focusing on their 'folk' activities (Schroeter 1978), or by creating 'career ethnics' with vested interests in perpetuating current multiculturalism programmes (Frideres & Goldenberg 1977). Nevertheless, reiteration of their commitment to the multiculturalism policy by recent Liberal and Conservative governments and the support the policy has received from all three major political parties suggests that the ideology persists and that the policy is likely to be continued.
7. The Canadian ideology with respect to 'ethnicity' appears to share much in common with the ideology with respect to 'race'. The major difference appears to be the greater degree to which the 'facts' of racial identity are taken to be innate and encoded in one's substance (for example, in 'blood' and 'colour'). It may be most appropriate, therefore, to regard 'East Indian'—like 'Black' and 'Native Indian'—as a racial-ethnic category label (though, in fact, many Canadians of Punjabi Sikh ancestry could easily 'pass' as white Canadians if colour were the only index).
8. This point deserves further elaboration. Parsons (1975, p. 65), quoting David Schneider, points out that in North America, 'ethnic status is conspicuously devoid of social content' and 'the markers of [ethnic] identity are in a very important sense 'empty symbols'. In other words, in North America, so long as a few general 'cultural markers' are retained, considerable 'cultural adaptation' can take place without bringing into question one's 'ethnic identity'.
9. While the separation of church and state is not as absolute in Canada as in the United States (and thus, for example, independent religious schools are eligible for public funds in British Columbia), multiculturalism funding is apparently not intended to support overtly-religious activities. Where religious institutions do receive public funds, it is usually specified as support for what are taken to be ancillary ethnic-cultural or ethnic-social service activities. Thus, in the early 1970s the KDS was briefly given a grant by the city of Vancouver to run an 'information centre' for new immigrants. The Vancouver gurdwaras have not sought further funds, even though the KDS Punjabi School might be eligible for funding from the Secretary of State (Multiculturalism) for its Punjabi language classes. KDS leaders give as a reason for not seeking such funding the fear of loss of autonomy. Since the Punjabi language and, especially, the Gurmukhi script are so intimately connected with the Sikh religion, it is hard to imagine the authorities being able to enforce the teaching of religiously-neutral Punjabi language classes at the gurdwaras.

10. In his comparative study of South Asia and the modern West, the French anthropologist Louis Dumont (1970) has admonished us to fully recognize and respect the contrasting ideologies of the two regions. Among other things, he has suggested that one significant contrast between South Asian and modern Western ideologies is in the latter's differentiation of social action and identity into a multitude of separate and distinct 'domains'. Inden & Nicholas (1977, p. xiv) even go so far as to suggest that the conventional distinction made in the modern West between the sacred and secular domains may not be present in South Asian cultures.
11. See Mayar (1959, pp. 8–9) for one discussion of the multiplicity of functions of the traditional Sikh gurdwara.
12. See Singh (1977, pp. 174–5) and Das (1923, p. 88) for accounts of some of the early activities of the Vancouver KDS.
13. For a detailed account of the KDS's efforts to achieve domiciliary rights for illegal South Asian immigrants in British Columbia, see KDS, 1947a.
14. For a detailed account of the KDS's efforts to achieve the federal, provincial, and municipal franchise for all 'Hindoos', see KDS, 1947b.
15. Lal (1976) contrasts the background of early would-be ethnic-political leaders (often highly educated non-Sikhs with considerable prior experience dealing with Westerners) with those of the masses (largely working-class Sikhs). Many of these political activists left Vancouver during the community's early years and found more receptive audiences elsewhere.
16. The Ghadar (Revolution) Party was active in Vancouver at this time. I have not considered it an ethnic-political institution of the Vancouver Sikh community, however, because (1) its primary orientation was towards the political situation in India rather than the situation of the community in Canada, and (2) while active in Vancouver, its organizational centre was in the United States.
17. All of the gurdwaras which were once the legal affiliates of the Vancouver KDS have now achieved their independence. At present the Western Sikh Samachar Society, publisher of the monthly *Sikh Samachar* journal aspires to be an umbrella organization for all the British Columbia (henceforth, BC) gurdwara societies.
18. The aims and objectives of the East Indian Canadian Citizens' Welfare Association as set out in its original Constitution and by-laws are:
    (a) To work for the social, economic, political and cultural advancement of the Canadian citizens of East Indian origin in Canada;
    (b) To act as an effective medium of cooperation between the members of the Indian Community in Canada and other Canadian citizens;
    (c) To interpret India, the people, traditions, and culture, to the people of Canada;

(d) To inculcate among the Canadian citizens of Indian origin, the responsibilities, duties, and rights of Canadian. citizenship;
(e) To promote better understanding and friendship between Canada and India by the exchange of mutual information;
(f) To establish centres for the purpose of cultural, recreational, social, and other community activities;
(g) To purchase,sell, take on lease, hire, mortgage, or otherwise acquire or deal in or foreclose property, land, and buildings, or any interest therein, for the purposes of the Association;
(h) To erect buildings on such lands, or any of them, to further the purposes of the Association;
(i) To buy, sell, deal in, hire, make or provide or maintain all necessary real or personal property or equipment for carrying out the objective of the Association;
(j) To publish periodicals, books, pamphlets and such literature as may be deemed necessary to promote the above-mentioned aims and objectives;
(k) To promote all other ancillary objects for the advancement of the above-mentioned aims (East Indian Canadian Citizens' Welfare Association 1954).

19. See Chadney (1976, pp. 154–68) for an account of the factors crucial to KDS leadership at the time of his study.
20. Sikhs from Vancouver continue to be well represented, however, on the national NACOI executive committee.
21. The East Indian Defence Committee represents an interesting case study since it is a group which apparently would like to take advantage of both Canadian and traditional Sikh ideologies of religion and ethnicity. Recognizing the importance of the gurdwaras to the Sikh community, the Defence Committee unsuccessfully sought control of the Vancouver gurdwaras during the mid-1970s. One of the arguments raised against Defence Committee involvement in gurdwara affairs was that as a 'political' organization and, as an affiliate of the Communist Party of Canada (Marxist-Leninist), an apparently 'anti-religious' organization, its participation in the affairs of a religious organization would be inappropriate. Having been rebuffed in efforts to secure a base in the gurdwaras, the Defence Committee sought to build a 'Memorial Hall' which would serve as a meeting hall and community centre commemorating the early martyrs of the Vancouver 'East Indian' community, the Indian Freedom Fighters, and recent Indian Naxalite activists. They found, however, that by installing a copy of the Guru Granth Sahib and allowing the building to be used for weddings, they could call it the Desh Bhagat Temple and thus (1) take advantage of the fact that 'houses of worship' are considered non-threatening by most

Canadians and are granted tax-exempt status under local statutes, and (2) keep open the channels of communication with those Sikhs who have need of a place to perform functions and do not object to this particular blending of religion and politics.

22. The Indian Peoples' Association of North American (IPANA) is affiliated with the Canadian Communist League-Marxist-Leninist (CCL-ML). The conflicts between the Defence Committee and IPANA (and between the CPC-ML and the CCL-ML) derive from splits in the Communist Party of India-Marxist (CPI-M) during the 1960s. The East Indian Workers' Association (EIWA) is modelled after the effective Indian Workers Association (IWA) in Britain.
23. It is interesting to note that there are no ethnic social-service organizations as such operated from within the 'East Indian' community. Traditionally, Sikhs have looked after their own either informally (for example, through family and village connections) or through the gurdwaras. Only recently in Vancouver has the long-standing resistance to turning to outside agencies for counselling or assistance begun to dissolve, this being both cause and effect of the breakdown of established patron/client and brokered relationships in a rapidly growing and diversifying Sikh population.
24. There is special irony in the election of the 1979 KDS executive committee. This was the first KDS election contested under new election procedures (membership fees, closed membership rolls, secret ballots) which had been pushed by 'modernists' as necessary to ensure fair elections but had been opposed by 'traditionalists' as a deviation from established electoral traditions (a show of hands by those present at the gurdwara on election day). The 1979 election was a hard-fought affair with the incumbent KDS leadership (which had strongly pushed the new procedures) and the 'orthodox' challengers (many of whom had opposed the new procedures) seeking to enrol as many new members as possible and to ensure that their supporters made it to the polls. Pre-election arithmetic forecast a close election which would probably be won by the incumbent group. Instead, the 'orthodox' group emerged with a clear majority of seats—and all major positions—on the new executive. The new election procedures appear to have backfired on the old-guard KDS leadership who, given the privacy of the voting booth, could no longer ensure the loyalty of those (for example, family members, village-mates, employees, clients) whom they had counted as their supporters.
25. The term 'orthodox' (with its specifically religious overtones) seems more appropriate in describing the present gurdwara leadership than the term 'traditionalist' (which speaks to a conservatism in a broad range of ethnic concerns). Whereas Sikh 'traditionalists' (represented at the organizational level in Vancouver by the Shiromani Akali Dal of

Canada) would insist on maintaining the gurdwara's traditional multi-functional role, the 'orthodox' leadership seems wary of mixing religion and politics. For instance, during recent provincial and federal elections, candidates who asked to address the *sangat* (congregation) at the KDS gurdwara (a traditional forum for courting the Sikh vote) were allowed to do so only after considerable debate on the part of the executive as to its propriety, and were instructed to speak only on the highly-charged issue of whether Sikhs should be exempted from hard-hat safety regulations on grounds that hard-hat requirements conflict with the Sikhs' religious duty and thus religious right to wear their turbans.

26. Some of these people argue that in this religiously-pluralistic society, 'modernist' and 'orthodox' branches of the Sikh religion should be allowed to co-exist institutionally in the same way that reformed/conservative/orthodox congregations exist within Judaism or the way denominational differences exist within Christianity. These people argue that there are other gurdwaras in the Vancouver area that the 'orthodox' could attend without taking over the KDS.
27. 'East Indian' students at the local colleges and universities appear to be extraordinarily active not only in their own 'East Indian' organizations but in campus politics generally. And there seems to be some carry-over between this activism and subsequent involvement with the community's ethnic-political organizations and the political parties of the wider society.
28. Along with marrying a *gora,* formal conversion to Christianity remains one of the surest ways to find oneself cut off from one's family and others in the Punjabi Sikh community. Few of these people have taken such a drastic step. Rather, many regard themselves as 'non-religious' (one of the options available in religiously-pluralistic Canada).
29. Most Canadian and American Sikh converts are members of the Healthy, Happy, Holy Organization (3HO), a group founded in 1969 in Los Angeles by a Sikh immigrant, Harbhajan Singh Puri (aka Yogi Bhajan; aka Siri Singh Sahib Bhai Sahib Harbhajan Singh Khalsa Yogi). The group was originally recruited on the basis of Puri's Kundalini and Tantric Yoga teachings and had a basically yogic identity (see Dusenbery 1973), but it has evolved over the course of the past decade into a small but dedicated group of people who regard themselves as upholders of Sikh orthopraxy in the West (see Dusenbery 1975). At present, perhaps as many as three to five thousand—but nowhere near the 250,000 claimed—Sikh converts live in over one hundred ashrams ('spiritual communes') throughout North America and in several cities abroad.

    In Vancouver, an ashram has existed since 1972. The orientation of the Vancouver ashram is split between involvement with the local 'East Indian' Sikh community and with the 'alternative lifestyles' subculture.

Relationships between 3HO and North Americans with Punjabi Sikh ancestries have often been strained, but the dozen or so members of the Vancouver 3HO ashram have been involved with Vancouver's Punjabi Sikhs both through the gurdwaras and through the Sikh Youth Federation of Canada (a joint Gora Sikh–Punjabi Sikh venture inspired and advised by Puri).

30. The converts regard 'caste consciousness' and the 'subjugation of women' as inconsistent with Sikh religious teachings. For a fuller discussion of North American and Punjabis perspectives on Sikh egalitarianism, see Dusenbery 1980.
31. In support of this idea that Sikhism is a religion with certain religious norms not legitimately subject to modification in any social setting, the converts point to the *rehat maryada*, which they term a Sikh 'code of conduct for living'. Formulated by a select group of distinguished Sikh historians and religious leaders as part of a general codification of Sikh religious principles earlier in this century, the *rehat* has been circulated by the Shiromani Gurdwara Parbandhak Committee. While the converts and some 'orthodox' leaders regard it as a definitive statement of Sikh religious norms, most Punjabi Sikhs in North America are unfamiliar with its details and would in any case consider them irrelevant to their assertion of Sikh identity.
32. Recent decisions confirming these 'religious rights' include: (I) the decision of the Crown to drop charges in the case of REGINA vs Khamba (1975) in which a Sikh had been charged with carrying a concealed weapon for wearing his *kirpan* (sword); the decision to drop charges was followed by a directive to all provincial police departments in B.C. not to treat the *kirpan* as a weapon unless used as such; (2) a settlement agreement before the Human Rights Board of B.C. wherein Pinkerton's of Canada Ltd. agreed to rehire a Sikh employee and allow him to 'in the course of his employment continue to follow his religious beliefs and in particular to wear a beard, turban and carry a Kirpan' (Aujila vs Pinkerton's 1978); (3) on the basis of a challenge from one of the gora Sikhs, the Canadian armed forces announced changes in recruitment and dress policies which will allow Sikhs entering the Canadian forces to retain their beards and turbans (*Canadian Human Rights Bulletin*, March 1979). Finally, at the time of this writing, the problematic issue of whether a Sikh's religious duty to wear a turban should exempt him from safety regulations requiring the wearing of a hard hat awaits resolution.

REFERENCES

Ames, Michael M. and Joy Inglis, 1973, 'Conflict and Change in British Columbia Sikh Family Life', *BC Studies*, vol. 20, pp. 15–49.

Buchignani, Norman L., 1979, 'South Asian Political Organization in Canada: 1906–20', Paper presented at the Biennial Canadian Ethnic Studies Association Meetings, Vancouver, B.C., 12 October.

Burnet, Jean, 1976, 'Ethnic Relations and Ethnic Policies in Canadian Society', in Frances Henry, (ed.), *Ethnicity in the Americas*, The Hague: Mouton, pp. 23–40.

Canada, 1960, 'An Act for the Recognition and Protection of Human Rights and Fundamental Freedoms', *Statutes of Canada*, (I) ch. 44, Ottawa: The Queen's Printer and Controller of Stationery.

———, 1971, 'Canadian Culture: Announcement of Implementation of Policy of Multiculturalism within a Bilingual Framework', *House of Commons Debates*, 8 October.

———, 1978a, 'Canadian Human Rights Act', *Canadian Gazette, Part III*, 2(7, ch. 33) proclaimed 1 march.

———, 1978b, 'Multiculturalism: Announcement of New Programs', *House of Commons Debates*, 21 March.

Chadney, James Gaylord, 1976, 'The Vancouver Sikhs: An Ethnic Community in Canada', Unpublished PhD dissertation, Department of Anthropology, Michigan State University.

———,1977a, 'Abstract: The Vancouver Sikhs', *Dissertation Abstracts International*, 37(9): 5912–A.

———, 1977b, 'Demography, Identity, and Decision-Making: The Case of the Vancouver Sikhs', *Urban Anthropology*, VI (3), pp. 187–204.

Cole, W. Owen and Piara Singh Sambhi, 1978, *The Sikhs: Their Religious Beliefs and Practices*, London: Routledge & Kegan Paul.

Das, Rajani Kauta, 1923, *Hindustani Workers on the Pacific Coast*, Berlin and Leipzig: Walter de Gruyter & Co.

Dumont, Louis, 1970, *Homo Hierarchicus: The Caste System and Its implications*, Chicago: The University of Chicago Press.

Dusenbery, Verne A., 1973, 'Why would anybody join...? A Study of Recruitment and the Healthy, Happy, Holy Organization', Unpublished senior Honors Essay, Department of Anthropology, Stanford University.

———, 1975, 'Straight→Freak→Yogi→Sikh: A "Search for Meaning" in Contemporary American Culture', Unpublished Master's thesis, Department of Anthropology, University of Chicago.

———, 1980, 'Hierarchy. Equality and the Assertion of Sikh Identity in North America', Paper presented at the 56th Annual Central States Anthropological Association Meetings, Ann Arbor, Michigan, 9–12 April.

East Indian Canadian Citizens' Welfare Association, 1954, Constitution and By-Laws (as adopted 7 December 1954).

Frideres, J. S. and Sheldon Goldenberg, 1977, 'Hyphenated Canadians: Comparative Analysis of Ethnic, Regional, and National Identification of Western Canadian University Students', *Journal of Ethnic Studies*, 5 (2), pp. 99–100.

Geertz, Clifford, 1973, 'Ideology as a Cultural System', *The Interpretation of Cultures*, New York: Basic Books, pp. 193–233.

Gordon, Milton Myron, 1964, *Assimilation in American Life: The Role of Race, Religion, and National Origins,* New York: Oxford University Press.

Inden, Ronald B. and Ralph W. Nicholas, 1977, *Kinship in Bengali Culture*, Chicago: The University of Chicago Press.

Isajiw, Wsevolod W., 1974, 'Definitions of Ethnicity', *Ethnicity*, vol. 1, pp. 111–24.

Khalsa Diwan Society, 1947a, *A Report of Correspondence and Documents relating to negotiations between 1939 and 1947, culminating in domiciliary rights being accorded to 210 members of the Indian Community by the Dominion Government*, Vancouver, B.C.: Khalsa Diwan Society.

———, 1947b, Report on Dominion, Provincial and Municipal Franchise for the Hindus in British Columbia, Victoria, B.C.: Khalsa Diwan Society.

Lal, Brij, 1976, 'East Indians in British Columbia, 1904–14: An Historical Study of Growth and Integration', Unpublished Master's thesis, Department of History, University of British Columbia.

Mayan, Adrian C., 1959, A Report on the East Indian Community in Vancouver, Working Papers, Institute of Social and Economic Research, University of British Columbia.

National Association of Canadians of Origins in India, 1977, Constitution and By-laws (as adopted at the Second Annual Conference, Vancouver, B.C., 27–8 August 1977).

Nicholas, Ralph W., 1973, 'Social and Political Movements' in Bernard J. Siegel, (ed.), *Annual Reviews in Anthropology*, vol. 2, Palo Alto: Annual Reviews Inc., pp. 63–84.

Parsons, Talcott, 1975, 'Some Theoretical Considerations on the Nature and Trends of Change in Ethnicity' in Nathan Glazer and Daniel P. Moynihan, (eds), *Ethnicity: Theory and Experience*, Cambridge, Mass.: Harvard University Press, pp. 53–83.

Porter, John, 1965, *The Vertical Mosaic: An Analysis of Social Class and Power in Canada*, Toronto: The University of Toronto Press.

———, 1975, 'Ethnic Pluralism in Canadian Perspective' in Nathan Glazer and Daniel P. Moynihan, (eds), *Ethnicity: Theory and Experience.* Cambridge, Massachusetts: Harvard University Press, pp. 267–304.

Schneider, David M., 1969, 'Kinship, Nationality, and Religion in American Culture: Toward a Definition of Kinship' in Robert F. Spencer, (ed.),

Forms of Symbolic Action. Seattle: The University of Washington Press (for the AES), pp. 116–25.

———, 1976, 'Notes Toward a Theory of Culture' in Keith Basso and Henry Selby, (eds), *Meaning in Anthropology*, Albuquerque: The University of New Mexico Press, pp. 195–221.

Schroeter, Gerd, 1978, 'In Search of Ethnicity: Multiculturalism in Canada', *Journal of Ethnic Studies*, 16(1), pp. 98–107.

Singh, Khushwant, 1977, *A History of the Sikhs. Volume 2: 1839–1974*. New Delhi: Oxford University Press.

Smith, Marian W. with Hilda W. Boulter, 1944, 'Sikh Settlers in Canada', *Asia and the Americans*, 44(8), pp. 359–64.

Srivastava, Ram P., 1974, 'Family Organization and Change Among the Overseas Indians with Special Reference to Indian Immigrant Families in British Columbia, Canada', in George Kurian, (ed.), *The Family in India: A Regional View*, The Hague: Mouton, pp. 369–91.

Wood, John, 1978, 'East Indians and Canada's New Immigration Policy', *Canadian Public Policy*, IV(4), pp. 547–67.

8

Socializing Sikhs in Singapore*

Soliciting the State's Support

In June 1992, an International Conference cum Exhibition on Punjabi/Sikh Heritage was held in the Republic of Singapore. The event, sponsored by the Sikh Advisory Board and the Singapore Sikh Education Foundation, had the twin goals of 'introduc[ing] Sikh children to their Punjabi/Sikh heritage in the context of national aspiration' and 'shar[ing] Punjabi/Sikh heritage with fellow Singaporeans'.[1] Twenty internationally renowned Punjabi and non-Punjabi scholars specializing in Punjabi/Sikh studies were brought from South Asia, North America, and Europe to present papers and to chair sessions; numerous local and international Sikh artists and artisans exhibited or performed; three government officials, including the Deputy Prime Minister, the Minister for Community Development, and a Sikh Member of Parliament, addressed the Conference; and several thousand Sikhs turned up for some or all of the three-day programme. The *Straits Times*, Singapore's government-controlled newspaper of record, described the event as 'the first of its kind in the world'; and its reports both highlighted the praise that Singapore's Sikhs received from government officials (for being 'generally better off than the rest of the population', for making contributions 'disproportionate to your numbers', and for '[having]

* First published in Pashaura Singh and N.G. Barrier, (eds), 1996, *The Transmission of Sikh Heritage in the Diaspora*, Columbia, Missouri: South Asia Publications and New Delhi: Manohar Publishers, pp. 127–64.

approached social problems affecting the community openly and frankly') and detailed the concerns of Sikh professionals (about 'alienation of the young . . ., social and educational problems among students and a lack of heritage awareness among young Sikh parents') that had prompted the Conference in the first place.[2]

This Conference cum Exhibition on Punjabi/Sikh Heritage was explicitly intended as a first step toward establishing a permanent Punjabi/ Sikh Heritage Centre 'where Sikhs and other Singaporeans can learn about the community, focusing not only on the past but also on how heritage can be used to advantage in the future.'[3] But subsequent talks with Bhajan Singh, the Chair of the Sikh Advisory Board and the Singapore Sikh Education Foundation, suggested that, in the minds of its organizers, the Conference and Centre were only part of an overall effort to identify and address concerns regarding transmission of Punjabi/ Sikh heritage in Singapore. In Bhajan Singh's analysis, the experience of Singapore's Sikhs has been common to Sikhs living outside India— to wit, relative material success in their new homes but challenges nonetheless in transmitting the Punjabi/Sikh heritage to subsequent generations; however, Sikhs in Singapore, as a mature and cosmopolitan community, are particularly well placed, Bhajan Singh would have it, to develop effective means of transmitting Punjabi/Sikh heritage that might serve as a model for others living in the pluralistic, English-speaking countries where most diasporan Sikhs now live.

It certainly would be hard to fault the overall material accomplishments of Singapore's approximately 15,000 Sikhs.[4] The city-state of Singapore, one of the so-called Asian tigers, has achieved one of the world's highest standards of living; and, according to statistics released by the Prime Minister in 1991, Singapore's Sikhs, who constitute barely one half of one per cent of the population, are better educated, more likely to be employed, and are better housed than the average Singaporean.[5] At the same time, research conducted in the late 1980s by a group of concerned Sikh professionals led by Bhajan Singh, purported to show a decline in educational standards among Sikh students, an increase in Sikh juvenile offenders, and a relatively high incidence of serious drug offences among Sikh male youth, all attributable in their analysis to 'an erosion of traditional Asian (Sikh) values among Sikh youth'.[6] It was, in fact, this disparity between the overall upward mobility and material success of Singaporean Sikhs and the discovery of an emerging Sikh underclass that has propelled the Sikh professionals into positions of leadership in the community over the past several years.

To address the perceived problems of this newly-discovered underclass, the professionals have consolidated their control over key Sikh community institutions, presented a Sikh action agenda to government authorities for their attention, and delivered on enough of this agenda to sustain their credibility both within the Sikh community and with state authorities.

In fact, Sikhs in Singapore have come in recent years to be regarded as something of a model minority. Then-Prime Minister Lee Kuan Yew, the father of modern Singapore, in public comments made on a visit to the Central Sikh Temple in 1991, praised Singapore's Sikhs for contributions to 'the well-being and stability of Singapore . . . more than in proportion to your numbers' and promised state support 'in preserving your distinctiveness'.[7] Similar statements of support for Sikh accomplishments, distinctiveness, and self-help efforts have been regularly forthcoming from other high-ranking government officials in recent years.[8] Significantly, these promises of state support appear to have yielded tangible opportunities for Sikhs to strengthen their Punjabi/Sikh heritage under the prevailing policies of multiracialism in Singapore. Thus, in recent years, Sikhs have been successful in having Sikh Studies included as an optional religious studies track in the schools, in having a separate 'Sikh' racial category as well as a 'Sikhism' religious category recognized for official purposes, and in having Punjabi accepted as a testable second language in the public schools. From the perspective of the local Sikh community, these are all major achievements that will help Singaporean Sikh youth preserve their heritage or, in the vocabulary of Singaporean multiculturalism, strengthen their 'cultural ballast'. Moreover, from the perspective of both Sikh and government officials, this preservation and promotion of a Punjabi/Sikh heritage and associated 'traditional Asian (Sikh) values' should, it is hoped, have a pragmatic payoff as well in counteracting the rise of a disaffected Sikh underclass in Singapore.

This paper analyses the Sikh experience in Singapore, asking how Sikhs have been able to achieve their ends, what the costs as well as benefits to Sikh interests have been, and whether the Singapore case can serve, as its proponents suggest, as a model for the transmission of Punjabi/Sikh heritage in the diaspora. I focus particularly on the ways in which the current Sikh institutional leadership has used the political system to advance its agenda of Sikh concerns within the context of the prevailing poetics and politics of multiculturalism in Singapore. And I argue that there are particular features of the corporatist political culture of Singapore that make Sikh 'successes' in Singapore dependent upon both a consensus among local Sikhs and a conjunction of interests with state officials. Thus I caution that, given the specifics of the Singaporean case, the Singapore Sikh model may be not only non-transportable to other settings in the diaspora, but also rather fragile in its Singapore setting.

***

The first Sikhs arrived in Singapore in the 1850s as political prisoners exiled to the British penal colony there after the Second Sikh War. Little is recorded of most of these prisoners, and none are known to have stayed on in Singapore. However, the most famous of these prisoners, Bhai Maharaj Singh (née Nihal Singh) is in the process of becoming a full-fledged local *shaheed* (martyr). Bhai Maharaj Singh was imprisoned in Singapore from 1850 until his death in 1856. According to a recent pamphlet on his life published by the Central Sikh Gurdwara Board in Singapore, 'Bhai Maharaj Singh was . . . not only a revolutionary fighter who tried to save the Sikh Kingdom [as a confederate of Mul Raj] but also a recognized religious personage of very high standing [as head of the Hoti Mardan Vali Sant Khalsa Sampardai], a true Saint of the Sikh Faith who died the death of a martyr.'[9] And, as Sikh Member of Parliament Davinder Singh notes in his foreward to this pamphlet: 'Like the other communities, we [Sikhs] are being encouraged to preserve our cultural heritage. This requires us to delve into our past to understand who we are, what we stand for, and how and when Sikhs came to Singapore. . . . Bhai Maharaj Singh is particularly special to us because of his brief residence in this country.'[10] Thus supported by Singaporean multiculturalism ideologies, Bhai Maharaj Singh's historical memory is being 'preserved' as that of a local *shaheed*, complete with a Bhai Maharaj Singh Memorial Gurdwara under construction, with government permission, as part of the renovation of the Silat Road Gurdwara complex.[11]

If Singapore's first memorialized Sikh was an anti-British martyr, those memorializing him today in Singapore are themselves largely the descendants of employees and functionaries of the British. Large-scale migration from Punjab to Southeast Asia dates to the British colonial period, especially to the period 1880–1920 when the changing political economy of Punjab pushed smallholder agriculturalists in central Punjab, particularly Sikh males from the Jat caste, to supplement family incomes through service in the British Indian army and/or international migration.[12] Sikhs and other North Indian 'martial races', having proven themselves in Hong Kong, were particularly sought after by the British to help provide internal security in the colonial plural society being created on the Malay peninsula. Thus, by the beginning of the twentieth century, following opportunities opened up by service to the British, Sikhs had already established a niche in the political economy of the Malay peninsula (including Singapore) as military, police, watchmen, and moneylenders.[13] While the first Sikhs had come as policemen in the Sikh Police Contingent and the Tanjong Pagar Dock Police Force or as militiamen in the Malay State Guides, others who followed them found work as private watchmen, bullock-cart drivers, and moneylenders. British patterns of recruitment for the police and military service and classic chain migration were important factors in determining the social make-up of the community in Singapore. Because of heavy recruitment in their home districts, Jats from Malwa and Majha dominated the early immigration; and they continue to predominate within the community in Singapore today.[14]

Most of the important Sikh institutions in Singapore, especially the gurdwaras, can be traced back to the opening decades of the twentieth century. The first gurdwaras were located in police barracks; but as increasing numbers of independent migrants arrived, gurdwaras came to be set up outside the barracks for the wider *sangat* (congregation). A premises on Queen Street was purchased for this purpose in 1912 and soon became the Central Sikh Temple.[15] A half-way house on Silat Road, founded by the Tanjang Pagar Dock Police, became Gurdwara Sahib Silat Road.[16] Until the mid-1920s, these two gurdwaras were the centre of community life, at least for those Sikh living outside the military bases.[17] However, during the 1920s and 1930s, factional disputes and concern over control of Central Sikh Temple by the Muhammadan and Hindu Endowments Board led to the establishment of region-specific gurdwaras among the Jats (Siri Guru Singh Sabha on Wilkie Road by Majhalis; Khalsa Dharmak Sabha on Niven Road by Malwais; Pardesi Khalsa Dharmak Diwan at Kirk Terrace by Doabis).[18] Mazhbis, offended by their treatment in the Jat-dominated gurdwaras set up their own gurdwara (Khalsa Jiwan Sudhar Sabha on Buffalo Road) in the 1930s.[19] Khatris and Aroras, a large number of whom settled in Singapore following India's partition in 1947, established their own gurdwara (Sri Guru Nanak Sat Sangh Sabha on Wilkinson Road in Katong) in the 1950s.[20]

Most of the original Sikh immigrants had come to Singapore as sojourners, as was typical of international migrants from Punjab in the early colonial period. But many of those who prospered in Singapore subsequently sent for wives and other family members. The early Singapore Sikh community, which was primarily made up of single males working multiple jobs and living frugally so as to remit generous sums to the family in Punjab, gradually became more gender equal, more concerned with raising families in Singapore, and more interested in building a future in Singapore. Thus the increase from fewer than 2,000 Sikhs in 1921 to around 3,500 Sikhs in 1931 to around 7,000 Sikh in 1957 went hand-in-hand with an increase in the number and percentage of women and minor children and significant advances in educational attainment and economic status.

One sign of the upward mobility of the Sikh community in Singapore was the organization in the 1920s of the Singapore Sikh Cricket Club, formed by Sikh schoolboys from Raffles Institution, Anglo-Chinese School, and St Joseph's Institution. After it was formally registered as Singapore Khalsa Association (SKA) in 1931, this sports and recreation club became a social centre for the emerging business and English-educated professional class among Singapore's Sikhs. By the 1950s, with an influx of commercial migrants from urban Punjab as new members and with English-educated civil servants in positions of leadership, activities expanded to include 'social dinners and receptions . . . to honour important visitors as well as to celebrate the achievements of fellow members, especially in career promotions.'[21] During the 1950s and 1960s, SKA also became involved in celebrating Sikh *gurpurbs*, Punjabi cultural evenings, and National Day. And the new SKA facilities eventually became a venue for Punjabi-language instruction in the 1970s and 1980s.[22]

By the early 1960s, Singaporean Sikhs and Sikh institutions were being forced to come to terms with the fact that almost all Singapore-born Sikhs were being educated in English-medium schools and that English was becoming their lingua franca. As a consequence, there was increasing concern about how to preserve and transmit Punjabi culture and Sikh religion. Various institutional responses were made or attempted. From the mid-1940s to the mid-1960s, the Sikh Missionary Society Malaya, based in Singapore, published 30 booklets for distribution not only in Southeast Asia but also in North America, Britain, and East Africa. Its intent was both to spread knowledge about Sikhism to other communities and to encourage Sikh youth to learn more about their own religion.[23] During the same period, the Singapore Sikh Partinidh Sabha (SSPS) promoted an ambitious plan to coordinate an institutional division of labour that would have had different gurdwara societies in Singapore take on responsibilities for different aspects of community welfare and socialization. Although their overall plan for amalgamating all the gurdwara societies under a single executive was ultimately rejected, two parts of the plan—a Khalsa English School on the premises of Khalsa

Dharmak Sabha and a Khalsa Punjabi School at Sri Guru Singh Sabha—were implemented.[24] In the mid-1950s, the Singapore Sikh Cultural Group (SSCG) organized cultural activities aimed at 'maintain[ing] a living sense of ethnic identity, especially among the [Sikh] youth'.[25] It was the subsequent incorporation of SSCG into the SKA that gave the latter its cultural focus in the 1960s and made it a logical recipient in the early 1970s of the SSPS library and its Punjabi-language classes.

Despite these efforts, the evidence suggests at best partial socialization of Singapore Sikh youth into Punjabi/Sikh heritage during the 1950s and 1960s. Two academic exercises conducted by Sikh students at the University of Singapore (one interviewing and observing a sample of twenty-five families; the other interviewing twenty-five university students) revealed that the average Sikh informant in Singapore in the late 1960s and early 1970s was more competent in English and Malay than in Punjabi, did not wear the 5Ks or a head scarf, was inclined to use Western rather than Punjabi names for his/her children, did not have a copy of the Guru Granth Sahib at home, etc.[26] The twenty-five Sikh university students interviewed in one of the studies, all second-or-third generation Singaporeans, recognized the 'deculturation' of their generation; and, while most thought it a 'bad thing', they also felt that there were 'no ways in which the culture could be preserved'.[27] And a seminar on Sikhism in contemporary Singapore held at the University of Singapore in 1971 revealed strong disagreements among speakers and participants about how to deal with such issues as the external symbols, language training and use, and gurdwara leadership and protocol.[28]

There is something of an irony here, of course. As elsewhere, the British in Singapore had exerted paternalistic control over Sikhs serving in their police and military forces, requiring Sikhs to maintain the visible Khalsa *bana* (uniform) and encouraging regular religious worship. Moreover, Sikh newcomers to Singapore had looked up and been beholden to those well-connected Sikhs—particularly the sergeants, *jemedar*, and *subedar*—who might sponsor them and find them a job. A Sikh Advisory Board, appointed through consultation with the ranking Sikh police official, served as a further paternalistic check on Sikh socialization and Sikh political activities in Singapore. However, as Sikhs increasingly moved into independent occupations and took control over their own community institutions (especially in the waning days of colonial rule), the clear-cut hierarchies of power and control were gradually undermined. Thus, Kernail Singh Sandhu, the late Director of the Institute of Southeast Asian Studies in Singapore, in a trenchant analysis, laced with biting indictment of post-colonial Sikh leadership in Singapore and nostalgia for the old order, rued the 'break-up of old economic, social, and power relations' which he saw as having led to 'a fragmented Sikh society . . . at a time when the Sikhs need at least a modicum of unity to attain and safeguard their legitimate cultural, social, economic and political requirements to ensure their longer-term survival and progress as *a community*.'[29] The recent efforts of Sikh professionals in Singapore to resurrect the Sikh Advisory Board and to reconstruct the old hierarchies of power between the state and the Sikh community in Singapore suggest interesting parallels in patterns and uses of state support of Punjabi/Sikh heritage in the paternalistic British colony of Singapore and in the corporatist post-colonial Republic of Singapore.

Of course, findings of 'deculturation' among Sikhs in Singapore are not unlike what one might have encountered among second-and third-generation Sikhs in British Columbia or California in the late 1960s and early 1970s. In California and British Columbia, it took a massive influx of Sikh migrants from Punjab (and the worldwide politicization of Sikh identity in the 1980s) to spark a significant 'revitalization' of Punjabi/Sikh culture in these settings.[30] However, unlike Britain, Canada, and the United States, Singapore has had no significant recent Sikh immigration. Since immigration laws were tightened in the 1950s, in-marrying female spouses and some independent professional class immigrants have been the only source of new permanent members added to the local Sikh community except through natural increase. Therefore, community leadership today derives primarily from a generation that has come of age in Singapore and represents a thoroughly Singaporean Sikh constituency.

However, despite their spatial and temporal distance from Punjab, Singapore's Sikhs remain well connected to Sikhs in Punjab and elsewhere through family connections, marriage ties, international travel, and communications links. News of events taking place in Punjab as well as news from elsewhere in the Sikh diaspora reaches Singapore with great rapidity. Moreover, local gurdwaras are largely staffed by temporary resident *granthis* brought over from India; *ragi jathas* from India and elsewhere regularly visit; and disco *bhangra* groups from Britain have even begun to include Singapore on their world tours. When Singapore's Sikhs decided to mount their International Conference cum Exhibition on Punjabi/Sikh Heritage, they were sufficiently well connected both to the wider Punjabi/Sikh community and to the political powers in Singapore to pull it off with great success.

But the Singapore case is interesting as a potential model, precisely because Singapore's is so truly a community of Sikhs who have come of age in the diaspora. Singapore's Sikh leadership confronts the challenge of transmitting to a new generation of Singaporean Sikhs a 'Punjabi/ Sikh heritage' that, given their own generation's socialization in Singapore in the 1950s and 1960s, they are at the same time rediscovering and reinventing for themselves. They thus are a potential harbinger of what Sikhs in Britain, Canada, and the United States may face in a coming generation. And what seems particularly notable about how Singapore's Sikh leadership has proceeded is the way that they have successfully solicited the state's support both to reinforce a distinctive Sikh identity and to help socialize Singaporean Sikhs into a version of Sikhism compatible with the teachings of the Sikh Gurus yet sensitive to the expectations of the modern nation-state.[31]

***

It is surprising that Sikhs in Singapore should be enjoying such success in pursuing their political agenda, because at first glance, Singapore's multiracialism as a state policy would not appear particularly favourable to Sikh self-assertion. After independence from Britain in 1959 and separation from Malaysia in 1965, Singapore embarked upon nationhood with a profound sense of its 'racial' pluralism. The colonial political economy had created Singaporean society primarily out of immigrant Chinese, Indian, and Malay labour. Colonial Singapore had been a classic plural society, stratified by race and class.[32] And local racial tensions and memories of past race riots lay close to the surface. At the same time, Singapore was now a Chinese-majority city-state located between two larger, Malay-dominated states, Malaysia and Indonesia, each experiencing tensions with its own Chinese minority. Singapore's new political leadership thus embarked on nation-building with what one Singapore-based political scientist has termed a 'garrison mentality'—that is, portraying Singapore as a nation-state surrounded by potentially hostile external forces and internally vulnerable to racial conflagration and disintegration.[33]

More positively, the image adopted of Singapore's multiracial society has been that of 'a rope braided together'—with the overall strength of the rope (that is, the Singaporean nation) dependent upon the unity and integrity of its constituent strands (that is, the different 'races'). Or, in the words and vivid illustrations of a Singapore Social Defence Forces video shown repeatedly on state-run television and in the public schools, Singapore's society is likened to a rope 'so strong when united, but so fragile when divided and individually frayed'. Singapore's rope thus provides a metaphor of pragmatic interdependence of diverse strands, and Singapore has approached its policies of 'multiracialism' as a utilitarian project.

Conventionally, the rope is shown with four strands, corresponding to what became known in Singapore as the CMIO categories. These 'racial' categories—'C' for the Chinese, who make up 77 per cent of the citizenry; 'M' for the Malays, who make up 14 per cent ; 'I' for Indians, who make up 7 per cent; 'O' for Others, who make up 2 per cent—became in the 1970s the taxonomic categories through which social difference in Singapore was recognized for official purposes. Rather than identify with one's dialect group or region of origin, Singapore's Chinese, Malay, and Indian citizens were encouraged to identify with what the state termed their 'race'. (In Singapore, racial identity is acquired through the patriline and listed on one's identity cards and other official documents.) Sikhs, who composed only a little more than 7 per cent of the 7 per cent of the population that was Indian, were thus rather invisible within the racial politics of the period.[34]

The state's policy at the time was not only to reify but also to reinforce these 'racial' categories, with the ultimate intent to create a unique species of 'Singaporean Chinese', 'Singaporean Malays', and 'Singaporean Indians' who did not look to ancestral homelands for reinforcement of their identities. Unity of the Singaporean nation through unity and harmonization of its racial communities ('many races, one people') became the goal. The Singaporean citizen was to identify with the positive cultural features and moral values of his/her ancestral Great Tradition without, however, retaining allegiances to or vested interests in the politics of the contemporary nation-states of one's ancestral homeland. Since it was assumed that language and culture were intimately connected, language policy became the favoured vehicle for reinforcing one's 'racial' identity. Thus, while English became the dominant working language of education, government, and commerce, Mandarin, Malay, and Tamil were also official languages, one language for each of the major local 'races'.

The association between race and language (and the reification of each) was further underlined with the 'speak Mandarin' campaign of the late 1970s and early 1980s. Rather than speak their native dialects—for example, Hokkein, Hakka, Cantonese — Singaporean Chinese were exhorted to learn Mandarin as the language appropriate to their race. A two-language policy implemented in the schools required each student to learn English and the 'mother tongue' (more accurately, a 'father tongue', since the race of the father determined the language class to which the child would be assigned). All Chinese students were required to learn English and Mandarin, regardless of the language that was spoken in the home. Malays were required to learn English and Malay. By the logic that tied each official race to one of the official languages, all Singaporean Indians were to learn Tamil, but North Indian speakers (including Punjabi Sikhs) argued vehemently that Tamil was of an entirely alien language group and that being required to learn Tamil would be too onerous a requirement. Eventually, they (along with Eurasians) were given permission to choose which of the official languages, in addition to English, they would submit for school testing purposes.[35]

The government's rationale for its language policy has usually had two components. One has been what might be termed 'political economic pragmatism': Mandarin and Malay (less so Tamil) are useful regional and international languages for trade and diplomacy; therefore, it behooves the country to have citizens fluent in these languages. The other has been what might be termed 'socio-cultural pragmatism'. Specifically, the argument has been that an 'Asian language' will serve as what Singaporeans call a 'cultural ballast', an antidote to creeping Westernization introduced through the use of English. Proficiency in English may be required on pragmatic grounds, since it is the international language of technology and commerce. But if Singaporeans are to avoid the decadence and destructive individualism of the West, they must have access to Asian cultural values that are thought to be transmitted through an Asian language.[36]

This search for a 'cultural ballast' was also an impetus to the introduction of various Religious Education tracks in the schools during the 1980s—the assumption being that if students were required to learn more about their ancestral religions, they would be less susceptible to Western secular humanism and Christian missionization. By the late 1980s, however, the government had changed its mind and decided that Religious Education was proving divisive, since it was fuelling religious revivalism.[37] The government subsequently decided to replace Religious Education (and its various tracks) with a common course of Moral Education based on 'national values' and, simultaneously, to introduce a Religious Harmony Act (establishing a Religious Harmony Council) that would counteract 'religious polarization' and would ensure that religion and politics be 'kept rigorously separate'.[38]

The government explained its search for a set of National Values as an attempt 'to identify a few key values which are common to all the major groups in Singapore and which draw on the essence of each of these heritages'. Once again, the argument was that this commitment to a set of implicitly Asian values would serve as an antidote ('cultural ballast') against creeping Westernization. The five National Values finally agreed upon were: (1) nation over community and society above the individual; (2) family as the basic unit of society; (3) regard and community support for individuals; (4) consensus instead of contention; (5) racial and religious harmony. One can legitimately ask to what extent these values are actually common to all the major groups in Singapore. Some analysts note that the list has a strongly Confucian bias. Nevertheless, it does articulate a set of values around which members of the society might orient themselves.[39]

This whole 'cultural ballast' and 'national values' discourse of the 1980s and early 1990s has proven quite useful to Singapore's Sikhs, who through their institutions have made a strong case for recognition and reinforcement of their distinctive Punjabi/Sikh heritage as congruent with the national agenda. For instance, consider the debate over language policy and the requirement that all students study in school an 'Asian language' as their race-appropriate 'mother tongue'. Not only were Sikhs, along with other North Indian Singaporeans, able to argue that it would put them at a competitive disadvantage to be forced to study Tamil, but they also could make the same argument of competitive fairness about being required to choose from among Mandarin, Malay, and Tamil. In fact, they attributed Sikh over-representation in the public school 'normal stream' during the 1980s to poor second-language scores.[40] Even more persuasively, they could make a case for being allowed to study Punjabi by noting that the solution of forcing them to choose from among the three official Asian languages did nothing to address their need for a 'cultural ballast' (since they had no special 'cultural' attachment to Tamil, Malay, or Mandarin), whereas allowing them to learn Punjabi tied them not only to the ancestral mother tongue but also to the language of Sikh religious texts. In fact, Sikhs had been making much this same argument since independence.[41] What had changed by the late 1980s was the ideological and institutional context for granting such a request.

***

In the late1980s the Singapore Sikh Resource Panel, a self-generated body of twelve Sikh professionals operating under the leadership of a secondary school principal, Bhajan Singh, had presented evidence both to the Sikh community and to the government suggesting that there existed a sizeable segment of Sikh youth who were not doing well in school, who were getting into trouble with the law, and/or who were marrying or converting out of the community and that this group was characterized by its estrangement from Sikh culture and from local community institutions. The Sikh professionals' public analysis of the problem addressed the perceived lack of a 'cultural ballast' among Singapore's Sikhs, particularly the youth. Sikhs did not identify with their community and its institutions; they knew little about their heritage; they were not learning Punjabi, the ancestral language and the language of the Sikh scriptures. And the Sikh Resource Panel promised an active programme to address these problems.[42]

The professionals sought to advance an agenda, first by gaining formal recognition from the Sikh Advisory Board (SAB), and then by taking control of the SAB to utilize it as a base from which to solicit state support for addressing the problems. As mentioned above, the Sikh Advisory Board originated as a quasi-governmental body established by British authorities in 1915. In its earliest incarnations, it included ten local Sikhs (including a senior Sikh police official as chair) appointed by the Governor of Singapore to advise the Settlement of Singapore 'on all matters affecting the Sikh religion and custom'.[43] From the 1920s until the Second World War, a British police official served as chair. When the Board was reconstituted thereafter, a Sikh was once again elected chair and membership consisted of three Sikhs directly appointed by the government and nine Sikhs chosen by the government from nominees forwarded from the various Sikh temple societies. After independence, the SAB became a statutory board established under the Ministry of Community Development with responsibilities 'to advise the Minister on matters concerning the Sikh religion and customs and the general welfare of the Sikh community.'[44]

During the 1980s, the Sikh Advisory Board had pressed the Ministry of Education to include Sikh Studies as part of the Religious Studies programme in the public schools. The government, which at first had not intended to include Sikh Studies, acquiesced on the condition that the Sikhs themselves prepare the teaching material, train the teachers, and foot the costs of offering a Sikh Studies option. Working from a pre-existing English-languge text (modified by a local panel and approved by the Ministry of Education), the SAB was able to see that Sikh Studies was offered as an elective track in the school's Religious Studies programme from 1983–9.[45] The old Board had less success, however, in getting the government to accept Punjabi as an optional, testable second language in the schools. And, from the government's perspective, the

SAB had failed in its responsibility to impress on Sikhs that anti-India and pro-Khalistan activities ('importing the politics of India into Singapore under the guise of religion') would not be tolerated in Singapore.[46]

In 1989, Bhajan Singh became one of the government's appointees to the Sikh Advisory Board and was immediately elected its chairman. Under Bhajan Singh's leadership, the Sikh Advisory Board (and its affiliate organizations, such as the Singapore Sikh Resource Panel and the Singapore Sikh Education Foundation, also controlled by Bhajan Singh and his fellow professionals) began systematically to court government officials, inviting senior ministers to attend such community functions as popular religious festivals, openings of new community institutions, and heritage gatherings. This allowed Sikhs to present themselves and their agenda to the government; it gave the government's imprimatur to the event, thereby gaining credibility for its sponsor in the eyes of a wider Sikh audience; and, given the publicity these visits garnered in the national media, it gained respect for Sikhs in the eyes of a wider Singaporean audience.

Thus, consider for example, the November 1990 visit by then-Prime Minister Lee Kuan Yew to the Central Sikh Temple. This was during the Prime Minister's last months in office, before he stepped up to become Senior Minister. The ostensible occasion was the 522nd birthday celebration for Guru Nanak, which in any case would have ensured a full house. In a carefully choreographed piece of political theatre (complete with Sikh bagpipers in tartan and turbans brought down from Malaysia to perform for the Prime Minister's benefit!), Sikhs honoured the retiring Prime Minister with presentation of a ceremonial turban and sword (whose purported meanings of 'honour, responsibility to family and nation' and 'dignity, power, fair play and justice' were carefully massaged to be congruent with National Values).[47] Sikh representatives, led by Bhajan Singh, also took the opportunity in their tribute to the Prime Minister to advance a Sikh agenda: specifically, a need for Punjabi-language testing in the schools, a need for collection and dissemination of Sikh-specific government data, a need for more Punjabi culture items in the (state-controlled) media, all justified as necessary to help combat 'the negative influences of western culture' and 'the erosion of traditional Asian (Sikh) values among the Sikh youth.'[48] And Singapore's Sikhs were, in turn, praised by the Prime Minister for contributions and successes as a 'distinctive group' who 'had been a credit to Singapore because by and large, they were law-abiding, hardworking and successful in educating their children to enter the professions and business'. At the end of his visit, the Prime Minister promised that 'the Government will support all your constructive schemes'[49]. This was accompanied by assurances that Punjabi was to be accepted as a testable second language option at the secondary school level through Cambridge University external examination, so long as Sikhs themselves produced the teaching materials, ran the classes, trained the teachers, and footed the bill. Subsequently, in 1993, similar permission was extended to allow Punjabi as a testable second language at the primary level, with the added caveat that the local Sikh community procure the evaluators as well.[50]

There are a number of reasons why the government has been willing to work with Bhajan Singh and his group of professionals to increase the power and credibility of the Sikh Advisory Board. Officials at the Ministry of Community Development with responsibility for overseeing the SAB and Sikh affairs were delighted that they were dealing with fellow professionals whose 'proactive' agenda reflected 'coinciding interests' with those of the government.[51] Sikh efforts to address the perceived needs of the Sikh underclass were entirely consistent with the government's 'self-help' campaign to get the different racial communities in Singapore to take care of their own educational and social welfare problems through their own community institutions. Although the Singapore Indian Development Association (SINDA) was formed in 1991 as the designated 'Indian' self-help institution, the kinds of self-help programmes being undertaken by the Sikh Advisory Board and its affiliated groups (Punjabi-language classes, educational scholarships, counselling of drug addicts, youth and senior activities, etc.) have earned consistent praise from government ministers for setting a positive example of community self-help.[52]

Government officials were also pleased that 'moderate' voices were in a position of authority within the Sikh community, rather than the pro-Khalistani elements that they had feared might take control of Sikh institutions in the mid-1980s. For instance, Prime Minister Lee Kuan Yew in his visit to the Central Sikh Temple had 'told the Sikhs that their wholehearted support for the Maintenance of Religious Harmony Bill [which mandated a strict separation of religion and politics] reflected their "realistic appreciation of Singapore's realities".'[53] Subsequently, Bhajan Singh, rather than a Sikh religious functionary or one of the old-guard temple society leaders or someone already involved in inter-religious affairs, was appointed to be the Sikh representative on the Religious Harmony Council.[54]

There were clear incentives from the government's side to be responsive to requests from Bhajan Singh and the Sikh Advisory Board, since a show of cooperation on the part of the government furthered the credibility of Bhajan Singh and his group of fellow professionals within the wider Sikh community. So long as the SAB could show continued progress on what Sikhs took to be pressing local needs, it would be difficult to mount a credible attack on the Sikh Advisory Board, as an institution, or its leadership, in particular. Moreover, with government officials appearing at various public events saying favourable things about Sikhs, praising their contributions to Singapore, and promising them respect for their distinctiveness, Khalistan supporters found it difficult to make a case for redress *in Singapore* of grievances against the government of India.

Thus, unlike the situation elsewhere in the diaspora, where local grievances and the impotence of Sikh leaders to address these grievances may have fed Sikh nationalist sensibilities, the successes of Sikhs in Singapore have helped keep Khalistani passions from consuming the agenda of the local community.[55] One of my Singaporean Sikh informants put it best. When I reported to him that the new matriculation forms at the National University of Singapore now list 'Sikh' as a separate 'race' as well as separate 'religion' (a change also reflected in the latest census categories), he commented, 'I guess the [Singapore] government has given us Khalistan.' If, as I suspect, sentiment for Khalistan is fed by a sense of besmirched honour in the diaspora as well as in India, the honour and respect accorded Sikhs in Singapore has had a palliative effect.[56]

Let me now summarize what I have and have not been arguing about Sikhs in Singapore. In Singapore, 'Sikh' as a distinctive social identity has become more widely know in recent years. Publicity—local, national, international—of events featuring identifiably 'Sikh' participants (including coverage of the Sikh nationalist movement and the crisis in Punjab) have ensured that the public at large is more cognizant now than it was a decade or so ago of the existence of the Sikhs as a distinct group. (Diasporan Sikhs, too, are probably more aware of their reported distinctiveness!) Thus, Singaporeans of other backgrounds are more likely to be aware that the old folk category 'Bangalee', used regionally for all North Indians (who were assumed to have arrived in Southeast Asia from Calcutta), is a misnomer and that Sikhs—also known locally as 'Singhs' or 'Bhais'—are a distinct group. More significantly, the state too seems to have recognized and validated that distinctiveness. Thus, in exercising its taxonomic control over difference, the Singaporean state, after failing to integrate Sikhs into a larger, synthetic 'Singaporean Indian' identity (which was largely South Indian, Hindu, Tamil-speaking), has acquiesced in accepting Sikh claims of distinctiveness to the point of recognizing Sikhs as a distinct 'race' (as well as 'religion') and in granting support for Sikh-initiated projects on the grounds that they will provide Sikhs with their own 'cultural ballast'. This has been seen, quite naturally, as a major accomplishment and a boon to the further transmission of Punjabi/Sikh heritage in Singapore. But there are inevitable tradeoffs to be made when ethnocultural groups play the 'politics of recognition' in different states. And the case of Sikhs in Singapore is no different on this count.

***

The post-colonial Republic of Singapore has variously been described as authoritarian, bureaucratic, administrative, and paternalistic. I follow the political scientist David Brown in characterizing the Singaporean state as 'inclusionary corporatist' and its politics of ethnic management as 'interventionist'. Corporatism, following Brown, 'refers to attempts by an avowedly autonomous state-elite to organize the diverse interest associations in society such that their interests can be accommodated within the interdependent and organic national community'. In a corporatist state, it is the state that empowers society. The classic corporatist state sought to organize competing economic interests so as to curtail populist participation. Singapore's corporatist state has increasingly sought to organize ethnic interest groups as well, by legitimating and enfranchising certain groups and individuals to participate in public affairs.[57]

Corporatist Singapore's interventions into the management of ethnicity include making a distinction between 'political authority . . . portrayed in monistic terms as absolutist loyalty to the nation-state, such that any other sub-national or cross-national political loyalties are deemed antithetical and illegitimate', 'cultural identity . . . seen as a layered or tiered structure, rather than as a monolith . . . such that various groups within the complex society are recognized as having values which differ from each other but which are compatible', and 'interest association' whereby the state recognizes, licenses, and in some cases actively creates the legitimate channels through which ethnic interests may be articulated.[58] Examples in Singapore include: depiction of society along racial or ethnic lines (for example, CMIO categories), but with subordination of ethnic political loyalties to the state; recognition of ethnic values (that is, 'cultural ballast') as congruent with National Values; the licensing of monopolistic ethnic institutions—for example, Chinese Development Assistance Council (CDAC), The Council for Malay Education (Mendaki), Singapore Indian Development Association (SINDA) and, in effect, the Sikh Advisory Board—as legitimate interest associations.

Sikh 'successes' in advancing a 'Sikh agenda' in Singapore must, therefore, be seen in the context of Singapore's 'inclusionary corporatism'. Since the late 1980s, the government has: (1) recognized Sikhs as a distinct 'race', (2) granted Sikhs permission to strengthen their 'cultural ballast' (for example, through Sikh studies, Punjabi language, Punjabi/Sikh heritage centre, etc.); and (3) fostered and licensed two legitimate channels for transmitting Sikh interests to the government and mobilizing Sikh support for government policies—the Sikh Advisory Board and its associated bodies, under the direction of Bhajan Singh (who also serves as the appointed Sikh representative on the boards of the Religious Harmony Council and the Singapore Indian Development Association);[59] and the elected Sikh 'minority' Member of Parliament, Davinder Singh, chosen under a system of Group Representation Constituencies introduced in 1988.[60] Both Bhajan Singh and Davinder Singh, it might be noted, come from the same generation of Singapore-raised professionals who became active in local Sikh affairs in the mid-1980s, and they have worked cooperatively to further Sikh political interests in Singapore.

At the same time, the government has cut its formal ties to potential alternative channels of Sikh interest articulation. The Central Sikh Gurdwara Board, the management body for the Central Sikh Temple and the Silat Road Sikh Temple, was granted its 'freedom' in 1987 from appointment and further oversight by the Ministry of Community Development, but with the understanding that as a religious body it could not involve itself in domestic or foreign political affairs.[61] The Singapore Khalsa Association has had its Punjabi-language classes incorporated into the National Punjabi Language Programme and its Khalsa Kindergarten tied to the Singapore Sikh Education Foundation through the financial leverage of the Singapore Indian Development Association.[62] And the long-time Sikh member of the Presidential Council for Minority Rights, retired Singapore Supreme Court Justice, Choor Singh, was quietly dropped from the Council at the expiration of his next term after he was suspected to have Khalistani sympathies.[63]

We thus see all the elements of Singapore's inclusive corporatism in its management of Sikh ethnicity: 'a distinction between ethnicity as the illegitimate political loyalties towards the Punjab; ethnicity as the identification with Sikh values which provide a cultural anchor and a basis for Singaporean identity; and ethnicity as the legitimate socio-economic interests of the Sikh community [articulated through state-licensed channels].'[64] But such distinctions are not always easy to comprehend and may be hard to sustain, especially in the face of a global flow of nationalist rhetoric asserting that Sikh religion, politics, culture, etc. are inseparable. Thus, Sikh 'successes' in Singapore are probably more fragile than they might first appear since, as discussed above, they depend on 'coinciding interests' of state-elite and community leaders.

Singapore's Sikhs—publicly united, nationally respected, and politically successful—might, therefore, wish to further ponder the price of their 'success' at playing the game of multiracialism in corporatist Singapore. What the corporatist state giveth it can taketh away, since it is the state that empowers society rather than the reverse. In the Singapore case, success in being able to promote their Punjabi/Sikh heritage requires Sikhs to make certain compromises to conform to the political culture of Singapore, including accepting a depoliticized Sikhism that promises to eschew overt political support for Sikh nationalism in India and to avoid all other forms of political action not explicitly sanctioned by the state. For those Sikh nationalists who argue that their religion, culture, politics are one, this may ultimately prove to be an unpalatable compromise. However, to assert themselves against the current leadership would be to jeopardize the recent local successes that have been gained, since the continued blessings of the state depend on the continuing judgment of state-elites that there are 'coinciding interests' between the state and Sikh organizations. Given that current successes are so tenuously tied in this corporatist state to the survival of the state-licensed moderate, professional Sikh leadership, the propensity for Sikh factionalism can hardly been taken as an auspicious omen.[65]

Moreover, in the euphoria over their 'successes' in playing the politics of recognition in Singapore, Sikhs have thus far largely avoided confronting potentially divisive questions over the kind and content of the 'Punjabi/Sikh heritage' to be transmitted to Sikhs in Singapore. Mention has already been made of the constraints on politicization that Singaporean Sikhs work under. When Sikh Studies was taught in the schools, G.S. Mansukhani's *Introduction to Sikhism* was 'revised and re-written to suit the needs of the Sikh pupils in Singapore' by a five-member panel appointed by the SAB, with the final text subject to approval by the Ministry of Education.[66] Now that almost all school-age Sikhs in Singapore are studying Punjabi, the National Punjabi Language Programme is developing curricular materials specifically for the Singaporean context rather than relying on textbooks imported from north India. Speaking with reporters during Prime Minister Goh Chok Tong's visit to the Central Sikh Temple in 1991, Bhajan Singh stated that 'there are cultural, contextual, environmental and emotional differences in the books and the way Sikhs here live. We hope to make the language, the values, more relevant, more familiar to our young here.' To which the Prime Minister responded, 'I am pleased to learn that your leaders have paid extra attention to promoting Singaporean Sikh values rather than adopt them lock, stock and barrel from overseas.'[67] Given fundamental differences among Sikhs about Punjabi-language pedagogy (whether, students should be trained to read the Adi Granth; to read and write secular Punjabi literature; to speak colloquial Punjabi) and this implicit distinction being made between Punjabi Sikh values and Singaporean Sikh values, one can easily envision battles to come over curricular content and teacher selection.[68]

Furthermore, there is little evidence yet that the positive feelings about Punjabi/Sikh heritage engendered by the activites of the Sikh Advisory Board, the Sikh Resource Panel, the Singapore Sikh Education Foundation, and the National Punjabi Language Programme have had a carryover effect in terms of reconciling Singaporean Sikh youth to the socialization practices prevalent in local gurdwaras. Singapore's gurdwaras remain social centres for the community. And the financial and moral support of the gurdwaras is crucial to the self-help activities initiated by the SAB and its affiliates. But the gurdwaras themselves have not been particularly innovative in their attempts to transmit 'Sikhism' as doctrine or practice relevant to the lives of Singaporean Sikhs. Recurrent calls for training and employing bilingual, Singapore-sensitive *granthis* who would be able to interpret religious texts, explain religious teachings, and perform a pastoral role to the *sangat* have been made for over a generation now by Singaporean Sikhs without much actual effect on gurdwara practices. Thus, a recent graduation exercise at National University of Singapore concludes, much like those conducted a generation earlier, that 'the gurdwaras have tremendous potential to act as agents of socialization among the Sikh youths. . . . But much of that potential is unrealized.' What does seem different from a generation ago, these findings suggest, are the ways in which state-licensed Sikh organizations have once again become a positive force in promoting a 'Sikh' identity. It is this 'ethnic revitalization' or 'ethnopoeisis', rather than Sikh religiosity, that appears to have been the main beneficiary of state support in Singapore.[69]

But Singapore's Sikhs may here want to factor in the costs—material and otherwise—incurred when the state 'downloads' responsibilities onto its ethnocultural communities. Funding and staffing Sikh education and social service internally is already proving to be a challenge in Singapore, and any perceived failure of Sikhs as a community to 'help themselves' and to continue their upward mobility in what the state represents as being a meritocratic society will now lie at the doorstep of the Sikhs rather than the state. In fact, it is by no means clear that providing a Punjabi/Sikh 'cultural ballast' will actually solve the problems of the newly-discovered Sikh underclass in Singapore, whose problems are in large part systemic (including residual institutional racism in this avowedly meritocratic society). Having bought into the 'cultural ballast' argument to advance their agenda, will Sikhs not be making themselves vulnerable to a 'blame the victim' attitude on the part of the state (and the Chinese majority) for any subsequent Sikh failures to achieve?

Finally, there are questions about the future of Singaporean multiracialism itself, particularly about the limits of public tolerance for the 'corporatism' and 'ethnic interventions' from which Sikhs appear to be benefiting. Academic specialists on Singapore now hold colloquia on the 'emergence of civil society' in Singapore, attest to the 'confusion' that the citizenry seems to experience over changing 'politics of ethnic management', query the 'racialization' of PAP politics, and speculate on the whether increasingly educated Singaporeans will become 'less receptive to the paternalism and authoritarianism of the PAP'.[70] No one knows to what extent the masses buy into the clearly self-serving set of National Values enunciated by the government. And while the government has set up Singapore as a defender of supposedly pan-Asian communal values against Western individualism run amok, racial and religious minorities like the Sikhs may find they have reason to value some of the 'decadent' rights that Westerners have against the tyranny of the majority. Given past policy changes, it is unclear what next moves in the 'politics of ethnic management' in Singapore might be. Singapore's 'inclusive corporatism' (for all its similarities to colonial rule in Singapore) is only the most recent manifestation of political culture in Singapore, not its necessary apotheosis.

All of which is not to denigrate the accomplishments of Singaporean Sikhs in revitalizing their Punjabi/Sikh heritage in Singapore but to be realistic about the conditions under which these accomplishments have taken place and the challenges that remain even in Singapore. Whether the Singaporean Sikh model is exportable to other societies is another matter. Singapore's 'inclusive corporatism' appears incompatible with the dynamic civil societies and pluralistic democracies of Britain, Canada, and the United States where most diasporan Sikhs now live. Where, as in Canada, the government has tried to license representatives for the articulation of ethnic-political interests, Sikhs have largely kept their distance from organizations seen to be 'government tools'.[71] Moreover, Sikh factionalism and the competition for honour—while serving, as Roger Ballard has argued, as a great spur to Sikh accomplishments both in Punjab and in the diaspora—mean that only under rare circumstances are Sikhs able to meet their own ideal of 'a closely knit, tightly organized, and comprehensively unified community'.[72] It, therefore, seems highly questionable whether the internally diverse and geographically dispersed Sikh populations of Britain, Canada, and the United States are in a position to set aside their differences to advance a unified Sikh domestic political agenda, especially in the absence of a move in these states toward more 'inclusionary corporatist' policy of ethnic management. Which is only to suggest that Sikhs in most diasporan settings will have to find ways to transmit Punjabi/Sikh culture without the kinds of state involvement experienced by Sikhs in Singapore.

In Singapore, most Sikh schoolchildren (and many of their previously 'deculturated' parents) are now taking Punjabi-language classes.[73] The Sikh Advisory Board and its affiliated self-help organizations are actively attacking Sikh social problems. An International Punjabi/Sikh Heritage Centre is on the drawing boards. Singaporean Sikhs continue to be the objects of public praise from government officials as a model minority. Sikhs in Singapore can rightfully be proud of these accomplishments; but they should also be aware of the conditions under which their successes were created, and they should not expect others to be in a position to borrow their model wholesale. A double socialization of Sikhs in Singapore has been taking place in recent years. On the one hand, they are being successfully socialized into the corporatist political culture of Singapore. On the other hand, their licensed leadership is socializing the next generation into a state authorized version of [Singaporean] Punjabi/ Sikh heritage. And while similar forms of double socialization will be taking place in other countries of the diaspora where Sikhs now live, the political cultures and the particulars of the Punjab/Sikh heritage that get transmitted are bound to differ. Thus, just as the Sikh Studies and Punjabi-language textbooks used in Singapore have been rewritten for the Singaporean milieu, so too these texts and those to follow will have to be rewritten for other diasporan audiences.

ACKNOWLEDGEMENTS

The research upon which this paper was based was conducted in 1992 and 1993 as part of a regional research project on Sikhs in Southeast Asia. This research was assisted by a Fulbright Southeast Asia Regional Research Award and by a grant from the Joint Committee on Southeast Asia of the Social Science Research Council and the American Council of Learned Societies with funds provided by the National Endowment for the Humanities and the Ford Foundation. I would like to thank the Institute of Southeast Asian Studies and its late Director, Kernail Singh Sandhu, for institutional affiliation and professional support in Singapore. I would also like to express my appreciation to Sikh institutions and individuals in Singapore (who shall remain unnamed to protect them from being held accountable for my interpretations) for their hospitality and cooperation during the course of my research. In addition to the audience at the University of Michigan Sikh Studies Conference on the Transmission of Punjabi/Sikh Heritage in the Diaspora, I would like to thank Yao Souchou and Gary Rodan for their insightful comments on earlier drafts of this material.

NOTES

1. From 'Message' of Bhajan Singh, Chairman of the Sikh Advisory Board and the Singapore Sikh Education Foundation, in the souvenir magazine of the 1992 International Conference cum Exhibition on Punjabi/Sikh Heritage.
2. 'Sikh concerns', *Straits Times*, 29 May 1992, p. 18; 'Sit on each other's committees, self-help groups told', *Straits Times*, 5 June 1992, p. 30; 'BG Lee: Govt wants more S. Asians to settle here,' *Straits Times*, 6 June 1992, p. 1; 'Sikhs praised again for self-help', *Straits Times*, 8 June 1992.
3. 'Sikh concerns', *Straits Times*, 29 May, 1992, p. 18.
4. The 1990 Census of Population (Table 15: Indian Resident Population by Age Group, Dialect Group and Sex) listed 12,771 under the category 'Sikh'. Another 2,307 were enumerated as 'Punjabi'. Given these as alternatives (along with 'Hindi', 'Urdu', and 'Hindustani', among other choices), it is not clear just who ended up in the 'Punjabi' category.
5. Speaking at the Central Sikh Temple on 21 November 1991, Prime Minister Goh Chok Tong announced: 'The Sikh community is generally better off compared to the total [Singaporean] population. A higher

proportion of Sikhs (45 per cent) has secondary or higher qualifications as compared to the population as a whole (39 per cent). The Sikh labour force participation rate is higher than the national average (63.3 per cent as against 62.1 per cent). The percentage of Sikhs living in private housing and four and five room flats is also higher than the national average (59 per cent as against 52 per cent). Also, 92 per cent of Sikhs own the houses they occupy as against 90 per cent for the total population.' For full text of the talk, see Goh Chok Tong, 'The Community Approach to Solving Problems', *Speeches*, 15, (6) Nov./Dec. 1991, pp. 4–7.

6. 'The Singapore Sikh Resource Panel and the Sikh Community, *The Singapore Sikh* (Nov. 1992), pp. 19–20.
7. 'PM: No reversal on bilingual policy', *Straits Times*, Saturday, 3 Nov. 1990, and 'Sikhs honour PM on birth anniversary of Guru Nanak', *Straits Times*, 3 Nov. 1990, p. 22. See also the account of a letter from Lee Kuan Yew to Bhajan Singh sent on the former's last day as prime minister ('Sikh community receives assurances from Lee Kuan Yew', *Straits Times*, 18 February 1991). Lee Kuan Yew's view of the Sikhs has been fairly consistent. At a Sikh function in 1967, he praised the Sikhs for their 'valuable contribution to the life, the vitality, the success and the prosperity of our society' and congratulated them 'on the success that you have made for yourselves in carrying out a desent [*sic*] livelihood for yourselves and your children' (quoted in *Tercentenary Souvenir*[Singapore: Sri Guru Nanak Sat Sang Sabha, 1967], n.p.). The only negative public stereotyping of Singapore's Sikhs by Lee Kuan Yew that I encountered occurred in the context of his justifying Singapore's Internal Security Act to a British reporter, when he stated that 'Sikhs in Singapore were outraged because the Golden Temple was attacked [in 1984]. We had to protect the Indian High Commissioner here from 40,000 [sic] Sikhs who would have bludgeoned him' ('Singaporeans expect firm and strong government, says PM', *Straits Times*, 22 Oct. 1989, p. 20).
8. In addition to comments made on the occasion of the International Conference (n. 2 above), public statements of support have been made by then-Minister of Community Development and Foreign Affairs Wong Ken Seng when the new Sikh Resource Panel held the first Singapore Sikh Lecture ('Sikhs set up panel to tackle community's problems', *Straits Times*, 17 Dec. 1989), by then-Acting Minister of Information and Arts B.G. Yeo at the launch of the Singapore Sikh Education Foundation ('Ethnic groups should set up own heritage centres: BG Yeo', *Straits Times*, 31 Dec. 1990, p. 16), by Prime Ministers Goh Chok Tong during a visit to the Central Sikh Temple on the occasion of Guru Nanak's birthday celebrations ('PM enjoys chapati and dhal with the Sikhs', 'PM Goh to self-help groups: rise above communal

interests,' and 'Sikhs to introduce own local textbooks', all in *Straits Times*, 22 Nov. 1991, p. 25), and by Minister for Law and Home Affairs S. Jayakumar, at Baisakhi Day celebrations ('Week of festivals for Sikhs, Hindus and Christians', *Straits Times*, 14 April 1992, p. 18).

9. Choor Singh, *Bhai Maharaj Singh: Saint-Soldier of the Sikh Faith*. (Singapore: Central Sikh Gurdwara Board, 1991), p. 17.
10. Davinder Singh, 'Foreward' in Choor Singh, *Bhai Maharaj Singh*, p. 2.
11. Construction of the memorial gurdwara within the Silat Road gurdwara grounds would replace a *samadh* (tombstone) currently residing on the grounds. The *samadh* was moved from the Singapore General Hospital grounds to the Silat Road Gurdwara in the 1960s. It is popularly known as the *samadh* of one Baba Karam Singh, a *karniwala* (possessor of supernatural powers). Nothing definitive is know of who Baba Karam Singh was. Some say the *samadh* was that of Bhai Maharaj Singh, built at the site of his cremation. The current management calls it a memorial to Bhai Maharaj Singh aka Baba Karam Singh. Those pushing the Bhai Maharaj Singh Memorial Gurdwara hope that its construction will put an end to what they see as the un-Sikhly practice of worshipping at a *samadh*.
12. On the circumstances favouring international migration from Punjab during the British colonial period, see Richard Fox, *Lions of the Punjab* (Berkeley: University of California Press, 1985), pp. 43–9; Verne A. Dusenbery, 1989 'Introduction' in N.G. Barrier and V.A. Dusenbery, (eds). *The Sikh Diaspora*, Columbia, Mo.: South Asia Publications, pp. 1–28; W.H. McLeod, 'The First Forty Years of Sikh Migration' in *The Sikh Diaspora*, pp. 29–48.
13. Regarding early Sikh migration to the Malay peninsula, see Kernail Singh Sandhu, 1970, 'Sikh Immigration into Malaya During the Period of British Rule' in J. Ch'en and N. Tarling, (eds), *Studies in the Social History of China and South-East Asia*, Cambridge: Cambridge University Press, pp. 335–54. On early Sikh history in Singapore, see Kernail Singh Sandhu, 'Historical Role of the Sikhs in the Development of Singapore' *Seminar Report on Sikh Youth and Nation Building* (Singapore: Sikh Advisory Board, 1989), pp. 24–40; Tan Tai Yong, 'A Historical Sketch of the Early Sikhs in Singapore', *The Varsity Sikh Journal*, 1 (1992), pp. 25–7. See also Seva Singh Gandharab, *Early Sikh Pioneers of Singapore* (Singapore: the author, 1986) and Mehervan Singh, *Sikhism: East and West* (Singapore: the author, 1979).
14. Subdividing Singaporean Sikhs according to locally-relevant caste and regional distinctions would generate the following, very rough estimates of the current Sikh population in Singapore: 5,000 Malwa Jats; 4,000 Majha Jats; 2,500 Doaba Jats; 1,000 Aroras; 500 Khatris; 500 Mazhbis; 500 Other (Chimbas, Nais, Cheors, Kamiars, etc.). Regional distinctions,

although becoming less important in marital matches, are still institutionalized in Singapore. Thus, for example, representation on the Sikh Advisory Board comes from gurdwara societies which are themselves regional or caste based.

15. In 1917, the Central Sikh Temple was vested in the Muhammadan and Hindu Endowments Board by order of the Governor (No. 715 of 1917). In 1940, The Queen Street Gurdawara Board of Trustees was granted control under the Queen Street Gurdwara Ordinance (No. 30 of 1940 [Cap. 311, 1955, ed.]). In 1961 an attempt to amalgamate the Queen Street and Silat Road Sikh Gurdwaras and place them under an incorporated board (L.A. 7 of 1961) failed when some Sikhs objected to the proposed make-up of the board. A subsequent attempt in 1981 to amalgamate the two boards into a single corporate body to be called the Central Sikh Gurdwara Board was successful (No. 17 of 1981; amended Act. No. 6 of 1987). In the late 1970s, the Singapore government appropriated the land at Queen Street, and the Central Sikh Temple was subsequently rebuilt on land supplied by the government at the intersection of Serangoon and Towner Roads.
16. Silat Road has since been renamed Jalan Bukit Merah. Silat Road Sikh Gurdwara was officially incorporated under a Board of Trustees through the Silat Road Sikh Gurdwara Ordinance (No. 23 of 1937; amended No. 4 of 1950 [Cap. 318, 1955 (ed.)]). Since 1981, Central Sikh Temple and Silat Road Sikh Temple have been jointly administered by the Central Sikh Gurdwara Board as per the Central Sikh Gurdwara Board Act (No. 17 of 1981, amended Act No. 6 of 1987).
17. Two smaller gurdwaras, Sembawang Sikh Temple near the British Naval Base and Gurdwara Sahib Jalan Kayu near the British Air Force Base, emerged to serve congregations in these locales in northern Singapore. Efforts are currently underway to consolidate these two societies and to cooperate on building a single, new gurdwara in Yushin.
18. Pardesi Khalsa Dharmak Diwan lost its home at Kirk Terrance when the government appropriated the land for redevelopment in the 1980s. They formally moved their gurdwara to a floor of a building on Geyland Road in 1991–2.
19. The Mazhbi Sikhs recently lost their gurdwara to redevelopment of the Serangoon Road area. They have not found a new institutional home.
20. Early (pre-partition) Khatri migrants to Southeast Asia specialized in sports shops, while Aroras specialized in textiles. The Arora community in Singapore is well connected to the thriving Arora community in Bangkok, Thailand.
21. Tan Tai Yong, *Singapore Khalsa Association* (Singapore: Times Books International for the SKA, 1988), p. 37.
22. In 1970, the SKA moved into a new five-storey building at Tessensohn and Balestier Roads. The building contains classrooms, facilities for

holding marriage and other celebrations, and an income-generating pub and gambling room open to the general public. See Tan Tai Yong, ibid., for further background on the SKA.

23. See, Singh, *Sikhism*, pp. 70–1.
24. Other SSPS proposals had been for an enlarged gurdwara at Central Sikh Temple, a Khalsa Press and Library at Pardesi Khalsa Dharmak Diwan, a Khalsa Sports and Game Centre at Khalsa Jiwan Sudhar Sabha, and a Khalsa Widows and Orphans Home at Silat Road Sikh Temple. The Khalsa English School and Khalsa Punjabi School had both folded by the early 1960s. The Khalsa English School, started in 1948 for overage students whose schooling had been interrupted by the War, had by the 1960s lost much of its student body to English-medium government schools. The Khalsa Punjabi School, started in 1947 for Sikh girls not attending public schools, had been undermined by the end of prejudice against Sikh girls attending English-medium schools. The latter also had lost government aid that it had received from 1958–62, when the Ministry of Education cut aid to schools not using one of the four official languages of Singapore. See Singh, *Sikhism,* pp. 45–6; Yong, *Singapore Khalsa Association*, pp. 41, 55.
25. Yong, *Singapore Khalsa Association*, p. 37.
26. Sarjit Singh, 'Some Aspects of Social Change in the Sikh Community in Singapore', BA exercise, Department of Social Work and Social Administration, University of Singapore, 1969; Surinder Jeet Singh, 'Culture Change Among the Sikh-Punjabis at the University of Singapore', BA exercise, Department of Sociology, University of Singapore, 1971.
27. Ibid., pp. 48, 54–5. Yong, *Singapore Khalsa Association*, p. 57 also reports concerns about 'deculturalisation' at this time.
28. *Seminar on Sikhism in Contemporary Singapore (University of Singapore, 1971): Communiqué and Papers.* Photostat at the Institute of Southeast Asian Studies Library, Singapore.
29. Sandhu, 'Historical Role of the Sikhs in the Development of Singapore', pp. 35, 38–9; emphasis in the original.
30. See, for example, Bruce La Brack, *The Sikhs of Northern California*. N.Y.: AMS Press, 1987.
31. One of the recurrent concerns running through the public addresses of the late K.S. Sandhu was how Sikhs might adapt the institutions and social practices of village Punjab to the new 'social ecology' of cosmopolitan, urban settings where most diasporan Sikhs now live. See, for example, 'Opening Address', *The Varsity Sikh Journal*, 1(1992), pp. 13–14. Similarly, Bhajan Singh has defined the challenge of adequately transmitting Punjabi/Sikh heritage to young people living in the diaspora as the greatest challenge facing Sikhs today (personal communication).
32. Within the colonial political economy, Sikhs as police and militia for the British and as petty moneylenders would hardly seem to have been in a

position to endear themselves to the average Chinese, Malay, or Tamil labourer. And many a Singaporean Chinese can tell you of having been told as a child that if they did not behave 'Babu Singh' would come to take them away. On the other hand, insofar as Sikhs were differentiated from Indian 'coolie' labour during the colonial period, the post-colonial Chinese leadership of Singapore seems to have adopted from the British some of the positive stereotyping of Sikhs as a 'race' apart from other Indians.

33. David Brown, *The State and Ethnic Politics in Southeast Asia* (New York: Routledge, 1994), p. 86.
34. On the CMIO categories and the logic of Singaporean multiracialism in the 1970s and early 1980s, see Geoffrey Benjamin, 'The Cultural Logic of Singapore's "Multiracialism" ' in Riaz Hassan, ed. *Singapore: Society in Transition*, (Kuala Lumpur: Oxford University Press, 1976), pp. 115–33; John Clammer, *Singapore: Ideology, Society and Culture* (Singapore: Chopman, 1985), pp. 107–17: and Sharon Siddique, 'Singaporean Identity' in K.S. Sandhu and P. Wheatley, (eds), *Management of Success: The Moulding of Modern Singapore*, (Singapore: ISEAS, 1989), pp. 563–77.
35. Singapore Supreme Court Justice Choor Singh was listed as among a group urging North Indians to accept Tamil as 'a vehicle for the maintenance and preservation of Indian cultural values in Singapore' ('Big drive to promote use of Tamil', *Straits Times*, 20 February 1980, p. 9); Jaswant Singh Gill, President of the SKA, was quoted as saying, 'There are no religious, social, cultural, or economic reasons for Punjabis to learn Tamil' ("No" to Tamil as link language for Indians here', *Straits Times*, 21 February 1980, p. 4). Susumu Awanohara, 'Singapore: Keeping Cultural Roots Alive', *Far Eastern Economic Review* (21 March 1980), p. 36.
36. On Singapore's linguistic policies and the ideology of language, see John Clammer, op. cit., pp. 133–7; Nirmala Puru Shotam, 'Language and Linguistic Policy' in *Management of Success*, op. cit., pp. 503–22; and Anne Pakir, 'English-Knowing Bilingualism', in Ban Kah Choon, Anne Pakir, and Tong Chee Kiong, (eds), *Imagining Singapore,* (Singapore: Times Academic Publishers, 1992), pp. 234–62.
37. 'New look at Religious Knowledge as a compulsory subject,' *Straits Times*, 21 March 1989, p. 17.
38. The intellectual justification for the Religious Harmony Act was provided by three National University of Singapore sociologists in a report prepared for the Ministry of Community Development (Eddie C.Y. Kuo, Jon S.T. Quah, and Tong Chee Kiong, *Religion and Religious Revivalism in Singapore*. Singapore: Ministry of Community Development, 1988). Subsequently, a government White Paper on the 'Maintenance of Religious Harmony' appeared (Republic of Singapore, Cmd. 21 of 1989), followed by passage of the Maintenance of Religious Harmony Act in 1990 (Republic of Singapore (Chpt. 167A), Act 26 of 1990, revised 1991). Quoted phrases come from the White Paper. The White Paper (Cmd. 21 of 1989) details

Hindu and Sikh activities in Singapore post-1984 which, although mild compared to activities elsewhere in the diaspora at the time, are presented as an example of religious groups in Singapore inappropriately 'importing foreign politics into Singapore' (par. 25–8).

39. The intellectual justification for the search for Singapore's National Values was provided by the Institute for Policy Studies in Singapore at the request of the government (Jon S.T. Quah, (ed.), *In Search of Singapore's National Values*. Singapore: Times Academic Press for the IPS, 1990). The government's White Paper on 'Shared Values' appeared the following year (Republic of Singapore, Cmd. 1 of 1991). Quotations above are taken from the White Paper. For other perspectives on the search for National Values, see Chua Beng Huat and Eddie C.Y. Kuo, *The Making of a New Nation: Cultural Construction and National Identity in Singapore*. Singapore: National University of Singapore, Department of Sociology Working Papers, no. 104, 1991; Gary Rodan, 'Singapore's Leadership Transition: Erosion or Refinement of Authoritarian Rule?, *Bulletin of Concerned Asian Scholars*, 24 (1), 1992, pp. 3–17, esp. pp. 9–11; and David Brown, op. cit, pp. 91 – 6 .
40. Malay emerged as the second language of choice for most Sikh schoolchildren in the 1980s.
41. See, example, the selection from SKA letter on Punjabi language to the Constitution Committee for the Safeguards for Minority Groups in 1966 in Yong, *Singapore Khalsa Association*, p. 42; also letter from SPSS to Ministry of Education cited in Yong, ibid., p. 68, n. 24.
42. Bilveer Singh, 'Singapore Sikh Resource Panel', *The Singapore Sikh* (December 1990), p. 5.
43. 'Appointments: Sikh Advisory Board, Singapore' in *Straits Settlements Government Gazette* (26 Nov. 1915), p. 1748.
44. *Rules for the Guidance of the Sikh Advisory Board* (Singapore: Sikh Advisory Board, n.d.), p. 1. The SAB consists of twelve members appointed for two-year terms by the Minister of Community Developement: three individuals directly nominated by the Minister; one representative chosen from among those nominated by Khalsa Jiwan Sudhar Sabha; and two representatives each chosen from among those nominated by Sri Guru Singh Sabha, Khalsa Dharmak Sabha, Pardesi Khalsa Dharmak Sabha, and Sri Guru Nanak Sat Sang Sabha. On the Sikh Advisory Board, see also: Mehervan Singh, op. cit. p. 54; Choor Singh, 'Sikh Advisory Board,' *The Singapore Sikh* (December 1990), p. 4.
45. 'Call to make Sikh studies 'O' level exam subject', *Straits Times*, 18 Feb. 1982. 'Sikh Studies now available as another option,' *Straits Times*, 4 Aug. 1983. The panel that wrote the textbooks was headed by Gobind Singh Mansukhani, and the textbooks they produced for use in Singapore public schools (G. S. Mansukhani et al., *Sikh Studies, Part I*. Singapore: Sikh Advisory Board, 1985; and G.S. Mansukhani et al., *Sikh Studies, Part II*. Singapore, Sikh Advisory Board, 1986) were based on Mansukhani's *Introduction to Sikhism*, Delhi: India Book House, 1968.

46. 'Sikh leaders warned not to create tension,' *Straits Times*, 11 Jan. 1989.
47. 'Sikhs honour PM on birth anniversary of Guru Nanak', *Straits Times*, 3 Nov. 1990, p. 22.
48. Letter of 2 November 1990 ('Tribute from the Sikh Community') from Bhajan Singh, Chair of Sikh Advisor Board, to Lee Kuan Yew, Prime Minister of the Republic of Singapore (author's files).
49. 'PM: No reversal of bilingual policy', *Straits Times*, 3 Nov. 1990.
50. The Minister of Education had announced in October 1989 that non-Tamil Indian pupils would be allowed to offer Punjabi, Bengali, Gujerati, Hindi, or Urdu as their second language at the N, O, and A-level in lieu of an official mother tongue. Sikhs quickly responded by creating a National Punjabi Language Programme which opened four language centres teaching Punjabi outside school hours. (See 'Panel set up to help Sikhs learn Punjabi as second language', *Straits Times*, 20 May 1990, p. 22.) A fifth centre was subsequently added by incorporating the Punjabi language classes at SKA. In July 1993, the government extended its permission for Punjabi to be taken at the Primary School Leaving Examination as well ('5 Indian languages for PSLE,' *Straits Times*, 27 July 1993, p. 21).
51. 'Proactive' and 'coinciding interests' were phrases used by Singapore Ministry of Community Development officials, Santanu Gupta and Nicholas Poh, to describe the relationship between the Ministry and the Sikh Advisory Board (interview of 26 July 1993).
52. In addition to the statements already noted (n. 7 above), see 'PM Praises Role of Self-Help in Communities', *Straits Times*, 4 Nov. 1990, in which it was reported that 'Mr. Lee Kuan Yew . . . singled out the great capacity for self-help among the Chinese and Sikhs in improving their well-being . . . . Mr. Lee said that this was the kind of dynamism—of the most successful helping the less successful—which was the secret of successful communities all over the world. It also explained why Sikh communities in Europe and elsewhere had done well, he said.'
53. 'PM: No reversal on bilingual policy,' *Straits Times*, 3 Nov. 1990.
54. 'First religious harmony body appointed,' *The Sunday [Straits] Times*, 2 Aug. 1992, pp. 1, 3. Others who may have considered themselves plausible candidates include: Mehervan Singh, a retired accountant and prolific author, long active as an officer of the Inter-Religious Organization (IRO); J.S. Sehgal, Chair of the Central Sikh Gurdwara Board and President of Sri Guru Nanak Sat Sang Sabha; Justice (Ret.) Choor Singh, who has taken to religious writings in his retirement. Clearly, Bhajan Singh's appointment was a demonstration of the state's corporatist management of ethnicity and religion, as it ensured a deliberate representational monopoly.
55. On the relationship between the local politics of recognition and Sikh nationalism in the diaspora, see my article, 'A Sikh Diaspora? Contested Identities and Constructed Realities' in *Nation and Migration: The Politics*

of Space in the South Asian Diaspora, Peter van der Veer, ed. (Philadelphia: University of Pennsylvania Press, 1995), pp. 17–42. Of course, Singapore's Internal Security Act and Religious Harmony Act also help keep any overt pro-Khalistan activities from taking place on Singapore soil.

56. Sikhs can freely enter 'Sikh' rather than 'Indian' as their 'race' on their identity cards; they can list themselves as 'Sikh' by 'ethnic/dialect group' on their census forms; and the 'race' category on the National University of Singapore matriculation form now provides the following choice: Chinese, Malay, Sikh, Sri Lankan, Other Indian, Eurasian, Other Asian, Caucasian, and Other. Of course, one of the effects of enumerating Sikhs separately by 'race' and by 'religion' might be to demonstrate that, contrary to the rhetoric of Sikh nationalists, 'race' and 'religion' are not coeval. My inquiry of the Department of Statistics, Ministry of Trade and Industry, Republic of Singapore generated the following response: 'Please be informed that the number of resident (citizen and permanent resident) *Sikhs* classified under Ethnic/dialect group in the 1990 Population Census was 12,771. However, basing on the 10 per cent sample data, the number of resident persons aged 10 and over having *Sikhism* as a religion in 1990 was 9,200'. In this case, the difference may be accounted for by those under 10 who would have had Sikhism listed as religion. It is true, however, that there are those in Singapore who would have returned 'Sikh' or 'Punjabi' for ethnicity and 'Christianity' or 'no religion' for religion. Conversely, some of the non-Punjabi spouses I met at the Sikh gurdwaras in Singapore would presumably have returned 'Sikh' for religion and 'Chinese' or 'Other Indian' for race or ethnicity.
57. Brown, *The State and Ethnic Politics in Southeast Asia*, pp. 66–111; quote on p. 67.
58. Ibid., pp. 70–1.
59. Bhajan Singh was recently the subject of a highly laudatory profile in the *Straits Times* that focused on his work as an innovative secondary school principal but also mentioned his leadership of the SAB and the Sikh Education Foundation, his membership on the Presidential Council for Religious Harmony and the Executive Council of SINDA, and his receipt in 1991 of the Bhai Vir Singh International Award for his community work in Singapore ('Si Ling's miracle worker', *The Sunday [Straits] Times*, 13 June 1993, p. 3).
60. Group Representation Constituencies were introduced in 1988 when it became apparent that, given the government's housing policy (which had the effect of dispersing the minority population throughout the island), all Members of Parliament would represent Chinese majority constituencies. Rather than nominate non-Chinese candidates who might have been challenged by Chinese candidates put up by opposition parties, the ruling PAP came up with Group Representation Constituencies (collapsing single member districts to form a larger

constituency where a team of four candidates would contest as a single slate) as a way to ensure the election of minority Members of Parliament without forcing them upon Chinese constituents. The Act mandated that at least one member of each slate represent Malay, Indian, or 'Other minority' communities. Davinder Singh Sachdev, a Sikh lawyer, was elected from Toa Payoh constituency in 1988 as an 'other minority' candidate on the PAP slate. There is currently a second Sikh Member of Parliament in Singapore, Dr Kanwaljit Soin, an orthopaeadic surgeon and a leading figure in the feminist organization, AWARE. She has sat since 1991 as one of four Nominated (that is, non-elected) Members of Parliament, having been appointed by the government to give women's concerns a voice in Parliament. Although one of the twelve professionals originally recruited by Bhajan Singh, she has been less active than Davinder Singh in publicly pushing an overtly Sikh agenda (since, for one thing, she thinks that Singaporean Sikhs, for pragmatic reasons, should be learning Mandarin as their second language); but she has raised concerns over quotas on admission of Indians into Law and Medicine faculties and gender bias in immigration law (which make it more difficult for females than males to sponsor foreign spouses) that have a direct affect on Singaporean Sikhs.

61. The Central Sikh Gurdwara Board Act of 1981 consolidated control over the Central Sikh Temple and the Silat Road Temple in the hands of a Board of Trustees, the initial Board of 25 to be appointed by the government and subsequent Boards to consist of 10 government appointees and 15 members elected from the Sikh community at large. When Sikhs objected to so strong a governmental role, the government amended the Act in 1987 'so that the administration and management of the temples are left entirely to the Sikh community.' (See n. 1 above.) Other gurdwaras in Singapore are categorized as 'social associations' rather than 'temples', and thus activities of their management committees are not covered by specific legislation or statute.
62. 'Sinda to give $54,000 grant to the Khalsa Kindergarten', *Straits Times*, 11 May, 1993, p. 25.
63. The Presidential Council for Minority Rights is responsible for considering whether any proposed legislation 'is, or is likely in its practical application to be, disadvantageous to persons of any racial or religious community and not equally disadvantageous to persons of other such communities, either directly by prejudicing persons of that community or indirectly by giving advantage to persons of another community' ('Report of the Presidential Council for the Twelve Months Ending 30th April 1972', Republic of Singapore Cmd. 18 of 1972). The Council is composed of five permanent members, plus a Chairman and up to ten temporary members serving three year (renewable) terms. In none of its annual reports has the Council suggested that any proposed legislation

was found to discriminate against racial or religious minorities in Singapore. Choor Singh served on the Council from its founding in 1973 until the conclusion of his term in 1991. On the origins and evolution of the Presidential Council for Minority Rights and its Constitutional authority, see S. Jayakumar, *Constitutional Law* (Singapore: Malaya Law Review, Faculty of Law, University of Singapore, 1976), pp. 17–28, 104–12.

64. Brown, *The State and Ethnic Politics in Southeast Asia*, p. 104.
65. Bhajan Singh is a Majha Jat, which has meant that some would-be Sikh leaders from among the more numerous Malwa Jats, who have historically controlled most community institutions, have felt their honour and that of other Malwais to be threatened by his prestige and success. Davinder Singh, a non-Jat, non-Punjabi speaker, with a non-Punjabi wife, would be potentially even more susceptible to factional intrigue, were it not for the fact that he is the government-licensed Sikh representative in Parliament.
66. Harbans Singh, 'Preface' to Mansukhani et al., *Sikh Studies, Part I.* One might usefully compare Mansukhani's original text (n. 45 above) with the textbooks produced for use in Singapore to analyse the changes introduced for the Singapore context.
67. 'Sikhs to introduce own local textbooks', *Straits Times*, 22 Nov. 1991, p. 25.
68. Insofar as those graduating from secondary school will be taking a Cambridge external examination, the curriculum along the way is constrained by the kinds of linguistic abilities judged by that exam.
69. Satvinder Singh, 'Sikh Organizations and Sikh Identity in Singapore,' BA exercise, Department of Sociology, National University of Singapore, 1993; quote on p. 49. Sikh Sewaks Singapore has been holding *samelans* (cultural cum religious camps) since 1982 in an attempt, only partially successful, to provide the religious education they feel is lacking in the gurdwaras (Ibid., pp. 44–6). As the author astutely notes: 'From the data collected there seems to be a tendency for the category "Sikh" to be seen in terms of "identity", not so much in terms of "religion". If this is the case, then the racial classification of "Sikh" used by the government for the Sikh community becomes paradoxically, rather apt, since the meaning attached to it is in terms of "identity", not "religion" (pp. 48–9).
70. See, respectively, 'Whither civil society in S'pore', *Straits Times*, 31 July 1993, p. 32; Brown, *The State and Ethnic Politics in Southeast Asia*, pp. 106–11; Bilveer Singh, *Whither PAP's Dominance?* (Petaling Jaya, Malaysia: Pelanduk Publications, 1992), pp. 155–9; Rodan, 'Singapore's Leadership Transition', p. 16.
71. Thus, in the late-1970s, when officials in Ottawa helped launch the National Association of Canadians of Origins in India (NACOI) as a pan-Indo-Canadian ethnic-political group, Sikhs largely boycotted the organization rather than use their numerical advantage to appropriate

it for their own ends. In the early 1990s, Multiculturalism-Canada floated a National Sikh Alliance, which was promptly repudiated by other Sikh organizations such as the World Sikh Organization-Canada (see, for example, Harbakhash Singh Sandhar, 'Canadian Government Launches New Sikh Body! . . . What Won't They Do to Please India?', *The Sword* [Spring/Summer 1992], pp. 26–9). Admittedly, cooperating with Canada's half-hearted corporatism is unlikely to bring the same sort of rewards as in Singapore, but Canadian Sikhs have not even tried to see what advantages might be derived from soliciting the state through licensed channels.

72. Roger Ballard, 'Differentiation and Disjunction Amongst the Sikhs in Britain' in *The Sikh Diaspora* (n. 12 above), pp. 200–34; quote on p. 230. In fact, historically, appeals to collective *izzat* (honour) in the face of an external enemy have been a way to unite the Sikh Panth or *qaum*. In corporatist Singapore, socio-economic competition with the other 'races' may serve the purpose of spurring Singaporean Sikhs to present a united front and, thus, to dampen factionalism.

73. In 1993, some 1,300 out of an estimated 1,540 Sikh schoolchildren were registered for Punjabi-language instruction. The assumption is that this percentage will increase with the acceptance of Punjabi as a testable second language at the primary level and as those who have been taking Malay as their second language pass through the system. While these children are in their classes, many of their parents have also begun studying Punjabi at the language centres.

9

The Poetics and Politics of Recognition*

Diasporan Sikhs in Pluralist Polities

One important new feature of global cultural politics . . . is that state and nation are at each's throats, and the hyphen that links them is now less an icon of conjuncture than an index of disjuncture.

—Arjun Appadurai, 'Disjuncture and Difference in the Global Cultural Economy'

Ethnic policy is heavily conditioned by this initial conceptualization of the relation of groups to each other and to the state. Of course, ethnic policy is also shaped by the particular institutional configurations within states, by interest groups, by the responses of ethnic groups to earlier policy, and by a variety of other influences. But what I wish to suggest here is that national ideologies, in combination with such other influences, are powerfully important.

—Donald L. Horowitz, 'Europe and America: A Comparative Analysis of "Ethnicity"'

In this essay, I am concerned with what Arjun Appadurai has termed 'the central feature of global culture today', to wit 'the politics of the mutual effort of sameness and difference to cannibalize one another' (1990, p.17). In particular, I examine the intersection of nationalist and multiculturalist discourses in the contemporary world, asking whether nationalist discourses that seek to take a diverse collection of individuals and conceptualize their fundamental unity as 'a people' and a polity—as 'national citizens'—must inevitably clash with multiculturalist discourses that, even if they presuppose a politically unified society, recognize internal diversity and legitimate the collective agency of constituent 'ethnocultural groups', 'a people' at another level of the polity?[1]

* First published in *American Ethnologist*, vol. 24, no. 4 (Nov. 1997), pp. 738–62.

Clearly, issues surrounding what has come to be called 'the politics of identity' or 'the politics of recognition' and the problems involved in adequately conceptualizing—let alone balancing—the rights and powers of the state, of ethnocultural groups, and of individuals, are pressing practical problems currently being wrestled with in pluralist polities around the globe. They are central features of what John Comaroff has called our contemporary 'Age of Revolution' (Comaroff 1995). Given their current political import, it is not surprising that the 'politics of identity' are also at the heart of theoretical consideration in all those disciplines—social theory (for example, Faubion 1995, p.12), political philosophy (for example, Taylor 1992, 1994), sociology (for example, Wolfe 1992), political science (for example, Weiner 1992), international relations (for example, Zalewski and Enloe 1995), and anthropology (for example, Comaroff 1995, Das 1995)—concerned with human social and political relations.[2] For anthropologists, in particular, the issue of the rights of 'cultural groups' is of compelling interest, since traditionally it has been such ethnocultural groups, rather than the state or the individual, that have been our objects of study. Indeed, some would argue that, for better or worse, our narratives of 'culture' have reinforced, if not impelled, claims to political agency by such collectivities.[3]

At issue, of course, in 'the politics of identity' are two, related matters: politics and identity. These concern the existence of ethnocultural groups as 'morphological categories' as well as 'subjects of rights' (Das 1995, p. 88). We are thus compelled to analyse those ethnosociologies through which difference is recognized in any particular social field as well as the political structures through which rights are allotted to groups or individuals. And since it is conventionally the state that has had power both to recognize difference and to endow difference with political import, our focus cannot fail to interrogate the state. Indeed, as my first epigram suggests, and as analyses such as Comaroff's (1995) make clear, most noticeable in global cultural politics is the increasing contestation of the legitimate power of the state to recognize and manage social difference. Yet as our second epigram suggests, and as Veena Das (1995, pp. 89–90) forcefully argues on historical grounds and Bruce Kapferer (1988) demonstrates comparatively, it would be unwise to assume that nation-states are all alike in their conceptualization of the relation of groups to each other and to the state. Nor, despite what post-sovereignty theorists such as Michael J. Shapiro (1994) and Jean-Marie Guehanno

(1995) may claim, can we assume the global death of the nation-state as a potent political force. We are, therefore, compelled to look closely in each case at how state hegemony is constructed and contested.[4]

I approach these issues surrounding the 'politics of recognition' through an investigation of the poetics and politics of nationalism and multiculturalism in two modern nation-states—Canada and Singapore. Each of these states in recent years has pushed an aggressive multiculturalist or multiracialist agenda in the face of insecurities about its national unity. Canada has had an official multiculturalism policy and related government support programmes in place since the early 1970s. Since its independence in 1965, Singapore has promoted itself as nation-state not only characterized by but committed to sustaining its racial, ethnic, and religious pluralism. In fact, each country has found it necessary to temporize on its multicultural policies; nevertheless, throughout the period each has presented itself to the world at large as a positive example of how a state can manage its internal diversity.[5]

I use the recent experiences of Sikhs in these two countries to examine how one small but visible minority with its own nationalist project has fared under the nation-building and multiculturalist regimes of these two modern nation-states. My focus is thus on the relationship between the state and its ideologies, policies, and practices of ethnic management on the one hand,and local Sikh institutions and their political aspirations on the other. My interest, in other words, is in the dialectic between the hegemonic powers of the state—in both material and ideological forms—to impose categories of identity on local residents and the culturally creative power of peoples to resist or deflect or work with these social and political categories. Since Canadian and Singaporean Sikhs have had to play the local 'politics of recognition' largely on terms not of their own making, I suggest that the contrasting experiences of Sikhs in the two countries can tell us something useful about the tensions inherent in reconciling nationalist and multiculturalist discourses.

A 'SIKH' DIASPORA: GLOBAL ETHNOSCAPE

Of course, even to begin by talking about a Sikh diaspora and 'Sikh' as a salient social category already begs the question of how a Sikh collectivity came to see itself as a unitary entity able to make claims on the state for recognition as a distinct cultural, ethnic, racial, and/or religious group. A full history is beyond the parameters of this paper, but is itself suggestive of the constitutive powers of, in the first instance, the pre-colonial and colonial state in India (see, for example, Fox 1985; Oberoi 1994). Today master narratives of 'Sikhs as a nation' and 'Sikhism as a world religion' circulate transnationally and provide the discursive underpinnings of claims to a unitary Sikh identity (see Dusenbery, forthcoming [1999]). But, as recent events in India indicate, such claims do not themselves compel the various postcolonial states where Sikhs currently reside to recognize 'Sikh' identity as socially salient and as a basis for the extension of political rights. As Arjun Appadurai points out, contemporary nation-states continue to 'exercis[e] taxonomical control over difference' (1990, p. 13). Thus, the extension or withholding of recognition is a powerful political act of the state. And in the 'battle of imagination' over how to conceptualize society and polity, 'micro-identities . . . have become political projects within the nation-state' (1990, pp.13, 14).[6] In fact, what follows in this essay is an account of how Sikhs in Singapore, but not in Canada, have been able to play the 'politics of recognition' so that a distinctive *Sikh* identity has been valorized, legitimated, and ultimately domesticated and disciplined within the local poetics and politics of multiculturalism.

Sikhs trace their origins as a people back to the disciples (Sikhs) drawn by the divinely-inspired teachings of a series of ten living gurus (preceptors), from Guru Nanak (1469–1538/9) to Guru Gobind Singh (1666–1708), who gained a following in the Punjab region of northwest India during the sixteenth and seventeenth centuries. Although the Sikh Panth (literally 'path' or 'way' that is, collectivity) was increasingly drawn into conflict with the Moghul rulers of the region, the Sikhs survived the fall of the Moghul Empire to see one of their own, Maharaja Ranjit Singh, consolidate rule over greater Punjab from 1799–1839. In the aftermath of Ranjit Singh's death and following two bloody Sikh wars, the British were finally able to incorporate Punjab into the British Empire in 1849.

Emigration from Punjab to Southeast Asia and to North America dates from the British colonial period, especially the period 1880–1920. At that time, the changing political economy of Punjab pushed smallholder agriculturalists in central Punjab, particularly Sikh males from the Jat caste, to supplement family incomes through service in the British Indian army and/or international migration (see Dusenbery 1989a; Fox 1985, pp. 27–51; McLeod 1989). By the turn of the century, following opportunities opened up by service to the British, Sikhs had already established a niche in the political economy of the Malay peninsula (including Singapore) as military, police, watchmen, and moneylenders (Sandhu 1970). Subsequently, some ten thousand Sikhs made their way to North America in the first decade of twentieth century, establishing themselves in lumber, mining, and railroad building in British Columbia and in agriculture pursuits in the central valleys of California before Canadian and American authorities enacted immigration restrictions to keep out 'the Hindoo [*sic*] hordes.'[7] Many important Sikh institutions in both Singapore and Canada, especially the gurdwara (temple) societies, can be traced back to the opening decades of this century. Subsequent immigration of families and independent migrants took place in both countries, especially following Indian independence and the partition of Punjab in 1947. The bulk of Canada's Sikh immigrant population, however, has arrived since Canadian immigration laws were liberalized in the mid-1960s.

Today, of the world's approximately 16–18 million Sikhs, perhaps one–third live outside the Indian state of Punjab and at least one million live outside South Asia (see Dusenbery 1989a). Sikhs are dispersed widely, especially in former British colonies. As many as half a million live in Britain itself. In Canada, Sikhs number approximately 150,000 out of 28 million citizens. And in Singapore, they number approximately 15,000 out of some 2.8 million citizens. Thus, by a convenient coincidence, Sikhs form almost exactly the same percentage of the population (approximately one half of one per cent) in each country.

Since the early 1980s, the political and security crisis engulfing India's Punjab—the Sikh spiritual homeland—and the movement for Khalistan—a separate Sikh nation-state imaginatively projected onto the map of South Asia—have been a source of ongoing concern to Sikhs around the world. As part of the global Sikh ethnoscape (cf. Appadurai 1990, 1991), Sikhs in Canada and Singapore are both consumers and producers of Sikh nationalist ideologies that circulate transnationally. Indeed, significant moral and material support for Khalistan has been said to derive from diasporan Sikhs (see, for example, Helweg 1989). However, Canadian Sikhs have been more overtly sympathetic to the nationalist cause than have their Singaporean counterparts. There are many reasons for this contrast, not the least of which, I would argue, is the difference in how Sikhs in Canada and Sikhs in Singapore have fared respectively under their local 'politics of recognition'.[8]

CANADIAN MULTICULTURALISM AND THE SIKHS: A PIECE OF ONE'S OWN

Public opinion surveys in Canada have consistently shown Sikhs, specifically, and, more generally, 'East Indians' or 'Indo-Canadians' (of whom Sikhs are still the largest component), to be among the least favourably viewed of all ethnic communities in Canada.[9] Sympathetic academic observers have discussed with some dismay the limited ability of Canadian Sikhs in recent years to organize collectively or to build coalitions with other groups to fight discrimination, to project a positive image, and to further their political interests within the Canadian context (see Buchigniani and Indra 1989, pp.167–8). And present and former public officials with whom I have spoken acknowledge that Sikhs have been rather ineffectual as a collective interest group in using the political and regulatory system to advance their public agenda.[10] Leaders of national and provincial Sikh organizations themselves express frustration at what they, too, consider to be their political marginalization and lack of collective voice in Canada.[11]

At first glance, it appears surprising that Sikhs should find themselves marginalized in multicultural Canada. The policy of 'multiculturalism within a bilingual framework', first announced by the Liberal Party government of Pierre Trudeau in October 1971 (and fully codified in the Multiculturalism Act of 1988, passed during the recent tenure of the Progressive Conservative Party), would seem favourable to Sikh collective aspirations for public recognition and articulation of the Sikh's political interests. The Royal Commission on Bilingualism and Biculturalism, whose work inspired the original policy, ultimately had come to reject the notion that Canada's so-called founding races (the British and the French) were the purveyors of an 'official culture' or that 'any group takes precedence over any other' (Canada 1971, p. 8545).[12] In fact, in announcing its policy, the government asserted, 'We believe that cultural pluralism is the very essence of Canadian identity. Every ethnic group has the right to preserve and develop its own culture and values within the Canadian context" ' (1971, pp. 8580–81). And, other than 'being given a chance to learn at least one of the two languages in which his [*sic*] country conducts its official business and its politics', the individual is free to 'adhere to one's ethnic group' (1971, p. 8545).

The operating metaphor of Canadian society, as projected over the past several decades, has been that of a 'mosaic': a collection of discrete pieces (the various 'ethnocultural groups'), equal in value if not equal in size, whose integrity is retained over time and who contribute crucially to the whole of Canadian society. The explicit contrast is with the image of the ethnic 'melting pot' in the United States, where ethnic communities are considered to lose their identities and their cultural integrity through processes of homogenization or assimilation. Unlike the case in the United States, so the social imagery suggests, ethnic groups in Canada can and do retain their distinct identities and their own cultural practices.[13] Moreover, the state will positively support the cultural activities of all ethnocultural groups through funding folk arts, historical preservation, and heritage language classes, since retention of cultural tradition is part of the contribution of each group to the mosaic.[14]

How these discrete ethnocultural groups are to be recognized and nurtured is left unspecified in the original policy documents, although the 1971 announcement of the implementation of the multiculturalism policy speaks of 'adherence to one's ethnic group' being determined 'by one's sense of belonging to the group' and by 'the group's "collective will to exist"' (Canada 1971, p. 8545). This Niezchean touch is appropriate to a document in which the language is that of 'possessive individualism' (see Handler 1988, p. 51), but one whereby both individuals and collectivities are endowed with agency, 'freedoms', rights, and liberties. Thus, in the originating text, individuals are posited as having freedom to choose their ethnicity and ethnocultural groups are free to will themselves into existence.

Given the inclusive imagery of the mosaic metaphor, the liberal language of the multiculturalism policy, and the very timing of its implementation, which coincided with a high point of Sikh and other 'visible minority' immigration, Sikhs had reason to expect that they would be officially recognized, consulted, and funded as a distinct ethnocultural group, should they express a 'collective will to exist' as such. The politics of recognition as actually practised in Canada, however, have proven more complex than the poetics might have suggested. Although the original announcement had rejected assigning Canadians to an ethnic group on the basis of 'one's origin or mother tongue' in favour of 'one's sense of belonging to the group' and 'the group's "collective will to exist"' (1971, p. 8545), in practice the state has exerted its considerable taxonomic control over difference. Rather than allow individual choice and collective will to exist' to splinter the mosaic into so many micro-identities as to become unmanageable (at least from the perspective of the government's bureaucrats), a notion of 'national origins' has provided the dominant basis of Canadian ethnic classification.[15] And Canadian Sikhs, whether because they have been viewed primarily as a multi-ethnic religious group (there now being non-Punjabi Sikh converts) or as merely a sub-group within mother India, have had considerable difficulty in gaining recognition as an ethnocultural group of separate 'national origins' with its own independent leadership licensed by the state and with quasi-governmental bodies to represent Canadian Sikh political interests.[16]

To briefly summarize a complex history, in the mid-1970s, after the federal government was inundated by conflicting representations from various 'East Indian' groups commenting on proposed changes to the Immigration Act, federal government officials actively supported the creation of a pan-'East Indian' ethnic-political organization, the National Association of Canadians of Origins in India (NACOI), to serve as an umbrella organization to articulate the collective interests of 'Canadians of origins in India'[17]. At the time, Indo-Canadian demographics were such that Sikhs could have dominated the national organization and its agenda. In the late 1970s, Sikh elites, especially Canadian-born and long-time residents with ties to the ruling Liberal Party, did participate in NACOI and urged other Sikhs to use it as a conduit to and from the federal government. Then, however, the Shiromani Akali Dal of Canada—an organization founded by and claiming to represent the mass of more recent Sikh immigrants—mounted a largely successful campaign against Sikh participation, arguing (even before the rise of a popular Sikh nationalist movement) that Sikhs constituted a separate ethnocultural group not to be conflated with other immigrants from the Indian subcontinent.[18]

Subsequently, in the early 1980s, some forty Sikh organizations (mainly temple societies) established an umbrella national ethnic-political organization to 'to promote, preserve, and maintain Sikh religion, culture, and heritage; to speak on behalf of the Canadian Sikhs at all levels of government; and to promote Sikh interests' (Narindar Singh 1994, p. 126). The Federation of Sikhs Societies, as it called itself, was briefly able to gain a measure of credibility with the Canadian Sikh masses and with the state, presenting briefs on issues of Sikh concern to federal and provincial bodies and successfully spearheading the fund-raising for a Sikh Studies position at the University of British Columbia that was funded jointly by the federal government and the Sikh community.[19] But before the Federation was able to consolidate its position as the legitimate representative of Canadian Sikh interests, the Federation was undermined by internal factionalism and by the rise of pro-Khalistan sentiments among Sikhs in Canada.

Throughout most of the 1980s and early 1990s, two pro-Khalistani organizations, the World Sikh Organization (WSO-Canada) and the International Sikh Youth Federation (ISYF), competed for control of local gurdwaras and other Sikh institutions. The major focus of both organizations has been the establishment of Khalistan.[20] Of the two groups, the WSO-Canada has been the more active in presenting Sikh interests to the Canadian public, although its lobbying has concentrated 'primarily on Sikh issues as they relate to Punjab' (Narindar Singh 1994, p.130). In the early 1990s, WSO-Canada was turned down for membership in the Canadian Ethnocultural Council (CEC)—the key national multiculturalism advisory, research, and monitoring body—on the grounds that NACOI, as the designated Indo-Canadian body on the CEC, already represented Canadian Sikh interests.[21]

At about the same time that WSO-Canada was being rebuffed by the CEC, the Canadian Ministry of Multiculturalism and Citizenship floated a National Sikh Alliance—a five-person committee constituted of Sikh professionals from Toronto, Edmonton, Montreal, Vancouver, and Ottawa—as a possible umbrella Sikh ethnic-political organization. But the Alliance was immediately repudiated by other Sikhs as unrepresentative of the community at large and as a tool of the Conservative Party and the Government of India.[22] As a consequence of this cool reception from Sikhs and the subsequent electoral defeat of the Conservative government in federal elections of 1993, the Alliance was never given the opportunity to deliver on such common Canadian Sikh concerns as immigration reform, Punjabi-language instruction in state-supported schools, Sikh studies in the public universities, and protection of Sikh religious rights (for example, to wear the turban and *kirpan* [sword] in public settings).

In short, over the past twenty years, Canada's Sikhs have not been able to sustain any popular organization recognized and licensed by the state's multiculturalism bureaucracy. Those organizations floated by the state (such as NACOI or the National Sikh Alliance) have failed to gain credibility with the Sikh grassroots because they were seen as unrepresentative and because they have failed to deliver on what Canadian Sikhs considered high-priority issues at the time. Conversely, those organizations with relatively broad appeal among Canadian Sikhs (such as WSO-Canada or the International Sikh Youth Federation) have failed to gain official recognition from the state because they have been considered too radical and too inimical to the ideal of Indo-Canadian cooperation and collective interest articulation.

In the view of many Canadian Sikhs, their efforts to address pressing issues of collective concern have been frustrated by the failure of the state to recognize the Sikhs as a distinct ethnocultural group and to license national organizations to speak on behalf of Sikh interests. In accounting for the slow progress, would-be national Sikh leaders cite disinformation campaigns orchestrated by the Government of India, lack of support from NACOI and other ethnocultural organizations, and the naiveté and/or bad faith of Canadian government officials as forces actively undermining Sikh interests.[23] While outsiders tend to agree that Sikh political lobbying in Canada has been generally less sophisticated and ultimately less successful than that of the Government of India or of NACOI, they also point out (1) that Canadian Sikhs have not spoken with a united voice; (2) that, unlike more successful aspirants for collective recognition—such as various Eastern European groups—Sikh groups have not been effective at building coalitions with other ethnic organizations that might help them advance their causes; and (3) that Sikhs have been impolitic in their handling of public responses to events in India and Canada—such as their failure to control, contest, or counteract in effective ways the images left by Sikhs publicly celebrating in Canadian cities after Indira Gandhi's assassination; by physical attacks perpetrated by Khalistan supporters on non-Khalistani Sikhs in Canada; by the bombing of an Air India flight originating in Canada; or by the landing in Nova Scotia of a boatload of Sikhs arriving from Europe to claim refugee status.

The irony is that actions (even fully legal ones, those not proven to be the work of Sikhs, or those demonstrably the work of a few Sikh individuals) in all the incidents I cite above have perpetuated a negative view of Sikhs as a collectivity in Canada. The result, as the Canadian anthropologists Norman Buchignani and Doreen Indra have put it, is that '[Canadian] Sikhs today are . . . strongly associated in peoples' minds with terrorism, with inappropriately bringing their home country disputes to Canada, and with being an inflexible, culturally different ethnic enclave' (1989, p. 162). Just how Sikhs are expected to counteract their negative image in the absence of publicly recognized and politically well-connected spokespersons licensed to speak on behalf of Sikhs, and just why being a 'culturally different ethnic enclave' should be a problem in multicultural Canada where cultural difference is proclaimed a virtue and where the state is officially committed to 'promote the reflection and evolving expression of those cultures' (as per the Canadian Multiculturalism Act), are questions to which we will return shortly.

SINGAPOREAN MULTIRACIALISM AND THE SIKHS: AN EVOLVING STRAND

In contrast to Sikhs in Canada, who are seen by the Canadian public as 'an inflexible, culturally different ethnic enclave' and who have been frustrated in their attempts to advance a distinctively Sikh political agenda, Sikhs in Singapore have in recent years come to be regarded as something of a model minority,[24] praised at the highest levels of government for contributions to 'the well-being and stability of Singapore . . . more than in proportion to your numbers' and rewarded with promises of state support 'in preserving your distinctiveness' (*Straits Times* 1990a).[25]

It is surprising that Sikhs in Singapore should be enjoying such success in pursuing their political agenda, because at first glance, Singapore's state 'multiracialism' policy would appear less favourable to Sikh self assertion and public recognition than would Canadian 'multiculturalism'. After independence from Britain and separation from Malaysia, Singapore embarked upon nationhood with a profound sense of its 'racial' pluralism. The colonial political economy had created Singaporean society primarily out of immigrant Chinese, Indian, and Malay labour. Colonial Singapore had been a classic plural society, stratified by race and class. And local racial tensions and memories of past race riots lay close to the surface. At the same time, Singapore was now a Chinese-majority city-state located between two larger, Malay-dominated states—Malaysia and Indonesia—each experiencing tensions with its own Chinese minority. Singapore's new political leadership thus embarked upon nation-building with what one political scientist has termed a 'garrison mentality'—that is, portraying Singapore as a nation-state surrounded by potentially hostile external forces and internally vulnerable to racial conflagration and disintegration (Brown 1994, p. 86).

More positively, the image adopted of Singapore's multiracial society has been that of 'a rope braided together': the overall strength of the rope—the Singaporean nation—depends on the unity and integrity of its constituent strands (the different local 'races'). Singaporean society, in the words and vivid illustrations of a Singapore Social Defence Forces video shown on state-run television and in government schools, comprises a 'common thread . . . strong when united, but so fragile when divided and individually frayed.' If Canada's mosaic provides a metaphor of aesthetic interdependence of diverse constituent units,

Singapore's rope provides a metaphor of pragmatic interdependence of diverse strands. One might want to unpack the metaphor even further to suggest a difference of attitude between Canada's view of multiculturalism as an aesthetic pleasure and Singapore's view of multiracialism as a utilitarian project.

Conventionally, the Singaporean rope is shown with four strands, corresponding to what became known as the CMIO categories. In the 1970s, these 'racial' categories—'C' for the Chinese, who make up 77 per cent of the citizenry; 'M' for the Malays, who make up 14 per cent; 'I' for Indians, who make up 7 per cent; 'O' for Others, who make up 1–2 per cent—became the taxonomic categories through which social difference in Singapore was reported and recognized for official purposes. Rather than identify with one's dialect group or region of origin, Singapore's Chinese, Malay, and Indian citizens were encouraged to identify with their state-defined 'race'. (In Singapore, racial identity is acquired through the patriline and listed on one's identity card and other official documents.) Sikhs, who composed only a little more than 7 per cent of the 7 per cent of the population that was Indian, were thus relatively invisible within the racial politics of the period.[26]

The state's policy at the time was not only to reify but also to reinforce these 'racial' categories, with the ultimate intention of creating a unique species of 'Chinese Singaporeans', 'Malay Singaporeans', and 'Indian Singaporeans' who did not look to ancestral homelands for the reinforcement of their identities. Unity of the nation through recognition and mutual respect of the constituent racial communities became a goal. Thus, for example, while English became the dominant language of education, government, and commerce, Mandarin, Malay, and Tamil were also official languages, one language for each of the major local 'races'. The association between race and language was further underlined with the 'speak Mandarin' campaign of the 1980s. Rather than speak their native dialects (Hokkein, Hakka, Cantonese, and others), Chinese Singaporeans were exhorted to learn Mandarin as the language appropriate to their 'race'. A two-language policy was soon implemented in the schools, requiring students to learn English and their respective 'mother tongues' (more accurately, 'father tongues', since the 'race' of the father determined the language class to which the child would be assigned). All Chinese students were required to learn English and Mandarin, regardless of the language spoken in the home. Malays were required to learn English and Malay. By the logic that tied each official race to one of the official languages, all Singaporean Indians should have been required to learn Tamil; and there were, in fact, initial efforts to require them to do so.

The government's rationale for its language policy has usually had two components. One has been what might be termed 'political economic pragmatism': Mandarin and Malay (less so Tamil) are useful regional and international languages for trade and diplomacy; therefore, it benefits the country to have citizens fluent in these languages. The other has been what might be termed 'sociocultural pragmatism'. Specifically, the argument has been that an 'Asian language' will serve as what Singaporeans call 'cultural ballast', an antidote to creeping Westernization introduced through the use of English. Proficiency in English may be required on pragmatic grounds, since it is the international language of technology and commerce. But if Singaporeans are to avoid the decadence and destructive individualism of the West, they must have access to Asian cultural values that are thought to be transmitted through an Asian language.[27]

This search for a 'cultural ballast' was also an impetus to the introduction of Religious Education in the schools during the 1980s—the assumption being that if students were to learn more about their ancestral religions, they would be less susceptible to Western secularism and Christian missionization. By the late 1980s, however, the government had changed its mind and decided that Religious Education was proving divisive, since it was fuelling religious revivalism. The government subsequently decided to replace Religious Education (and its various tracks) with a common course of Moral Education based on 'national values' and, simultaneously, to introduce a Religious Harmony Act (establishing a Religious Harmony Council) that would counteract 'religious polarization' and would ensure that religion and politics be 'kept rigorously separate'.[28]

The government explained its search for a set of national values as an attempt 'to identify a few key values which are common to all the major groups in Singapore and which draw on the essence of each of these heritages' (Singapore 1991b, p. 3). Once again, the argument was that this commitment to a set of 'Asian values' would serve as an antidote ('cultural ballast') against creeping Westernization. While one may legitimately ask whether the five National Values on which agreement was finally reached—'(1) nation over community and society above the individual; (2) family as the basic unit of society; (3) regard and community support for individuals; (4) consensus instead of contention; (5) racial and religious harmony' (Singapore 1991b, p. 10)—are actually common to, and reflect the essence of, all the major groups in Singapore, there can be no doubt that they articulate a set of values around which members of the polity might wish to orient themselves.[29]

In keeping with the third National Value ('community support of individuals'), in recent years the state has begun to devolve social welfare responsibilities onto its 'racial' communities, arguing that each community is best placed to identify the problems of, generate support from, and deliver services to its own members. Thus quasi-governmental self-help organizations have been established for each of the major races: The Council for Malay Education (Mendaki), the Chinese Development Assistance Council (CDAC), and the Singapore Indian Development Association (SINDA).

Given the state's ideological and institutional efforts since the 1970s to nurture an inclusive Singaporean Indian identity (albeit one largely Tamil and Hindu in content) and its explicit repudiation of politicized religion (including a quick crackdown on Singaporean Sikh supporters of Khalistan in the mid-1980s), it is surprising to find that the Sikhs as a distinct community have gained the official recognition and support of the Singaporean state in recent years. In fact, however, the 'cultural ballast', 'national values', and 'self-help' discourse of the past ten to fifteen years has proved quite useful to Singapore's Sikhs, who, through the professional leadership of key institutions, have made a strong case for recognition and reinforcement of their distinctive Punjabi/Sikh heritage as congruent with the national agenda.

In the late-1980s a Sikh Resource Panel, a self-generated body of twelve Sikh professionals operating under the leadership of a secondary school principal, Bhajan Singh, presented evidence both to the Sikh community and to the government suggesting that there existed a sizeable underclass of Sikh youth who were not doing well in school, who were getting into trouble with the law, and/or who were marrying out of the community; that this group was characterized by its estrangement from Sikh culture and from local community institutions. The group of Sikh professionals used these survey findings and a fresh set of proposals to address 'the problem' by transmitting the Punjabi/Sikh heritage, in order to gain a significant degree of credibility both within the Sikh community and with the government.

The Sikh professionals' public analysis of the problem and their proposed solutions addressed the perceived lack of 'cultural ballast' among Singapore's Sikhs, particularly the youth. Sikhs did not identify with their community and its institutions; they knew little about their heritage; and they were not learning Punjabi, the ancestral language and the language of the Sikh scriptures. The professionals sought to advance an agenda, first by taking control of a key institution, the Sikh Advisory Board (SAB), and then by using it as a base from which to begin soliciting state support for addressing the community's problems.

The Sikh Advisory Board is a quasi-governmental body dating from British colonial days. In its earliest incarnations, it included ten local Sikhs (including a senior Sikh police official as chair) appointed by the governor of Singapore to advise the Settlement of Singapore 'on all matters affecting the Sikh religion and custom' (Straits Settlement 1915: 1748). From the 1920s until World War II, a British police official served as chair. When the Board was reconstituted after the War, a Sikh was once again elected chair and membership consisted of three Sikhs directly appointed by the government and nine Sikhs chosen by the government from nominees put forward by Sikh temple societies. After independence, the SAB became a statutory board established under the Ministry of Community Development with responsibilities 'to advise the Minister on matters concerning the Sikh religion and customs and the general welfare of the Sikh community' (Sikh Advisory Board n.d.). In 1989, Bhajan Singh was made one of the government's appointees to the SAB. He was immediately elected its chairperson, serving the maximum six years before stepping aside in October 1995.

During the 1980s the SAB had pressed the Ministry of Education to include Sikh studies as part of the religious studies programme in the state-run schools. The government, which at first had not intended to include Sikh studies, acquiesced on the condition that the Sikhs themselves prepare the teaching material, train the teachers, and foot the costs of offering a Sikh studies option. Working from a pre-existing English language text (which they translated into academically—and politically—acceptable Singaporean English), the SAB was able to see that Sikh studies was offered as an elective track in the schools' Religious Studies programme from 1983–9.[30] The old Board had less success, however, in getting the government to accept Punjabi language as an optional, testable subject in the schools.

In the debate over language policy and the requirement that all students study in school an 'Asian language' as their race-appropriate 'mother tongue', Sikhs, along with other North Indian Singaporeans, had successfully argued against being forced to study Tamil (which was to have been the designated Singaporean Indian language). The government's fallback position—that they be allowed to choose from among Mandarin, Malay, and Tamil—was still felt by most Singaporean Sikhs to leave them at a competitive disadvantage in the classroom. Bhajan Singh and the Sikh professional leadership, however, advanced the argument for a Punjabi option not on competitive grounds, but rather on the grounds that forcing Sikhs to choose from among the three official Asian languages did nothing to address their real need for 'cultural ballast' (since they had no special linguistic-cum-cultural attachment to Tamil, Malay, or Mandarin), whereas allowing them to learn Punjabi in government schools as their testable second language would tie them not only to their Asian mother tongue but also to the language of Sikh religious texts.

At the same time, the Sikh Advisory Board (and sister organizations, such as the Sikh Education Foundation and the more recently formed Sikh Welfare Council, all controlled by Bhajan Singh and his fellow professionals) began systematically to court government officials, inviting senior ministers to attend such community functions as popular religious festivals, openings of new community institutions, and international Punjabi/Sikh heritage gatherings. The visits served multiple purposes: (1) allowing Sikhs to present themselves and their agenda to the government; (2) providing the government's imprimatur to the event, thereby gaining credibility for its sponsoring organization in the eyes of a wider Sikh audience; and, (3) given the publicity these visits garnered in the national media, gaining a measure of respect for Sikhs in the eyes of a wider Singaporean audience.

Consider, for example, the November 1990 visit by then-Prime Minister Lee Kuan Yew to the Central Sikh Temple. This was during the prime minister's last months in office, before he stepped up to become senior minister. The ostensible occasion was the 522nd birthday celebration for Guru Nanak, the founder of the Sikh religion, which in any event would have ensured a full house. In a carefully choreographed piece of political theatre (complete with Sikh bagpipers in tartan and turbans brought down from Malaysia to perform a piece of colonial nostalgia for the Prime Minister's benefit!), Sikhs honoured the retiring prime minister with their presentation of a ceremonial turban and sword, the purported meanings of which—'dignity and justice' and of 'responsibility to family and nation'—were carefully massaged into conguence with Singaporean National Values.

Sikh representatives, led by Bhajan Singh, also took the opportunity in their tribute to the prime minister to advance the local Sikh agenda: specifically, the need for Punjabi-language training in the schools, for collection and dissemination of Sikh-specific government data, and for more Punjabi culture items in the (state-run) media all justified as necessary to help combat 'the negative influences of [W]estern culture' and 'the erosion of traditional Asian (Sikh) values among the Sikh youth'[31]. And Singapore's Sikhs were, in turn, praised by the prime minister for contributions and successes as befitted a 'distinctive group' who 'had been a credit to Singapore because by and large, they were law-abiding, hardworking and successful in educating their children to enter the professions and business' (*Straits Times*, 3 Nov. 1990, p. 50). At the end of his visit, the prime minister promised, 'The Government will support all your constructive schemes.' This commitment was accompanied by assurances that Punjabi would be made a testable option at the secondary school level as long as Sikhs themselves produced the teaching materials, ran the classes, trained and paid the teachers, and procured the evaluators. Subsequently, in 1993, the same permission was extended to allow Punjabi as a testable second language at the primary level.

There are a number of reasons why the government has been willing to work with Bhajan Singh and his group of professionals to increase the power and credibility of the Sikh Advisory Board. Officials at the Ministry of Community Development with responsibility for overseeing the SAB and Sikh affairs were delighted that they were dealing with fellow-professionals whose 'proactive' agenda reflected 'coinciding interests' with those of the government.[32] In the context of the state's attempt to devolve many social services onto state-sanctioned ethnic self-help organizations, the Sikh Advisory Board's agenda of social uplift for the Sikh underclass was consistent with evolving government welfare initiatives.[33] Government officials were also pleased that 'moderate' voices were in a position of authority within the Sikh community, rather than the pro-Khalistani elements that they had feared might take control of Sikh institutions in the mid-1980s. Indeed, during his visit to the Central Sikh Temple Lee Kuan Yew had pointedly 'told the Sikhs that their wholehearted support for the Maintenance of Religious Harmony Bill [which mandated a strict separation of religion and politics] reflected their 'realistic appreciation of Singapore's realities' (*Straits Times*, 1990a).[34]

This show of recognition and cooperation on the part of the government in turn furthered the credibility of Bhajan Singh and his group of fellow professionals within the wider Sikh community. So long as the SAB could show continued progress on what Sikhs took to be their most pressing local needs, it would be difficult to mount a credible attack on the Sikh Advisory Board as an institution or its leadership in particular. Moreover, with government officials publicly saying favourable things about Sikhs, praising their contributions to Singapore, and promising them respect for their distinctiveness, Khalistan supporters found it difficult to make a case for redress in Singapore of grievances against the Government of India.

Thus, unlike the situation in Canada, where lack of recognition and the impotence of Sikh leaders to address grievances have fed Sikh nationalist sensibilities, the successes of Sikhs in Singapore have dampened Khalistani sentiments (see Dusenbery 1995). One of my Singaporean Sikh informants expressed the situation especially well. When I reported to him in 1993 that the new matriculation forms at the National University of Singapore now listed 'Sikh' as a separate 'race' as well as separate 'religion' (a change also reflected in the latest census categories), he commented, 'I guess the [Singapore] government has given us Khalistan.' If, as I suspect, sentiment for Khalistan is fed by a sense of besmirched honour in the diaspora as well as in India, the honour and respect accorded Sikhs in Singapore has had a palliative effect.[35]

Let me now summarize precisely what it is that I have and have not been arguing in this contrast between the experience of Sikhs in Canada and Singapore. In both countries 'Sikh' as a distinct social identity has become more widely recognized in recent years. Publicity—local, national, and international—of events featuring identifiably 'Sikh' participants, publicity that includes coverage of the Sikh nationalist movement and the political crisis in Punjab, has ensured that the public at large is more cognizant now than they were a decade or two ago of the existence of the Sikhs as a distinct group. (Diasporan Sikhs, too, are probably more aware of their reported distinctiveness.) Thus, other Canadians are much less naive about an undifferentiated category of 'East Indians' than they were when I first did fieldwork there in the 1970s. Similarly, Singaporeans are more likely to be aware that the old folk category 'Bangalee', used regionally for all North Indians (who were assumed to have arrived in Southeast Asia from Calcutta), is a misnomer and that Sikhs (also known locally as 'Singhs' or 'Bhais') are a distinct group.

What differs in the two cases is the manner in which the state has exercised its taxonomic control over that difference. In the case of Singapore, the government, after failing to integrate Sikhs into a larger, synthetic 'Singaporean Indian' identity (which was largely Tamil-derived) has acquiesced in accepting Sikh claims of distinctiveness to the point of recognizing Sikhs as a distinct 'race' (as well as 'religion') and in granting support for Sikh-initiated projects in language, education, welfare, and heritage on the grounds that they will provide Sikhs with their own 'cultural ballast'. In Canada, although individual Sikh temples and local organizations have partaken of multiculturalism funds set aside for folk arts, ethnic history, and heritage language programmes, state bodies have largely resisted claims by Sikh organizations to represent a distinct ethnocultural group with its own agenda. They have based their refusal on the grounds that Sikhs are but a subset of the larger community of Indo-Canadians.

The differences between these two cases, I want now to argue, in part reflect differences between the two states and the ways in which they have gone about their nationalist and multiculturalist projects. And they highlight the kinds of tradeoffs that ethnocultural groups must make if they are to play a successful 'politics of recognition' in different states.

CANADA'S MULTICULTURALISM: LIMITING THE 'COLLECTIVE WILL TO EXIST'

According to the Multiculturalism Act of 1988, it is the declared policy of the Government of Canada to 'recognize and promote the understanding that multiculturalism reflects the cultural and racial diversity of Canadian society and acknowledges the freedom of all members of Canadian society to preserve, enhance and share their cultural heritage' (Canada 1988, p. 3). Yet Canadian Sikhs find themselves stigmatized as an 'inflexible, culturally different ethnic enclave', marginalized from effective participation in the political culture of Canada, and increasingly disillusioned with Canadian multiculturalist policies despite a considerable 'collective will to exist' as a distinct ethnocultural group. How can the promise of Canada's Multiculturalism Act be reconciled with the experience of Canadian Sikhs?

In their perceptive analysis of Canadian ethnic and race relations as they have affected Sikhs in Canada, Buchignani and Indra have argued that the failure of Sikhs to use Canadian political institutions to their advantage (particularly by comparison to other ethnocultural groups) reflects the failure of Canadian Sikhs to adopt a collective strategy, to build internal and external coalitions, and to lobby effectively. In their words:

> Contemporary [Canadian] Sikhs have been almost totally unable to organize for a long term, developmental, coordinated fight against discrimination or to better relations with others. . . . [T]his problem is representative of a more deep organizational difficulty endemic to Sikhs in Canada: the structural inability to develop long-term community planning, to institutionalize planning objectives, and to develop broad-based community support for such institutions (Buchignani and Indra 1989, pp. 167–8).

But what are the implications of blaming the Sikhs for the fact that they have not enjoyed the same political successes of other ethnocultural groups in Canada? Should we be surprised at the way Sikhs have organized and presented their case to government bodies and to the general public? Should Sikhs necessarily be expected to speak with one voice, build lasting coalitions with other groups, publicly lobbying officials for support—all the sorts of things that they are accused of failing to do effectively in Canada? After all, Jat Sikhs in Punjab are known for their factionalism, their litigiousness, their individualistic political culture (see Pettigrew 1975; 1995, pp. 187–8). Are they not then simply being 'true to their culture'? And is this not perfectly acceptable behaviour according to a multiculturalist ideology that suggests that there is no 'Canadian culture' apart from the plurality of cultures of its constituent ethnocultural units? Or is it perhaps possible that the overt message sent by multicultural ideologies and policies to Canadian Sikhs is, in fact, misleading and maladaptive for them—that there exists a distinctive political culture in Canada, and that the unequal value assigned to different political styles in a liberal democracy like Canada's effectively marginalizes groups like the Sikhs?

In recent years, something of a backlash has developed against Canadian multiculturalism in English-speaking Canada, not just from reactionary Anglo-Canadians nostalgic for an era of Anglo-hegemony but also from 'visible minorities' disenchanted with the failure of the policy to live up to its promise. Analyses of the problems with Canadian multiculturalism vary, but one common complaint voiced by 'visible minority' spokespersons is that there is an element of bad faith in asserting that there is no dominant culture to which one must accommodate, when clearly there are culturally-appropriate ways to advance one's cause. In the words of the novelist Bharati Mukherjee, herself a one-time Indo-Canadian:

> I sometimes think that liberal whites, out of their need to appease guilt of some sort, want the non-European to preserve her or his original culture.

Multiculturalism, in a sense, is well intentioned; but it ends up marginalizing the person. . . .

I blame some of that [racism against South Asian Canadians] on the mosaic theory of absorbing immigrants . . . where the government and the national mythology encourage the newcomer to hang onto old-world cultures, old-world psyches. The intention was good. But if, in a multicultural system, unequal value is put on the various cultures, then I'm afraid that marginalization tends to work against the nonwhite immigrant. [Mukherjee, as quoted in Moyers 1990, pp. 5–6]

Well-intentioned liberal whites in Canada, like sociologists Augie Fleras and Jean Elliott, dismiss most attacks on Canadian multiculturalism policy as 'represent[ing] a thinly veiled disguise for the restoration of a largely anglo-centric ideological system' (1992, p. 280). But the argument of the 'visible minority' critics is no call for 'restoration' of Anglo-centric ideological hegemony. It is about acknowledging the twin facts that Canada already has evolved a liberal democratic political system with some corporatist elements that may be different from that previously known to its recent non-European immigrants and that there are limits to the accommodation offered different ethnic practices within the Canadian system. It is about recognizing that immigrants are not only disadvantaged if they are not quickly familiarized with its all-too-implicit expectations of appropriate conduct but may actively marginalize themselves by believing themselves free to practise politics according to the conventions of other political cultures.

In the words of Neil Bissoondath, a Canadian multiculturalism critic of Indo-Trinidadian descent:

Multiculturalism [in practice] seems to offer at best provisional acceptance, and it is with some difficulty that one insists on being a full—and not just an associate—member. Just as the newcomer must decide how best to accommodate himself or herself to the society, so the society must in turn decide how it will accommodate itself to the newcomer. [1993, pp. 383–4]

To the extent that Canada is a Western liberal society, there are lines to be drawn. Sikhs are unlikely to achieve the removal of tenured faculty members from Canadian public universities for perceived 'blasphemy' or 'insensitivity' in their academic writings. Nor are they likely to be granted a separate 'personal law' that would shield them on 'cultural' grounds from spousal or child abuse charges. As the distinguished Canadian political philosopher, Charles Taylor, puts it: 'Liberalism is not a possible meeting ground for all cultures, but is the political expression of one range of cultures, and quite incompatible with other ranges .... Liberalism can't and shouldn't claim complete cultural neutrality .... (It) has to draw the line' (1992, p. 62). And the line is already there, if only implicitly. Some Sikhs see it; but others, having understood Canadian multiculturalism as making few demands of them, are then surprised and frustrated to find the state unresponsive to—what they take to—be legitimate demands they make of it.

Defenders of Canadian multiculturalism ideology and policies argue that the Canadian multiculturalism policy since 1985 has increasingly turned away from support of 'expressive culture' toward social, political, and economic 'mainstreaming', a tacit acceptance of the need to socialize Canadians into the operations and expectations of the dominant political culture. Thus, since the creation of a new Department of Multiculturalism and Citizenship in 1990, they note that:

> government discourse on multiculturalism is couched increasingly in terms of citizenship ... focused on (a) what it means to be a Canadian citizen, (b) the rights, duties, and obligations of citizenship in a multicultural society, and (c) the necessity to highlight ethnocultural differences and human rights as essential ingredients of Canadian citizenship. (Fleras and Elliott 1992, p. 79)

But the possibility of mixed messages is still strong, given the long-standing celebration of 'folkloric culture' as the essence of Canadian multiculturalism. For the ethnic minorities themselves, to say nothing of the wider Canadian public, it is still the case that, despite the redirection of money and energies toward these 'mainstreaming' activities, 'the folkloric aspects of multiculturalism appear to hold sway—issues related to language, culture, and identity remain paramount' (Fleras and Elliott 1992, p. 93). And it is only if one supposes that 'expressive' or 'symbolic' aspects of culture are divorced from 'instrumental' or 'political' culture, as is perhaps the case for Euro-Canadians of many generations standing, that it makes sense simultaneously to promote the two as if they were entirely unrelated or mutually compatible. Sikh popular folklore and religious hagiography, like that of any living culture, is a means of socialization into a world view—involving, in the Sikh case, a fusion of religious and political authority, complete with images of heroic martyrdom on behalf of collective honour—that may or may not be compatible with the dominant political culture of Canada (see Dusenbery 1981, pp.102–4; 1990). Is it any wonder that Sikhs are confused when their heroic political culture is subsidized as folk culture but repudiated as inappropriate to political action in liberal Canada, where a separation of religion and politics is taken for granted?

Sikhs note that those Sikhs who have succeeded within Canadian electoral or appointive politics have mainly done so by de-emphasizing their Sikhness—for example, by being clean-shaven or running in electoral ridings with few Sikh constituents—and by taking care not to give the impression of representing Sikh interests or as being pro-Khalistan. At the same time, many Sikhs see that those most visibly identified as Sikhs and associated with overtly Sikh causes are excluded both electorally and administratively from the corridors of power.[36] To recognize, affirm, and fund Sikh folklore and 'expressive culture' as fully worthy of respect and nurturance in the Canadian context but then to turn around and deny the appropriateness of that very culture for informing public actions of Sikhs in Canada has had the effect of feeding Sikh cynicism about the ideology and politics of Canadian multiculturalism.

Given the comparatively recent arrival in Canada of most Sikh immigrants, their relative lack of state socialization into the political culture of Canada by the state, and the long history of anti-Asian prejudice in Canada, one should perhaps not be surprised at the corresponding failure of Sikhs in Canada to articulate and advance their political agenda. The greater sophistication of Canadian Jews, Ukrainians, and other Euro-Canadian groups in using the politics of multiculturalism to their own advantage is probably a consequence of multiple factors, including greater opportunity to learn how to work the Canadian political system, a smaller cultural distance between the political cultures of these groups, and old-fashioned racism that distinguishes European immigrant groups from 'visible minorities' in the first place.[37] By contrast, in Singapore, where the majority of Sikhs are locally-born, where the state has spelled out more explicitly its expectations of them, and where Sikhs are 'fellow Asians', Sikhs have proven to be relatively successful at furthering their own political agenda by working the system to their advantage. Here, the issue that Sikhs must confront is how to work the corporatist state without being co-opted by it.

SINGAPORE'S MULTIRACIALISM: DOMESTICATING DIFFERENCE IN A CORPORATIST STATE

Singapore's state has been variously described as authoritarian, bureaucratic, administrative, and paternalistic. I follow the political scientist David Brown in characterizing the Singaporean state as 'inclusionary corporatist' and its politics of ethnic management as 'interventionist' (see Brown 1994, pp. 66–111). Corporatism, following Brown, 'refers to attempts by an avowedly autonomous state-elite to organize the diverse interest associations in society such that their interests can be accommodated within the interdependent and organic national community' (Brown 1994, p. 67). In a corporatist state, it is the state that empowers society. The classic corporatist state sought to organize competing economic interests so as to curtail populist participation. Singapore's corporatist state has increasingly sought to organize ethnic interest groups as well, by legitimating and enfranchising certain groups and individuals to participate in public affairs.

Corporatist Singapore's interventions into the management of ethnicity include making a distinction among (1) 'political authority . . . portrayed in monistic terms as absolutist loyalty to the nation-state, such that any other sub-national or cross-national political loyalties are deemed antithetical and illegitimate'; (2) 'cultural identity . . . seen as a layered or tiered structure, rather than as a monolith . . . such that various groups within the complex society are recognized as having values which differ from each other but which are compatible'; and (3) 'interest association' whereby the state recognizes, licenses, and in some cases actively creates the legitimate channels through which ethnic interests may be articulated (1994, pp. 70–1). Examples in Singapore include: depiction of society along racial or ethnic lines (for example, CMIO categories), but with subordination of ethnic political loyalties to the state; the recognition of ethnic values (that is, 'cultural ballast') as congruent with National Values; and the licensing of monopolistic ethnic institutions (for example, Chinese Development Assistance Council, The Council for Malay Education, Singapore Indian Development Association) as legitimate interest associations.

Sikh 'successes' in advancing a 'Sikh agenda' in Singapore must , therefore, be seen in the context of Singapore's 'inclusionary corporatism'. Since the late 1980s, the government has: (1) recognized Sikhs as a distinctive 'race', (2) granted Sikhs permission to strengthen their 'cultural ballast' ('for example' through Sikh studies, Punjabi language, Punjabi/Sikh heritage centre, etc.); and (3) fostered and licensed two legitimate channels for transmitting Sikh interests to the government and mobilizing Sikh support for government policies: (a) the Sikh Advisory Board and its affiliates, under the direction of Bhajan Singh (who also serves as the appointed Sikh representative on the boards of the Religious Harmony Council and the Singapore Indian Development Association), and (b) the elected Sikh Member of Parliament, Davinder Singh (of the ruling Peoples Action Party [PAP]). Davinder Singh was chosen under a system of Group Representation Constituencies introduced in 1988, whereby a slate of four candidates, including at least one 'minority' (that is, non-Chinese) representative, is elected from a single constituency as a team. Both Bhajan Singh and Davinder Singh, it might be noted, come from the same group of Sikh professionals who became active in Sikh affairs in the mid-1980s.

At the same time, the government has cut its formal ties to two potential alternative channels of Sikh interest articulation: (1) the Central Sikh Gurdwara Board, an elective body representing two open-membership Sikh temple societies in Singapore, which was granted its 'freedom' from government control by the Ministry of Community Development in 1987 but with the understanding that as a religious body it was not to involve itself in domestic or foreign political affairs; and (2) the long-time Sikh member of the Presidential Council for Minority Rights, retired Singapore Supreme Court Justice Choor Singh, who, once he was suspected of Khalistani sympathies, was quietly dropped from the council at the expiration of his next term.[38]

We thus see all the elements of Singapore's inclusive corporatism in its management of Sikh ethnicity:

> a distinction between ethnicity as the illegitimate political loyalties towards the Punjab; ethnicity as identification with Sikh values which provide a cultural anchor and a basis of Singaporean identity; and ethnicity as the legitimate socio-economic interests of the [Singaporean] Sikh community [articulated through state-licensed channels]. (Brown 1994, p. 104)

But such distinctions are not always easy to comprehend and may be hard to sustain, especially in the face of the global flow of nationalist rhetoric asserting that for Sikhs religion and politics are inseparable. Thus Sikh 'successes' in Singapore are probably more fragile than they might first appear since, as I have shown, they depend on 'coinciding interests' of state officials and Sikh community leaders respectively.

CONCLUSIONS

Canada's Sikhs—internally factionalized, socially marginalized, and politically unrecognized—might wish that the Canadian state in its management of multiculturalism was either a bit more inclusive and interventionist in its ethnic corporatism (and that it had consequently laid down explicit criteria by which to play 'the politics of recognition' and receive the blessings of the state) or a little less corporatist (and so inclined to follow its original liberal rhetoric of recognizing and supporting all groups with 'a collective will to exist'). As matters stand, Sikhs in Canada seem caught in a vicious circle from which they cannot easily extricate themselves. So long as they demand recognition as a distinct ethnocultural group, apart from other Indo-Canadians, they reinforce the stereotype of Sikh intransigence, insularity, and political radicalism.

Sikh marginalization and lack of recognition from the state, however, only strengthens those community members who argue for Sikh nationhood as a solution to Sikh dishonour in India and in Canada. In the end, Sikhs who enjoy success in Canadian electoral and party politics largely do so by distancing themselves from what are identified as overtly 'Sikh causes', and Sikhs who attain administrative and bureaucratic appointment largely do so as Indo-Canadians. In short, multiculturalism in Canada has not been particularly empowering of Sikhs qua Sikhs. As a result, there is considerable grumbling about 'bad faith' in Canadian multiculturalism ideology and policies. But would Canada's Sikhs be any better served under a more fully corporatist system with the state fostering and licensing legitimate Sikh intermediaries, as it did in the case of NACOI or attempted with the National Sikh Alliance?[39]

Singapore's Sikhs—publicly united, nationally respected, and politically successful—might wish to further ponder the price of their 'success' at playing the game of multiracialism in corporatist Singapore. What the corporatist state giveth, it can taketh away, since it is the state that empowers society rather than the reverse. In the Singapore case, success in promoting Punjabi/Sikh heritage requires Sikhs to make certain compromises to conform to the political culture of Singapore. These include accepting a de-politicized Sikhism that promises to eschew overt political support for Sikh nationalism and to avoid all other forms of political action not explicitly sanctioned by the state. For those Sikh nationalists who argue that their religion, culture, and politics are one, this may ultimately prove to be an unpalatable compromise. By asserting themselves against the current leadership, however, they would jeopardize their recent local successes: the continued blessings of the state depend on the continuing judgment of state-elites that there are 'coinciding interests' between the state and Sikh organizations. Given that in this corporatist state successes are so tenuously tied to the survival of the state-licensed, moderate, professional Sikh leadership, the history of Sikh factionalism in Singapore can hardly be taken as an auspicious omen.

Moreover, Singapore's Sikhs must take into account the costs—material and otherwise—incurred when the state 'downloads' responsibilities onto its ethnocultural communities. Internal funding and staffing of Sikh education and social service is already proving to be a challenge for Sikhs in Singapore, and any perceived failure of Sikhs as a community to 'help themselves' and to continue their upward mobility in what the state represents as being a meritocratic society will now lie at the Sikhs' doorstep rather than at the state's. In fact, it is by no means clear that providing a Punjabi/Sikh 'cultural ballast' will actually solve the problems of the newly-discovered Sikh underclass in Singapore, a class whose problems are in large part systemic and include residual institutional racism in this avowedly meritocratic society. Having accepted the 'cultural ballast' argument as a means of advancing their agenda, are Sikhs not making themselves vulnerable to a 'blame the victim' attitude on the part of the state—and the Chinese majority—for any subsequent Sikh failures to achieve their ends?

For Canada, the increasing public disaffection of both Anglo-Canadians and 'visible minorities' with the policies and practices of multiculturalism in Canada is yet another challenge to a nation-state already made vulnerable by French-Canadian and First Nations separatisms. It is legitimate to ask whether the country can survive without a public commitment to any collective values other than multiculturalism (cf. Fleras and Elliott 1992, pp. 132–4). It is also fair to question the curious amalgam of liberal democratic and corporatist tendencies in the way multiculturalism policies have been implemented and to query the problematic blurring of individual and collective agency in such documents as the Multiculturalism Policy of 1971, the Human Rights Act of 1985, and the Multiculturalism Act of 1988. Like other liberal western democracies, Canada is clearly struggling with how to combine respect for the rights and freedoms of individuals with attempts to empower culturally defined groups.[40] Given that Canada has shown corporatist tendencies, as in the creation of NACOI, it is somewhat surprising that the state has not taken the tactic of Singapore—that is, to recognize Sikhs as a distinct ethnocultural group but to domesticate and discipline difference by licensing 'moderate' Sikhs as institutional spokespersons for Sikh interests. Perhaps it is too late for that now—or so the recent failure of the National Sikh Alliance suggests.

For Singapore, there are serious questions too, particularly about the limits of public tolerance for 'corporatism' and 'ethnic interventions'. Academic specialists on Singapore now query the 'racialization' of PAP activities (B. Singh 1992, pp. 155–9), hold colloquia on the 'emergence of civil society' in Singapore (Girling 1993), attest to the 'confusion' or 'unease' that the citizenry seems to be experiencing over changing 'politics of ethnic management' (Brown 1994, pp.106–11; Vasil 1995, pp. 152–5), and speculate on the whether the political quietism of the masses will survive the end of the current economic boom and the next leadership transition (Rodan 1992). And while the government has set up Singapore as a defender of supposedly pan-Asian communal values against rampant Western individualism, racial and religious minorities like the Sikhs may find they have reason to value some of the 'decadent' rights that Westerners have against the tyranny of the majority. For all their frustrations over the 'politics of recognition' in Canada, Canadian Sikhs have made effective use of their legal rights as individual litigants to challenge race-based or religion-based discrimination in educational access, employment practices, and public accommodation, areas in which Singaporean Sikhs have not always been free to challenge existing legal and social conventions.[41]

Clearly, multiculturalism and nationalism are discourses of the moment. And, just as clearly, we have not one but many multiculturalist and nation–building projects in contest with each other. And they all raise difficult problems for the modern pluralistic nation-state, which must justify its balance of power between the state, ethnocultural groups, and individual citizens. Myron Weiner has recently noted that 'it remains to be seen whether ideals of unity and diversity, that is, political unity and cultural diversity can be the foundations of modern states' (personal communication). Canada and Singapore would presumably both claim that they can and that the balance is being achieved in their cases. But liberal Canada and corporatist Singapore appear to have started from different places in their attempts to achieve a political unity that accommodates cultural diversity. And the differences in their respective conceptualizations of power as evolving upward from individuals or devolving downward from the state put ethnocultural groups in very different, if equally problematic, situations in the two cases.

Nevertheless, in both instances, minority ethnocultural communities like the Sikhs must ultimately accommodate themselves to that power that continues to reside with the state and its intermediaries; power, the exercise of which they are most unlikely to control directly. If I have emphasized in this paper the way that Sikhs have sought to use the poetics and politics of nationalism and multiculturalism to gain recognition from the state, I want to end by emphasizing the way in which the state has used its recognition or non-recognition of the Sikhs as a way both of demonstrating its power and of imagining the national self.[42] In Singapore, Sikhs have been constituted as a model minority, the ethnic Other—now delinked from the negatively stereotyped 'other Indians' (that is, Tamils)—most like the valorized and idealized industrious, responsible, successful Chinese Singaporean majority.[43] By contrast, Sikhs in Canada constitute an 'inflexible, culturally different ethnic enclave'; they are the negatively stereotyped ethnic Other who, in offending the self-image of the liberal (white) Canadian majority, is deemed undomesticable and, therefore, literally unrecognizable.

For anthropologists and other ethnographers of 'the politics of recognition', it is important in particular socio-historical situations to be sensitive both to the agents who command the power to name and control difference and to the terms under which recognition is extended. Having focused so long on ethnocultural groups as primary objects of study, anthropologists have rightfully been accused both of reifying 'culture' and of undertheorizing 'power'. Clearly, no bounded, unitary Sikh collectivity (in either the 'homeland' or the 'diaspora') exists as a natural fact; it is always an 'imagined community', an integral component of our human capacity for self-creation. Nor can any individual or organization truly speak for all Sikhs, a notoriously pluralistic and factionalized community (as are most). Nevertheless, as we have seen in the two cases at hand, governments grant ethnocultural communities collective recognition and empower individuals to speak on behalf of those communities. And since, as Appadurai reminds us, 'the central paradox of ethnic politics in today's world is that primordia . . . have become globalized' (1990, p. 15), anthropologists can never hope to capture global ethnoscapes by sitting in one place but can only hope to map the relationship between ethnic politics and 'primordial' identities in their particular, context-dependent forms. Thus, I present this modest attempt here at doing an ethnography of the poetics and politics of recognition at two nodes in this intersection of global ethnoscapes and pluralist polities.

ACKNOWLEDGEMENTS

This research was supported, in part, by a CIES Fulbright grant (91–64961) through the Southeast Asian Regional Research Program, by an Advanced Research Award from the Joint Committee on Southeast Asia of the Social Science Research Council and the American Council of Learned Societies with funds provided by the Ford Foundation and the National Endowment for the Humanities, and by a Hannah grant from Hamline University. Earlier versions of this paper were presented at Hamline University, at the University of Minnesota, at the 47th Annual Meeting of the Association for Asian Studies, and at the Institute for Southeast Asian Studies in Singapore. I thank these multiple audiences, my Sikh and non-Sikh friends and informants in Singapore and Canada, and the editors and reviewers at the *American Ethnologist*—Donald Brenneis, Michael Herzfeld, Richard Fox, and three anonymous reviewers—for comments and suggestions (not always heeded) on this paper. I take full responsibility for the interpretations presented herein.

NOTES

1. For reviews of the anthropology of nationalism, see Fox (1990); Foster (1991). On anthropology and multiculturalism, see Chicago Cultural Studies Group (1992), Lee (1995), and Turner (1993).
2. For recent anthropological overviews or review articles on the politics of identity, see Alonso (1994) and Smith (1994).
3. On the mutual entailment of anthropological and nationalist concepts of 'culture' and the political uses thereof see, for example, Handler (1985), Turner (1993), Williams (1993).
4. Within the literature on transnationalism and globalization, there appears something of a split between the post-sovereigntists, who would argue that the state has lost its legitimacy as the source of social recognition and the arbiter of rights, and others—such as Nina Glick Schiller, Linda Basch and Cristina Szanton Blanc (Basch et al. 1994; Glick-Schiller et al. 1992)—who emphasize the configuring hegemonic powers of nation-states. Arjun Appadurai's writings provide a middle ground, taking as an open question the ultimate outcome of battles between states and social groups over recognizing and managing difference in the 'global ethnoscape' (see, 'for example' Appadurai 1990, pp. 13–14; 1993, 1996), even as he encourages us to 'think ourselves beyond the nation' (1993, p. 411).
5. On the positive example of ethnic management in Canada, see Fleras and Elliott (1992). On the same in Singapore, see Vasil (1994 [1990]).

6. On this point, Appadurai's transnational perspective appears quite similar to that of Glick-Shiller, Basch and Blanc-Szanton (1992) in emphasizing, as do I, the dialectic between the hegemonic powers of the state—in both material and ideological forms—to impose categories of identity on local residents and the culturally creative power of diasporic peoples to resist or deflect these impositions.
7. Terms such as *Hindoo hordes* appeared regularly in the popular press of the period (see, for example, Indra 1979). On the early history of South Asian immigration to North America, see Buchignani and Indra (1985) and Jensen (1988). Whether the migration from colonial Punjab is best seen as primarily a 'Sikh' or a 'Punjabi' exodus remains a hotly contested issue (Dusenbery 1995; Leonard 1989; McLeod 1989) because clear-cut normative differences between Hindu, Sikh, and Muslim Punjabis were only beginning to be delineated in the colonial period. In both Singapore and Canada, however, Sikhs attempted at times to play upon the positive stereotypes that the British had of Sikhs—as good soldiers and loyal subjects—to differentiate themselves from other Indian immigrants, including other Punjabis.
8. In an earlier article, I deal in some detail with the concepts of a 'Sikh diaspora' and a 'Sikh nation' and their mutual construction and naturalization in relation to a territorialized Sikh homeland (Dusenbery 1995). I also advance the argument that the longing for Khalistan is for some diasporan Sikhs a means of and to belonging in their current country of residence.
9. See, for example, the attitudinal surveys discussed in Buchignani and Indra (1989, pp. 157–63) and in Kashmeri & McAndrew (1989, pp. 149–50).
10. In their conversations with me, both Amyn B. Sajoo, formerly of the Canadian Human Rights Commission, and Anna Chiappa, executive director of the Canadian Ethnocultural Council, spoke of difficulties encountered by Sikh organizations in getting their concerns addressed by these institutions. A major source of the problem, in their view, is the Sikh insistence that they are a separate ethnocultural group and thus their apparent unwillingness or inability to 'work through' or 'work with' other recognized ethnocultural organizations.
11. This statement is based on conversations in 1993–4 with past and present officials or spokespersons of the Federation of Sikh Societies, the National Sikh Alliance, the World Sikh Organization-Canada, and the Ontario Council of Sikhs.
12. In recounting the work of the Royal Commission on Bilingualism and Biculturalism, the Minister of State for Multiculturalism states that the commission was charged with inquiring into and reporting on bilingualism and biculturalism in Canada. It was to recommend what steps should be taken to develop an equal partnership between the

founding races, taking into account the contributions made by other ethnic groups to the cultural enrichment of Canada. (Canada 1978, p. 9) The Québecois have often represented Canadian multiculturalism as a diversion from the more important issues of federalism. For a historical overview, see Berry and Laponce (1994), Fleras and Elliott (1992), and Hryniuk (1992); compare Bissoondath (1994).

13. For further discussion of the Canadian mosaic metaphor, from the perspective of strong proponents of Canada's multiculturalism policies, see Fleras and Elliott (1992, pp. 64–6).
14. According to Fleras and Elliott, 'nearly $200 million was set aside between 1971 and 1987 for specific initiatives in language and culture maintenance' (1992, p. 74).
15. By the time that the Canadian Multiculturalism Act of 1988 was passed, 'will to exist' had explicitly given way to 'common origins' as a basis of group classification. Thus, the Act commits the state to 'recognize the existence of communities whose members share a common origin and their historic contribution to Canadian society, and enhance their development' (Bill C-93, 3(1)(d)). But since 'common origin' is not further defined in the Act, the decision as to which ethnocultural groups merit recognition in practice can appear ad hoc and arbitrary.
16. The existence of a small but visible group of non-Punjabi Sikh converts in North America complicates the case for those who would argue that Sikhs constitute a 'nation' or an 'ethnic group' (see Dusenbery 1981; 1995, pp. 35–6). But the major difficulty here seems to arise from the fact that Sikhs are 'lumped together with about fifty other groups—as "East Indians"' (N. Singh 1994, p. 119).
17. On the origins of NACOI, see NACOI (1977), Paranjpe (1986), and Wood (1978). On early Vancouver Sikh reactions to NACOI, see Dusenbery (1981, pp. 107–10).
18. The factional differences at the national level paralleled a similar factional dispute at the time over control of the Khalsa Diwan Society in Vancouver, the oldest and largest Sikh gurdwara society in Canada (see Dusenbery 1989b, pp. 99–105).
19. For a listing of briefs and position papers presented by the Federation, see N. Singh (1994, pp. 126–7). The Federation was a signatory to the agreement with the secretary of state for multiculturalism and the University of British Columbia; the agreement set up a chair in Sikh and Punjabi Studies at UBC. Both the state (through the Multiculturalism Directorate) and Sikhs (through the Federation) contributed money towards the chair. The fact that the Federation has since become largely a paper organization has complicated efforts of those Canadian Sikhs seeking to oust the initial holder of the chair and to exert control over the activities and teachings of the chair.
20. A third pro-Khalistan organization, Babbar Khalsa, was also active in Canada during this period. Babbar Khalsa members in Canada were

implicated in 'terrorist' activities, although their actual involvement in criminal activities has been contested (see, for example, Kashmiri and McAndrew 1989; N. Singh 1994, pp. 127–8). Unlike WSO-Canada and ISYF, Babbar Khalsa was not a mass organization seeking control of established community institutions in Canada.

21. The Canadian Ethnocultural Council describes itself as 'a non-profit, non-partisan organization representing 38 national ethnocultural organizations. . . [that] in turn represent over 2,000 ethnic associations across Canada.' Fleras and Elliot characterize the council as 'a catalyst and advocate for minority issues,. . . [that] seeks to advance multiculturalism in Canada through public education, the submission of briefs, appearances before House of Commons committees, lobbying, conferences, research, and publications' (1992, p. 74). According to Anna Chiappa, the executive director, CEC membership is determined on whether the organization in question: (1) represents a 'unique community based on nationhood or peoplehood', (2) has a national scope, and (3) is not already represented by another group that can speak for it. In the final analysis, the council decides whom it will admit to its ranks. In addition to NACOI, the Federation of Pakistani Canadians is represented. But just as WSO-Canada was rejected on grounds that NACOI already speaks for Sikh interests, Macedonian Canadians were turned down in the early 1990s on grounds that the Hellenic Canadian Congress already spoke for them (Anna Chiappa, personal communication, 30 August 1993).
22. The proposed National Sikh Alliance was regarded as too overwhelmingly dominated by non-Jats to suit many in the Jat Sikh majority. On the charge that it was too close to the Conservative party and insufficiently critical of the Government of India, see Sandhar (1992).
23. These explanations arose in a series of conversations in 1993–4 with the long-time Secretary of the Federation of Sikh Societies, Gucharan Singh. But perusal of the Canadian Sikh media will quickly show the same sort of analysis to be voiced by other Sikh leaders. In fact, the charges against the Government of India may be well-founded. An investigation by two reporters, one from the *Toronto Globe and Mail* and other from the *Toronto Star* (Kashmeri and McAndrew 1989), uncovered evidence that during the 1980s the Government of India's intelligence operatives in Canada 'engaged in a devious and ruthless operation to manipulate and destabilize Canada's Sikh population . . . [that] has left the Sikh community estranged from Canadian society' (1989: v).
24. For a more detailed account of Singaporean ideologies, policies, and practices of ethnic management and of the Sikh–state relations in postcolonial Singapore, see Dusenbery (1996).

25. These quotations come from public comments made by the father of modern Singapore, the then-prime minister, Lee Kuan Yew, shortly before his retirement to the position of Senior Minister (*Straits Times* 1991). But similar comments, reflecting official appreciation of disproportionate Sikh contributions and promising government support of Sikh initiatives can be found in the subsequent comments of then-Acting Minister of Information and Arts, B.G. Yeo (*Straits Times* 1990c) and Prime Minister Goh Chok Tong (*Straits Times* 1991). Lee Kuan Yew's view of the Sikhs has been fairly consistent. At a Sikh function in 1967, he praised the Sikhs for their 'valuable contribution to the life, the vitality, the success and the prosperity of our society' and congratulated them 'on the success that you have made for yourselves in carrying out a desent [sic] livelihood for yourselves and your children' (Sri Guru Nanak Sat Sang Sabha 1967). The only negative public stereotyping of Singapore's Sikhs by Lee Kuan Yew that I encountered occured in the context of his justifying Singapore's Internal Security Act to a British reporter, when he noted that 'Sikhs in Singapore were outraged because the Golden Temple was attacked [in 1984]. We had to protect the Indian High Commissioner here from 40,000 [sic] Sikhs who would have bludgeoned him' (*Straits Times* 1989).
26. On the CMIO categories and the logic of Singaporean multiracialism, see Benjamin (1976), Clammer (1985, pp. 107–17), Lai (1995, pp. 178–87) and Siddique (1989).
27. On Singapore's linguistic policies and the prevailing ideology of language, see Clammer (1985, pp. 133–7), Pakir (1992), and Puru Shotam (1989).
28. The intellectual justification for the Religious Harmony Act was provided by three National University of Singapore sociologists in a report prepared for the Ministry of Communiy Development (Kuo et al. 1988). Subsequently, a government white paper on the 'Maintenance of Religious Harmony' appeared (Singapore 1989), followed by passage of the Maintenance of Religious Harmony Act in (1990) (Singapore 1991a). Quoted phrases are from Singapore (1989).
29. The intellectual justification for the search for Singapore's National Values was provided by the Institute for Policy Studies in Singapore at the request of the government (Quah 1990). The government's white paper on 'Shared Values' appeared the following year (Singapore 1991b). For other perspectives on the search for National Values, see Chau and Kuo (1991), Rodan (1992), and Brown (1994, pp. 92–6).
30. The panel that wrote the text was headed by Dr Gobind Singh Mansukhani (Mansukhani et al. 1985, 1986), and the text itself was based on Mansukhani (1968).

31. These issues are drawn from a letter of 2 November 1990 ('Tribute from the Sikh Community') from Bhajan Singh, chair of Sikh Advisor Board, to Lee Kuan Yew, prime minister of the Republic of Singapore (author's files).
32. 'Proactive' and 'coinciding interests' were phrases used by Singapore Ministry of Community Development officials, Santanu Gupta and Nicholas Poh, to describe the relationship between the Ministry and the Sikh Advisory Board (personal interview, 26 July 1993).
33. In October 1995, a Punjabi/Sikh Welfare Council was launched by the Sikh Advisory Board. Structurally, this would make it parallel to the self-help organizations of the other recognized 'races'.
34. Subsequently, Bhajan Singh was appointed to be the Sikh representative on the Religious Harmony Council, even though plausible cases could be made for one of the old-guard temple society leaders or of someone already involved in inter-religious affairs. Clearly, Bhajan Singh's appointment was a demonstration of the state's corporatist management of ethnicity and religion, as it ensured a deliberate representational monopoly.
35. One of the effects of enumerating Sikhs separately by 'race' and 'religion' is to provide evidence suggesting that, contrary to the rhetoric of Sikh nationalists, 'race' and 'religion' do not perfectly coincide (see Dusenbery 1996, p. 143).
36. Prominent examples of candidates who have succeeded within Canadian politics by de-emphasizing their Sikhness are Moe Sahota and Ujjal Dosanjh, members of the British Columbia provincial cabinet; Gurcharan Singh Bhatiar, a 'visible minorities' appointee to the Canadian Human Rights Commission; Sangat Singh, the current President of NACOI; and Herb Dhaliwal, Liberal Party MP from British Columbia.

    Gurbax Malhi, Liberal Party MP from Ontario, is the first turbaned Sikh elected to the Canadian Parliament. But even he has stated publicly that he does not consider himself to be representing the Sikh community or the Khalistan issue (see interview in *Mehfil Magazine*, Dec./Jan. 1994, p. 29). Contrast this with the expectation in Singapore that Davinder Singh, elected as a 'minority' (i.e., non-Chinese) member of Singapore's Parliament through a system of Group Representation Constituencies, will represent both his electoral constitutency and the Singaporean Sikh community at large.
37. Clearly, Asians and other 'visible minorities' are represented on the CEC. But the distinctions among European-derived groups are apparently considered more salient than similar distinctions among, for example, South Asian Canadians. Here, the Canadian politics of recognition appears to take on a racial cast. Hence, the view of Gucharan Singh, of the Federation of Sikh Society, is that the CEC is basically a 'European

organization' and his assertion is that 'the [Canadian] Sikh community . . . has been effectively cut off from all federal government funding . . . [because of] these discriminating (and to a large extent racist) policies against them' (personal communication, 21 September 1993).

38. The Presidential Council for Minority Rights is responsible for considering whether any proposed legislation

> is, or is likely in its practical application to be, disadvantageous to persons of any racial or religious community and not equally disadvantageous to persons of other such communities, either directly by prejudicing persons of that community or indirectly by giving advantage to persons of another community. [Singapore 1972]

The council is composed of five permanent members, a chairman, and up to ten temporary members serving three year (renewable) terms. In none of its annual reports has the council suggested that any proposed legislation was found to discriminate against racial or religious minorities in Singapore. On the origins and evolution of the Presidential Council for Minority Rights and its constitutional authority, see Jayakumar (1976, pp. 17–28, 104–12).

39. Sikh successes adapting both to the corporatist political culture of Singapore and to the liberal political culture of the United States suggest that it may be, in part, the hybrid nature of Canadian political culture that has proven so problematic for Canadian Sikh interest articulation. (I am appreciative of Luther Gerlach for suggesting that I make this three-way comparison.)
40. John Comaroff (1995) identifies what he calls 'hetero-nationalism' as an incipient third way between 'Euro-nationalism' and 'ethno-nationalism' and suggests that newly-independent South Africa may take the lead in showing the world how this could work in practice. But Comaroff's analysis, while suggestive, is short on specifics of how the hetero-nationalist state would balance individual rights and group claims.
41. Thus, for example, the racial quotas limiting Indian admission into the law faculty at National University of Singapore or the advertisements based on race and gender in the *Straits Times* or the de facto exclusion of non-Chinese from the government's SAP (super assistance programme) schools are all likely to be subject to successful legal challenge in Canada.
42. See Chicago Cultural Studies Group 1992. I am grateful to Yao Souchou for encouraging me to emphasize the various Otherings going on here.
43. Note, for example, the then-prime minister Lee Kuan Yew's comments on the occasion of his 1990 visit to the Central Sikh Temple: 'Mr. Lee Kuan Yew . . . singled out the great capacity for self-help among the Chinese and Sikhs in improving their well-being. . . . Mr. Lee said that this was the kind of dynamism . . . which was the secret of successful communities all over the world' (*Straits Times* 1990b).

REFERENCES

Alonso, Ana Maria,1994, 'The Politics of Space, Time and Substance: State Formation, Nationalism, and Ethnicity', *Annual Review of Anthropology*, vol. 23, pp. 379–405.

Appadurai, Arjun,1990, 'Disjunction and Difference in the Global Cultural Economy', *Public Culture*, 2 (2), pp. 1–24.

———, 1991, 'Global Ethnoscapes: Notes and Queries for a Transnational Anthropology' in Richard G. Fox, (ed.), *Recapturing Anthropology*, Santa Fe: School of American Research, pp. 191–210.

———, 1993, 'Patriotism and Its Futures', *Public Culture*, vol. 5, pp. 411–29.

———, 1996, 'Sovereignty Without Territoriality: Notes for a Postnational Geography' in Patricia Yaeger, (ed.), *The Geography of Identity*, Ann Arbor: University of Michigan Press, pp. 40–58.

Basch, Linda, Nina Glick Schiller, and Cristina Szanton Blanc, (eds), 1994, *Nations Unbound*, Langhorne, Pennsylvania: Gordon and Breach Publishers.

Benjamin, Geoffrey, 1976, 'The Cultural Logic of Singapore's "Multiracialism"' in Riaz Hassan, (ed.), *Singapore: Society in Transition*, Kuala Lumpur: Oxford University Press, pp. 115–33.

Berry, J.W. and J.A. Laponce, (eds), 1994, *Ethnicity and Culture in Canada*, Toronto: University of Toronto Press.

Bissoondath, Neil, 1993, 'A Question of Belonging: Multiculturalism and Citizenship' in William Kaplan, (ed.), *Belonging: The Meaning and Future of Canadian Citizenship*, Montreal: McGill-Queens University Press, pp. 368–87.

———, 1994, *Selling Illusions: The Cult of Multiculturalism in Canada*, Toronto: Penguin Books.

Brown, David, 1994, *The State and Ethnic Politics in Southeast Asia*, New York: Routledge.

Buchignani, Norman L. and Doreen M. Indra, 1985, *Continuous Journey: A Social History of South Asian in Canada*, Toronto: McClelland and Stewart Ltd.

———, 1989, 'Key Issues in Canadian-Sikh Ethnic and Race Relations: Implications for the Study of the Sikh Diaspora' in N. Gerald Barrier and Verne A. Dusenbery, (eds), *The Sikh Diaspora*, Delhi: Chanakya Publications and Columbia, MO: South Asia Publications, pp. 141–84.

Canada, 1971, 'Announcement of Implementation of Policy of Multiculturalism Within Belingual [*sic*] Framework', House of Commons Debates, 115, 187 (8 October), pp. 8545–48, 8580–85.

———, 1978, *Multiculturalism and the Government of Canada*, Ottawa: Minister of State for Multiculturalism

———, 1985, *Canadian Human Rights Act*, R.S., 1985, c. H-6.

———, 1988, *Canadian Multiculturalism Act*, Bill C-93, Statutes of Canada, 2, C-18.7 3(1)(2). [R.S. 1985, c.24 (4th supp.)]

Chicago Cultural Studies Group, 1992, 'Critical Multiculturalism', *Critical Inquiry*, vol. 18, pp. 530–55.

Chua, Beng Huat and Eddie C.Y. Kuo, 1991, *The Making of a New Nation: Cultural Construction and National Identity in Singapore*, Singapore: National University of Singapore, Department of Sociology Working Papers No. 104.

Clammer, John, 1985, *Singapore: Ideology, Society and Culture*, Singapore: Chopmen Publishers.

Comaroff, John L., 1995, 'Ethnicity, Nationalism and the Politics of Difference in an Age of Revolution' in John L. Comaroff and P.C. Stern, (eds), *Perspectives on Nationalism and War*, Luxembourg: Gordon and Breach Publishers, pp. 243–76.

Das, Veena, 1995, *Critical Events*, New Delhi: Oxford University Press.

Dusenbery, Verne A., 1981, 'Canadian Ideology and Public Policy: The Impact on Vancouver Sikh Ethnic and Religious Adaptation', *Canadian Ethnic Studies*, 13(3), pp. 101–19.

———, 1989a, 'Introduction: A Century of Sikhs Beyond Punjab' in N. Gerald Barrier and Verne A. Dusenbery, (eds), *The Sikh Diaspora*, Delhi: Chanakya Publications and Columbia, MO: South Asia Publications pp. 1–28.

———, 1989b, 'Of Singh Sabhas, Siri Singh Sahibs, and Sikh Scholars: Sikh Discourse from North America in the 1970s' in N. Gerald Barrier and Verne A. Dusenbery, (eds), *The Sikh Diaspora*, Delhi: Chanakya Publications and Columbia, MO: South Asia Publications, pp. 90–119.

———, 1990, 'On the Moral Sensitivities of Sikhs in North America' in Owen M. Lynch, (ed.), *Divine Passions*, Berkeley: University of California Press, pp. 239–61.

———, 1995, 'A Sikh Diaspora? Contested Identities and Constructed Realities' in Peter van der Veer, (ed.), *Nation and Migration,* Philadelphia: University of Pennsylvania Press, pp. 17–42.

———, 1996, 'Socializing Sikhs in Singapore: Soliciting the State's Support' in Pashaura Singh and N. Gerald Barrier, (eds), *The Transmission of Sikh Heritage in the Diaspora,* New Delhi: Manohar Publishers and Columbia, MO: South Asia Publications, pp. 127–64.

———, 1999, ''Nation' or 'World Religion': Master Narratives of Sikh Identity' in Pashaura Singh and N. Gerald Barrier, (eds), *Sikh Identity*, New Delhi: Manohar Publishers, pp. 127–44.

Faubion, James D., 1995, 'Introduction' in James D. Faubion, (ed.), *Rethinking the Subject*, Boulder, CO: Westview Press, pp. 1–27.

Fleras, A. and Jean L. Elliott, 1992, *Multiculturalism in Canada*, Scarborough, Ontario: Nelson Canada.

Foster, Robert J., 1991, 'Making National Cultures in the Global Ecumene', *Annual Review of Anthropology*, vol. 20, pp. 235–60.

Fox, Richard G.,1985, *Lions of the Punjab*, Berkeley: University of California Press.

———, 1990, 'Introduction' in Richard G. Fox, (ed.), *Nationalist Ideologies and the Production of National Cultures*, Washington, DC: American Ethnological Society Monograph Series, (2), pp. 1–14.

Girling, John, 1993, 'Whither Civil Society in Singapore?' Paper presented at the Institute of Southeast Asian Studies, Singapore, July.

Glick Schiller, Nina, Linda Basch, and Cristina Blanc-Szanton,1992, 'Transnationalism: A New Analytic Framework for Understanding Migration' in Nina Glick Schiller, Linda Basch, and Cristina Blanc-Szanton, (eds), *Towards a Transnational Perspective on Migration*, New York: Annals of the New York Academy of Science, pp. 1–24.

Guéhenno, Jean-Marie, 1995, *The End of the Nation-State*, Minneapolis: University of Minnesota Press.

Handler, Richard, 1985, 'On Dialogue and Destructive Analysis: Problems in Narrating Nationalism and Ethnicity', *Journal of Anthropological Research*, vo. 41, pp. 171–82.

Helweg, Arthur W., 1989, 'Sikh Politics in India: The Emigrant Factor' in N. Gerald Barrier and Verne A. Dusenbery, (eds), *The Sikh Diaspora*, Delhi: Chanakya Publications and Columbia, MO: South Asia Publications, pp. 305–36.

Horowitz, Donald L.,1989, 'Europe and America: A Comparative Analysis of "Ethnicity"', *Revue Européenne des Migrations Internationales*, 5(1), pp. 47–61.

Hryniuk, Stella, (ed.),1992, *Twenty Years of Multiculturalism: Successes and Failures*, Winnipeg, Manitoba: St. John's College Press.

Indra, Doreen M., 1979, 'South Asian Stereotypes in the Vancouver Press', *Ethnic and Racial Studies*, 2(2), pp. 166–89.

Jayakumar, S., 1976, *Constitutional Law*, Singapore: Malaya Law Review, Faculty of Law, University of Singapore.

Jensen, Joan, 1988, *Passage From India: Asian Indian Immigration to North America*, New Haven: Yale University Press.

Kapferer, Bruce, 1988, *Legends of People, Myths of State: Violence, Intolerance, and Political Culture in Sri Lanka and Australia*, Washington, DC: Smithsonian Institution Press.

Kashmeri, Zuhair and Brian McAndrew, 1989, *Soft Target: How the Indian Intelligence Service Penetrated Canada*, Toronto: James Lorimer & Co.

Kuo, Eddie C.Y., Jon S.T. Quah, and Tong Chee Kiong, 1988, *Religion and Religious Revivalism in Singapore*, Report Prepared for Ministry of Community Development, Singapore: Ministry of Community Development.

Lai, Ah Eng, 1995, *Meanings of Multiethnicity: A Case Study of Ethnicity and Ethnic Relations in Singapore*, Kuala Lumpur: Oxford University Press.

Lee, Benjamin, 1995, 'Critical Internationalism, *Public Culture* 7, pp. 559–92.

Leonard, Karen, 1989, 'Pioneer Voices from California: Reflections on Race, Religion and Ethnicity' in N. Gerald Barrier and Verne A. Dusenbery, (eds), *The Sikh Diaspora*, Delhi: Chanakya Publications and Columbia, MO: South Asia Publications, pp. 120–40.

Mansukhani, Gobind Singh, 1968, *Introduction to Sikhism*, Delhi: India Book House.

Mansukhani, Gobind Singh, Kirpal Singh, Naranjan Singh, Meharvan Singh, Nirmal Tej Singh Chopra, and Harbans Singh, 1985, *Sikh Studies*, Part 1, Singapore: Sikh Advisory Board.

———, 1986, *Sikh Studies*, Part 2, Singapore: Sikh Advisory Board.

McLeod, W.H., 1989, 'The First Forty Years of Sikh Migration: Problems and Some Possible Solutions' in N. Gerald Barrier and Verne A. Dusenbery, (eds), *The Sikh Diaspora*, Delhi: Chanakya Publications and Columbia, MO: South Asia Publications, pp. 29–38.

Mehfil Magazine, 1994, *'Your Voice on the Hill?* 5(1) December/January, pp. 28–9.

Moyers, Bill D with Andie Tucher, (ed.), 1990, *Bill Moyers: A World of Ideas* II, New York: Doubleday.

NACOI (National Association of Canadians of Origins in India), 1977, Constitution and By-laws, Ottawa: NACOI.

Oberoi, Harjot, 1994, *The Construction of Religious Boundaries: Culture, Identity and Diversity in the Sikh Tradition*, New Delhi: Oxford University Press and Chicago: The University of Chicago Press.

Pakir, Anne, 1992, 'English-Knowing Bilingualism in Singapore', Ban Kah Choon, Anne Pakir, and Tong Chee Kiong, (eds), *Imagining Singapore*, Singapore: Times Academic Publishers, pp. 234–62.

Paranjpe, A.C., 1986, 'Identity Issues among Immigrants: Reflections on the Experience of Indo-Canadians in British Columbia' in Richard Harvey Brown and George V. Coelho, (eds), *Tradition and Transformation: Studies in Third World Societies*, Williamsburg, VA: College of William and Mary, pp. 71–94.

Pettigrew, Joyce, 1975, *Robber Noblemen: A Study of the Political System of the Sikh Jats*, Boston: Routledge & Kegan Paul.

———, 1995, *The Sikhs of the Punjab: Unheard Voices of State and Guerrilla Violence*, London: Zed Books Ltd.

Puru Shotam, Nirmala, 1989, 'Language and Linguistic Policies' in Kernail Singh Sandhu and Paul Wheatley, (eds), *Management of Success*, Singapore: Institute of Southeast Asian Studies, pp. 503–22.

Quah, Jon S.T., (ed.),1990, *In Search of Singapore's National Values*, Singapore: Times Academic Press for the Institute of Policy Studies.

Rex, John,1995, 'Ethnic Identity and the Nation State: The Political Sociology of Multi-Cultural Societies, *Social Identilites,* 1(1), pp. 21–34.

Rodan, Garry, 1992, 'Singapore's Leadership Transition: Erosion or Refinement of Authoritarian Rule?', *Bulletin of Concerned Asian Scholars*, 24(1), pp. 3–17.

Sandhar, Harbakhash Singh, 1992, 'Canadian Government Launches New Sikh Body!... What Won't They do to Please India?', *The Sword*, Spring/ Summer, pp. 26–9.

Sandhu, Kernail Singh, 1970, 'Sikh Immigration into Malaya During the Period of British Rule' in Jerome Ch'en and Nicholas Tarling, (eds), *Studies in the Social History of China and South-East Asia*, Cambridge: Cambridge University Press, pp. 335–54.

Shapiro, Michael J.,1994, 'Moral Geographies and the Ethics of Post-Sovereignty', *Public Culture*, vol. 6, pp. 479–502.

Siddique, Sharon, 1989, 'Singaporean Identity' in Kernail Singh Sandhu and Paul Wheatley, (eds), *Management of Success*, Singapore: Institute of Southeast Asian Studies, pp. 563–77.

Sikh Advisory Board (Singapore), n.d., *Rules for the Guidance of the Sikh Advisory Board*, Singapore: SAB.

Singapore, Republic of, 1972, *Report of the Presidential Council for the Twelve Months Ending 30th April, 1972*, Cmd. 18 of 1972.

———, 1989, *Maintenance of Religious Harmony*, White Paper, Cmd. 21 of 1989.

———, 1991a, *Maintenance of Religious Harmony Act* (Ch. 167A), Act 26 of 1990. Rev. edn.

———, 1991b, *Shared Values*, White Paper, Cmd. 1 of 1991.

Singh, Bilveer,1992, Whither PAP's Dominance? Petaling Jaya, Malaysia: Pelanduk Publications.

Singh, Narindar,1994 , *Canadian Sikhs*, Ottawa: Canadian Sikhs' Studies Institute.

Smith, Anthony D.,1994, 'The Politics of Culture: Ethnicity and Nationalism' in Tim Ingold, (ed.), *Companion Encyclopedia of Anthropology*, New York: Routledge, pp. 706–33.

Sri Guru Nanak Sat Sang Sabha (Singapore),1967, *Tercentenary Souvenir in Honour of Sri Guru Gobind Singh Ji*, Singapore: Sri Guru Nanak Sat Sang Sabha.

Straits Settlement, 1915, Appointments: Sikh Advisory Board, Singapore. Straits Settlements Government Gazette, Nov. 26, 1748.

Straits Times, 1989, 'Singaporeans Expect Firm and Strong Government, Says PM', October 22, pp. 20.

———, 1990a, 'PM: No Reversal on Bilingual Policy', 3 November, p. 50.

———, 1990b, 'PM Praises Role of Self-help in Communities', 4 November, p. 22.

———, 1990c, 'Ethnic Groups Should Set up Own Heritage Centers: B.G. Yeo', December 31, p. 16.

———, 1991, 'PM Enjoys Chapati and Dhal with the Sikhs', 22 November, p. 25.

Taylor, Charles, 1994 [1992], 'The Politics of Recognition' in Amy Gutmann, (ed.), *Multiculturalism and the 'Politics of Recognition'*, Princeton, New Jersey: Princeton University Press, pp. 25–73.

Turner, Terrence, 1993, 'Anthropology and Multiculturalism: What is Anthropology That Multiculturalists Should Be Mindful of It', *Cultural Anthropology*, vol. 8, pp. 411–29.

Vasil, Raj, 1994 [1990], 'Ethnic Peace: A Unique Contribution' in Derek da Cunha, (ed.), *Debating Singapore*, Singapore: Institute of Southeast Asian Studies, pp. 35–9.

———, 1995, *Asianising Singapore: The PAP's Management of Ethnicity*, Singapore: Heinemann Asia for the Institute of Southeast Asian Studies.

Weiner, Myron, 1992, 'Peoples and States in a New Ethnic Order?', *Third World Quarterly*, vo. 13, pp. 317–33.

Williams, Brackette F., 1993, 'The Impact of the Precepts of Nationalism on the Concept of Culture: Making Grasshoppers of Naked Apes', *Cultural Critique*, Spring, pp. 143–91.

Wolfe, Alan, 1992, 'Democracy versus Sociology: Boundaries and Their Political Consequences' in Michele Lamont and Marcel Fournier, (eds), *Cultivating Differences*, Chicago: The University of Chicago Press, pp. 309–25.

Wood, John, 1978, 'East Indians and Canada's New Immigration Policy', *Canadian Public Policy*, vol. 4, pp. 547–67.

Zalewski, Marysia and Cynthia Enloe, 1995, 'Questions about Identity in International Relations' in Ken Booth and Steve Smith, (eds), *International Relations Theory Today*, University Park: The Pennsylvania State University Press, pp. 279–305.

10

Diasporic Imagings and the Conditions of Possibility*

Sikhs and the State in Southeast Asia

One of the more interesting debates within the burgeoning social scientific literature on transnationalism and diasporic communities concerns the role of the state. For some theorists the current academic interest in transnational social formations is itself both sign and symptom of the decline of the sovereign nation-state as the primary institution of social life. Thus, in books like Jean-Marie Guéhenno's *The End of the Nation-State* (1995) and articles like Michael J. Shapiro's 'Moral Geographies and the Ethics of Post-Sovereignty' (1994), we are advised to think ourselves beyond '[s]tate-centric political discourses' since such discourses are said to reflect a world on the wane and only serve to 'legitimate the authority of the state system' (ibid., p. 479). Whether the end of the nation-state is seen in emancipatory terms (as in Shapiro's vision of 'post-sovereign ethics') or as a potential threat to personal liberties (as in Guéhenno's vision of what he calls 'the imperial age'), these theorists advise us to rethink the analytical primacy we attribute to what they take to be an institution of declining global importance.

Yet other theorists of transnationalism and global diasporas reject this reading of historical trends and emphasize the continuing hegemonic powers of the state. Thus, Kachig Tölölyan, in his introduction to the inaugural issue of the journal, *Diaspora*, tells us that

* First published in *SOJOURN: Journal of Social Issues in Southeast Asia*, vol. 12, no. 2 (October 1997), pp. 226–60. Reproduced here with kind permission of the publisher, Institute of Southeast Asian Studies, Singapore.

to affirm that diasporas are the exemplary communities of the transnational moment is not to write the premature obituary of the nation-state, which remains a privileged form of polity. (1991, p. 6)

And Nina Glick Schiller, Linda Basch, and Cristina Szanton Blanc argue that

despite the internationalization of capital and the transnationalization of populations, nation-states and nationalism persist and must be the topic of further analysis . . . [since] transnational migrants exist, interact, are given and assert their identities, and seek to exercise legal and social rights within national structures that monopolize power and foster ideologies of identity. (Glick Shiller et al. 1992, p. 15; c.f. Basch et al. 1994, p. 30)

It is in the dialectic between the powers of the state—in both material and ideological forms—to impose categories of identity upon local residents and the culturally creative power of diasporic peoples to resist or deflect these impositions in their self-imagings that should be our analytic focus.

If, as Arjun Appadurai advises us, we must 'think ourselves beyond the nation' (1993, p. 411) to imagine 'a post-national geography' (1996) of 'global ethnoscapes' (1991), we still must recognize, as Appadurai has also noted, that contemporary nation-states continue to 'exercis[e] taxonomical control over difference' (1990, p. 13) and 'have not given in readily to the emergence of nonnational, transnational, or postnational markets of loyalty' (1996, p. 49). Thus, while

the global competition for allegiances now involves all sorts of non-state actors and organizations and various forms of diasporic and multilocal allegiance (1996, pp. 48–9)

the nation-state remains a powerful actor both as an arbiter of global flows and as a source of social recognition. And thus it is not surprising that in the 'battle of imagination' over how to conceptualize society and polity, 'micro-identities . . . have become political projects within the nation-state' (1990, pp. 13, 14).

Of course, as Ulf Hannerz and others remind us, not every nation-state possesses the same power 'to constrain transnational cultural flow' or 'to impose its will and implement its [cultural] policy' (1992, pp. 236, 237). The state's hegemony is rarely complete and is frequently contested, especially in our contemporary 'Age of Revolution' (Comaroff

1995).[1] So, researchers must be attentive to the different abilities of nation-states to constrain transnational flows and impose conditions of possibility upon their citizenry. The pluralistic polities of Southeast Asia provide an interesting series of case studies of the dialectic between diasporic imagings and state power since, as the recent comparative works of Brown (1994), Sajoo (1994), and DeBernardi and Tarnowski (1995) make clear, these nation-states have pursued different policies for managing their ethnic and religious pluralism.

This paper takes a look at the 'battle of imagination' between diasporic Sikhs and the state in three post-colonial nation-states in Southeast Asia—Singapore, Malaysia, and Indonesia. My argument is that Sikh identities are being (re)made at the intersection of transnational discourses of Sikh collective identity and the discursive practices of ethnic/religious pluralism in these nation-states. That is, local Sikhs are negotiating a public identity responsive both to global self-imagings of what it means to be part of a transnational Sikh community and to the representational conditions of possibility created by various nation-states through their ideologies, policies, and practices of nationalism and ethnic/religious management. The very different experiences of Sikhs in post-colonial Indonesia, Singapore, and Malaysia, despite historical commonalities, demonstrates the power of the State in Southeast Asia to impose conditions of possibility upon Sikh self-representations. At the same time, these experiences demonstrate the creative abilities of Sikhs to fashion self-identities in different fields of power.

IMAGES OF A 'SIKH DIASPORA' AND SIKH IMAGINGS IN THE DIASPORA

The story of how immigrants from different regions of Punjab settled at different points in time in different parts of the globe have come to see themselves as part of a Sikh diaspora is a complex one. As I have argued elsewhere, the 'Sikh diaspora' is a relatively recent and contested social category (Dusenbery 1989, p. 18; 1995). It depends on the emergence of normative 'Sikh' identity that was itself the historical product of late nineteenth and early twentieth century social forces. We know now that the Punjabi village of the time was 'no place to go looking for clear-cut normative identities' (McLeod 1989, p. 42; see also Oberoi 1994) and that early international migrants from colonial Punjab did not necessarily see themselves as part of a 'Sikh' diaspora (see Leonard 1989, p. 120). My argument has been that the colonial and diasporan experience introduced a modernist discourse of identity that, in conjunction with political economic forces, made it possible over the course of this century for Sikhs to come to regard themselves and represent themselves to others as a unitary 'community' and ultimately as constitituting a captive 'nation' with its own global 'diaspora'.[2]

The first significant Sikh migration from Punjab to insular Southeast Asia dates from the British colonial period, especially to the period 1880–1920 when the changing political economy of Punjab pushed smallholder agriculturalists in central Punjab, particularly Sikh males from the Jat caste, to supplement family incomes through service in the British Indian army and/or international migration (see Fox 1985, pp. 27–51, McLeod 1989, Dusenbery 1989). Sikhs and other North Indian 'martial races,' having first proven themselves in Hong Kong, were preferentially recruited by the British to help provide internal security in the colonial plural society being created on the Malay peninsula.[3] Thus, by early in twentieth century, following opportunities opened up by service to the British, Sikhs had already established a niche in the political economy of the Malay peninsula as military, police, watchmen, and moneylenders (see Sandhu 1970). British colonial policy, which sought to cultivate qualities valued in the preferred 'martial races' and to police the ethnic population through local race-based Advisory Boards, had the effect of reinforcing Malay Sikhs in their identities as *Sikhs* (from either the Majha or Malwa region of Punjab), despite the fact that most locals lumped all north Indians together as 'Bengalis'.

During the same period, Sikhs and other Punjabis began making their way to north Sumatra and Batavia (Jakarta), arriving either directly from Punjab or after a brief stay in Malaya. Many of those who settled near Medan and Aceh became dairy farmers, while those arriving in Batavia worked mainly as watchmen and petty moneylenders. Unlike the majority of Sikhs on the Malay peninsula, most early migrants to Sumatra and Java arrived as independent migrants rather than as recruits for Malay or British security forces. And Dutch authorities worked their system of indirect rule over Indian and Chinese migrants through appointment of a series of Indian and Chinese Kapitans charged with accepting or rejecting other potential migrants and with policing their 'own' communities. Appointment to this position allowed the Kapitan to excercise a gatekeeper function, which meant that the individual was able to shape the subsequent demographic make-up of the local community. With less external motivation to conform to a single 'Sikh' standard as in British Malay and Straits Settlement police and military regiments, Punjabi enclaves in the regions of Aceh, Medan, and Batavia took on distinctive characters depending on the background of the local Kapitan.

In the colonial plural societies of the Dutch East Indies, the Straits Settlements, and British Malaya, Sikhs soon came to fill classic middleman economic niches in a political economy divided by race and class. Such roles as policeman, watchman, and moneylender tended to put them in an adversarial relationship with the Chinese, Malay, and Tamil working classes. And except among Sikh dairymen and petty traders in the rural areas of Malaya and Sumatra, there was little intimacy between Sikhs and the local population. In fact, 'Bengali devils' (as Sikhs were sometimes called) were feared by many Malays and Chinese who had experienced or heard about how Sikh troops put down labour unrest for the British or how Sikh moneylenders dealt with defaulters. Chinese informants in Malaysia and Singapore still tell stories of having been frightened into obedience by parents who threatened to call 'Babu Singh' to take them away.

Over time, Sikhs began to invest in English-language education as a means of professional advancement. Those male soujourners who chose to settle in Southeast Asia rather than return to Punjab began to send for wives and children from India and to raise a locally-born second generation. On the Malay peninsula, Sikhs sought entry into English-medium schools run by the British. In Indonesia, the Sikh-run Khalsa English School in Medan and Metropolitan English School (later, Gandhi Memorial School) in Jakarta were among the premier English-medium schools in the region in the 1930s–50s. And Southeast Asian Sikhs educated in English-medium schools in country or in India or the UK increasingly sought and found employment in the professions and the colonial civil service.

With decolonization, Sikhs were forced to make a choice about committing to the new independent states then coming into existence. Some, including a number active in the battles for independence, enthusiastically took up offers of citizenship or permanent resident status. Others hedged their bets by retaining British or Indian passports. Thousands chose to depart for a newly independent India, whose independence many had fought for as members of the Indian National Army. At the same time, some Sikhs displaced by the creation of Pakistan, largely those from merchant castes, chose to join relatives already settled in Southeast Asian urban centres. The late 1940s and early

1950s were thus a time of turnover and transformation of the Sikh population in Indonesia, Singapore, and Malaysia.

Southeast Asia was not itself a major destination for immigrants from Punjab in the 1950s and 1960s, since the emerging nation-states did not encourage further Indian emigration and Sikhs were unsure of their political and economic futures in the region. Instead, Sikhs moved in large numbers from Punjab to the UK (in the 1950s and early 1960s) and to North America (in the late 1960s and early 1970s). And some Southeast Asian Sikh joined this migrant flow to countries in the West. In the process, Punjabi migrants established new enclaves and revitalized old Sikh communities in England, Canada, and the US. Whereas Sikhs in Southeast Asia had remained relatively wellconnected to and played active roles in events in Punjab during the colonial period (see Barrier 1989, pp. 65–7), in the early post-colonial period they were largely peripheral to the transnational flows of Sikh labour, capital, images, and ideas. Having chosen to settle and throw their lot with the emerging nations in Southeast Asia, most Sikhs seem focused on upward economic mobility and local political concerns.[4]

This began to change by the late 1970s and early 1980s. The increased wealth of Sikh communities in India, Britain, North America, East Africa, and Southeast Asia and new global transportation and communication linkages facilitated an ever greater transnational flow of Sikh spouses, religious teachers, cultural productions, publications, capital, and so forth. Sikh social networks became increasingly transnational, with increased flows not simply between Punjab and Sikh communities abroad but also across nodes of the diaspora. This stimulated lively comparative discussion about how Sikhs were faring in different places, and it generated critiques of state policies and practices as experienced not only in India but also in diasporan settings. Although states in Southeast Asia filtered some of this transnational flow, Southeast Asian Sikhs were becoming more attuned to discourses of ethno-nationalism and of religious and cultural revival running through the diaspora. It was in this context that both calls for an independent Khaḷistan (a sovereign Sikh nation-state) and calls for greater attention to the transmission of Sikh heritage began to be articulated, especially by diasporan Sikhs.[5]

As I have suggested elsewhere (Dusenbery 1995), 'diaspora' and 'nation' are in many ways reciprocating terms which both serve to naturalize one another and are mutally implicated in contemporary global politics of recognition. It is not surprising, therefore, that Sikhs outside

Punjab might increasingly think and talk of themselves as belonging to a 'Sikh diaspora' at the same point that they have begun to join in imaginatively projecting an independent Sikh nation-state of Khalistan upon the map of South Asia.[6] Although Southeast Asian Sikhs were not as vocal or visible in their support of Khalistan as were Sikhs in Canada, the UK, and the US, the attack on the Golden Temple in 1984 by Indian Army troops and the slaughter of innocent Sikhs in India following Indira Gandhi's assassination provoked Sikhs everywhere to see themselves as an embattled collectivity and to reflect on what it meant to be a Sikh. At the same time, interrogation of the Indian state went hand-in-hand with interrogation of other nation-states as to how their ideologies, policies, and practices were affecting the lives of their Sikh citizens.

The global politicization of Sikh identity was largely complete by the late 1980s. Circulating images of besmirched honour and heroic martyrdom—in religious iconography, poster art, grainy home videos—reminded Sikhs everywhere both of their vulnerabilities as a visible minority and their collective history of struggles against oppressive states. Stories of atrocities taking place in Punjab were relayed by visiting relatives or by touring *ragi jathas* (religious musical troups) or by young Sikh men being spirited out of or into Punjab. Maps, declarations, constitutions, and even passports and money of the imagined Khalistan went into global circulation. Speeches and interviews with Sant Jarnail Singh Bhindranwale (killed in the attack on the Golden Temple and considered a martyr by many Sikhs) were disseminated widely on audio-cassette. Political and religious tracts circulated in print and over computer networks. And Sikhs in Southeast Asia were a part of this flow of images, serving not only as consumers but sometimes even as producers of Sikh nationalist ideologies circulating transnationally.[7]

By no means has all of this transnational flow been about Khalistan. Another set of images has focused on religious and cultural revival and, especially, the future of *Sikhi* (Sikh religious practices) and Punjabi cultural forms in the modern, cosmopolitan world. This concern with 'Sikh identity' and 'the transmission of heritage' has been especially pronounced in the diaspora, where Sikhs in various countries attempt to fashion images of what it is to be a Sikh and to practise the Sikh religion that they can comfortably live with and pass on to their children. This has led Sikh intellectuals, religious entrepreneurs, and cultural performers in the diaspora, often with an assist from the multiculturalist state, to attempt to translate images of Sikh life previously grounded in

Punjabi realities into idioms that will be accessible to Sikhs growing up in the diaspora.[8] And here, because they are a relatively mature diasporan community (that is, well settled and with no recent mass influx from village Punjab), Southeast Asian Sikhs have been among the leaders in producing images of cosmopolitan Sikhism.[9]

Today Sikhs constitute a small minority of the total population in contemporary Indonesia, Singapore, and Malaysia. There are an estimated 6,000 Indonesian Sikhs, 15,000 Singaporean Sikhs, and 40,000 Malaysian Sikhs.[10] The overwhelming majority are multi-generational residents and citizens of these post-colonial states. At the same time, many maintain social relationships (through kinship networks, business connections, religious organizations) with other Sikhs across national borders. And, especially since the early 1980s, Sikhs in Southeast Asia have increasingly come to see themselves as part of a global Sikh diaspora. But the extent and nature of Sikh involvement in the global and local 'politics of identity' has inevitably been affected by prevailing ideologies, policies, and practices in their country of residence. Since Sikhs are a small minority in Indonesia, Singapore, and Malaysia, few state policies in these countries have been implemented specifically with Sikhs in mind. Nevertheless, state ideologies, policies, and practices have served both to filter global flows and to set conditions of possibility for Sikh self-representation and political mobilization.

Let us look, therefore, at Sikh imagings and the conditions of possibility as experienced in each of these three states.

Indonesian Sikhs and the Indonesian State

Indonesian Sikhs live primarily in and around Medan and Jakarta. The present-day community of fewer than three thousand Sikhs in Medan and its environs is sustained by what informants playfully call 'the 3S's'—*susu* ('milk'; that is, dairying and, more recently, cattle raising), *sport* (proprietorship of wholesale and retail sporting goods outlets), and *sekolah* ('school'; that is, proprietorship of private English-language courses). The community, which is politically factionalized, maintains four gurdwaras (Sikh temples) in Medan proper and three in surrounding towns. The two thousand plus Sikhs around Jakarta include a group owning sports shops and related import/export business operating out of the Pasar Baru area and a number of Sikh professionals (many with training from Khalsa English School in Medan) who have found jobs in the expanding and rapidly internationalizing local economy. Jakarta Sikhs appear in many ways to constitute three somewhat distinct social communities with different migration histories, divergent class interests, and separate religious institutions. Despite internal divisions (by caste, class, regional origins in Punjab, factional allegiances, political ties, religious practices, and so forth), most Indonesian Sikhs would nevertheless recognize one another as part of a broader Sikh collectivity. At the same time, many Sikhs would express frustration at their marginalization both within the Sikh diaspora and within the Indonesian society and polity.[11]

It has been argued that Sikhs in Indonesia 'have tended to maintain their exclusive religious-cultural existence' (Arora 1982, p. 121), but this is clearly more true of the original migrants than of the post-colonial generation, who are 'at an important juncture of having to find a way to keep their religion and identity while becoming Indonesian' (Mani 1993a, pp. 86–7; see also Mani 1993b). The Indonesian state ideology, encapsulated in the Pancasila ('Five Principles') and actively expressed in the commitment to Bahasa Indonesia as an incorporative national language, requires supra-ethnic participation on the part of all citizens (*warga negara*). Indonesian Sikh attempts to maintain or to assert a distinctive religious and/or ethnic identity have thus had to confront certain challenges from state ideology, policies, and practices which, despite the national slogan of the post-colonial Indonesian state, *Bhinneka Tunggal Ika* ('Unity in Diversity'), have tended to promote assimilation and neo-patrimonial political involvement, especially for non-Malay minorities. Like the Chinese, Sikhs have often felt themselves to be provisional members of the national community. And Sikhs, who are viewed by other Indonesians as a relatively prosperous but somewhat insular section of the Indian populace, must fear the scapegoating that the Chinese have long been subject to in Indonesia.[12] Not surprisingly, many of the state policies and practices that Sikhs identify as impediments to asserting and sustaining their Sikh identity in Indonesia—especially those concerning immigration, citizenship, language use, and property ownership—were primarily intended to force the assimilation of Chinese in the post-1965 New Order.

Let me briefly list and discuss seven areas that at least some Indonesian Sikhs identified as ideologies, policies, and practices of the state that serve to shape how they live their lives as Sikhs in Indonesia.

1. In Keeping with the Pancasila Belief in 'one God', the State's Official Recognition of Five World Religions (Islam, Protestantism, Catholicism, Buddhism, and Hinduism) to which an Indonesian Should Belong

The failure to recognize Sikhism as a separate world religion coming within the perview of the Department of Religion (Departmen Agama R.I.) forces Sikhs to accept categorization and treatment as a Hindu sect. (The rationale for this categorization, according to officials at the Department, is that Sikhs are listed as Hindus under Hindu Personal Law as per Article 25 of the *Indian* Constitution. This rationale is particularly irritating to Sikh nationalists, for whom Article 25 is a long-standing grievance. In fact, Sikh delegates refused to sign the Indian Constitution after independence because of their objections to this very clause.)

One practical effect for Indonesian Sikhs of being placed within the Hindu–Buddhist section of the Department of Religion is that few resources and little effort have yet gone into the production and dissemination of Sikh religious materials, since the section is largely staffed by and oriented toward the concerns of the large Balinese Hindu population. A second effect of this categorization, combined with Indonesia's neo-patrimonial political culture, is that leaders from the Sikh Temple in Pasar Baru (Jakarta), the most Hinduized gurdwara in Indonesia (by virtue of its joint Sindhi and merchant-caste Sikh membership) have been taken as representing and speaking on behalf of Indonesia's Sikhs, despite protests to the Department of Religion from other Indonesian Sikhs asserting that Sikhs are religiously distinct from Hindus and that certain practices at the Pasar Baru gurdwara do not fully conform to Sikh orthopraxy.

2. Nationalization of Private Schools (as per Regulation 158 from the Ministry of Education) + Promotion of Bahasa Indonesia as the Medium of Instruction in Indonesian Schools + Restrictions on Indonesian Nationals Attending Local International Schools.

The combined effect of these three educational policies pursued as part of the nationalist agenda since independence has been effectively to kill off Khalsa English School and Khalsa Punjabi School in Medan (which now teaches the national curriculum in Bahasa Indonesia) and to make it difficult if not impossible to get local Sikh children into Gandhi

Memorial School in Jakarta/Ancol (which has become a school for Indian nationals). Most Indonesian Sikh children now attend state-run schools where they are taught the national curriculum in Bahasa Indonesia. Without access to educational institutions like Khalsa English/Punjabi School or Gandhi Memorial School, it has become more difficult to train Sikh children in English (the language of international commerce and, increasingly, of Sikh communication in the diaspora) and in Punjabi (the traditional language of Sikh religion and culture). The effect, as perceived by many Indonesian Sikhs, has been downward educational and career mobility for Indonesian Sikh youth (who are not as fluent in English as their parents) plus a further distancing of Indonesian Sikhs from their cultural and religious heritage (since so little material on Sikh religion or history is available in Bahasa Indonesia).

3. Suppression of Materials Deemed to give Offence to Another Religion (Sensitive Issues Concerning Ethnic [*suku*], Religious [*agama*], and Racial [*ras*] Harmony).

Combined with the subordination of Sikh concerns within the Department of Religion, the experience of having had Sikh materials challenged as offensive to some other religious community has had a dampening effect on the production of Sikh religious materials in Bahasa Indonesia.[13] Officials at the Department of Religion claim that assistance is available and that Sikhs have been 'too proud' to come to the Ministry for help in preparing religious materials. Sikhs express concern that such materials might be adulterated to conform to the government's or some other community's version of what constitute non-offensive Sikh teachings.

4. Immigration Restrictions on the Entry of Foreign Religious Teachers

While this policy may have been directed at other religious groups, its effect has been to make it nearly impossible for Sikh gurdwaras (Sikh temples) in Indonesia to acquire and maintain a permanent, well-trained staff of religious functionaries. Most gurdwaras have no *granthi* (one who cares for and reads from the sacred text) and, therefore, must rely exclusively on members of the congregation to lead services or have only a temporary *granthi*, whose residence status is insecure. This has had the effect of rendering much of the Indonesian Sikh community religiously illiterate, since there are few well-trained religious teachers and little means of locally training new ones.

5. Immigration Restrictions on the Entry of Foreign Spouses

This policy effectively forces Sikhs to find spouses from within the rather restricted field of other Indonesian Sikhs, to marry a non-Indonesian Sikh and move abroad, or to marry a non-Sikh Indonesian. The latter option, although increasingly common, is still regarded as problematic by most Indonesian Sikhs. It is especially problematic in the case of females, where it has a negative affect on family honour. Transnational marriage networks stand at the heart of the Sikh diaspora, connecting and revitalizing Sikh communities around the globe. Consequently, this policy feeds an overall Indonesian Sikh sense of isolation (from the larger Sikh world) and entropy (within the Indonesian Sikh world).

6. Neo-patrimonial Involvement of Instruments of the State in Civil Society.

David Brown has emphasized that

> the inherent fragilities of the neo-patrimonial state generate the development and politicization of communalism . . . in the form of integrative communal patronage networks. (1994, p. 112)

And Indonesian Sikhs have on several occasions sought to use the neo-patrimonial Indonesian state and its patronage in contest for control of Sikh institutions. In both Medan (in the 1960s) and Jakarta (in the 1980s) insurgent factions sought legitimacy for attempts to take over Sikh institutions on the grounds that locally-registered organizations should be controlled by Indonesian nationals (as per Law No. 8/1985 of Mass Organisations) and that the incumbent group was led by 'Indian Sikhs' (that is, permanent residents who had retained Indian citizenship). What was notable about these two disputes was that all the Sikh factions sought to actively involve allies in the Indonesian military, police, national security agency, and various government departments to bolster their position. And, in fact, the resolution of these two factional disputes had more to do with relative ability to moblize patrons within state organs than the merits of the case under Law No. 8.[14] This has fed a certain cynicism about whether community leaders owe their positions to popular will or to their ability to control key Sikh institutions by calling on state connections.[15]

7. Policing of Public Speech and Political Assembly and an Ideology of Non-involvement by Indonesian Citizens in the Internal Political Affairs of Foreign States

Indonesian Sikhs seeking to express their anger over the Government of India's attack on the Golden Temple in 1984 were not allowed to demonstrate publicly. Instead, the officially-sanctioned local Sikh response was limited through negotiations with Indonesian and Indian govenment officials to a single letter of protest delivered to the Indian Embassy in Jakarta by a small delegation of Indonesian Sikhs. This may not have been a sufficient venting of local Sikh anger, as the subsequent murder in Jakarta of an Indian diplomat posted to the Indian Defense Attache's Office was attributed to 'Sikh extremists' (see the article in the *Indonesia Times*, 29 November 1986). Knowing of the government's concerns over signs of Indonesian Sikh involvement with Khalistani activities, both sides in the factional battles in Jakarta in the 1980s suggested to Indonesian officials that the other faction harboured Khalistan sympathizers. At the very least, Sikhs in Indonesia have not been indifferent to what is happening to Sikhs elsewhere in the world, even if the conditions of possibility for them to express their concerns are limited by the state.

SINGAPOREAN SIKHS AND THE SINGAPOREAN STATE

Like Sikhs in Indonesia, Singapore's Sikhs have experienced the ideologies, policies, and practices of the state both as a resource to be appropriated to advance collective interests and as a constraint on pursuing collective interests. Which of the two characterizations of the state any Singaporean Sikh might wish to emphasize probably varies widely from person to person and from issue to issue. My argument would be that Singaporean Sikhs in recent years have skilfully solicited the state to advance collective interests but that the state has exacted certain concession or imposed certain conditions in return. Thus, the positive public image that Sikhs are able to project in Singapore is carefully controlled by the corporatist state through its licensing of Sikh organizations and leaders.[16]

It certainly would be hard to fault the overall material accomplishments of Singapore's approximately 15,000 Sikhs. According to statistics released by the prime minister in 1991, Singapore's Sikhs, who constitute barely one half of one per cent of the population, are better educated, more likely to be employed, and are better housed than the average Singaporean (Goh Chok Tong, 'The community approach to solving problems' in *Speeches* 15, no. 5 (November/December 1991), pp. 4–7). In fact, Singapore's Sikhs have in recent years come to be regarded as something of a model minority—recognized as a distinctive group, praised at the highest level of government for their contributions to the nation, and promised state support for their initiatives (see, for example, comments of then-Prime Minister Lee Kuan Yew in the *Straits Times*, 3 November 1990, p. 50).

This is a somewhat surprising turn of events, since Sikhs were rather invisible in the post-colonial state's early policy of multiracialism. In the 1970s, Chinese/Malay/Indian/Other (CMIO) were the taxonomic categories through which social difference was reported and recognized for official purposes. And the state actively sought to reify and reinforce these categories to create a unique species of 'Singaporean Chinese', 'Singaporean Malays', and 'Singaporean Indians' who did not look to ancestral homelands for reinforcement of their identities. Given demographic realities, the inclusive 'Singaporean Indian' identity that the state nurtured was largely South Indian, Hindu, and Tamil-speaking in content; and, at least at the outset, north Indians (including Sikhs) were urged to learn the Indian 'official language' — Tamil.[17] As little more than 7 per cent of the 7 per cent of the population labelled 'Indian', Sikhs hardly appeared to be well placed to gain the state's recognition of their own micro-identity.

But the state's ideological rationale for requiring an 'Asian language' of its citizens rested heavily on the perceived need for what Singaporeans called a 'cultural ballast'. The assumption was that Asian cultural values would be transmitted through the Asian language and that this would serve as an antidote to Western values introduced through English. Subsequently, the search for a set of National Values was phrased as a commitment to a set of shared 'Asian values' that would serve as a cultural ballast and antidote against decadent Western values. As I suggest below, this state ideology provided Sikh leaders in Singapore an opportunity to make their case to the state elite for recognition of their distinct 'Punjabi/Sikh heritage' and reinforcement of their own 'traditional Asian (Sikh) values'—especially as a means to addressing a newly-discovered Sikh underclass, whose existence was conveniently attributed to 'the negative influences of Western culture' and 'an erosion of traditional Asian (Sikh) values among Sikh youth' ('The Singapore Sikh Resouce Panel and the Sikh Community', *The Singapore Sikh*, November 1992, pp. 19–20).

This 'discovery' of a Sikh underclass in Singapore propelled a group of Sikh professionals into leadership of key community organizations in the late 1980s. And their 'proactive' agenda for addressing the problems of the underclass through community-building activities found a generally sympathetic hearing from state elites. What is particularly notable is not that Sikhs have advanced concerns about the effects of state policies and practices on their community but that Singapore's 'inclusionary corporatist' state (a) has seen fit to seriously entertain Sikh concerns when advanced through state-licensed channels (the Sikh Advisory Board and its affiliates or the Sikh Members of Parliament) and (b) has responded positively where state elites have identified 'coinciding interests' between the state's agenda and that of the Sikhs.[18] However, even in those cases that Sikhs judge to be successes, the state has often imposed certain costs in return for Sikh gains in Singapore.

The following are concerns over state policies and practices identified by Singaporean Sikh organizations or representatives and brought to the attention of state elites and the public in recent years:

1. **CMIO racial categories.** Racial characterization on national ID cards, in census data, on National University of Singapore matriculation forms, and so forth tended to follow the CMIO categories in the 1970s, with Sikhs incorporated into the inclusive 'Indian' category. With the global politicization of Sikh identity in the 1980s, Singaporean Sikhs pushed hard for reclassification as a distinct racial/ethnic group. The Sikh plan to address the welfare of the Sikh underclass coincided with the state's interest in providing a 'cultural ballast' and the state's plan to devolve welfare responsibilities to race-based self-help groups. Singaporean Sikhs were thus empowered by state authorities to list 'Sikh' as their 'race''(as well as 'Sikhism' as their 'religion') on official documents. As a separate 'racial'group, however, Sikhs have been made responsible through Sikh organizations for the welfare of Sikhs in Singapore.
2. **Second language education and testing in state-run schools.** A two-language policy implemented in the schools requires each Singaporean student to learn English and one's Asian 'mother tongue' from among the state's 'offical languages' (Mandarin, Malay, and Tamil). When the policy was first instituted, Sikhs

and other North Indians vehemently protested being forced to learn Tamil, and they were eventually given permission to choose which of the official languages, in addition to English, they would submit for school testing purposes. But Sikhs still felt themselves to be at a competitive disadvantage. Recently, by arguing their need for 'Asian (Sikh) values' transmitted through the Punjabi language, Sikhs have gained permission for Punjabi to be considered as a testable second language at the primary and secondary level. However, the state requires the Sikh community to run the classes outside of school time, to provide the teaching materials, to train the teachers, to procure the outside evaluators, and to absorb all associated costs.

3. **Religious and moral education in state-run schools.** Religious Education was instituted in the schools during the 1980s as a means of reinforcing students' 'cultural ballast'. The government had not intended to include Sikh Studies until pushed to do so by the Sikh Advisory Board. Even then, the state acquiesced only on the condition that Sikhs prepare the teaching materials, train the teachers, and foot the costs of offering a Sikh Studies option. By the late 1980s, the state had judged Religious Education to be potentially divisive and replaced it with a common course of Moral Education based on shared 'National Values'. Some Sikhs privately complain that the National Values (nation over community and society over individual; family as the basic unit of society; regard and community support for individuals; consensus instead of contention; racial and religious harmony), although represented as pan-Asian, reflect a Confucian bias.
4. **Depoliticization of religion** (as per the Maintenance of Religious Harmony Act + Ministry of Community Development policies on supervision of religious organizations). The Maintenance of Religious Harmony Act of 1990 sought to counteract 'religious polarization' and to ensure that religion and politics be 'kept rigorously separate.' Passage of this Act followed publication of a government White Paper (Cmd 21 of 1989) that included details of Hindu and Sikh incidents in Singapore post-1984 which, although mild compared to activities elsewhere at the time, were presented as examples of religious groups in Singapore inappropriately 'importing foreign politics into Singapore' (par. 25–8). Public acceptance of the Act by Sikh leaders was cited by then-Prime Minister Lee Kuan Yew as

reflecting a 'realistic appreciation of Singapore's realities (*Straits Times*, 3 November 1990, p. 50). The Central Sikh Gurdwara Board was granted its 'freedom' in 1987 from appointment and further oversight by the Ministry of Community Development, only after agreeing that as a religious body it would not involve itself in domestic or foreign political affairs. Some Sikhs, whose nationalist vision includes the fusion of religion and politics, find such accommodations to Singapore's realities problematic.

5. **Surveillance under the Internal Security Act.** In one of his few public comments reflecting negatively on Sikhs, Lee Kuan Yew justified Singapore's Internal Security Act to a British reporter by stating that

   > Sikhs in Singapore were outraged because the Golden Temple was attacked. We had to protect the Indian High Commissioner here from 40,000 [*sic*] Sikhs who would have bludgeoned him. (*Straits Times*, 22 October 1989, p. 20)

   Some Sikhs argue that the security officials overreacted in 1984 and that they continue to over-estimate the security threat posed by Singaporean Sikhs.

6. **Gender bias in immigration law.** Immigration policy allows Singaporean men the right of residence and citizenship for foreign wives, but Singaporean women are not automatically allowed the same for their foreign husbands. This has had the effect of creating a class of educated women unable to find husbands. This is a gender issue that crosses racial lines, but it is a particular concern of Sikh women in Singapore since (a) Sikh men tend to marry women of lesser educational status and (b) Singaporean Sikh men, but not women, can enhance their marital prospects on the global Sikh marriage market by offering their spouses a Singapore connection.

7. **Racial quotas on admissions to the law and medical faculties at universities.** Limitation of the number of spaces available to Singaporean Indians in the law and medical faculties at Singapore's universities adversely affects Sikhs (who are, for this purpose, still included under the 'Indian' quota) and is seen as flying in the face of the state's meritocratic rhetoric.

What is notable about this list, beside the fact that some of the issues have already been resolved to the general satisfaction of the community, is that the appropriate routes for articulation of Sikh concerns—the Sikh Advisory Board and Sikh Members of Parliament—were clearly signalled by the state.[19] This provides an incentive for Sikhs to put aside factional differences—and Singaporean Sikhs are factionalized like Sikhs elsewhere—in favour of articulating ethnic-political interests through state-licensed representatives. As I have argued elsewhere,

> Singaporean Sikhs are being successfully socialized into the corporatist political culture of Singapore . . . [and] into a state-authorized version of (Singaporean) Punjabi/Sikh heritage. (1996, pp. 152–3)

MALAYSIAN SIKHS AND THE MALAYSIAN STATE

The Sikh population in Malaysia is both larger and more widely dispersed than in either Indonesia or Singapore. Malaysian Sikhs, numbering perhaps 40,000, are concentrated in and around such urban centres as Kuala Lumpur, Penang, Ipoh, and Johor Bahru.[20] Sikhs, however, constitute an even smaller proportion of the total 'Indian' population in Malaysia (of 1.4 million and 8 per cent) than they do in Singapore. And, in contrast to the numbers in Singapore, Malaysian Sikh numbers may actually be declining as a result of emigration outpacing natural increase. Destinations of choice for Sikh emigrants from Malaysia include the United Kingdom, North America, and (increasingly) Australia. This itself is a telling commentary on how many Malaysian Sikhs, especially the upwardly mobile middle-class and professionals, have experienced the post-independence period. In fact, Malaysian Sikhs may enjoy somewhat greater religious autonomy than do Sikhs in either Indonesia or Singapore, but they feel that their political and economic interests are being actively undermined by post-colonial policies favouring the majority Malays.

British colonial policies—which not only created a classic plural society in Malaya but also assisted in sub-communal separation among Indians (Stenson 1980, pp. 142–3) and ongoing contacts with the home country—which 'made it possible for the retention of not only their Indian identity but also sub-ethnic and caste identities' (Rajoo 1982, p. 59)—meant that Sikhs in Malaysia were neither 'indigenized' nor 'Indianized' before independence. Instead, they largely held themselves apart both from other Indians and from the Chinese and Malays. Although post-colonial policies pushed Indians to form a collective identity and organize politically as a single 'ethnic community' (structurally equivalent to the Chinese and Malays), both cultural/religious practices and class interests of the largely urbanized and increasingly middle-class and professional Sikhs have continued to separate them from the dominant rural, working-class, Hindu Tamils. As a consequence, Sikh participation in the Malaysian Indian Congress (MIC) of the ruling United Malays National Organization (UMNO) coalition has weakened in the years since independence, as the MIC has itself broadened beyond its roots in the English-speaking Indian bourgoise. As a consequence of their relatively small numbers and their effective estrangement from the designated 'Indian' communal party, Malaysian Sikhs have had little political voice as a collective interest group in national politics.

Reflecting back on the years since independence (and, especially, the post-1969 transition to the New Economic Policy and its successors), Malaysian Sikhs are accutely aware that language, education, and employment policies favouring Malay/*bumiputera* advancement have taken their toll on Sikh social and economic opportunities. Among the policies and practices most often noted as detrimental to Sikh interests include:

1. **The promotion of Malay as the *lingua franca*, the country's official language, and the preferred language of commerce, education, and administration.** Although less totalistic than the similar nationalist language policy in Indonesia, policies privileging Bahasa Malaysia, as per the Malayan Federal Constitution of 1957, have nevertheless been experienced as a hardship for middle-class Sikhs who, more so than other Indians and Chinese, had invested heavily in English-language education under the British.[21]

2. **Preferences in scholarships and college admissions for Malays/ *bumiputera* + Sharp limits on educational opportunites for Malaysian Indian and Chinese citizens.** As a community that had experienced upward educational and economic mobility (from watchmen and moneylenders to doctors and lawyers) under the British, Sikhs have found the inability to ensure educational opportunities for the next generation a major frustration and a frequent cause of Sikh emigration. And Malaysian Sikhs who have sent their children for education in India now find themselves confronted with the possibility that the government will no longer recognize educational credentials from Indian medical schools, as has long been the case with Indian law schools.[22]

3. **Sharp limits on public sector employment for Malaysian Indian and Chinese citizens.** The attempt to increase the proportion of Malays/*bumiputera* in the armed forces and in the civil service has been adversely felt by Malaysian Sikhs. Because they were over-represented in police and armed forces under the British, attempts to change the ethnic make-up of these forces in favour of the Malays have led Sikhs to be decommissioned and not replaced (see, for example, 'Take more Indians into Forces: Samy Vellu', *New Straits Times*, 4 May 1987). Moreover, the sharp fall from 1970 to 1988 in the Indian share of administrative and managerial jobs (from 7.8 to 4.6 per cent of the workforce) probably understates the hit that Sikhs took, given their historic overrepresentation vis-à-vis other Indians in administrative postions.[23]

In the area of the state's religious policies, the Malaysian Sikh experience is more equivocal. Although the Malayan Constitution of 1957 recognized Islam as the official religion in a secular state, the state ideology enunciated in the *Rukunegara* of 31 August 1970 committed Malaysia to

> a liberal society in which its members are free to practice and profess their own religions, customs and cultures consistent with the requirements of national unity. (quoted in Sajoo 1994, p. 46)[24]

In practice, this has meant that non-Muslim religions have been subject to policing by the state to ensure that they remain apolitical (at least in the domestic sphere) and that they do not intrude upon Malay/Muslim social space (for example, through proselytization or building religious sites), but at the same time this has not stopped both 'moves to seek non-Muslim unity' and 'a high degree of experimentation [within non-Muslim religions], often resulting in the formation of many competing movements' (Ackerman and Lee 1990, p. 41). The Malaysian Consultative Council for Buddhism, Christianity, Hinduism, and Sikhism (MCCBCHS), formally launched in 1984 after several years of informal consultation, has served as one vehicle for making representations to the government on behalf of non-Muslims. Sikhs thus have a second recognized route, in addition to the MIC, for articulating their concerns to the government. And the MCCBCHS has, in fact, brought to public attention a number of concerns shared by many Malaysian Sikhs.[25] These include the following concerns:

4. **Applications for non-Muslim places of worship turned down.** During the past fifteen years, non-Muslims have expressed repeated concern that their applications for permission to build religious places of worship and burial or cremation sites have been turned down disproportionately by state officials, despite Article 11 of the Malayan Federal Constitution, which specifies that

   every religious group has the right to (a) manage its own religious affairs, (b) to establish and maintain institutions for religious and charitable purposes; and (c) to acquire, own property and hold and adminster it in accordance with law.

5. **No provision for non-Islamic teachings or teaching about non-Islamic civilizations in state-run schools.** Non-Muslims, including many Sikhs, see a double standard in teaching non-Muslims about Islam but not teaching Muslims about other religious traditions. The introduction of 'moral education', they argue, is not sufficient balance.

6. **Insufficient entry permits for religious resource personnel from overseas.** Like other non-Muslim groups, some Sikh societies have had trouble getting the required permits processed to allow them to sponsor work permits for trained religious functionaries to staff Sikh *gurdwaras*.

7. **Islamic copyright of certain exclusively 'Islamic words'.** In the 1980s, Malaysian authorities produced a list of twenty-five words and nine expressions that were deemed exclusively 'Islamic' and not to be used by other religious groups. Although initially targeted at translations of the Christian Bible, the policy had the effect of making illegal all texts of the Sikh holy scripture, the Adi Granth, since in the original Gurmukhi script (let alone in Bahasa Malaysia translation) it contains the word '*Allah*' and many other prohibited words (Means 1991, p. 104). Sikhs ultimately convinced state authorities to exempt the Adi Granth from seizure by assuring them that the text would not be allowed to intrude on Malay/Muslim social space. This incident may, however, help explain why English, rather than Punjabi or Bahasa Malaysia,

has become a major medium of religious education and sectarian competition amongst Malaysian Sikhs.

8. **Federal government power to act against any religious group deemed a danger to public order** (as per amendments in 1982 to the Penal and Criminal Codes). While this move was directed primarily toward dissident Muslim groups, it nevertheless strengthened the state's hand in dealing with non-Muslim groups (Ackerman and Lee 1990, p. 161). And, in fact, the state was able to use the existence of these powers to induce Malaysian Sikhs to moderate their initial response to the 1984 Government of India attack on the Golden Temple.

Despite common irritations over what are perceived to be unjust limitations by the state on religious freedoms, Malaysian Sikhs have never been able to sustain any pan-Sikh organizations to represent Sikh religious interests in Malaysia. Regional rivalries between Sikhs who trace their ancestry to the Malwa and Majha regions of Punjab and a long-standing tradition of autonomy of Sikh temples have continually thwarted previous attempts, such as that of the Malaysian Sikh Union (established 1949; revived 1985), to speak with one voice through a single Sikh body to the government.[26] In turn, the Malaysian government has been much less concerned with regulating internal religious activities of non-Muslims than with eliminating competition between Muslim and non-Muslims and articulating Islam with the modern state. As Ackerman and Lee point out (1990, pp. 160–5), this relative indifference to issues of doctrinal orthodoxy in the non-Muslim field has allowed non-Muslims relative freedom to fashion a religious message and to compete with one another for adherents.

In many ways, therefore, Malaysian Sikhs are freer than their Singaporean and Indonesian counterparts from direct state intervention in religious organizations or state policing of internal religious discourses. In turn, this has made for free-wheeling discussions of religious issues and much religious innovation among Malaysian Sikhs, with multiple Sikh youth groups promoting quite different visions of Malaysian Sikhism, drawing upon different diasporan discourses, and competing with one another for the allegiances of Malaysian Sikhs.[27] At the same time, the 'laissez-faire conditions surrounding the non-Muslim field' (Ackerman and Lee 1990, p. 164) have resulted in Sikh conversions to other religions. According to Manjit S. Sidhu, Sikh religious functionaries in Malaysia, noting high rates of conversion and out-marriage, have grown pessimistic about the future Sikh religion in Malaysia (Sidhu 1991, pp. 128–9). My perspective is somewhat different, although I found Malaysian Sikhs suffering from ethnic politics as it has played out to their detriment in recent years, I was impressed at the religious dynamism I saw. This is just the opposite of the situation in Singapore, where Sikh successes as an ethnic or 'racial' community were not yet matched by a corresponding dynamism and experimentation in local religious institutions (see Dusenbery 1996, p. 150).[28]

CONCLUSIONS

However much globalization may be transforming the world order, the death of the nation-state is much exaggerated. Whether we look at transnational diasporic imagings or at the promotion of micro-identities within a given polity, contemporary identity politics continue to be refracted through a world of nation-states. Those transnational theorists telling us to stop talking about the state might be well advised to direct some of their attention to Southeast Asia. Sikhs in Indonesia, Singapore, and Malaysia would certainly testify that the post-colonial state and its agents, however much the state's power to recognize and manage social difference may be contested, are significant factors in their lives.

In Southeast Asia, as David Brown points out (1994, pp. 25–32), post-colonial states are relatively resilient, having turned themselves from 'weak' into 'strong' states through a successful 'combination of democratic legitimation with bureaucratic-authoritarian political control' (p. 28). For pluralist polities in Southeast Asia, transnational links have long been somewhat suspect as a source of potentially destabilizing influences. And this has lead to what Brown has called a 'garrison mentality' (p. 86), with state efforts both to ensure that political loyalties of ethnic minorities lie with the nation-state rather than the ancestral homeland (the paradigmatic case in the region being that of the 'overseas Chinese') and to limit the influence of outside religious parties with global agendas (for example, Islamic 'radicals' or Christian missionaries). The ideologies, policies, and practices of nationalism and nation-building in Indonesia, Singapore, and Malaysia have thus commonly sought to filter what flows to local citizens from the outside world.[29] At the same time, they have sought 'to accommodate, manage or manipulate' ethnic and religious affiliations within their plural societies so as to avoid confrontations that might threaten the survival of the state (p. 28).

Of course, even the most authoritarian state is unable totally to block or to filter the flow of ideas and images emanating from outside its borders. Global imagings of Sikhs controlling their own nation-state, Khalistan, have spread through transnational networks among Sikh. This, in turn, has raised Sikh sensitivities to the comparative politics of identity in diasporan settings where Sikhs now live.[30] Not surprisingly, this has led Sikhs in Southeast Asia to reflect upon and to question how they are empowered to pursue their interests as Indonesian, Singaporean, or Malaysian Sikhs. And this has made them aware of both constraints and opportunities opened up by the conditions of possibility set down through their own government's management of ethnicity and religion.

In Indonesia, the assimilationist policies and neo-patrimonial practices of the state have meant, on the one hand, that ethnic groups cannot articulate collective interests through ethnic-based political organizations and that ethnic patrons derive their leverage over their clients through personal ties to patrons among the state elite. On the other hand, certain religious communities are recognized by the state and are expected to work through appropriate sections of the Department of Religion. For Indonesian Sikhs this has meant that thus far it has been expedient (a) to accept—at least publicly—religious categorization as 'Hindu', and (b) to address the state through patronage links. Although these conditions may please those Sikh power-brokers whose position derives from access to state officials and may serve to forestall some factional battles over religious orthopraxy among Sikhs, it has left many Indonesian Sikhs feeling that they lack sufficient control over their own communal institutions so as to fashion a life consonant with their ideal image of what it means to be a Sikh.

In Singapore, the state's inclusionary corporatist management of ethnicity has taken the form of legitimating and enfranchising certain groups and individuals to participate in public affairs. At the same time, religious groups have been depoliticized. For Singapore's Sikhs, this has meant that their ability to push a Sikh agenda has depended on (a) gaining recognition from the state as a legitimate racial/ethnic interest group, and (b) articulating collective concerns through state-licensed channels. To the extent that Sikhs have been able to accomplish the above and to make their agenda coincide with that of state elites, Sikhs have been generally successful in advancing their local political interests. On the other hand, this success has come at the cost of accepting both the devolution of education and welfare activities onto the community and a radically depoliticized Sikhism. The latter may prove to be the hardest to reconcile with the dominant global self-imagings of what it means to be a Sikh.

In Malaysia, ethnicity is considered a legitimate basis for the articulation of political interests. And ethnic coalitions within the ruling party seek to balance ethnic interests through ethnic patronage, but with an overall 'racial restructuring' in favour of Malay socio-economic interests. At the same time, state policies of religious management seek to protect Islam from incursions from other religions, but offer nominal freedom of worship to non-Muslim religions. Malaysian Sikhs have seen their influence within the Indian ethnic political party wane, and they have been unsuccessful in sustaining a pan-Sikh party that might speak directly to the state. Consequently, many Sikhs have felt victimized by state policies and feel relatively impotent either to shape or to protest. On the other hand, Malaysian Sikhs sustain a lively variety of religious organizations and have made use of the non-Muslim religious coalition to advance religious concerns to the government.

In sum, we see striking cross-national differences in how diasporan Sikhs live their public lives in Southeast Asia. This suggests that the conditions of possibility laid down by state ideologies, policies, and practices continue to influence diasporan peoples. At the same time, we know that diasporan peoples are increasingly attentive to their relative ability to fashion lives in accord with global self-imagings. Hence, our attention here to the 'battle of imagination' between Sikhs and the state in Southeast Asia.

ACKNOWLEDGMENTS

Research conducted in 1992–3 was supported, in part, by a CIES Fulbright grant (91–64961) through the Southeast Asian Regional Research Program and by an Advanced Research Award from the Joint Committee on Southeast Asia of the Social Science Research Council and the American Council of Learned Societies with funds provided by the Ford Foundation and the National Endowment for the Humanities. I am particularly appreciative of the late Professor Kernial Singh Sandhu for arranging affiliation at the Institute of Southeast Asian Studies, where he was the long-time director, and for providing me with contacts in the region, where he was a deeply respected diasporan Sikh figure. I regret that he did not live to impart his wisdom to my analyses.

In addition to the participants in the ISEAS/SSRC Conference on Southeast Asian Diasporas, I would like to thank John Bowen, Elizabeth

Coville, Jean DeBernardi, Gordon Means, Garry Rodan, and Greg Setterholm for comments on an earlier draft of the paper. All mistakes and misinterpretations are my own.

NOTES

1. In what Comaroff has termed our contemporary 'Age of Revolution', characterized by 'globalization and the crisis of the nation-state', we are witnessing—simultaneously and dialectically—assertions of state sovereignty *and* the rise of identity politics within national communities (1995, pp. 258–60). Thus, depending on whether looked at from the global or the local level, it may appear that allegiances to the nation-state are under challenge from transnational allegiances—for example, 'to the national imaginary of diasporic populations' (Appadurai 1996, p. 50)—or from sub-national allegiances—for example, to 'micro-identities' (Appadurai 1990, p. 13).
2. As elaborated in Dusenbery (1995). I argue there that 'the colonial and diasporan experience has confronted South Asians with an alternative modernist discourse of identity that would have them possess . . . a fixed, superordinant 'cultural'/'ethnic'/'national' identity, such that Sikhs have increasingly come to represent themselves as an 'ethnoterritorial community'' at the expense of pre-modernist understandings of personal and group identities (p. 19).
3. Sikh migration to the Malay peninsula is discussed in Sandhu (1970). On the history of the (mainly Sikh) Malay States Guides, see Inder Singh (1965).
4. Thus academic exercises from the period done at the University of Malaya and the University of Singapore depict Sikhs in Malaysia and Singapore as locally-focused and relatively less invested in Punjabi language and culture or Sikh religion at this time. See Sarjit Singh (1969), Surinder Jeet Singh (1971), Ranjit Singh Malhi (1977).
5. For an overview of the emergence and dynamism of the Sikh diaspora, see Barrier and Dusenbery (1989). On the role of diasporan Sikhs in promoting Khalistan and influencing the politics of Punjab, see especially the articles in this volume by Helweg (1989) and La Brack (1989). As I acknowledged in my introduction (Dusenbery 1989), our overview underrepresented the experiences of Sikhs in Southeast Asia.
6. I suggest that this reciprocal construction of 'nation' and 'diaspora' is not a mechanical one but rather follows from the way in which modern pluralist states recognize and allot political rights to ethnic communities. For Sikhs in the diaspora to be recognized and heard as a separate 'ethnocultural group' under various multiculturalist regimes, it helps to have a recognized 'country of origin'. Hence, 'the 'longing' for Khalistan is for some Sikhs a means to 'belonging' in their country of residence' (Dusenbery 1995, p. 34).

7. During fieldwork in Indonesia in 1992, I acquired a 1992 calendar put out by a *gurdwara* (Sikh temple) in Canada intended as a 'salute to those Brave Heroes, who Sacrificed their Lives for Khalistan.' In Singapore, retired Supreme Court Justice, Choor Singh, publishes nationalist tracts based in part on the works of Punjab-based scholars and of other diasporan Sikh nationalists (see, for example, Choor Singh 1994, pp. 20–5; 1995).
8. One of the recurrent concerns of K.S. Sandhu, late director of ISEAS, was how Sikhs might adapt the institutions and social practices of village Punjab to the new 'social ecology' of cosmopolitan, urban settings where most diasporan Sikhs now live. See, for example, Sandhu (1992). Similarly, Bhajan Singh, Chair of the Singapore Sikh Education Foundation and Chair of the Singapore Sikh Advisory Board from 1989–1995, identified transmission of Punjabi/Sikh heritage in the diaspora as the greatest challenge facing Sikhs today (personal communication).
9. Attempts to fashion and to promote the images of cosmopolitan Sikhism were on display at the International Conference cum Exhibition on Punjabi/Sikh Heritage held in Singapore in June 1992 (under the sponsorship of the Sikh Advisory Board and Singapore Sikh Education Foundation) and the International Sikh Conference on Identity in Crisis held in Kuala Lumpur the same month (in conjunction with the twenty-fifth anniversary celebration of Sikh Naujawan Sabha Malaysia).
10. These are my guess-timations. Singapore numbers are based on the 1990 Population Census figures. interestingly, the number listed in the Singapore Census as 'Sikh' by 'ethnic/dialect group' is not the same as the number given for 'Sikhism' as 'religion'. The number of Sikhs in Indonesia dropped significantly at independence and again during the turmoil of the mid-1960s. As I discuss below, the number of Sikhs in Malaysia may have fallen in recent years as educated Sikhs seek to relocate to North America, Europe, or Australia. Only in Singapore do the numbers show a relatively steady natural increase.
11. One Indonesian Sikh informant, bemoaning the tendency of travelling Sikh missionaries (*pracharak*) and religious musicians (*ragi jathas*) to bypass Indonesia in favour of Malaysia and Singapore, called Indonesian Sikhs 'the forgotten *sangat* (congregation)'. At the same time, the Indonesian state has not made it easy to invite such visitors.
12. If Sikhs appear insular and largely unassimilated to other Indonesians, they appear to an outsider to be exceptional in their degree of social integration. Not only is the incidence of intermarriage with non-Punjabis relatively high (over 20 per cent by most estimates) but so is the degree of acceptance of in-marrying spouses and their children by the local Sikh community.
13. One of the key prayers from the Sikh scriptures, *Djapdji (Karya Guru Nanak)* was translated into Bahasa Indonesia by D. Pratap Singh (former principal of Khalsa School in Medan) and was subsequently published

by the Gurdwara Parbandhak Committee-Delhi State in 1969. The same year, Yayasan Sikh Gurdwara Mission in Jakarta published a book on the founder of Sikhism and the Sikh way of life. The book, *Guru Nanak dan Agama Sikh*, was authored by a Balinese Hindu, Njoman S. Pendit. Unfortunately, the Vice-Chairman of the Central Executive Board of Muhammadiyah subsequently requested that the government ban circulation of the book on the grounds that it gives offence to Islam (see the letter-to-the-editor by Lukman Harun in the *Indonesia Times* of 3 July 1987). The book was eventually re-issued in 1989 bearing a testimonial of approval from the Director General of Hindu and Buddhist affairs.

14. In Medan, the insurgent faction, with active assistance from Indonesian military and police forces, took control of the Teuku Umar *gurdwara* and Khalsa School. In Jakarta, the incumbent faction retained control of Pasar Baru and Tanjang Priok *gurdwaras* with the backing of the Department of Religion officials.
15. According to an account in the *Straits Times* (21 May 1993, p. 20), the Indonesian Co-ordinating Minister for Political Affairs and Security has urged religious communities in Indonesia to resolve their internal disputes without inviting government intervention. But it is unclear whether this will be sufficient to change established practices. Since both patrons and clients are complicit in Indonesia's neo-patrimonial political culture, it seems that government officials would also have to be constrained from intervening in such internal disputes.
16. For a more detailed account of the relationship between Sikh organizations and the Singaporean state, see Dusenbery (1996).
17. See, example, 'Big Drive to Promote Use of Tamil' in the *Straits Times* (20 February 1980, p. 9). While English became the language of education, government, and commerce in Singapore, Mandarin, Malay, and Tamil (one language for each of the major local 'races') were also official languages.
18. See Dusenbery (1996) for fuller elaboration of this point. 'Proactive' and 'coinciding interests' were phrases used by Singapore's Ministry of Community Development officials, Santanu Gupta and Nicholas Poh, to describe the relationship between the Ministry and the Sikh Advisory Board (interview of 26 July 1993). 'Inclusionary corporatist' is David Brown's term for Singapore's policies of ethnic management (1994, pp. 70–1).
19. Davinder Singh, a Sikh lawyer, has been elected to Parliament as one of the PAP 'minority' representatives in his Group Constituency. Kanwaljit Soin, an orthopaedic surgeon, has served as an appointed MP, selected by the government to represent women's concerns in Parliament.
20. On Malaysian Sikh demographics, see the work of Manjit S. Sidhu (1991).
21. On the marginalization of the Malaysian Indian middle class and elite since independence, see Muzaffar (1993). As Muzaffar notes, 'the more

pervasive role of the Malay language and Malay culture has, without doubt, affected the status and prestige of those non-Malay elite, whose facility in English was one of the advantages they had over some Malay elite' (1993, p. 225).

22. According to statistics reported in the *Far Eastern Economic Review* (10 June 1993, p. 15), in any given year, only one in four eligible non-Malays finds a place in any of the national universities. And out of 450 medical seats, Indians are given fifteen (Samy Vellu quoted in *Asiaweek*, 30 March 1990, p. 31).
23. See 'Striving for a Better Deal' in *Asiaweek* (30 March 1990, p. 30). On the vulnerability of Malaysian Indians to government policies concerning public sector employment, see Puthucheary (1993).
24. Susan Ackerman and Raymond Lee argue that at independence recognition of Islamic supremacy was exchanged for the legitimization of the citizenship status of non-Malays (1990, p. 41).
25. These issues were first raised at the founding seminar of the MCCBCHS in 1984 (see Putra et al. 1984); and most of these same issues were brought up again at the 10th anniversary dinner in 1994, as reported in the *Star*, 3 April 1994, p. 12.
26. See Sandhu (1993, pp. 164–7) on the contemporary challenges to establishing an organization speaking collectively on behalf of Malaysian Sikhs.
27. Competition between Sri Guru Gobind Singh Ji Khalsa Garh Malaysia and Sikh Naujawan Sabha Malaysia has drawn the intervention of both Punjab-based Sikh authorities and other diasporan Sikhs.
28. A recent National University of Singapore graduation exercise on Sikh organizations in Singapore notes that 'Sikh youths have certain needs which the *gurdwaras* [Sikh temples] have not been able to address' (Satvinder Singh 1993, p. 45).
29. Examples would include Indonesian censors blackening Chinese characters in international news magazines and recently announced efforts to police internet content in Singapore (see, for example, Rodan 1996).
30. For another comparative take on this issue, see Dusenbery (1997), which contrasts the poetics and politics of recognition as they affect Singaporean Sikhs and Canadian Sikhs.

REFERENCES

Ackerman, Susan E. and Raymond L.M. Lee., 1990, *Heaven in Transition: Non-Muslim Religious Innovation and Ethnic Identity in Malaysia*, Kuala Lumpur: Forum.

Appadurai, Arjun., 1990, 'Disjunction and Difference in the Global Cultural Economy', *Public Culture*, 2 (2), pp. 1–24.

———, 1991, 'Global Ethnoscapes: Notes and Queries for a Transnational Anthropology', *Recapturing Anthropology*, Richard G. Fox, (ed.), Santa Fe: School of American Research, pp. 191–210.

———, 1993, 'Patriotism and its Futures', *Public Culture*, vol. 5, pp. 411–29.

———, 1996, 'Sovereignty Without Territoriality: Notes for a Postnational Geography' in Patricia Yaeger, (ed.), *The Geography of Identity*, Ann Arbor: University of Michigan Press, pp. 40–58.

Arora, B.D., 1982, 'Indians in Indonesia' in I.J. Bahadur Singh, (ed.), *Indians in Southeast Asia*, Delhi: Sterling Publishers, pp. 119–29.

Barrier, N. Gerald, 1989, 'Sikh Emigrants and Their Homeland' in N. Gerald Barrier and Verne A. Duenbery, (eds), *The Sikh Diaspora*, Delhi: Chanakya Publications and Columbia, Missouri: South Asia Publications, pp. 49–89.

Barrier, N. Gerald and Verne A. Dusenbery, (eds), 1989, *The Sikh Diaspora: Migration and the Experience Beyond Punjab*, Delhi: Chanakya Publications and Columbia, Missouri: South Asia Publications.

Brown, David, 1994, *The State and Ethnic Politics in Southeast Asia*, New York: Routledge.

Choor Singh, 1994, *Understanding Sikhism*, Singapore: Central Sikh Gurdwara Board.

———, 1995, *Bhindranwale: Martyr of Sikh Faith*, Singapore: The author.

Comaroff, John L., 1995, 'Ethnicity, Nationalism and the Politics of Difference In an Age of Revolution' in J.L. Comaroff and P.C. Stern, (eds), *Perspectives on Nationalism and War*, Luxembourg: Gordon and Breach Publishers, pp. 243–76.

DeBernardi, Jean and Christopher Tarnowski, 1995, 'Managing Multicultural Societies: The Status of Minority Groups in Singapore, Malaysia, and Thailand' in Amitav Acharya and Richard Stubbs, (eds), *New Challenges for ASEAN*, Vancouver: UBC Press, pp. 73–113

Dusenbery, Verne A., 1989, 'Introduction: A Century of Sikhs Beyond Punjab' in N. Gerald Barrier and Verne A. Dusenbery, (eds), *The Sikh Diaspora*, Delhi: Chanakya Publications and Columbia, MO: South Asia Publications, pp. 1–28.

———, 1995, 'A Sikh Diaspora? Contested Identities and Constructed Realities' in Peter van der Veer, (ed.), *Nation and Migration*, Philadelphia: University of Pennsylvania Press, pp. 17–42.

———, 1996, 'Socializing Sikhs in Singapore: Soliciting the State's Support' in Pashaura Singh and N. Gerald Barrier, (ed.), *The Transmission of Sikh Heritage in the Diaspora*, New Delhi: Manohar Publishers and Columbia, MO: South Asia Publications, pp. 127–64.

———, 1997, 'The Poetics and Politics of Recognition: Diasporan Sikhs in Pluralist Polities', *American Ethnologist*, vol. 24, pp. 738–62.

Fox, Richard G., 1985, *Lions of the Punjab*, Berkeley: University of California Press.

Glick Schiller, Nina, Linda Basch, and Cristina Blanc-Szanton, 1992, 'Transnationalism: A New Analytic Framework for Understanding Migration' in Nina Glick Schiller, Linda Basch, and Cristina Blanc-Szanton, (eds), *Towards a Transnational Perspective on Migration*, New York: Annals of the New York Academy of Science, pp. 1–24.

Guéhenno, Jean-Marie, 1995, *The End of the Nation-State*, Victoria Elliott, (trans.), Minneapolis: University of Minnesota Press.

Hannerz, Ulf, 1992, *Cultural Complexity*, New York: Columbia University Press.

Helweg, Arthur W., 1989, 'Sikh Politics in India: The Emigrant Factor' in N. Gerald Barrier and Verne A. Duenbery, (eds), *The Sikh Diaspora*, Delhi: Chanakya Publications and Columbia, Missouri: South Asia Publications, pp. 305–36.

Inder Singh, 1965, *History of Malay States Guides*, Penang: Cathay Printers Ltd.

La Brack, Bruce, 1989, 'The New Patrons' in N. Gerald Barrier and Verne A. Duenbery, (eds), *The Sikh Diaspora*, Delhi: Chanakya Publications and Columbia, Missouri: South Asia Publications, pp. 261–304.

Leonard, Karen, 1989, 'Pioneer Voices from California' in N. Gerald Barrier and Verne A. Duenbery, (eds), *The Sikh Diaspora*, Delhi: Chanakya Publications and Columbia, Missouri: South Asia Publications, pp. 120–40.

Linda Basch, and Glick Schiller Nina and Cristina Szanton Blanc, (eds), 1994, *Nations Unbound*, Langhorne, Pennsylvania: Gordon and Breach Publishers.

Malhi, Ranjit Singh, 1976/77, 'The Punjabi Newspapers and Sikh Organizations of Kuala Lumpur', BA exercise, Department of History, University of Malaya.

Mani, A., 1993a, 'Indians in North Sumatra' in K.S. Sandhu and A. Mani, (eds), *Indian Communities in Southeast Asia*, Singapore: ISEAS/Times Academic Press, pp. 46–97.

———, 1993b, 'Indians in Jakarta' in K.S. Sandhu and A. Mani, (eds), *Indian Communities in Southeast Asia*, Singapore: ISEAS/Times Academic Press, pp. 98–130.

McLeod, W.H., 1989, 'The First Forty Years of Sikh Migration' in N. Gerald Barrier and Verne A. Duenbery, (eds), *The Sikh Diaspora*, Delhi: Chanakya Publications and Columbia, Missouri: South Asia Publications, pp. 120–40.

Muzaffar, Chandra, 1993, 'Political Marginalization in Malaysia' in K.S. Sandhu and A. Mani, (eds), *Indian Communities in Southeast Asia*, Singapore: ISEAS/Times Academic Press, pp. 211–36.

Means, Gordon P., 1991, *Malaysian Politics: The Second Generation*, Singapore: Oxford University Press.

Oberoi, Harjot, 1994, *The Construction of Religious Boundaries: Culture, Identity and Diversity in the Sikh Tradition*, New Delhi: Oxford University Press and Chicago: The University of Chicago Press.

Puthucheary, Mavis, 1993, 'Indians in the Public Sector in Malaysia' in *Indian Communities in Southeast Asia*, K.S. Sandhu and A. Mani, (eds), Singapore: ISEAS/Times Academic Press, pp. 334–66.

Putra, Tunku Abdul Rahman et al., (eds), 1984, *Contemporary Issues on Malaysian Religions*, Petaling Jaya: Pelanduk Publications.

Rajoo, R., 1982, 'Indians in Peninsular Malaysia' in I.J. Bahadur Singh, (ed.), *Indians in Southeast Asia*, Delhi: Sterling Publishers, pp. 52–78.

Rodan, Garry, 1996, 'Information Technology and Political Control in Singapore', Ms available at *http://www.nmjc.org/jpri/*

Sandhu, Kernial Singh, 1970, 'Sikh immigration into Malaya during the period of British rule' in Jerome Ch'en and Nicholas Tarling, (eds), *Studies in the Social History of China and Southeast Asia*, Cambridge: Cambridge University Press, pp. 335–54.

———, 1992, 'Opening Address', *Varsity Sikh Journal*, vol. 1, pp. 13–14.

———, 1993, 'Sikhs in Malaysia: A Society in Transition', K.S. Sandhu and A. Mani, (eds), *Indian Communities in Southeast Asia* in Singapore: ISEAS/ Times Academic Press, pp. 558–67.

Sajoo, Amyn B., 1994, *Pluralism in 'Old Societies and New States'*, Occasional Paper No. 90, Singapore: ISEAS.

Sarjit Singh, 1969, 'Some Aspects of Social Change in the Sikh Community in Singapore', BA exercise, Department of Social Work and Social Administration, University of Singapore.

Satvinder Singh, 1993, 'Sikh Organizations and Sikh Identity in Singapore', BA exercise, Department of Sociology, National University of Singapore.

Shapiro, Michael J., 1994, 'Moral Geographies and the Ethics of Post-Sovereignty', *Public Culture*, vol. 6, pp. 479–502.

Sidhu, Manjit S., 1991, *Sikhs in Malaysia*, Malacca: Sant Sohan Singh Ji Melaka Memorial Society.

Stenson, Michael, 1980, *Class, Race and Colonialism in West Malaysia: The Indian Case*, Vancouver: University of British Columbia Press.

Surinder Jeet Singh, 1971, 'Culture Change Among the Sikh-Punjabis at the University of Singapore', BA exercise, Department of Sociology, University of Singapore.

Tololyan, Khachig, 1991, 'The Nation-Sate and its Others', *Diaspora*, vol. 1, pp. 3–7.

11

Sikh Positionings in Australia and the 'Diaspora' Concept*

Diasporas, according to Kachig Tololyan, are 'the exemplary communities of the transnational moment' (1991, p. 5). And one of the major appeals of the concept 'diaspora', has been in helping scholars break from the territorialization of such prior analytic concepts as 'culture', 'nation', and 'society'. However, I would argue, we now run the risk of doing to 'diaspora' what an earlier anthropology did to 'culture'.

American cultural anthropologists developed the 'culture' concept to help escape the totalizing and biologizing concept of 'race'. Yet, over time, 'culture' itself became reified, so that, used as a collective noun, it began to obscure internal differences and human agency, creating the impression of 'common-denominator people' compelled to enact imperatives deriving from 'their [territorialized] culture'. Just as cultural anthropologists have become rightly suspicious of such collective claims ('the Balinese do X' or 'in Balinese culture people believe Y') and increasingly attentive to differential agency and power and imagination within social fields, scholars of diasporas should be suspicious of generalizing claims made in the name of 'the—diaspora' and more attentive to differences of interest and identity amongst those so labelled.

This case study of Sikh positioning in Australia is intended as reminder that we must be careful in how we use the diaspora concept.

* First published in Melvin Ember, Carol R. Ember, and Ian Skoggard (eds), *Encyclopedia of Diasporas*, Kluwer Academic Plenum Publishers New York: vol. 1. 2004, pp. 485–91.

Sikhs in Australia form a part of the larger imagined community sometimes referred to, both by outsiders and by insiders, as 'the Sikh diaspora'.[1] As I suggest here, however, Sikhs dispersed around the globe are positioned in different ways in the nation-states where they reside and may imagine their political interests and their communities of belonging in quite different ways.

IMMIGRATION

The overwhelming majority of Sikhs in Australia—17,401 of whom were officially enumerated at the 2001 census—have either arrived in the three decades since the end of the White Australia policies or have been born to these recent immigrants. The history of Punjabi Sikhs in Australia, however, dates back to the period before Federation in 1901, when the first of the 'grandfathers' arrived from India. During the first half of the twentieth century, Sikhs with rights to domicile in Australia (by virtue of their British passports and/or their presence in the colonies before Federation) commonly moved back and forth between wage labour in Australia and familial responsibilities in their natal villages in Punjab. These were classic male 'sojourners' for whom the village in Punjab remained 'home' and for whom wages from labour in Australia was remitted or brought back to support and enhance family well-being and honour in the natal village. Wives and children remained in the Punjabi village, with sons perhaps joining fathers in Australia at maturity. Given the prevailing Australian rhetoric and practices of Asian exclusion and the Punjabi's prime motivation to enhance family honour and expand the homestead in Punjab, it is hardly surprising that these Sikh sojourners in Australia saw themselves as *pardesi* ('foreigners') and did not seriously consider making Australia their permanent home.

It was only in the 1950s and 1960s that Sikh sojourners began to consider the possibility of establishing deeper roots in Australia. Political and economic changes in Australia and India (including lessening discrimination in Australia and rising land prices in Punjab) made it possible for Sikhs to envision investing some of their resources in Australia rather than remitting everything to Punjab. Thus, for example, Sikhs previously reliant on cane cutting and other itinerant labour in Queensland and northern New South Wales took jobs as labourers on banana plantations in the Woolgoolga, New South Wales, area starting in the 1940s. During the 1950s, these Sikhs increasingly began to take advantage of the opportunity to share crop and, ultimately, to purchase local banana farms. It was only in the 1960s, however, that most saw fit to bring wives and minor children to Australia, leaving property in India to be managed by relatives and fellow villagers. Thus, although Sikh immigration goes back to the nineteenth century, Sikh family life in Australia and thus the coming of age of a fully Australian-born and raised generation of Sikhs is a relatively recent phenomenon.

The 1950s and 1960s also saw the arrival in Australia's capital cities of a number of Punjabi Sikh students, both those brought through the Commonwealth's Colombo Plan and those arriving independently. Some of these Sikhs stayed on by virtue of marriage to an Australian citizen or through the extension of domicile privileges to 'distinguished and highly-qualified' — later 'well-qualified' – Asians. With further liberalization of immigration policies in 1966 and official annulment of the White Australia policy in 1973, the opportunities for Sikh immigration were further expanded. Those Sikhs benefiting in the 1970s and 1980s from the no longer racially discriminatory but still 'selective and controlled' migration opportunities included both extended family members of the earlier migrants and skilled independent migrants. The latter category included many Sikhs from East Africa, Singapore, Malaysia, and the United Kingdom who possessed the 'education level, English fluency, youth, skill level, and employability' emphasized in the selection system.[2]

In the 1980s and1990s, direct migrants from India (refugees, skilled migrants, spouses, family members, students, and visa overstayers) became a more pronounced component of the Sikh migrant stream. The political violence in Punjab in the 1980s and early 1990s, surrounding the separatist movement for an independent Khalistan, led many young Sikh males to seek refugee status in Australia, as in other countries with liberal refugee policies. Economic dislocations in Punjab, both those arising from productive transformation of the agricultural economy and those following from the political violence, were also an impetus for educated unemployed or underemployed Sikhs to seek opportunity abroad.[3] On paper, if not always in the reality of the job market, Australia was a relatively appealing destination for those who could qualify as skilled migrants. Family stream migration, especially given the ability of both males and females in Australia to bring in spouses and family members, led to arranged marriages between the rising generation of Australian Sikh citizens or permanent residents and Sikhs from India—and, to an extent, from elsewhere in the Sikh diaspora. Finally, the possibility of entering Australia as a student legally entitled to work twenty hours a week, has in recent years led to a considerable influx both of legitimate degree-seeking Sikh students and of economic sojourner 'students' who may or may not wish to make Australia their home.

As this brief overview of Sikh immigration and settlement suggests, a changing world political economy and changing Australian policies have produced an internally diverse Australian Sikh population, not a homogenous 'diasporan Sikh' community in Australia. Presumably, all would be categorized as of 'non-English-speaking background' (NESB) and as 'Asians' within the official and folk categories of Australian multiculturalism. And, as Ghassan Hage (1994) reminds us, NESB Australians—especially Asians—are precariously positioned within the Australian national space as the, at best, 'tolerated' Other. Yet it should be clear that Australian Sikh relationships to the English language and to their Punjabi roots are actually quite diverse.

POSITIONINGS

So how are different Punjabi Sikh migrants and their descendants positioned in Australian society? And how do these different positionings affect their sense of belonging in multicultural Australia?[4]

The Cosmopolitan

Let me begin with those Australian Sikhs whom I would term 'cosmopolitans'. Following Ulf Hannerz (1990), I understand cosmopolitans to be exemplary figures in transnational cultures of the global ecumene, analytically distinguishable not only from 'locals' but also from 'ordinary labour migrants'. Cosmopolitans 'are "the new class", people with credentials, decontextualized cultural capital . . . [that] can be quickly and shiftingly recontextualized in a series of different settings' (Hannerz 1990, p. 246). Cosmopolitans challenge the dualism of 'home' and 'abroad', since they are competent operating in various spatial and cultural contexts and are comfortable interacting with those from different localities and diverse cultural backgrounds.

Cosmopolitan Sikhs in Australia tend to come from among those who originally migrated as independent skilled entrants (post-1975) or those who first came as post-graduate students (pre-1975). They are likely to be employed in business or a profession or in a managerial position in Australia. Most live dispersed in upper middle-class suburbs of the capital cities, especially in north and east Sydney and east and south Melbourne. The often twice (or thrice or more) migrants from Singapore/

Malaysia, East Africa, and the UK are over-represented amongst cosmopolitan Australian Sikhs, having acquired prior to arrival the cultural capital (for example, English-language fluency, educational qualifications, financial wherewithal, professional experience) and the cosmopolitan state of mind to facilitate their move to and within Australia.

These cosmopolitan Sikhs are for the most part now comfortably settled in Australia. They are economically well off and socially integrated, but they are also able and willing to relocate as employment or educational opportunities require. In addition to acquiring Australian citizenship, they may retain passports or residence status elsewhere. They are likely to have family members living, working or studying in various countries. Their marriage networks span the Sikh diaspora. They travel and communicate globally. In short, they are potentially 'at home' in any cosmopolitan urban setting. Or, as it was put to me by a cosmopolitan Australian Sikh—born elsewhere, living in Sydney, travelling widely in the Asian-Pacific region for his transnational employer—'home is where I tie my turban'. In many ways, they thus reflect the 'postnational consciousness' (Appadurai 1996) and 'flexible citizenship' (Ong 2000) that some consider exemplary of the coming era.

Given their cosmopolitan 'cultural capital' and 'willingness to engage with the Other'(Hannerz 1990, p. 239), these Australian Sikhs may, in fact, aspire, like their European-descended 'cosmo-multiculturalist' neighbours and co-workers, to 'governmental belonging' (Hage 1998). That is, they may not be content with simple 'tolerance' by others of their 'passive belonging' in Australia, but may actively cultivate and accumulate 'national capital' (Hage 1998, p. 54) that can be used in ethnic lobbying and mainstream politics to affect policy-making and nation-building. In addressing various levels of government, they naturally seek to influence Australian policies as these affect their own situation, for example, in the areas of citizenship (dual citizenship, travel permits), immigration (visas for spouses, religious functionaries), multiculturalism/anti-racism (racial tolerance, educational and economic opportunity, exemptions for religious symbols, permits for religious sites), and education (recognition/support of Punjabi as a Language Other Than English (LOTE)). Their cultural capital and willingness to engage with the Other also makes it possible for the Sikh cosmopolitan to serve as cultural 'brokers' (Hannerz 1990, p. 248) advancing somewhat different political agendas for other Australian Sikhs with the cosmo-multiculturalist establishment.

Finally, with respect to the discourses of belonging circulating in the Sikh diaspora, cosmopolitan Australian Sikhs are most likely to be moved by the relatively deterritorialized and non-essentializing master narrative of 'Sikhism as a world religion' (Dusenbery 1999). Cosmopolitan Sikhs are relatively comfortable with the idea and reality of Sikhs of different racial, cultural, and national backgrounds. And, because of their own attenuated ties to Punjab (which is the 'ancestral homeland' and 'spiritual holy land' but no longer actively 'home'), they may be suspicious of discourses of belonging that make Punjabi-ness and Punjabi territory central to the identity of a Sikh. Although they may want their children to learn Punjabi so that they can read the Sikh scriptures, they are normally not averse to the use of English as a first language and a component of Sikh services. And they, along with the western Sikh converts, have often been at the forefront of those seeking to distinguish universal Sikh religious practices (*Sikhi*) from what they take to be (parochial) Punjabi culture practices.

The (Bi)local

Hannerz goes on to distinguish 'cosmopolitans' from 'locals', primarily in terms of the former's greater willingness to become involved with the Other and greater competence with regard to alien cultures (1990, p. 240). Clearly, in the case of Australian Sikhs, these are crucial factors in differentiating the cosmopolitan's position from that position that I am calling the '(bi)local'.

By '(bi)local', I suggest a Sikh who literally has 'two homes', one in the village in Punjab and the other in the ethnic neighbourhood in Australia, but who participates in a single social network and cultural frame of reference encompassing both homes. The paradigmatic case here would be the banana farmer in Woolgoolga who travels frequently between houses and land in the natal village in Punjab and the village of Woolgoolga (Bhatti and Dusenbery, 2001). Such people may, in fact, be deeply rooted in Australia. Their financial and emotional investments in Australia are often much heavier than that of the cosmopolitan. In the case of those in Woolgoolga, their grandfathers were sojourners; their parents were settlers; they are locals. But they are at home in Australia in a very different way than the cosmopolitans.

Arjun Appadurai reminds us not to image 'the local' as a residual or passive category of residence but to recognize that locals as subjects and agents must construct their place in the world—their 'homes' and 'neighbourhoods'—through what he calls 'techniques for the *spatial* production of locality' (1995, p. 205). In the case of Australian Sikh (bi)locals, this requires the 'production of locality' in both locales—the Australian neighbourhood and the Punjabi village. Some of 'the processes by which locality is materially produced', including constructing and maintaining houses, cultivating fields, and building temples, are activities which (bi)locals are likely to undertake in two settings. At the same time, 'space ... [is] socialized and localized through complex and deliberative practices of performance, representation, and action' (Appadurai 1995, p. 206). In the case of Australian Sikh (bi)locals, this may involve various rituals of belonging to assert one's place in either or both local spaces—for example, wedding ceremonies conducted first in the village in Punjab and then again back in Australia, cremation in Australia but ashes sent to Punjab to be sprinkled in rivers there, ritual first haircuts taken in Punjab, or ritual objects brought from Punjab to Australia.

Appadurai goes on to note that 'the production of a neighbourhood is inherently colonizing' (1995, p. 209). In so far as Australian Sikhs may seek to make a neighbourhood of local space, it can involve them in conflict with others who claim the same space or, at the very least, it may require negotiation with others over the sharing of that space. Hence, getting a permit to build a Sikh temple or to hold a procession through local streets or to wear a *kirpan* (sword worn by an initiated Sikh) in public or to get signs in Punjabi put up in the local school, may be politically challenging, with success in these matters seen as a sign of belonging and rejection taken as a sign of exclusion. In this manner, the quarter century long battle to get the local Returned and Services League of Australia (RSL) Club in Woolgoolga to allow turbaned Sikhs as members must be understood to be a symbolic struggle for the right of Sikhs to claim 'local belonging' in Woolgoolga.[5]

* Sikhs intent on raising their children as keshdhari (literally 'hair bearing') Sikhs, obviously would not take their children to Punjab for a ritual first haircut but rather would take them for the distinctively Sikh ritual first turban-tying ceremony (*dastar bandana*). However, as an ethnographic fact, most of Woolgoolga's Sikhs are neither Amritdhari nor Keshdhari Sikhs. Strictly speaking only the Amritdharis are obliged to follow the Sikh Rahit Maryada (the Khalsa code of belief and conduct), although in practice the Keshdharis are expected to observe it and to uphold the explicit taboo on 'dishonouring the hair'. Some Sikh families from Woolgoolga do, in fact, take their children to the Punjab for 'first haircuts' without thinking that this implies making them non-Sikhs.

Sikh (bi)locals inevitably encounter other Australians in the course of producing the neighbourhood. But for (bi)locals, the strongest social connections are maintained with other Sikhs (both in their Australian neighbourhood and back in the Punjabi village) rather than with local non-Sikh Australians. In fact, *gora* (white) Australian society, as the ethnic Other, is actively stigmatized and efforts made to patrol the social (if not Spatial) borders with it. Gossip, ostracism, and even more coercive practices, limit social relationships with other Australians that might cause dishonour to the family or community. And this reinforces and protects the Sikh (bi)locals' sense of social difference and moral superiority.

Sikh (bi)locals are thus party to sustaining an 'Indians' versus 'Aussies' mentality. Thus, for example, in Woolgoolga (a single town made up of two local communities—Sikhs and non-Sikhs), an annual cricket match is held between the 'Indians' (that is, local Australian Sikhs) and the 'Aussies' (that is, local non-Sikh Australians). In 1999, when Woolgoolga's Sikhs held a procession through the town in honour of the 300th anniversary of the founding of the Khalsa (that is, the order of initiated Sikhs), the headline in the local paper, *The Advertiser,* on 6 April 1999 read 'Sikhs invite Locals'—as if Sikhs were not themselves locals. A non-Punjabi Woolgoolgan, when asked what she thought about the Sikh procession and whether she would attend it, said that 'the Sikhs have their procession, and we [non-Sikhs] have ANZAC' (that is, the annual Australian and New Zealand Army Corps (ANZAC) parade celebrating Australian and New Zealand military sacrifices)—as if it were unthinkable that Australian Sikhs might also claim ownership of ANZAC.

For the most part, Australia's Punjabi Sikh (bi)locals are content with mere 'passive belonging'—that is, the expectation of 'hav[ing] the right to benefit from the nation's resources, to 'fit into it' or 'feel at home' within it' (Hage 1998, p. 45). Thus, the 'tolerance' of difference characteristic of Australian multiculturalism, which Hage points out gives the power of 'governmental belonging' primarily to White cosmo-multiculturalists, is normally sufficient for Australian Sikh (bi)locals. Indeed, like locals generally, the (bi)local is happy with a notion of multiculturalism that 'allows all locals to stick to their respective cultures' (Hannerz 1990, p. 250).

This, of course, makes (bi)locals suspicious of cosmopolitans, who seem to move easily between cultures. As Hannerz notes, 'for most locals, the cosmopolitan is someone a little unusual, one of us and yet not quite one of us' (1990, p. 248). This certainly describes the relationship between Australian Sikh cosmopolitans and (bi)locals: although recognizing one another as fellow Punjabi Sikhs, the latter see the former as dangerously close to *gora* (white) society and as insufficiently committed to Punjabi village values.[6] In so far as Australian Sikh cosmopolitans possess forms of social and cultural capital that can be used in advancing their interests, (bi)locals may seek out or accept the cosmopolitan's contacts to advance concerns with, for example, the Australian Department of Immigration and Multicultural Affairs (over spousal approvals, family reunification, citizenship) or even with the Government of India (over its treatment of Non-Resident Indians). Not surprisingly, the Australia-born children of the (bi)local run the risk that higher education, occupational mobility, and travel will make them too cosmopolitan to fit into the local community, and they can find themselves caught between the model of their parents and the example provided by Sikh cosmopolitans.[7]

In the end, the Australian Sikh (bi)local is likely to be moved by the Punjabi discourse of *des pardes* (literally 'home for home' or 'at home abroad'), which asserts the ability and commitment of the migrant to pursue his or her own culturally-appropriate goals in whatever foreign country of residence.[8] For the (bi)local, who aspires to be 'at home abroad' in both Australian and Punjabi locales, this is a discourse that validates the 'honour' that is maintained in keeping a certain distance from *gora* (that is, Western) ways, in carving out a place for one's family in a sometimes hostile and challenging environment, and in sustaining practices and ties Punjabi in the face of covert or overt assimilative pressures.

The Transnational Labour Migrant

In contrast to the (bi)local, who is 'at home abroad', what I am calling the 'transnational labour migrant' is positioned 'in' but not yet fully 'of' Australia. In fact, in this case, there may be only provisional acceptance of 'national belonging' by the migrant as well as by other Australians. Here, I am thinking of the recent, opportunistic migrant (whether arriving as student, refugee, skilled migrant, family member, illegal) who might well have gone elsewhere in the global labour market if better opportunity had presented itself and who might still uproot oneself should better opportunities arise—or should Australian authorities deport him or her.

Like cosmopolitans, then, transnational labour migrants are not as deeply rooted in Australia as are (bi)locals. Unlike cosmopolitans, however, transnational labour migrants may not possess even 'passive belonging', let alone 'governmental belonging', in Australia, since Sikh transnational labour migrants commonly lack both the cultural capital and the comfort of interaction with the Other that provide Sikh cosmopolitans with their relatively easy landing in Australia.

Hannerz suggests that 'most ordinary labour migrants do not become cosmopolitans. . . . A surrogate home is again created with the help of compatriots, in whose circle one becomes encapsulated' (1990, p. 243). What commonly characterizes transnational labour migrants is their substantial political and socio-economic marginalization. Opportunities in Australia may have appeared better than in India (given the changing political economy of Punjab) or than in other optional migration destinations, but the realities of Australian labour market for those arriving with accented English, foreign degrees, and no 'Australian experience' often lead to underemployment or to taking jobs of lesser status, even for 'skilled' direct migrants from India. Thus, one finds PhDs from Punjab Agricultural University driving taxis and working as train guards in Sydney. Although Sikh labour migrants rarely stay unemployed for long, they normally do not possess the cultural capital and comfort to move as easily as the Sikh cosmopolitans into 'national belonging' in Australia. They are thus liable to remaining 'encapsulated' in a circle of compatriots; but, unlike similarly 'encapsulated' (bi)locals, they do so without a self-sustaining economic base within the village economy in Australia or Punjab. Given their social and economic insecurities, they are not yet 'at home abroad'.

Nina Glick Schiller and her colleagues have pointed out that, even in an age of globalization, 'transnational migrants exist, interact, are given and assert their identities, and seek to exercise legal and social rights within national structures that monopolize power and foster ideologies of identity' (Glick Schiller et al. 1992, p. 15). Transnational Sikh labour migrants consequently are likely to have a number of concerns with various Australian policies affecting their rights and identity, such as equal opportunity employment laws (recognition of foreign qualifications), immigration policies (student visas, refugee status, social/financial support for new immigrants), human rights (legal protections for Sikh symbols of identity—turban, sword, etc.—especially in the Australian workplace), and foreign affairs (India's human rights record in Punjab). Unless Sikh cosmopolitans take up their political agenda, however, these migrants are at a disadvantage in pushing their case with Australian authorities, since they are less likely than other Australian Sikhs to know how the political/bureaucratic system works or to have the cultural capital necessary to work the system to their advantage.

The appeal of Khalistan (a sovereign Sikh nation-state imaginatively projected onto the map of South Asia) and the master narrative of 'Sikhs are a nation' can be especially compelling to these transnational labour migrants. This accounts for the high proportion of young, male 'students', refugees, and recent direct migrants from India among those wearing Khalistan buttons at the 1999 procession in Sydney marking the tricentenary of the founding of the Khalsa and attending the International Sikh Youth Federation (a pro-Khalistan group) annual meeting at the Parklea Sikh temple. Given political marginality and economic insecurities experienced in both Punjab and Australia, these migrants may find that the emotional appeal of nationalist visions can relieve their 'longing for belonging' (van der Veer 1995).

The imagined Khalistan thus serves as an ideal site of utopian projection, complete with a moral economy that provides an honourable place for the migrant—in contrast to the dishonour attendant to his or her current situation. Moreover, as I have argued elsewhere (1995), the imagined Khalistan may be envisioned as possessing the political standing and will to act (as against the presumed indifference and impotence of the Government of India) to protect and improve the labour migrant's 'place' in Australian society. In short, belonging to the 'Sikh nation' is consolation to the transnational labour migrant for the indignities and insecurities suffered first in India and now in Australia.

CONCLUSION

The discourse of 'diaspora' runs the risk of fetishizing historical 'homelands' and ancestral 'roots' and of assuming a commonality of interests and identity amongst those who bear collective labels such as 'Sikh' or 'Jew' or 'Armenian' or 'Chinese' (to name some of the paradigmatic diasporas). This case study suggests that Sikhs in Australia neither share identical political interests nor inevitably imagine what it means to be Sikh in the same manner. Instead of discourses of diaspora that assume such commonalities, perhaps students and scholars of diasporas should be asking: when, where, for whom, and in what form is the imagined transnational community of the 'diaspora' compelling?[9]

NOTES

1. As co-editor of a volume entitled *The Sikh Diaspora* (Barrier & Dusenbery 1989), I was complicit in the construction of this object of study. In another essay (1995), I have discussed some of the implications of our non-reflective use of this term.
2. Qualification criteria for Asian immigrants as discussed in Jayasuriya and Pookong (1999).
3. Not coincidentally, Punjab at the onset of its recent political troubles had the highest proportion of educated unemployed in India. Jat Sikhs in particular were disadvantaged by the capitalization of agriculture, decommissionings from the military, and the lack of off-farm employment opportunities.
4. The positionings that I lay out below do not pretend to map the actual empirical Sikh subject—despite whatever ethnographic exemplifications I might provide. But they do reflect analytic distinctions that follow internal lines of differentiation that Australian Sikhs recognize in talking about the Australian Sikh population (without however including all distinctions of persons that Sikhs might make). These are clearly dynamic positionings.
5. The fact that this was a symbolic battle for local belonging was driven home by the fact that once the right to membership was won, few local turbaned Sikhs were actually interested in taking up membership or booking functions at the Woolgoolga RSL Club. The community was content to continue to patronize the Woolgoolga Bowling Club, which had opened its membership to all Sikhs earlier.
6. This is to say nothing of historical Punjabi caste, class, and urban/rural differences that may faurther overlay and complicate the relationship.
7. Thus, the challenge that some university-educated Sikhs in Woolgoolga have had in returning to *either* village. For example, Rashmere Bhatti's published article based on her own life, "The Good Indian Girl" (1992) reflects a (bi)local's sense of belonging in both the Punjabi village and the Australian village, as well as a sence of ambivalence and lack of full belonging in "my western world". Ironically, Rashmere Bhatti's subsequent career as Coordinator, Community Services Settlement officer, and Department of Immigration and Multicultural Affairs representatives at the Woolgoolga Neighbourhood Centre and co-editor of a government-supported social history of the Woolgoolga Sikhs (Bhatti and Dusenbery 2001) has given her a more cosmopolitan outlook and sense of "governmental belonging" that might lead her to write a different account of her positioning today.
8. Unlike the territorial nationalist intent of the *-stan* of Khalistan (literally "[home]land of the pure"), *desh* here connotes not the nation-state but rather the ancestral village or *pind.* Although such a discourse is

accommodative of the system of nation-states, the discourse is essentially sub-national and antiassimilationist. It speaks to the ability of Sikh migrants, drawing on their cultural heritage, especially the imagined values of village Punjab, 'to rebuild their lives [in migrant settings] *on their own terms*' (Ballard, 1994, p. 5; emphasis in the original).

9. Brain Axel (2001) advances a somewhat similar argument, although one framed in quite different terms.

REFERENCES

Appadurai, A., 1995., 'The Production of Locality' in R. Fardon, (ed.), *Counterworks,* New York: Routledge, pp. 205–25.

——1996, *Modernity at Large: Cultural Dimensions of Globalization*, Minneapolis: University of Minnesota Press.

Axel, B.K, 2001, *The Nation's Tortured Body: Violence, Representation, and the Formation of a Sikh 'Diaspora'*, Durham, NC: Duke University Press.

Ballard, R, 1994, 'Introduction: The emergence of *desh pardesh*' in R. Ballard, (ed.), *Desh Pardesh: The South Asian Presence in Britain*, London: Hurst and Company, pp. 1–34.

Barrier, N.G. and V. A. Dusenbery, (eds), 1989, *The Sikh Diaspora: Migration and the Experience Beyond Punjab*, Delhi: Chanakya Publication and Columbia, MO: South Asia Publications.

Bhatti, R., 1992, 'The Good Indian Girl' in K. Herne, J. Travaglia, and E. Weiss, (eds), *Who Do You Think You Are? Second Generation Immigrant Women in Australia*, Broadway, NSW: Women's Redress Press, p. 131–6.

Bhatti, R. and V.A. Dusenbery, (eds), 2001, *A Punjabi Sikh Community: From Indian Sojourners to Australian Citizens*, Woolgoolga, NSW: Woolgoolga Neighbourhood Centre.

Dusenbery, V.A, 1995, 'A Sikh Diaspora? Contested Identities and Constructed Realities' in Peter van der Veer, (ed.), *Nation and Migration: The Politics of Space in the South Asian Diaspora*, Philadelphia: University of Pennsylvania Press, pp. 17–42.

—— 1999, 'Nation' or 'World Religion',? Master Narratives of Sikh Identity' in P. Singh and N.G. Barrier, (eds), *Sikh Identity: Continuity and Change*, New Delhi: Manohar Publishers, pp. 127–44.

Glick Schiller, N., L. Basch, and C. Blanc-Szanton, 1992, 'Transnationalism: A New Analytic Framework for Understanding Migration' in N. Glick Schiller, L. Basch, and C. Blanc-Szanton, (eds), *Towards a Transnational Perspective on Migration*, New York: Annals of the New York Academy of Science, (645), pp. 1–24.

Hage, G., 1994, 'Locating Multiculturalism's Other: A Critique of Practical Tolerance', *New Formations*, vol. 24, pp. 19–34.

—— 1998, *White Nation: Fantasies of White Supremacy in a Multicultural Society*, Annandale, NSW: Pluto Press.

Hannerz, U., 1990, 'Cosmopolitans and Locals in World Culture' in M. Featherstone, (ed.), *Global Culture: Nationalism, Globalization and Modernity*, London: Sage Publications, pp. 237–51.

Jayasuriya, L. and K. Pookong, 1999, *The Asianisation of Australia?,* Carlton South, Vic: Melbourne University Press.

Ong, A., 2000, *Flexible Citizenship: The Cultural Logics of Transnationality*, Durham: Duke University Press.

Tololyan, K., 1991, 'The Nation-state and its Others: In Lieu of a Preface', *Diaspora*, vol. 1, pp. 3–7.

Veer, P. van der, 1995, 'Introduction', in P. van der Veer, (ed.), *Nation and Migration: The Politics of Space in the South Asian Diaspora*, Philadelphia: University of Pennsylvania Press, pp. 1–16.

12

Who Speaks for Sikhs in the Diaspora?*

Collective Representation in Multicultural States

Let me begin with a three observations.[1]

My first, quite obvious, observation is that Sikhs have, in little more than a century, become quite widely dispersed beyond the ancestral homeland of Punjab. In fact, Sikhs can be seen as a paradigmatic modern transnational 'imagined community'—that is, a people who maintain a sense of their common identity and global interconnected-ness despite being dispersed across many contemporary nation-state borders.[2] Of course not every PSO ('person of Sikh origins') retains a strong connection with the Sikh *qaum* (collectivity; literally, 'those who stand together'), but most do so, even if they do not follow all the same Sikh practices. It is in that sense that I will be talking of a 'Sikh diaspora', as the imagined connection of Sikhs outside India not only to fellow Sikhs back in Punjab but also to Sikhs living elsewhere in the world—however those connections may be imagined.[3]

My second observation, also quite obvious, is that Sikhs, in whichever nation-state they may reside, are everywhere a demographic minority—usually a quite small minority, and often a minority within a larger local minority category of 'Indians' or 'South Asians' or 'Asians'. The movement for Khalistan, to the extent that it imagined a sovereign Sikh-majority nation-state, was obviously one attempt, on the part of some Sikhs, to change that demographic fact. But most contemporary Sikh

* Also published in Gurupdesh Singh (ed.), *Diasporic Studies: Theory and Literature*. Amritsar: Guru Nanak Dev University Press, 2007, pp. 68–83.

politics and political consciousness in the diaspora has been about self-representation *in the local context* in light of the fact of being a minority—and often a quite 'visible minority' at that (to use the Canadian terminology).[4]

My third initial observation is that many of the countries where diasporan Sikhs reside are themselves pluralist polities, often having explicit multiculturalist ideologies, policies, and practices intent on incorporating minority groups within the nation-state. Indeed, we can see that the challenge of fully incorporating minority ethnic and religious groups into the polity has become a pressing issue in many contemporary nation—states. Yet, since Sikhs are often a relatively small minority group, the fact is that policies in the countries where Sikhs now reside are often made with little thought as to how they might affect Sikhs (as we have seen, for example, in the fallout affecting Sikh schoolchildren from the French government's recent decision to ban 'ostentatious' religious symbols from state schools).

Thus, with these three observations behind us, I come to the topic at hand: the challenge that Sikhs living in the diaspora have had of representing themselves, in the double sense that the word 'representation' has. That is, I am interested in both the discursive aspect of representation (how one's story gets told to outsiders through discourse about the collectivity) and the political aspect of representation (how collective interests get articulated in the political arena). Both the discursive and political aspects of representation involve issues of power. And thus I want to consider the question of who speaks for Sikhs in the diaspora—that is, (a) who seems to have the authority to represent Sikhs as a collectivity in the public sphere and (b) how is that authority attained, sustained, or undermined under the different muticulturalist regimes prevailing in the nation-states where Sikhs live. In exploring these questions, I draw primarily from my own fieldwork with Sikhs in North America, Southeast Asia, and Australia.

SIKH DISPERSION FROM PUNJAB

According to Darshan S. Tatla, of a global population of approximately 20 million Sikhs, over 10 per cent live permanently outside Punjab—and of that 10 plus per cent, half live outside India, with the most sizeable current populations in the UK, Canada, and the United States.[5] Others have suggested that the total number of Sikhs living outside India might actually be over two million.[6]

During the colonial period, the British, either directly or indirectly, were the initial conduits for much Sikh migration abroad. The late nineteenth century saw Sikh troops and police in Malaya and Hong Kong, some of whom stayed on to found the current communities in Southeast and East Asia. Some moved on and encouraged others also to move as independent migrants across the Pacific to the west coasts of Canada and the United States and down to Australia and New Zealand to found the beachhead communities in North America and Oceania. British recruitment of craftsmen to build the railways of East Africa brought Sikh communities to East and southern Africa, many of whose descendents have since migrated to the UK, Canada, Australia, and elsewhere. Partition provided an impetus for further migration, as some of those uprooted from west Punjab moved not only to east Punjab or Delhi or other Indian states but also to Southeast Asia or elsewhere abroad.

Migration to Britain began in earnest after the Second World War with the labour requirements of rebuilding the industrial base opening up the island to large-scale Punjabi migration in the 1950s and 1960s. Canada and the United States received large numbers of Sikh immigrants after liberalization of their immigration laws in the mid-1960s. Because of how the laws were written, initially at least, Canada tended to get the more working class and the US the more professional class from among these migrants. And, of course, the economic consequences of the agrarian transformation in Punjab and the political violence of the 1980s and early 1990s, led to a new wave of economic migrants and political refugees seeking domicile in the UK, Canada, the US, Europe, Australia, and elsewhere. At the same time, recruitment of Indian labour for the Gulf economies has drawn additional Sikh migrants, especially from the less well-off or well-connected sectors of the community.

Thus, in the early twenty-first century, we find Sikh settlements of some size and historical depth in the UK, Canada, and the US; long-standing Sikh communities in Southeast Asia and in East and Southern Africa; growing Sikh settlements in mainland Europe, the Gulf, Australia, and even Latin America. And, given the different waves of primary and secondary migration, we find many settlements with complex demographic make-ups—including third-fourth, and even fifth-generation descendants of early migrants; twice and thrice migrants who have already criss-crossed the globe; and new independent migrants and family members freshly arrived from Punjab.[7]

The diversity of this migration history (to say nothing of the class, caste, and sectarian differences amongst diasporan Sikhs) creates a challenge for Sikhs in any locality in telling a collective story and in choosing public leaders to articulate a common agenda. And, to further complicate matters, the nation-state itself often has its own expectations of who should speak for an imagined 'Sikh community'.

FOUR MULTICULTURALIST REGIMES

Let me turn now to some of the multiculturalist regimes that diasporan Sikhs encounter in their countries of residence. (By 'multiculturalist *regimes*' here, I refer to the prevailing ideologies, policies, and practices of ethnic and religious management pursued by the state in culturally and religiously pluralist polities.) And let me suggest four different models of multiculturalism pursued by nation-states where Sikhs now live. These four I pick not only because I know them fairly well but also because they seem to form something of a continuum.

On the one end, we find Singapore with a corporatist model of ethnic and religious management built on a bureaucratic framework inherited from the British. On the other end, we find the United States with a laissez-faire model, which largely leaves it to ethnic and religious groups to find their own way in multicultural civil society. Between these two extremes, one finds a quasi-corporatist model of multiculturalism in Canada and a quasi-liberal model of multiculturalism in Australia. Let me elaborate.

In calling what Singaporean's term their policy of 'multiracialism' a corporatist model, I mean that the state sees society as made of ethnic or racial communities as corporate groups (each with their own, separate 'cultures' and political interests) and treats them as such. Originally, this meant recognizing Chinese, Malays, Indians, and Others as the four corporate groups in Singapore, each with its own sanctioned socio-political organizations and leadership. But, as I will explain below, Sikhs in recent years have gained provisional recognition as yet another distinct corporate group.

In saying that the United States follows a laissez-faire model of ethnic and religious management, I mean to suggest that there is no official multiculturalism policy in place. The state does not attempt to formally recognize groups and leaders. It is left to ethnic and religious communities to represent themselves both to the state and within civil society. Such groups are free to organize and to mobilize collectively as they see fit (within the legal limits – tightened after 9/11), but the state does not presume to select or authorize certain organizations or persons to speak on behalf of the community as a whole. Thus, multiple voices may vie to represent the collectivity to the state (for example, in legislatures, courtrooms, and bureaucratic settings) and in civil society.

Australia *does* have an official multiculturalism policy but, unlike Singapore, it does not perceive ethnic or religious communities to be corporate entities and it does not license official national spokespersons for such groups. Rather, local organizations can make appeal to the federal and state agencies for funding of proposed initiatives that would serve their community or to make representation to the government on how policies might affect them. It is in this sense, of a policy predicated on many discrete cultures (that is, multiculturalism) but without an attempt to treat each culture as unitary (that is, having a single, shared culture and political agenda) or to license official spokespersons for the collectivity that I term Australia's a quasi-liberal model.

Canada, on the other hand, has had what I would call a quasi-corporatist model. Canadian multiculturalism, as outlined in its originating documents was predicated on the liberal assumptions of self-representation raised to the collective level. That is, each group within the multicultural mosaic deserves to be recognized and to be heard by the state. In practice, however, Canadian multiculturalism officials have tried to manage the resulting cacophony (including, one might note, the many Sikh voices struggling to be recognized and to be heard) by attempting to create and license certain groups and individuals to represent the interests of collectivities recognized by the state. This corporatist model grafted onto liberal principles is what I have termed quasi-corporatist.

One could go on to add additional models (for example, the cronyism model of Indonesia under Suharto or the separate-and-unequal model of Malaysia under Mahathir), but I hope to have suggested that Sikhs in the diaspora live and must attempt to represent themselves collectively under quite varied multiculturalist regimes.[8] And, I would argue, these different conditions of possibility have affected how Sikhs have gone about negotiating the local 'politics of representation'.

REPRESENTATIONAL CHALLENGES FACED BY SIKHS IN THE DIASPORA

What, then, have been the representational challenges that Sikhs have faced in the diaspora in negotiating these different multiculturalist regimes?

Diffused authority within the Sikh Panth means that there exists no obvious apex authority or ecclesiastical hierarchy to represent Sikh collective interests to outside parties. Since the death in 1708 of the last living, human Sikh Guru, Guru Gobind Singh, the Guruship has been seen as residing in the Guru Granth (the Word inscribed in the holy book) and the Guru Panth (the collectivity of gursikhs). But, in practice, this has left open the issue of who has the authority to speak for the Panth, either globally or locally.

Neither the appointed *jathedar* of the Akal Takht (the highest seat of Sikh temporal authority) nor the elected president of the Shiromani Gurdwara Parbandhak Committee (the statutory body in charge of historic shrines in Punjab), sometimes put forth as appropriate apex authorities, is fully accepted as having the legal authority and/or the moral standing to represent Sikhs abroad.[9] As a consequence, unlike the case in the Roman Catholic Church, there is no formal line of command to sanction certain diasporan Sikhs as local representatives of the Panth. Moreover, the egalitarian and competitive Sikh ethos mitigates against easy acceptance of claims of authority to represent the collectivity made by individual Sikhs—the 'who elected you Guru' charge.[10]

At the same time, even the most corporatist of multicultural states has yet to introduce an electoral system that would allow minority groups, such as the Sikhs, to elect their own political representatives.[11] Electoral systems in most modern polities are based on territorial, not ethnic or religious, constituencies; thus, like other small and dispersed minority groups, Sikhs are not able to elect Sikh-*qua*-Sikh leaders. Those Sikhs who have enjoyed electoral success in the diaspora owe their position in large measure to their selection by non-ethnic and non-religious political parties and to their election from local, usually non-Sikh-majority, constituencies. Even if they command wide respect among their fellow Sikhs (some do, some do not), they are not elected from a national or even local Sikh constituency and thus stand as rather imperfect representatives of the Sikh collectivity at the nation-state level.

As a consequence of this internal Sikh religious anti-structure and of the electoral political structures of modern nation-states, state bureaucrats in charge of mutliculturalism are faced with the challenge of how to deal with Sikhs in their midst. Should they regard Sikhs as a separate and distinct cultural/ethnic/religious/racial group? And, if so, who are they to recognize as speaking for Sikhs and advancing Sikh interests?

In Singapore, this has meant revitalizing the colonial-era Sikh Advisory Board as conduit to and from the government. In the late 1980s and early 1990s, state bureaucrats in the Ministry of Community Development and Sikh professionals found 'coinciding interests' in putting moderate, professional Sikhs into positions of power in a revitalized Sikh Advisory Board (and its affiliate education and welfare organizations) and in simultaneously de-authorizing potentially competing local centres of Sikh power and authority (such as local gurdwara societies); in return for giving up some political and associational rights and in suppressing local factionalism and separatist politics, Sikhs were granted official recognition as a distinct 'race' (apart from 'Indian') on their identity cards, the ability to use Punjabi (rather than Mandarin, Malay, or Tamil) as a second language for school testing purposes, and expanded coverage in the state-run media as the local 'model minority'. In addition, the state moved to introduce multi-member electoral districts requiring that one of four candidates for each slate be from a 'minority' (that is, non-Chinese) community, thereby manoeuvreing into parliament Sikh and other minority candidates who ended up serving not only as representatives of their territorial constituency but also as de facto representatives of their 'racial' group.[12]

In Canada, on the other hand, the failure of state attempts to create umbrella organizations and license spokespersons that Sikhs would accept led Canadian Sikhs, during the same period that they were being praised in Singapore as a model minority, to be seen in Canada as an 'inflexible . . . ethnic enclave'. Sikhs, taking Canadian multiculturalism to mean, as per its liberal rhetoric, that each cultural group has its right to self-representation, resisted attempts by the multicultural bureaucracy to use the National Association of Canadians of Origins in India (NACOI) as a conduit for Sikh interests. While the state took 'national origins' to be the logical basis of ethnocultural affiliation, Sikhs argued for separate representation. By the time that Canadian officials were willing to float a separate National Sikh Council, Sikhs had grown suspicious of state intentions and state-selected leaders, especially as the Canadian Ethnocultural Council, in deference to NACOI, continued to resist grassroot Sikh organizations' attempts to join this key multiculturalism advisory council. In the end, elected officials—such as former British Columbia premier and federal minister, Ujjal Dosanjh; former federal minister, Herb Dhaliwal; long-time Member of Parliament, Gurbax Singh Mahli, and other provincial and federal politicians of Sikh backgrounds—have come to serve as rather imperfect and sometimes reluctant representatives of Sikh collective interests in Canada.[13]

In Australia, the state multiculturalism bureaucracy has thus far avoided any attempt to create or to recognize a national umbrella 'Sikh' organization or to force Sikhs to use an umbrella 'Indian' one to advance their interests with the government. Instead, multiculturalism funding at the federal and state level is open to any ethnocultural organization that might wish to apply, and grassroot groups are invited to present their concerns directly to the government. Moreover, the government has tried to 'mainstream' ethnic and religious minorities through aggressive recruitment of their members into government bodies. In practice, this has meant that the more cosmopolitan Sikhs and their organizations have had an advantage in advancing their interests (for example, funding of heritage language classes or acceptance of professional qualifications from abroad) with the state, since they have the social, cultural, and financial capital to get 'heard' by state multiculturalism functionaries and, in fact, to be enlisted into the multiculturalism bureaucracy itself; other, lesscosmopolitan Sikhs only get their somewhat different interests (for example, ESL classes or protection of the 5Ks in the workplace) represented to the extent that 'cosmo-multiculturalist' Sikhs are willing to advance their interests in the name of Sikh solidarity. Such dependence, of course, can lead to a degree of tension and suspicion among differently positioned Australian Sikhs.[14]

Finally, in the United States, there is no official multiculturalism policy and thus no direct multiculturalism funding or corresponding multiculturalism bureaucracy. As befits the American privileging of civil society and market capitalism, individuals and organizations are relatively free to organize, to promote themselves, and to lobby for their agendas in the public 'marketplace of ideas'. And the dynamism of civil society in the US and the organizational acumen of Sikh American professionals is such that one finds a multitude of Sikh advocacy, development, and public education groups—for example, The Sikh Media and Resource Task Force (SMART) and its successor, the Sikh American Legal Defense and Education Fund (SALDEF), the Sikh Council on Religion and Education (SCORE), United Sikhs, The Sikh Coalition, the Sikh Communications Council (SikhCom), the Sikh Heritage Foundation, and so forth. All of these are active US-based NGOs or PVOs, many of which sprang into action impressively to counter anti-Sikh violence and harassment in post-9/11 America. But, despite would-be claimants, there is no obvious apex organization or identifiable individual who can be said to speak for Sikh Americans.[15] Within the American system, sophisticated voices, fancy titles, media savvy, political connections, and a healthy checkbook go a long way in getting one's message amplified through the US media and in US corridors of government—but without any assurance that those with the power to speak truly represent collective Sikh interests or sentiments.

In each of these four cases I have been considering, there are obvious trade-offs for Sikhs in how they go about getting heard and in how their interests get publicly articulated. Sikhs in Singapore get recognition and goodies from the state but must accept state-sanctioned leadership and constraints on their autonomy. Sikhs in Canada resist subordination of their interests by the state but at the cost of being seen as difficult and of having to use elected officials who happen to be Sikh as de facto representatives to carry their agendas. Sikhs in Australia can seek state support for local initiatives but must depend on cosmopolitan Sikhs amongst them to carry the agenda for all the differently-positioned Australian Sikhs. Sikhs in the United States are free to organize and to represent themselves in the civil and political spheres, without state support and with minimal state interference; but they, then, are dependent on individuals and groups with the means and wherewithal to broadcast their message and to advance their agenda.

CONCLUSION

What then are we to conclude about the challenges that diasporan Sikhs have faced in representing themselves collectively in the multicultural nation-state where they now live? Let me end with six conclusions that follow from the four cases I have outlined above:

The multicultural nation-states where Sikhs now live have varied ideologies, policies, and practices of ethnic and religious management. And these ideologies, policies, and practices have affected Sikh collective representations, even though they have rarely been constructed with their effects on Sikhs in mind.

None of these multicultural nation-states, even if they conceptualize their societies and polities as being made up of discrete cultural groups, has put in place a system of political representation such that local minorities elect their own representatives democratically based on ethnic or religious constituencies.

Whether speaking globally or locally, Sikhs themselves have neither an ecclesiastical hierarchy nor, since the days of the living, human Gurus, any indigenous system for constituting an apex organization or selecting a spokesperson with the unquestioned authority (both internal and external) to represent Sikhs as a collectivity. Nor are they likely in the near term to be able to fashion one, despite recurrent attempts to do so.[16]

Given these conditions of possibility, diasporan Sikhs, in typically energetic and pragmatic fashion, have successfully pursued *different* strategies of collective representation in different places—for example, using the Sikh Advisory Board professionals in Singapore, Sikh elected officials in Canada, Sikh 'cosmo-multiculturalists' in Australia, and Sikh donors and public advocacy groups in the United States.

Despite what some diasporan Sikhs might like to believe and to promote, there is not now—and there is unlikely ever to be—a one-size-fits-all strategy of effective collective representation for diasporan Sikhs to follow. And thus what has worked for Sikhs in Singapore will not necessarily work in the United States—and vice versa.

My sixth and final point is more a reflection on the entire notion of collective representation in multicultural nation-states. Both the multiculturalist state and the transnational Sikh community are invested in imagining ethnocultural groups as discrete and internally homogenous—sharing an essential 'culture' and presumed common political interests. But we know that, in reality, Sikhs, like any imagined community, are heterogeneous in their ideas, practices, and interests. Thus, any claim to represent the collectivity, discursively or politically, is inherently problematic, reflecting the subject position of the individual or organization making the claim and thus inviting counter-claimants. If we understand that, as positioned subjects, one may speak 'as a Sikh' but not necessarily 'for Sikhs', how does that change things? At the very least, understanding this social fact invites further attention to the power *to* represent, a social construction of authority that is shared between Sikhs and the nation-state. It is that historical *co*-construction that I have sought to analyse here.

NOTES

1. An earlier version of this paper was presented as the 13th Vidvatva Fulbright Lecture in New Delhi on 6 October 2005. It was subsequently presented, in revised form, at the seminar on 'Diasporic Studies: Theory, Literature and Arts' at Guru Nanak Dev University on 16 December 2005.
2. Arjun Appadurai has said of the Sikhs that, in their dispersion and interconnection, they can be seen to have been constructing a 'new, postnational cartography' (Appadurai 1996, p. 50).

3. The basis of Sikh 'identity' has been a repeated topic of investigation and debate on the part of Sikh studies scholars. I have argued that Sikhs constitute a genus of people by virtue of shared 'worship substances' but that Sikh persons simultaneously belong to other human genera based on other shared coded-substances (occupational, territorial, gendered); this suggests that a 'Sikh diaspora' comes into being only when and where globally-dispersed Sikhs recognize and valorize their commonalities *as Sikhs* (see Dusenbery 1995). Brian Axel has argued that circulating images of tortured amritdhari Sikh bodies created a diasporic consciousness amongst Sikhs during the 1980s and 1990s (see Axel 2001).
4. 'Visible minorities' was the term used by Canadian officials in the early years of Canadian multiculturalism to distinguish the non-European from the European descended minority populations. Canadian usage refers more to racial than religious emblems of identity.
5. Tatla 1999.
6. Mann 2005, p. 21.
7. For an overview of this migration history, see Dusenbery 1989 and Tatla 1999.
8. Dusenbery (1997b) contrasts the Sikh experiences under the differing Singaporean, Indonesian, and Malaysian state ideologies, policies, and practices of ethnic and religious management.
9. The SGPC is a 175-member statutory body elected through adult franchise by Sikhs in Punjab. It chooses its own president. The SGPC also approves the appointment of the jathedar of Akal Takht. Sikhs outside Punjab, including those living abroad, point out that they are thus not part of the political process through which the SGPC president or the Akal Takht jathedar are chosen. And recent attempts at giving diasporan Sikhs a formal consultative status with the SGPC have come to naught.
10. The late Yogi Bhajan (aka Siri Singh Sahib Bhai Sahib Harbhajan Singh Khalsa Yogiji; nee Harbhajan Singh Puri) created an ecclesiastical hierarchy for his *gora* (white) Sikh followers of 3HO/Sikh Dharma, with himself constituted as 'the chief religious and administrative authority for the Sikh dharma in the western hemisphere'. While this self-proclaimed title may have been the reason that Yogi Bhajan was invited to appear on American television in 1984 to give the American Sikh response to the assassination of Indira Gandhi, other North American Sikhs were quick to challenge his claim to represent Sikhs in the United States or elsewhere in the western hemisphere (see Dusenbery 1988).
11. The Scandinavian countries of Norway, Sweden, and Finland might appear to contradict this claim, insofar as they have introduced electoral representation for the indigenous Sami peoples via a separate 'Sami

Parliament' in each state (with the Sami Parliament in Sweden serving as both a popularly elected body and a government authority); however, these states have not extended this system of collective electoral representation to other minorities, including Sikhs, nor have they used ethnic representation as a basis for election to their national parliaments.

12. I develop this analysis of the Singaporean Sikh experience in greater detail in Dusenbery (1996).
13. I develop this analysis of the Canadian Sikh experience, and its contrast with the Singaporean Sikh experience, in greater detail in Dusenbery (1997a). The claim that Canadian Sikhs by the late 1980s had developed a public reputation as an 'inflexible . . . ethnic enclave' comes from Buchignani & Indra (1989, p. 162).
14. I develop this analysis of the Australian Sikh experience in greater detail in Dusenbery (2004). I am indebted to Ghasan Hage (1998) for the term 'cosmo-multiculturalist' to refer to those ethnic cosmopolitans who have gained what he terms 'national belonging', including incorporation in the multiculturalism bureaucracy. Recently, a would-be umbrella organization, the Sikh Council of Australia, has been launched to represent Australian Sikhs to the state and in civil society; it is too early to judge its representational effectiveness.
15. Even to name possible recent claimants—the late Yogi Bhajan and his 3HO/Sikh Dharma organization; Gurmit Singh Aulaukh of the Council of Khalistan; Didar Singh Bains when he was World Sikh Organization-U.S. president; the current president of the fledgling American Gurdwara Parbandhak Committee—is to expose how fraught with controversy such claims to represent Sikh Americans would be.
16. The most recent attempt, spearheaded by the Institute of Sikh Studies in Chandigarh, was the launching of an 'International Sikh Confederation (Proposed Sikh Apex Body)' in November 2005. According to the IOSS: 'The doctrine of 'Guru Granth—Guru Panth' proclaimed by Guru Gobind Singh demands the setting up of such a body without which the Panth cannot discharge its responsibilities or exercise its authority' (IOSS 2005, p. 4).

REFERENCES

Appadurai, Arjun, 1996, 'Sovereignty without Territoriality: Notes for a Postnational Geography' in Patricia Yeager, (ed.), *The Geography of Identity*, Ann Arbor: University of Michigan Press, pp. 40–58.

Axel, Brian Keith, 2001, *The Nation's Tortured Body: Violence, Representation, and the Formation of a Sikh 'Diaspora'*, Durham, NC: Duke University Press.

Buchignani, Norman L. and Doreen M. Indra, 1989, 'Key Issues in Canadian-Sikh Ethnic and Race Relations: Implications for the Study of the Sikh Diaspora' in N. Gerald Barrier and Verne A. Dusenbery, (eds), *The Sikh Diaspora*, Delhi: Chanakya Publications and Columbia, Missouri: South Asia Publications, pp. 141–84.

———, 1988, 'Punjabi Sikhs and Gora Sikhks: Conflicting Assertions of Sikh Identity in North America' in Joseph T. O'Connell, Milton Israel, and Willard G. Oxtoby, (eds), *Sikh History and Religion in the Twentieth Century*, Toronto: Centre for South Asian Studies, University of Toronto, pp. 334–55.

———, 1989, 'Introduction: A Century of Sikhs Beyond Punjab' in N. Gerald Barrier and Verne A. Dusenbery, (eds), *The Sikh Diaspora: Migration and the Experience Beyond Punjab*, Columbia, Missouri: South Asia Publications and Delhi: Chanakya Publications, pp. 1–28.

———, 1995, 'A Sikh Diaspora? Contested Identities and Constructed Realities' in Peter van der Veer, (ed.), *Nation and Migration: The Politics of Space in the South Asian Diaspora*, Philadelphia: University of Pennsylvania Press, pp. 17–42.

———, 1996, 'Socializing Sikhs in Singapore: Soliciting the State's Support' in Pashaura Singh and N. Gerald Barrier, (eds), *The Transmission of Sikh Heritage in the Diaspora*, Columbia, Mo.: South Asia Publications and New Delhi: Manohar Publishers, pp. 127–64.

———, 1997b, 'Diasporic Imagings and the Conditions of Possibility: Sikhs and the State in Southeast Asia', *SOJOURN: Journal of Social Issues in Southeast Asia*, 12(2) October, pp. 226–60.

———, 1997a, 'The Poetics and Politics of Recognition: Diasporan Sikhs in Pluralist Polities', *American Ethnologist*, 24(4) November, pp. 738–62.

Dusenbery, Verne A., 2004, 'Sikh Positionings in Australia and the 'Diaspora' Concept' in M. Ember, C. R. Ember, and I. Skoggard, (eds), *Encyclopedia of Diasporas*, New York: Kluwer Academic/Plenum Publishers, pp. 485–91.

Hage, Ghassan, 1998, *White Nation: Fantasies of White Supremacy in a Multicultural Society*, Annandale, NSW, Australia: Pluto Press.

Institute of Sikh Studies (IOSS), 2005, *International Sikh Confederation (Sikh Apex Body): Its Need and Proposed Constitution*, Chandigarh: Institute of Sikh Studies.

Mann, Gurinder S., 2005, 'Sikh Educational Heritage', *Journal of Punjab Studies*, 12, (1) Spring, pp. 1–28.

Tatla, Darshan Singh, 1999, *The Sikh Diaspora: The Search for Statehood*, London: UCL Press.

Appendix

A SELECT LIST OF REVIEW ESSAYS, BOOK REVIEWS, AND APPRECIATIONS

2006 'Review of Kamala E. Nayar's *The Sikh Diaspora in Vancouver: Three Generations amid Tradition, Modernity, and Multiculturalism*' in *Journal of Asian Studies*, 65(1) February, pp. 211–12.

2005 'Review of Constance Waeber Elsberg's *Graceful Women: Gender and Identity in an American Sikh Community*' in *Contemporary Sociology*, 34 (2) March, pp. 141–2.

2004 'Review of Brain Keith Axel's *The Nations Tortured Body: Violence, Representation, and the Formation of a Sikh "Diaspora"*' in *American Anthropologist*, 106 (1) March, pp. 178–80.

2002 'Review of Crispin Bates, (ed.), *Community, Empire and Migration: South Asians in Diaspora*' *Pacific Affairs*, 75(1) Spring, pp. 129–30.

1999 'Review of Karen Isaksen Leonard's *The South Asian Americans*' *Pacific Affairs*, 72(2) Summer, pp. 318–19.

1997 'Political Violence and the Politics of Ethnography' (Review essay on Joyce J.M. Pettigrew's *The Sikhs of Punjab: Unheard Voices of State and Guerilla Violence* and Cynthia Keppley Mahmood's *Fighting for Faith and Nation: Dialogues with Sikh Militants*), *American Anthropologist*, 99(4) December, pp. 831–3.

1997 'Cultural Studies Meets Ethnography' (Review essay on Marie Gillespie's *Television, Ethnicity, and Cultural Change*), *Current Anthropology*, 3(1) February, pp. 148–9.

1996 'Review of Barbara-Sue White's *Turbans and Traders: Hong Kong's Indian Communities*' in *International Journal of Punjab Studies*, 38 (2) July–December, pp. 250–3.

1995 'Review of K.S. Sandhu and A. Mani, (eds), *Indian Communities in Southeast Asia*', *International Journal of Punjab Studies*, 2(1) Jan.–June, pp. 119–21.

1994 'Review of W.H. McLeod's *The Sikhs: History, Religion, and Society*', *Journal of Asian Studies*, 53 (2)May, pp. 600–02.

1994 'Review of Darshan S. Tatla's *Sikhs in North America: An Annotated Bibliography*', International Journal of Punjab Studies, 1(1) April, pp. 159–61.

1994 'Kernail Singh Sandhu: An Appreciation', *International Journal of Punjab Studies*, 1(1) April, pp. 163–5.

1998 'Review of Richard G. Fox's *Lions of the Punjab: Culture in the Making*', *American Ethnologist*, 15(2) May, pp. 386–7.

1998 'Review of Arthur W. Helweg's *Sikhs in England* (second edition)', *South Asia in Review*, 12(2–3) January, pp. 4–5.

1985 'Review of Harish K. Puri's *Ghadar Movement: Ideology, Organisation & Strategy*', *South Asia in Review*, 9(3) March, p. 5.

Index